Interventions is produced on the land of the Wurundjeri people of the Kulin Nation. We acknowledge the Traditional Owners of country throughout Australia and recognise their continuing connection to land, waters and culture. We pay our respects to their Elders past, present and emerging. Their land was stolen, never ceded.

It always was and always will be Aboriginal land.

First published 1993 by Bookmarks Australia
2nd edition 2012 by Interventions
3rd edition 2023 by Interventions Inc

Interventions Inc is a not-for-profit, independent, radical book publisher. For further information:
www.interventions.org.au
info@interventions.org.au
PO Box 963
Coffs Harbour NSW 2450

Design and layout of cover and interior of this edition by Viktoria Ivanova
Front cover images clockwise from top left: Anti-Fraser artwork, AMWSU, Ken Mansell ephemera collection; ACTU Medibank poster, Ken Mansell ephemera collection; Anti-Kerr rally poster 1976, Ken Mansell ephemera collection; Honeymoon mine rally May 1982, John Ellis Collection, University of Melbourne Archives, 1999.0081.00918; Give Frazer the Razor, poster Michael Callaghan, Earthworks Collective; Demonstration at nursing home, John Ellis Collection, University of Melbourne Archives, 1999.0081.00358; Anti-Fraser banner December 1975, John Ellis Collection, University of Melbourne Archives, 1999.0081.00452; Anti-Kerr poster 1976, Ken Mansell ephemera collection.

Back cover image: Poster: Give Fraser the Bullet, Martin Hirst, 1977

Author: Tom O'Lincoln

Title: Years of Rage
ISBN: 978-0-6452535-0-4: Paperback
ISBN: 978-0-6452535-1-1: ebook

© Tom O'Lincoln 2023

The moral rights of the author have been asserted.
All rights reserved. Except as permitted under the Australian Copyright Act 1968 (for example, a fair dealing for the purposes of study, research, criticism or review), no part of this book may be reproduced, stored in a retrieval system, communicated or transmitted in any form or by any means without prior written permission.

All inquiries should be made to the publisher.

 A catalogue record for this book is available from the National Library of Australia

Years of Rage

Social conflicts in the Fraser era

Tom O'Lincoln

INTERVENTIONS

Dedication

This third edition of *Years of Rage* is dedicated to two activists from the Fraser years who died too young.

Dave Shaw (1955 - 1978)

Dave was a committed socialist and union militant all his short life. Starting out as a member of the Communist Party of Australia he was on the Sydney District Committee until 1976 when he resigned from the party because of its rightward drift. He joined the International Socialists later that year. Dave was a leading militant as a builders' labourer, actively supporting green bans and other industrial action. He was also active in the anti-uranium movement.

After the intervention into the NSW BLF in 1975, many good militants became demoralised and conditions deteriorated on the building sites, with an increasing number of accidents and deaths. Dave Shaw, who was active in the ongoing rank and file resistance, was one of those killed on the job. When he fell off some scaffolding on 20 December 1978 at the age of 23 he left a memory still vivid to his friends and comrades today.

Jeff Goldhar (1947 - 1997)

Jeff Goldhar became politically active in Melbourne in the 1960s as a member of the Labour Club at Melbourne University and was active against the Vietnam War. In the early 1970s he joined the International Socialists (now Socialist Workers Party) in the UK. On his return to Melbourne, Jeff joined the fledgling Australian organisation, Socialist Workers Action Group, and was involved in many of the struggles against Fraser. He can be seen in the image on page 197. Jeff was a committed activist and socialist until he died from cancer in 1997. Jeff had an important insight: he left a special bequest to 'allow us to bring our history and ideas to those receptive to them'. Set up at the end of 1998, the Jeff Goldhar Project financed the publication of many books, including most of Tom O'Lincoln's works. In 2015 Interventions took over the publication project and has continued to support Jeff's vision: 'We have a proud history ... I'd like our history to be remembered. I'd like our ideas to be available.'

YEARS OF RAGE

Contents

Preface i

Author's introduction 1993/2012 v

Introduction to third edition 2023 vii

1	Contending classes	1
2	A new era of conflict	23
3	Coup in Canberra	53
4	Fraser on the offensive	83
5	In the trenches	113
6	Workers, peace and the environment	145
7	'Work or riot': the unemployment crisis	185
8	Queensland: battle with Bjelke	219
9	The oppressed fight back	257
10	Issues on the left	317
11	A union revival	349
12	The more things change…	383

Appendix: The roots of economic crisis 411

Afterword 415

Acronyms and abbreviations 429

Endnotes 433

Image credits 457

Preface

This book was first published in 1993 and reprinted with only minor changes in 2012. Unfortunately, the references were left out of the second edition. Tom O'Lincoln gave the following explanation in his Introduction to the 2012 edition:

> The 1993 edition contained copious references, which were lost in reformatting the text. To key them all in again seemed a thankless task, since most of the facts are in themselves undisputed and most of the disputed ones can't be resolved by checking footnotes. Accordingly, this edition doesn't have footnotes. If you do wish to check sources, there are copies of the first edition in libraries around Australia, especially university libraries.[1]

How times have changed in the intervening 10 years! Most routine checks of references today can be done without personal visits to the library. In issuing a new edition, we felt that the task of inserting the missing references was essential, and we were able to draw on the professional expertise of Eris Harrison, whom we thank for carrying out this 'thankless' task.

The content of this new edition is, in essence, the same as the previous two. The text has not been substantially edited or updated to include more recent publications and sources, but remains in terms of content where it stood in 1993. This means that the analysis does not have the benefit of hindsight, but it does have the benefit of having been written not long after the events by a participant; it retains the eyewitness feel of the original.

However, the text has been reworked to some extent. We have improved expression and made a number of minor corrections. We have recognised modern language conventions – particularly in regard to oppressed groups – and changed some wordage which might not be clear to a younger audience. Spelling and punctuation now accord with Interventions' style. We feel certain that all of this would have met with Tom's approval. His main aim was always clear and accessible English for a broad readership.

Modernising the language in relation to the various queer and non-binary groups proved tricky. At the time the book covered, and during the period in which it was written, recognition was mainly given to gay men and Lesbians, although bisexuals and others (cross dressers) were recognised to some extent. After some consideration, we decided not to replace all 'gay and Lesbian' references with 'LGBTQI+', because this would be an anachronism. Instead, the words have been left as they appear in the original, with the terms used at the time Tom was writing.

We have modernised all references to Indigenous people where they occur in the text. How to handle quotes can be a debatable subject; however, we at Interventions choose not to edit actual quotes. We leave them as they are, unless there is ambiguity. This practice has been retained in the present volume.

Terms related to the country that used to be the Union of Soviet Socialist Republics (USSR) are another dilemma. The terms USSR and Soviet Union are not as familiar today as they were when Tom wrote this book. Because that entity actually contained several countries apart from Russia, it is desirable to avoid the use of Russia and Russian. But, because the Stalinist regime had nothing in common with genuine soviets, it is also desirable to avoid the word Soviet. This leads to an impasse, where no names present themselves as suitable. For the present work, we decided to keep the terms in use at the time the book was written. The arguments presented centrally relate to politics in Australia, and changing the term used to refer to another country is really a side issue.

Rick Kuhn has provided a new Introduction and an Afterword outlining the main political events since the end of the Fraser era in 1983. He shows how the essential themes from that period continue today.

Graphics and photos from the period enhance this edition. This has been a pleasure to research and assemble, because they represent a history at which many of us were present. All of us who were around then will never forget the many Fraser cartoons, including the wonderful ones by Mark Matcott. Tom's colourful presentation of events is further heightened by the images of memorable actions that many of us participated in and that had a profound influence on our development.

Many people provided comments or assisted in other ways in each of the editions of this book. Combining all together, we would like to express our gratitude to: Alison Anderson, Mick Armstrong, Sandra Bloodworth, Tom Bramble, Verity Burgmann, Alex Ettling, John Dawes, Carole Ferrier, David Glanz, Jeff Goldhar, Phil Griffiths, Graeme Haynes, Ken Howard, Alec Kahn, Rick Kuhn, Richard Lane, Tess Lee Ack, David Lockwood, Tanya McConville, John Minns, Dave Nadel, Judy McVey, Natasha Proctor, Ian Rintoul, Liz Ross, Vicki Spiteri, Janey Stone, Walter Struve, Les Thomas, Herb Thompson, Jane Tovey, Bob Weatherall, Phillip Whitefield, Graham Willett, George Wragg, Rob Zocchi and the staff of both the Victorian State Library and the State Library of NSW, particularly Bruce Carter.

Janey Stone
January 2023

A good red. Tom O'Lincoln early 1970s

Author's introduction 1993/2012

Malcolm Fraser's greatest achievement was probably to put class struggle back at the top of the political agenda.

Few serious students had ever doubted that Australian society was unequal. The country's long history of strikes and social conflicts was well known, and the years since 1968 had seen industrial disputes and social movements at high levels. But Fraser's daring grab for power in 1975 polarised the contending forces into two great camps, giving the labour movement in particular a sharply defined enemy. On the day of Fraser's 'Canberra Coup', social theorist Raewyn Connell wrote:

> If there remained any lingering doubt about the class nature of Australian politics, the events of 1975 must have resolved it. There is hardly a clearer case...of the way a threatened ruling class is able to mobilize fragments of state power, business connections, financial resources, and the legitimacy given them by the dominant culture, in a campaign to remove an offending government.[1]

Yet 1975 created more dilemmas than it resolved. Fraser's capitalist backers expected him to end the country's economic crisis, squash protest movements and smash the unions; his foes, mostly in and around the labour movement, expected the unions and the Australian Labor Party (ALP) to wage a fierce struggle to dislodge the usurper and teach the bosses a lesson. None of these expectations was met. While many in the labour movement did 'maintain the rage', seven years of strife brought the exhaustion of the contending forces and the triumph of new political leaders preaching 'national reconciliation'.

Since then, Hawke and Keating's 'reconciliation' has lost credibility. Australian society remains divided between workers and bosses, oppressors and oppressed; and, since the conflict between them is so enduring, we need to learn from the last round of struggle. To study why neither side could prevail during the Fraser era may help in determining how workers can take the offensive today.

This study argues the importance of organisation, leadership and politics. Neither camp, capital nor labour, had mobilised effectively for the struggle. Neither had a coherent leadership willing, or able, to take the offensive in sustained fashion, partly because neither side understood the dimensions of the economic crisis. Today, the last point is clearer, and the other issues are beginning to confront us once again. In the coming struggles, workers and oppressed people will need new kinds of organisation. Without them, we will at best repeat the disappointments of the 1970s; at worst, we will suffer shattering defeats, should our opponents learn the lessons of that era while we do not.

We need organisations and leaders of a revolutionary stamp, fighting to overturn the social order and put an end to class society. If this view is generally implicit rather than explicit in the following pages, it's because the forces that fought for it in the Fraser era were generally too marginal to shape events. That is precisely what must change.

After two chapters that set the scene and introduce the players, chapters 3-5 discuss the main industrial and political confrontations of the early Fraser era, ending in defeat for the labour movement. The final two chapters resume this central theme by recounting a second period of conflict between the 'big battalions' of labour and capital, which resulted in Fraser's defeat, but not necessarily victory for the working class. The middle section of the book (chapters 6-10) considers social movements and the distinctive struggles in Queensland, along with the development of ideas and theories on the left. I was on the scene of many of the events described. The backdrop to this entire complex drama was the global economic crisis of the 1970s and early 1980s. In that regard, the similarities with today will be obvious.

Tom O'Lincoln
July 1993/January 2012

Introduction to third edition 2023

Very partisan and extremely disinterested, Tom O'Lincoln's account of struggles in Australia under the conservative government of Malcolm Fraser in *Years of Rage* is a model of incisive Marxist analysis. He argues that this period, from late 1975 to early 1983, was ultimately one of class stalemate. Fraser came to office in a ruthless constitutional coup and talked tough. For a few years, his government did inflict significant defeats on the working class. But, from the end of the 1970s, there were more successful struggles by workers. Ultimately, Fraser was unable to decisively undermine the capacity of the working class to fight – and especially its workplace traditions of militancy and organisation. Sections of the capitalist class, which supported Labor in the 1983 elections, recognised this. The achievement of their aspirations – to seriously weaken workers' means of resistance and morale and to erode their living standards and working conditions – was the 'achievement' of Bob Hawke's and Paul Keating's Labor governments, in collaboration with the bulk of the trade union bureaucracy.

Tom's book remains the best history of social conflict in Australia under Fraser. The arguments it makes about political strategy on the left continue to be valid. In particular, the detrimental consequences for workers of the union bureaucracy's shift to policies that rely much more on Labor governments than on class struggle. This third edition is not only a very readable story about a time past, but also a valuable political guide for the present. Even more so because the useful reference notes, lamentably absent from the second edition, have been restored.

Years of Rage was the product not only of Tom's impressive individual efforts and considerable talents, but also of the socialist organisations he belonged to and led. These groups provided a vital framework for discussion and debate over theoretical and practical issues, both internally and with other forces. You can read about his background and experiences, through to the 1990s, in his memoir *The Highway is For Gamblers*. I benefited from that kind of framework too. Tom was a founder and particularly influential, although far from the only leader and theoretician, of the current that gave rise to Socialist Alternative. Of the individuals involved, it was from Tom that I learned the most about politics (and writing style).

A basic strength of these organisations, despite the inevitable misassessments and mistakes, was their collective capacity to make sober political judgements. Commitment to fundamental social change – the realisation of the working class's interest, not only in improving its conditions under capitalism, but in the revolutionary overthrow of the existing order – combined with impatience with the pace of developments can give rise to illusions about how good or bad a group's prospects and the current situation are. Our current has, by and large, avoided that danger. We don't kid ourselves about what is going on in the world or our own significance. *Years of Rage* embodies the insight and intellectual sobriety, but also the passion and humour, that are vital elements in the struggle for working class self-emancipation.

In his introduction, Tom writes: 'This study argues the importance of organisation, leadership and politics'. His convincing case is sustained by the use of powerful Marxist concepts. They include the irreconcilability of workers' and capitalists' fundamental interests; capitalist society as the foundation of contemporary gender, racial, religious and other forms of oppression; the distinctive place of the trade union bureaucracy in the class structure; and the nature of the Australian Labor Party as a capitalist workers' party. These provided the basis for the important conclusions Tom drew from his analysis in Chapter 12:

> Exhausted in partial struggles, led down blind allies by the Hawkes and Halfpennies, the increasingly discouraged militants were tempted by the hope that collaboration between governments, capital and labour could solve their problems. Over the following decade of ALP government, we learned how false that hope was; and by the early 1990s Australian society was again in crisis. It was time to revive the rage.

Such a revival may have been justified and desirable; but it didn't happen. And, since the late 1980s, there have only been relatively brief episodes of rage that gave rise to large-scale struggles, particularly under conservative governments. Tom's analysis of class relations and major social conflicts during the 1970s and 1980s and his framework provide the basis for understanding later surges in resistance by workers and the oppressed – and their limitations. I have chronicled them briefly in my afterword.

Rick Kuhn
January 2023

1.

The contending classes

There is always plenty to fight about in Australia, starting with economic inequality – because the country's wealth has always been concentrated in a few hands. In the 1970s, one percent of the population owned 22 percent of personal wealth, while the top 5 percent owned more than the bottom 90 percent.[1] This was vested in ownership not only of luxuries but, more importantly, of capital. A 1979 study of listed companies found that the largest 20 shareholders in half of them held at least half the shares, with the average standing at nearly 53 percent.[2] Thus, a minority owned a disproportionate share of industry; and, because the remaining shares were dispersed, this minority had effective control of the means of production in factories, offices, mines and mills.[3]

That control could be highly concentrated, as, for example, in the media industry: Fairfax controlled the *Sydney Morning Herald*, the *Financial Review*, the *Sun-Herald*, the *National Times* and numerous other publications, along with 10 TV stations, a controlling interest in the Melbourne *Age* plus one-third of the Macquarie radio network. The Herald and Weekly Times organisation controlled 50 percent of daily newspaper circulation, together with radio and TV interests. News Ltd controlled five metropolitan dailies, eight metropolitan weeklies, 14 country newspapers, six magazines and two TV stations. Needless to say, these companies wielded considerable political power, although they did not always apply it in concerted fashion.

The owner–controllers were linked together in relationships which help us to see them as more than a collection of individuals: they begin to take shape as a ruling class, known in Marxist terminology as the bourgeoisie. In 1973, 30 percent of shares held by large shareholders in the biggest firms were held by companies, with institutions and nominees holding another 14 percent. Individuals held only 2.5 percent.[4] Overlapping equity was matched by interlocking directorships. Anne Game and Raewyn Connell studied the top 50 companies, listing all common directors, then working out the 'density' of links between them; this demonstrated strong ties between finance, manufacturing and mining.[5]

Control of industry enabled this class to make crucial decisions affecting the lives of large numbers of people. Firms might sack hundreds of employees without so much as a word of warning; and, as Raewyn Connell and Terry Irving pointed out, the frantic redevelopment of central Sydney during the 1960s and early 1970s 'resulted from a series of decisions made in the boardrooms of perhaps twenty companies', about which ordinary workers and residents had little or no say.[6] Although public companies were supposedly subject to democratic control by the shareholders, the concentration of big share holdings alongside the dispersal of the others ensured that, in practice, the same narrow bourgeois interests prevailed.

While governments claimed to regulate industry in the public interest, in reality, the top levels of public administration collaborated closely with company management in capital's own interest – not surprisingly, because senior business people had close ties to top bureaucrats and politicians. One analysis of 418 members of various elites and their personal links revealed a 'central circle' consisting of about 31 percent business leaders, 20 percent senior public servants and 27 percent politicians, plus media, judges and a handful of union officials.[7] Predictably, the senior public servants assisted their 'client base' in industry. H. C. Coombs, then Reserve Bank governor, remarked:

> It is difficult to be intimately involved in the workings of the financial system without coming to feel identified with it... I remember the wife of an Asian central banker asking me, 'What exactly do central bankers achieve other than to protect the wealth of the wealthy?'[8]

When business interests were threatened, the state could deploy its police, courts and other mechanisms of control in their defence. During most of the postwar years, for example, governments had used penal powers to restrict strikes; these nominally included provision for sanctions against miscreant employers, but the latter were almost never used. Similarly, the police might be used against picket lines but were not known to arrest employers who sacked workers. Class bias in the operation of the state machinery was accompanied

THE CONTENDING CLASSES

by subtle mechanisms of social and ideological control, beginning with the mass media, which was itself part of big business, and including the schools, which socialised people to accept the dictates of people in authority while propagating the ideology of the system.

Even so, this ruling class domination was seldom untroubled. Firstly, the bourgeoisie was divided. Rural and mining capital had interests distinct from those of the urban bourgeoisie, and those two great camps were fragmented between industry sectors (finance, manufacturing, agriculture, mining and so on) and between states and regions. The divisions were reflected in a plethora of competing employer organisations which were sometimes bitterly hostile to each other. Within industry sectors, despite an element of monopolisation, competition and conflict could be equally fierce.

If the bourgeoisie's industrial leadership was fragmented, so was its political leadership. Rural and mining capital oriented to the Country Party (later renamed the National Party), while urban business looked to the Liberals. The

Sydney stock exchange in the 1970s. A convenient target for anti-Fraser protests

two parties maintained an uneasy coalition at the federal level but not always at state level; because of the need to reconcile differing interests, their joint policy framework was generally pragmatic at best, makeshift at worst. There was also a gap between business and its political representatives. It was true that business was directly involved in party machines, particularly Liberal Party finance committees:

> In the state of Victoria, they have included Sir Ian Potter, one of Australia's leading stockbrokers; Sir Maurice Nathan, chairman of the furniture retailing firm of Patersons Ltd; Sir George Coles, founder and director of the retail chain...; Herbert Taylor, chartered accountant, company director and a past president of the Associated Chambers of Commerce of Australia; F.E. Lampe, former president of the Australian Council of Retailers; H.G. Brain, chairman of T&G Life Assurance Co [and others].[9]

But senior business leaders seldom entered parliament, preferring to leave it to professional politicians who, for their part, had other constituencies as well. The parties drew their mass memberships from the ranks of the middle classes and smaller farmers, whose aspirations were often quite different to those of banks, or big mining companies. In addition, the politicians had ties to the bureaucracy and other sections of the state machine, each of which had interests of its own. The result was a certain relative autonomy for the politicians. In some ways, this had advantages for the long-term survival of capitalism, ensuring that at least a few political leaders had wider horizons than did entrepreneurs fixated with the 'bottom line'. They might even say so openly: Menzies himself had once taken a jab at what he termed 'reactionary' laissez-faire.[10]

Australia's relations with the rest of the world economy produced additional contradictions. The domestic economy was too small to generate enough capital for the rate of national development the country's rulers wanted. From colonial times, therefore, Australian industry had relied on large dollops of overseas capital, bringing with it considerable foreign ownership. In 1967, foreign-owned manufacturing plants accounted for over 25 percent of output. The late 1960s saw a boom in foreign investment in mining. By 1973, foreign capital controlled nearly 62 percent of value added in that industry.[11] While those who benefited naturally welcomed the inflow of funds, others feared the competition and worried that the Australian state might lose control of sections of the economy; the result was a surge of economic nationalism among sections of the ruling class, resulting in attempts by the Gorton Government to place greater controls on foreign capital. John Gorton's efforts led to his political demise, however, leaving the economic nationalist field open to Labor – traditionally the party of specifically Australian (as opposed to British) nationalism.

The gaps and contradictions made for a messy and confusing picture. In a crisis, it could be difficult for any one group to unite the ruling class and lead it. The bourgeoisie was not too bad at uniting against governments whose measures they disliked: in the late 1940s, the finance industry had mobilised support throughout the business community and the political right to torpedo Labor PM Ben Chifley's plans to nationalise the banks. In 1975, the Whitlam Government faced something similar. Formulating and implementing a positive program at a time of crisis, however, was something Australia's capitalist class found rather more difficult. During World War II, the bourgeoisie had turned not to its own parties but to the Labor Party, partly because the ALP could enlist working class support for the war, but partly also because it was sufficiently independent of each of the warring bourgeois factions that it could make a reasonable fist of uniting all of them.

Finally, the Australian ruling class was ideologically vague. Despite occasional hairy-chested rhetoric about the dangers of 'socialism' and the glories of free enterprise, business was generally quite well-disposed to the state and the public sector. Large sections of secondary industry depended on tariff protection or bounties, while rural interests counted so heavily on rural subsidies as to provoke jokes about 'Country Party socialism'. Their political representatives behaved accordingly, with Menzies maintaining high tariffs and the Country Party presiding over handouts to its constituency.

If business and conservative politicians still persisted in anti-socialist rhetoric, much of it was just propaganda. Red-baiting and dire warnings about supposed Russian and Chinese threats served to rally the public behind the state and its overseas interests in a world divided by the Cold War. It proved equally useful in the domestic sphere, in fomenting a certain paranoia about the ALP left and in justifying attacks on the more militant trade unions. (Socialism was understood by leaders of both capital and labour as meaning either Russian-style 'communism' or nationalisation by ALP governments; Karl Marx's own perspective of democratic workers' power was little known.)[12]

Red-baiting also provided emotional comfort to the conservatives' middle-class voting base, 'a form of symbolic reassurance to interests and individuals supporting the [Liberal Party] whose demands could not be met' because, ultimately, the politicians' first loyalty was to the ruling class.[13] It did not mean

Hancock family free enterprise seminar, Wentworth Hotel, Sydney, June 1982. Left to right: Andrew Peacock, Fraser government minister; Petr Beckman, University of Colorado; George Roche, Hillsdale College, Michigan; Gina Hancock; Lang Hancock. The crude clichés of economic liberalisation as promoted by Beckman and Roche were aligned with business objectives such as uranium mining and nuclear power

that many capitalists or conservative politicians were prepared for open class warfare. Why should they be? Postwar experience suggested that, while sections of the union movement and the ALP sometimes liked to talk about socialism, in practice they could achieve gains within the existing system; this was their real objective. It was only with the onset of economic crisis that the potential for a more fundamental conflict arose.

It was true that the need to fight for its interests against organised labour had forced capital to tighten both its industry organisation and its ideology in the 1960s. Concern about growing union militancy had spurred the creation of a National Employers' Industrial Committee, which intervened in the arbitration system and lobbied the government, with the metal bosses playing a leading role because their award was a benchmark in wage fixing. The employer bodies began using economists to brush up their ideology, and experts such as D. H. Whitehead of La Trobe University provided sophisticated arguments against wage rises. These played an increasing role as the employers faced more sophisticated advocacy from the Australian Council of Trade Unions (ACTU) and, more importantly, growing industrial pressure from unions whose bargaining power was rising steadily in a buoyant economy. Even so, the employers were only preparing for more vigorous jostling over income shares within an economy that was expected to go on growing. They were not developing a battle plan for imposing austerity on the working class.

The conservative politicians were little help before 1975, because the Liberal Prime Ministers who followed Menzies were all mediocrities: Holt achieved little, Gorton fell out with large sections of his own party, and Billy McMahon floundered in the face of the relatively mild 1972 recession. Amid the crisis of the 1970s, the ruling class desperately needed a strong leader with some sort of political vision. At first, some of them thought that they had found one in Gough Whitlam. They later believed for a time, after 1975, that Malcolm Fraser could do the job.

The working class in the 1970s

The Australian working class is the one group in society capable of challenging the hegemony of capital; most of the time, however, it lacks awareness of its potential power. Most people work for wages and salaries, and a fairly big section of these belong to an organised labour movement. In the 1970s, Australian unions were quite large by comparison with those in other Western societies; the country's 2,800,000 union members made up 55 percent of the workforce in

THE CONTENDING CLASSES

1976 – partly because of an arbitration system which institutionalised unions even where workers were not actively involved. The public sector was very strongly unionised – up to 88 percent in telecommunications.[14]

One characteristic was particularly important in defining labour as a class: employees' relationship to the process of production. Whereas the employers controlled the means of production (plant, equipment, materials) and sold the products to make a profit, workers typically owned no means of production – apart, perhaps, from a set of tools – and had to sell their labour for a wage.

This had profound social implications. Donald Horne wrote of blue collar labour:

> there was a sense of estrangement from work itself. Work was something over which they had no control and in which there was little or no inherent interest... They were simply working for other people, and, more likely than not, they saw their bosses as bastards and what they said as bullshit.[15]

A similar atmosphere predominated in many offices. Superficial observers might think that strikes were just about money. Actually, this sense of alienation often fuelled them, and so industrial disputes contained the seeds of social and political radicalism.

The alienation was not some vague malaise but was rooted in tangible realities. The bosses had the right to hire and fire; they tried to keep wages low; sexual harassment of women employees was common; and many workplaces were sweatshops. And the bosses were arrogant, as a leaked 1971 Broken Hill Proprietary Company (BHP) report illustrated, suggesting that management should use 'emotional blackmail' to prevent strikes and introduce 'a system of moving workers who express dissatisfaction sideways' and proposing the use of suggestion boxes to 'identify such people' as well as to allow workers to 'let off steam'. Because survey results showed that most of BHP's Whyalla employees were unhappy with work arrangements, the report called for jolly posters and better social and sporting facilities as an alternative to raising wages: 'This is the lottery principle of encouraging people to live on hope.'[16]

No wonder a lot of workers hated the employers. A study of Broken Hill mine employees in the early 1960s found that they had some time for foremen and shift bosses, who were themselves close to the workforce; but, when it came to management: 'as the authority increased, the proportion of favourable comments decreased.'[17] Class resentments such as these gave a sharp edge to the industrial struggles that broke out after 1968.

In 1976, some 30 percent of the workforce were in the 'skilled trades', an increase on 24 percent 10 years earlier. Sixteen percent were in the clerical sector, an increase of 11 percent. Only one percent were miners, but many of these were exceptionally well organised and combative. The trades declined during the Fraser years as manufacturing suffered from recession, but the clerical or 'white collar' figures edged upward. These included managers, professionals with ties to capital but also many others such as teachers, nurses or other members of the 'lower' professions whose conditions were no longer so very different from those of blue collar workers, and whose trade union consciousness was growing. Large numbers of clerks received wages similar to those of industrial workers, while mechanisation had created vast numbers of office jobs no less repetitive than factory work. Clerks, too, were becoming union conscious.

A similar process was underway in the technical professions, where one computer programmer told a researcher:

Sydney building workers c1976

> I'm by no means a socialist, and I don't particularly like the idea of mass bargaining...but over the years the income and social standing of salaried staff has been gradually eroded...it's only logical to join a union.[18]

Women made up only 23 percent of clerical workers in 1966, but that rose to 31 percent five years later. Among adults, married women were an ever-increasing section of the workforce, exceeding the 20 percent mark during the Whitlam years. The unions were often slow to accept women as 'real' unionists, a reflection of both sexist attitudes and conservative craft traditions, but the 'feminisation' of large sections of the union movement was too strong a tide to be resisted for long. The growth of the white collar and service sectors brought a growing union participation by women, and thousands of these joined strikes during the Fraser years – their confidence boosted by their numbers and the knowledge that industry needed them – and their ideas often radicalised by women's liberation or the other political movements of the time.

The workforce was young and growing younger. Workers aged under 34 years made up 42 percent in 1971, and more than half 10 years later.[19] These young people, who had grown up during the postwar economic boom, shared high expectations about living standards and quality of life, while their political ideas were often left of centre. Malcolm Fraser would not find it easy imposing his reactionary policies on them.

One-quarter of the workforce had been born overseas, with a heavy concentration of migrants in 'blue collar' jobs and in the urban centres. Many of those from non-English-speaking backgrounds had language difficulties, and some lacked education, leading them to 'factory fodder' jobs and a disproportionate share of the unemployment; the Henderson Report found poverty nearly twice as prevalent among newly arrived migrants as it was in the general population.[20] Their newness to the country and the raw deal it offered them meant that they often felt less commitment than Australian-born workers to a range of institutions in society, including the formal structures of the trade unions.

Migrants had only begun to assert themselves in the unions in the early 1970s, with Migrant Workers' Conferences in 1973 and 1974. The unions did begin to publish multilingual literature, and the labour movement began to notice the influence of migrant community organisations such as the Federation of Italian Workers and their Families (*Federazione Italiana Lavoratori Emigrati e famiglie*; FILEF). Moreover, migrants' relative lack of ties to the existing union structures was not always a negative factor: when they went on strike, they could often be more militant precisely because they weren't weighed down by the conservative traditions of some unions. The same was frequently true of women. In subtle ways, the migrants also changed the outlook of Australian-born workers, by relating their experiences of oppression and struggle overseas. Unfortunately, the labour movement made little effort to build systematically on this infusion of new knowledge.

Aboriginal and Torres Strait Islander Australians made up a small proportion of the workforce. They were concentrated in rural jobs, and large numbers were unemployed; but a growing number worked as clerks, sales staff, tradespeople, process workers and labourers as more Black people came into cities and towns. Almost all Indigenous workers were unambiguously working class – Australia in the 1970s had no Black middle class to speak of, let alone Black capitalists. Moreover, Indigenous workers suffered appalling inequality even within the working class. A 1972 study found white truck drivers being paid $70 a week, while their Indigenous counterparts got $20; for mechanics, the figures were $65 and $24, and for painters, $65 and $16.[21]

Still, the Black struggles of the 1960s had some impact: the first Aboriginal person known to hold a full-time union position was appointed in 1965; in the next few years, several others followed him. The left-wing unions expressed sympathy for Indigenous people, occasionally organising job meetings or collections in support of their struggles. The wider labour movement, however, not only failed to educate its members on issues of racism but was itself guilty at times of racial discrimination against Black people and also migrants. The struggle against prejudice had to be waged within the labour movement itself.

Working class organisation

Workers had built the trade unions primarily to fight for their interests against the employers; but, given that objective, these organisations had huge built-in limitations. By their nature, they existed to confront the employers on the terrain of the capitalist system itself, bargaining over wages rather than seeking to abolish the wages system. They were also highly fragmented and seemed, at the time, likely to remain so. There were 313 unions in Australia in 1976, compared with 356 in 1936; by the end of the Fraser era, the total had managed to grow. This had much to do with craft jealousies – competition between groups of workers which showed just how deeply the unions had absorbed the ethos of capitalism. On top of that were bureaucratic rivalries between the full-time officials who dominated the union movement.

The union leaders posed other, equally serious problems. They represented an intermediary layer between the workers themselves and the capitalist system and so were an important mechanism for ensuring that organised labour did not challenge that system. While union officials claimed to represent the workers, their social position was quite different. They usually enjoyed better pay or perks, but more important was their different social role as brokers between capital and labour, which gave them an interest in resolving industrial conflicts – whereas the rank and file had an interest in winning them.

The officials wielded power not only through formal structures but also through access to information and resources. A 1979 study of meetings in two major unions covering building and metal workers showed full timers not only proposed most initiatives but also made a sizeable proportion of opposing remarks.[22] The full timers could hold office for long periods; quite a few were not even drawn from the rank and file – university graduates could be (and were) 'parachuted in' to join union staff because of political connections. Additionally, many organisers were appointed, rather than elected. It is easy to see how entrenched union leaderships could fend off even quite strong rank and file challenges.[23] This bureaucratic layer generated an ideology of class collaboration reflecting its position as broker between capital and labour: most union officials not only argued, but believed, that industrial conflict was best resolved through quiet dialogue presided over by themselves.

Nationalism provided an important ideological cement for class collaboration, as unions formed alliances with employer groups to defend protective tariffs against foreign competition, and the officials seized on the burst of economic nationalism after 1967 to try to maintain common ground between the bosses and the most militant sections of the rank and file. In the Fraser years, agitation against the supposed conspiracies of multinationals, sparking projects for alliances with 'patriotic' capitalists, contributed to confusing and dampening the class struggle against the employers.

None of this suggests that rank and file members were uniformly more militant or politically advanced than their officials. If the unions were capitalist institutions, designed to achieve improvements for members within the existing social order, this largely reflected the expectations of the members themselves; the majority of members were relatively conservative and apathetic much of the time, because the pressures of daily life under capitalism were largely conservatising. People working all day in factories and offices, having to cope with the stresses of family life in an oppressive society, normally didn't get around to developing visions of social change. Despite its oppressive features, they accepted the existing social framework – if only by default. But this could begin to change if their immediate personal aspirations or the mere defence of their living standards brought them into direct conflict with the system, as occurred in the 1970s. Large numbers of workers were then impelled to challenge the system in practice. Most of them did not fully grasp the implications of their actions, but a minority did, and some of them looked for systematic ideas to justify their new stance. Unfortunately, even the most left-wing union leaders failed to provide them with the answers.

If there were problems with the industrial leadership of the working class, there were even greater ones with organised labour's political leaders. Overwhelmingly, those workers who wished to fight the bosses in the political sphere looked to the Labor Party. Labor had held power in the past, including long stretches at the state level, without unsettling the bourgeoisie; but two decades of conservative rule in Canberra had allowed hopes to rise among some Labor supporters – and fears among conservatives – that a socialist tiger lurked somewhere within the ALP. These views were not entirely illusory, because the Australian party system did reflect class divisions.

True, some workers voted Liberal, and Labor could win over middle-class voters, but two academic observers could still write confidently:

> class, whether objectively or subjectively defined, remained the most powerful predictor of the vote...the primacy of occupational class is the rock on which the party system rests.[24]

And, when it came to the party organisation, the ALP's class character was equally obvious. Only a small minority of Labor voters were party members, and a smaller minority were active. Nevertheless, an army of blue and white collar workers canvassed and attended branch meetings; during the polarised elections of the 1970s, these activities sometimes took on the dimensions of a religious war.

Party activists were often rank and file leaders in other spheres, as shop stewards on the job or leaders of protest campaigns, giving the party deep roots in unions and social movements. Labor's internal factions had rank and file followings too; and, for every careerist looking for parliamentary preselection, there was someone else acting on conviction – especially in the party's sizeable left-wing current, strongest in Victoria, which did not hesitate to describe itself as socialist.

Of course, working class people are not automatically more left wing or militant than others. But the industrial conflicts of the late 1960s, alongside the antiwar movement of the time, had created a more left-wing climate. Most of the party's members and supporters looked to Labor to bring significant social change. Thus, the base of the party had a potential for political radicalism and for struggle. Unfortunately, the ALP structures were not a suitable vehicle for either of these.

The party was highly fragmented, with much power concentrated at state level, and fairly bureaucratic. The trade unions controlled a solid majority of votes at annual conferences, typically about 60 percent. This was a reflection of the party's class basis, but a distorted one which did not involve control by rank and file workers; rather, it placed considerable power in the hands of full-time union officials, who normally decided the make up of delegations. Although some union leaderships took fairly radical left-wing stances, they were balanced by stronger centre and right-wing forces, especially at the national level. Bold party leaders, pursuing right-wing policies backed by the media and vested interests, might find ways to get around these structures, but the rank and file had little hope of doing so.

Labor politicians were generally even further removed from the rank and file than the union officials. In government, they administered the capitalist state and tried to regulate the capitalist economy. In opposition, they kept trying to establish their suitability for government. Like the union officials, they had a political outlook corresponding to their social position: an emphasis on going through 'proper channels' – complemented at most by cautious, orderly and generally limited protest actions – and, above all, an orientation to the ballot box. Whatever the issue, however stormy the conflict, you could always rely on Labor politicians to suggest waiting for the next election.

Because the unions were organisations stuck on the terrain of the capitalist system; because their full-time officials were largely committed to that system; and because the ALP was based firmly on the trade union structures, it followed inexorably that Labor itself would perpetuate, rather than challenge, the basic institutions of capitalist society. So, while it was understandable that some saw the ALP as a vehicle for radical change, such hopes or fears were largely misplaced. As Labor moved closer to government under Gough Whitlam's leadership, the party actually moved steadily to the right, and the experience of government was to accelerate the trend.

The small groupings to Labor's left could offer no serious political alternative. The Communist Party of Australian (CPA) had once enjoyed considerable strength in industry. By the 1970s, it had fragmented and was in terminal decline.[25] Although the fragments retained a certain influence, both in the unions

CPA leaders John Halfpenny and Bernie Taft 1974

and (informally) inside the ALP, their politics – apart from various international affiliations – largely blended into those of the Labor left. Important Communist union leaders like John Halfpenny and Laurie Carmichael were actually more moderate than some ALP officials. There were small groups of organised revolutionaries with some influence among students, but they remained at the margins of the labour movement.

Thus, while capital and labour were by far the most important forces in Australian politics, each in its own way was too confused, too fragmented, too poorly led to be prepared for an era of class warfare. Yet that was just what awaited them after 1968. The conflict became sharply polarised after 1975, because the rising expectations of workers and Labor voters clashed with the imperatives of a ruling class faced with economic crisis and no longer prepared to make concessions.

About the 'middle classes'

Australia's class structure would be worth a book on its own; this chapter seeks only to introduce the main combatants. From that point of view, the various social layers located between capital and labour are comparatively

Students rally for civil rights for Indigenous people outside Parliament House Sydney 7 July 1964. Note the prevalence of ties on the men

unimportant, because the acute polarisation after 1975 drove most politically active people towards an alliance with one or another of the two main classes.

Some will disagree with my view. Influential political science theories see Western society since the 1960s as shaped by the rise of new social movements (peace, green, feminist, etc.) which are allegedly carried by a 'new middle class' consisting of students, intellectuals and professionals. These are sometimes thought to be displacing the labour movement as the main challenger to the social order. But, while the middle classes have taken on some new contours in recent decades, they did not play the role sometimes claimed for them in the social movements of the Whitlam and Fraser years.[26]

It is certainly true that students had become an important political force in the 1960s, reflecting their increasing numbers amid a massive expansion of tertiary education. Enrolments in tertiary institutions, including Colleges of Advanced Education, had risen by 75 percent in the 1950s and climbed by

187 percent in the 1960s. As their numbers grew, students became more assertive and even began to see themselves as taking the lead in changing society. When a group called Student Action was set up at Melbourne University in 1961 to campaign against the White Australia policy, one of its leaders wrote that students had 'shown several times in the past twelve months that they are prepared to give a moral lead.'[27] During the 1960s' political radicalisation, students became an important source of activists for the antiwar movement and a recruiting ground for various radical currents. After graduation, many of the same people went on to become active in white collar or professional organisations or emerged as leaders of various social movements.

Students, however, cannot be defined statically as 'middle class', because each generation of students goes on to join the workforce. The radical students of the late 1960s and early 1970s had generally found work by the time Fraser replaced Whitlam, a large proportion of them entering professional and white collar jobs as teachers, health workers, public servants and the like. These sections of the workforce, as we have seen, were not part of a 'new middle class' but rather represented new sections of the working class. A large proportion of the people joining, for example, anti-uranium demonstrations in the 1970s were workers of this kind.

Other ex-students became managers, joined professional elites such as doctors and lawyers or went into business, but these groupings showed little bent for social radicalism. On the contrary, some of them undoubtedly supported the reactionary anti-union mobilisation discussed in Chapter 11.

Finally, some of the university-trained '1960s generation' became career intellectuals and did indeed play an important role in setting the ideological tone among feminists, peace campaigners or environmentalists from the 1970s onwards. Unfortunately, their influence generally accelerated the decline of these movements by pushing them away from links with the working class and socialist politics, a process we will consider in Chapter 10. The student movement itself had little staying power and declined sharply from the early 1970s, intimidated by a rapidly slackening job market for university graduates. Suddenly, good marks really mattered.

Far from being sustained by a 'new middle class', the strongest social movements always had direct or indirect connections with the labour movement. The social radicalisation of the late 1960s and early 1970s would not have been so powerful were it not for a more or less simultaneous strike movement in the working class and the involvement of the ALP left in the antiwar campaign; similarly, the anti-uranium movement of the early Fraser era owed its considerable political impact to trade union support. As various social movements turned away from a working class orientation, their social weight declined, even if their numbers held up. Even the large disarmament rallies of the early 1980s were comparatively ineffectual precisely because the peace movement tried to orient to a supposedly more enlightened middle-class constituency. The only really effective middle-class mobilisation was the battle to save the Franklin River – a campaign in which the environmentalists enjoyed support from sections of the bourgeoisie.

In all the decisive conflicts of the Whitlam and Fraser years, capital and labour were the forces that really mattered, as they always will be while the capitalist system endures.

2.
A new era of conflict

After a decade and a half of relative social peace, Australia began changing quickly in the late 1960s.

A major defeat in the 1949 coal strike, followed by cold war witch hunts, had put the unions on the defensive. The Menzies Government kept them there through penal powers which enabled the Arbitration Commission to virtually ban strikes. The postwar economic boom had allowed conservative governments to consolidate a right-wing social consensus until around 1967, and the resulting union quiescence had misled observers such as Craig McGregor, who wrote in his *Profile of Australia* that 'the climate of class warfare is rapidly receding'.[1] But industrial disputes began to multiply in 1967. By 1968, the number of strike days had topped one million; in the industrially fateful year of 1969, it was nearly double that.

Prosperity had initially underpinned a conservatisation of society because, in the aftermath of working class defeats, rising living standards offered workers some consolation for submitting to the indignities of capitalist exploitation and Liberal Party rule. By the mid-1960s, however, a decade and a half of accumulated prosperity had laid the basis for a new militancy. Steadily increasing affluence, along with years of relative job security, had begun to boost workers' confidence, while a new generation of union militants, unscarred by the defeats of the past, had emerged. They did not feel inclined to tolerate the oppression that capitalism inflicted on them at work. The boom era had also created new expectations about what constituted an acceptable living standard. The new combativeness was part of an international trend dramatised by the massive general strike in France in 1968 and continuing through the 1974 British miners' strike to the 1974–75 upheavals in Portugal.

Economic factors fuelled the worldwide industrial upsurge, but the contradictory development of international capitalism also gave it a political edge. The prosperity and stability of the boom years had been unevenly distributed. Japan and Germany began to outstrip the USA economically; when the USA attempted to reassert its hegemony through massive military intervention in Vietnam, it provoked a huge political revolt, both within the USA and internationally. Less developed sections of Europe, such as Greece, Ireland, Spain and Portugal underwent political crises, while the more backward southern states of the USA were rocked by Black people's struggle for civil rights, which then spilled over into ghetto riots in the northern cities. The call for Black liberation further contributed to demands for women's liberation some years later.[2]

Despite Australia's geographic isolation, the big events overseas all found some resonance in this country. The Vietnam issue was as big here as in the USA, but other international events were fairly significant for important sections of the working class, too. The car factories were full of Italians and Greeks who were used to voting communist, some of them veterans of big struggles in the old country. Migrants from the British Isles knew all about the unrest in Northern Ireland or the miners' defeat of Heath's Tory government; Aboriginal people heard the message about 'Black power' from the USA; Australian women and homosexuals (with 'lesbians and gay men' these are the terms we used back then) did not take long to respond to the example set by US liberation movements.

Thus, in numerous subtle ways, the ferment abroad affected the Australian working class. So it was in response to international trends as well as the growing strike wave at home that Laurie Aarons, secretary of the CPA, insisted at the start of 1969: 'The time has come for a determined, militant confrontation with the employer–arbitration–Government class structure.'[3]

An occasion presented itself within months, when Victorian Tramways Union secretary Clarrie O'Shea was jailed for defying the penal powers. Twenty-seven unions struck in Victoria, three interstate Trades and Labour Councils followed suit, and a special union meeting bluntly informed the government that it:

> must recognise that it can no longer pursue its traditional adherence to these penal provisions in the face of this determined attitude by the Australian trade union movement.[4]

The shackles had been broken. Strike days topped three million by 1971 and, after a lull in 1972, were to peak at more than six million in 1974. The employers capitulated repeatedly to union demands for higher wages, shorter hours and

BLF march to NSW Premier Robert Askin's office, October 1973

better conditions, while the conservative governments of the time were largely impotent in the face of the working class offensive.

Victoria was the most militant state. When some of its more combative unions grew tired of being held back by the right wing in Melbourne's Trades Hall, they struck out on their own. In 1967, 27 of them withheld affiliation fees. After the Council suspended them, the 'rebel unions' became an alternative trade union centre – spearheading the strikes in defence of Clarrie O'Shea. These unions rejoined Trades Hall in the 1970s but continued to represent the most important left-wing pole in the Australian labour movement. In NSW, the general union scene was more conservative, but there were militant enclaves such as the South Coast. Here, the Trades and Labour Council was left wing, the local wharfies and coal miners had strong communist and left ALP leaderships, and a reform group had deposed the right-wing Federated Ironworkers' Association (FIA) leaders. Elsewhere in the state, the power industry had an outstanding shop committee movement. In Sydney, all eyes were on the Builders Labourers Federation (BLF).

The BLF had once been weak and corrupt, but communists of different stripes had begun cleaning it up in the 1960s. In Victoria, the pro-Chinese communist Norm Gallagher was in power; in NSW, a reform group led by mainstream communist Jack Mundey won leadership. The labourers had also gained greater industrial muscle with the advent of high rise construction, new technology and a runaway building boom. The BLF became famous for stopping environmental destruction with their Green Bans; unfortunately, as the building boom came to an end, the different factions in the union became locked in bitter conflicts until, in 1974, the Gallagher-controlled federal office intervened in NSW with the backing of the employers, leaving a huge legacy of bitterness in Sydney.

Some people on the right saw the new ACTU leader Bob Hawke as the evil genius behind the union surge of 1969–74. NSW Premier Bob Askin, for example, called him 'power drunk and strike happy'.[5] More realistically, Hawke's abrasive style suited the new mood, while his capable advocacy in arbitration helped translate the unions' industrial muscle into formal awards. He was no militant, simply an opportunist. Biographer John Hurst pointed out that Hawke 'had no time for the jargon of the class war'; indeed, he was a good friend of employer advocate George Polites:

> Boozing with his union mates, Hawke would happily join in a raucous rendition of 'Keep the Red Flag Flying'. Boozing with Polites the two could sing with great gusto, 'The working class can kiss my arse, I've got the foreman's job at last'.[6]

The behaviour of Gallagher and Hawke, supposedly representing progressive strands in the union movement, gave early indications of just what an obstacle even the better union leaders could be; but, before the early 1970s, the bureaucratic conservatism of the union officialdom did not prevent the labour movement from making important advances. In the 1960s and early 1970s, an expanding capitalism was able to grant many of workers' demands. So long as gains could be won with relative ease, some union officials could even lead quite militant struggles, knowing that this did not really involve challenging the system.

A new left

The industrial militancy intersected with a political radicalisation, which gave birth to a new left independent of the ALP and even of the CPA. It was part of a wider youth 'counter-culture' whose partisans often combined the politics of sex, drugs and rock and roll with Chairman Mao or Leon Trotsky in confusing fashion. Although only a small minority were clear on what 'the revolution' might mean, many more sympathised with it, especially on the campuses.

The students' growing numbers had increased their political confidence to the point where they sometimes spoke of 'student power'. They set up

Student Action for Aborigines bus Bogabilla NSW February 1965

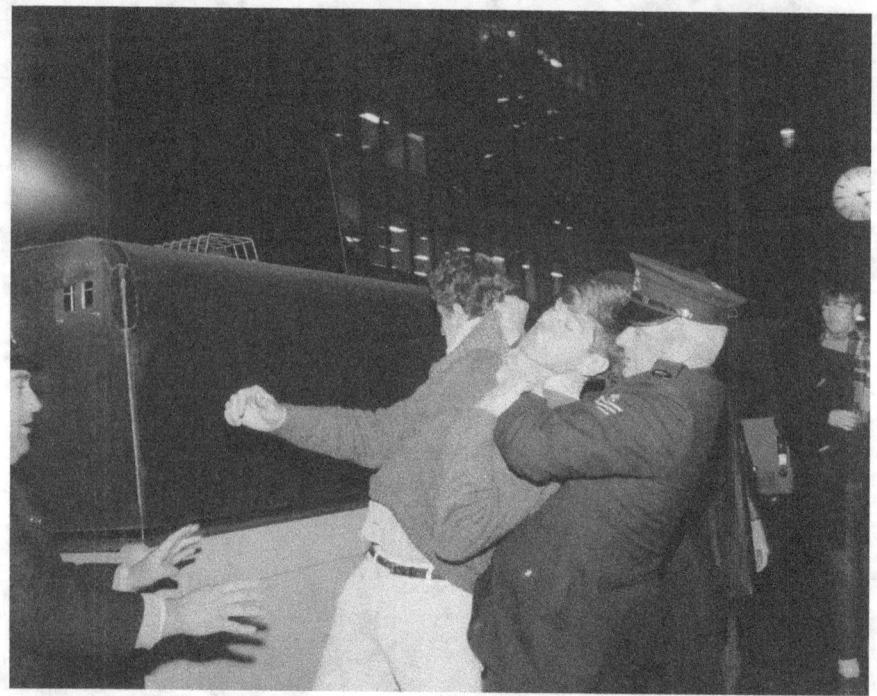

Anti-Vietnam Rally, July 1968

radical organisations such as Students for a Democratic Society, Students for Democratic Action and various Labor Clubs. Fighting racism was a common aim, whether it be 'Freedom Rides' with Aboriginal people or demonstrations against the Springboks. These themes blended with specific campus issues. To challenge restrictive curricula and political bias, they set up a 'free University' in Sydney. At Monash, disciplinary action against Labor Club members raising money for the Vietnamese National Liberation Front led to a strong campaign in their support. Nothing, however, was as important for the 'new left' as the campaign against the Vietnam war. It was part of an international struggle, but direct Australian military involvement also gave the war issue a strong domestic cutting edge from 1965. In the development of this movement, the 1966 election proved a major turning point.

Because Labor leader Arthur Calwell had declared himself against the war, the radicalising youth hoped for an ALP victory. Calwell's defeat shattered them and made them question whether change could come through parliament. Revolutionary politics rapidly gained a hearing, although the precise politics varied: in Melbourne, Maoism won supporters; in Sydney, it was Trotskyism; in Brisbane, a libertarian current. While the proliferation of factions led to sectarian conflict, there was still much common ground. Everyone hated the prevailing social order, and there was immense sympathy for the third world and for Indigenous people. In the early 1970s, a groundswell of support for women's liberation complemented this.

In 1970, the more moderate peace forces initiated mass Moratorium marches around Australia. In Melbourne, ALP left leader Jim Cairns had called for people to 'occupy the street' on 8 May. A worried government attempted desperately to frighten people away from the marches with talk of violence, but to no avail. The 70,000 people who marched in Melbourne – and 120,000 nationwide – showed that the country was turning against the war.[7]

Despite strong union support, the antiwar movement was by no means organised along class lines. It did, however, strengthen left-wing political sentiment among workers, who took action of their own in some cases. Seamen on two ships, *Jeparit* and *Boonaroo*, refused to handle cargo bound for Vietnam. During Moratorium marches, delegations of maritime unionists and other workers stopped work and marched up separately to join the main contingent. Workers also agitated on the job, as in the case of:

> a Yank guard on *Jeparit*, who was sweltering in full combat gear, bristling with guns, while a seaman with only a pair of shorts on casually leaned over the rail giving him a lecture on why he should not be in Vietnam. The Yank kept nodding in agreement all the time and said: 'You don't have to tell me, Bud. I wish I could get out of here right now.'[8]

With the labour and antiwar movements advancing, there was also more space for oppressed people to assert themselves.

Over decades, the original genocidal policies towards Indigenous people had been replaced by concepts of 'assimilation' and 'integration', according to which Australia's Black people were to blend into the national mainstream. This policy was racist: it contemptuously dismissed Indigenous people's desire to maintain their own culture. It was also dishonest: the miserable wages paid to Black workers (when they could get work) made a mockery of integration. Amid the 1960s mineral boom, 'assimilation' was really intended to limit Aboriginal people's rights to mineral-rich land – if they were 'like everyone else', they would have no special right to control the land or extract royalties.

Protesters in front of US President Johnson's car Sydney 1969

The 1960s saw a growing mobilisation against Aboriginal oppression. Black and white students from Sydney University joined 'Freedom Rides', demonstrating against race discrimination in country towns such as Moree and Walgett. In 1966, stockmen on Northern Territory stations struck for equal pay, and the trade union movement organised demonstrations and meetings as well as raising funds. After this strike won a partial victory, the Gurindji people left the stations to settle at Dagu Ragu (Wattie Creek), then demanded 500 square miles of land; when the Liberal government knocked them back, there were further strikes.

This stage of the struggle reached a symbolic peak with the establishment of the Aboriginal tent embassy outside Parliament House, after the McMahon Government again refused to grant land rights. Each time police tore it down, hundreds of Black and white demonstrators defied them and put it up again.

From about 1969, a new movement for women's rights not only demanded equality but put forward a vision of liberation. The movement was partly inspired by overseas examples, but it was also a product of women's changing position in Australian society: as more women entered paid employment, demands grew for equal pay. Theoretically, the government and the unions were committed to this principle; but, apart from teachers and some clerks, there was little progress until 1969, when new test cases before the Arbitration Commission put the issue on the agenda.

The 1969 equal pay decision was a stingy concession applying only to workplaces where women were not in the majority. By now, however, women had raised their expectations. Increasingly, they knew that the economy needed their labour, and boom conditions meant that the bosses could afford to pay; women were not prepared to accept the setback. In a famous action, Zelda D'Aprano and two friends chained themselves to the Commonwealth Building in Melbourne in protest at the decision; when attempts to win official union support for bigger actions fell on deaf ears, they formed the Women's Action Group:

> The type of women's organisation we envisaged was a militant organisation. We had passed the stage of caring about a 'lady-like' image because women had for too long been polite and lady-like, and were still being ignored.'[9]

By 1970, the Women's Action Group was joined by Sydney Women's Liberation, meeting in 'a small room with a bare light globe,'[10] and similar groups were springing up nationwide; 1972 saw the first International Women's Day marches inspired by the new movement.

The activists took an interest in the class struggle, organising support for strikers at Melbourne's Everhot factory and inviting shop steward Edith Turnewitsch to speak on International Women's Day. By 1975 – International Women's Year – there was also a Working Women's Centre in Melbourne and a Women's Trade Union Commission in Sydney. Meanwhile, equal pay for work of equal value had formally arrived, with two landmark arbitration decisions in 1972 and 1974. These still left large numbers of women without equal wages in practice, but they did widen the criteria compared to the 1969 decision – an advance reflecting women's struggles and the general climate of working class mobilisation.

Strongly influenced by women's liberation and by the 'sexual revolution' of the 1960s, a gay movement had arisen in the USA, and Australia didn't lag far behind. In September 1970, Sydney activists established the Campaign Against Moral Persecution (CAMP) to campaign for civil rights and provide support for their community. But it was not long before the more radical ideas of the Gay

Liberation Front, which addressed the wider social context, superseded CAMP's cautious tactics and its limited analysis of homosexual oppression as due merely to prejudice. Caught between homophobia in the women's movement and misogyny among male gays, lesbians also began organising separately.

While the new left sometimes spoke of challenging the existing leaders of the labour movement, its actual impact on the working class was mostly cultural. That, however, was still very important. There was racism, sexism and homophobia aplenty in the working class, as elsewhere in society, but it was being challenged on a mass scale. The general atmosphere of struggle and radical demands was infectious. Women workers, for example, who might not feel ready to join a liberation movement, were still heard more and more frequently to say, 'I'm not a women's libber, but...'

The Whitlam Government

Gough Whitlam rode to power in December 1972[11] on a swell of social unrest, with his government marking a peak of expectations among workers and Labor supporters. Yet, at the same time, more than a few employers had high hopes, for he had cultivated them rather well. *The Australian* reported that, at a 1969 meeting with the business community:

> Gough Whitlam strode into the grand ballroom of one of Australia's finest hotels...and greeted members of the Company Directors' Association of Australia like brothers.[12]

Whitlam intended to resolve the crisis in Australian society through collaboration between capital and labour and by coopting the radicals into administering social programs. Sections of business, aware that the conservative parties had run out of answers, thought this alternative worth a try. For the first time in 23 years, Canberra saw that peculiar phenomenon which Labor governments represent: the official leadership of the working class solving problems for capital.

Whitlam taxed capitalism with sins 'of omission rather than commission,'[13] believing that his government could redress them by restructuring industry, developing the welfare state and bolstering national capital against its foreign rivals. Tariff cuts would force industry to shape up to foreign competition; retraining schemes would help workers make the leap to new jobs; equal pay, child care and parental leave would help more women enter the workforce, which would reduce the country's dependence on immigration; and, through 'resources diplomacy', the government would mobilise commodity producers and help them to present a united front to world markets. There was also a Prices Justification Tribunal (PJT) to combat monopoly pricing, although it did little for consumers – its Chair told them bluntly that the Tribunal 'was not designed as an answer to inflation'.[14]

Whitlam's ability to deliver social and welfare policies depended on delivering economic growth. In his first year, the economy did expand, and the government pressed on with its program. Whitlam raised pensions in line with plans to peg them at 25 percent of average weekly earnings, doubled education spending, trebled outlays on urban development and quadrupled expenditure on housing. Health spending rose by 20 percent, with Medibank yet to come. It seemed that the country's postwar prosperity was being lifted to new heights. Alas, 1974 brought the beginnings of an economic slump savage enough to destroy the government.

As the recession developed, Labor retreated steadily from its programs, but the early stages of the government have nevertheless left behind the myth of Whitlam the daring reformer, with Fraser cast as his nefarious opposite. It is true that Fraser took a meat cleaver to much of the Whitlam legacy. At the same time, however, there were deeply equivocal features to that legacy, as well as important elements of continuity between what were, after all, two capitalist governments. Just as the Whitlam regime was a living contradiction, seeking to mesh incompatible demands from capital and labour, so its reforms managed to be progressive yet – at the same time – to harbour dubious and even regressive elements.

Traditional welfare philosophy had favoured only a minimal safety net for those who couldn't cope in the free market so that, in Liberal PM John Gorton's magnanimous phrase, 'they do not need blankets to be provided for them in winter.' By contrast, the Whitlam Government intended its measures to embrace the entire people. Its programs, said ALP Senator John Wheeldon, were of 'benefit to all Australians and not just those below the poverty line'.[15] Such an approach clearly had its progressive side; yet it effectively precluded a redistribution of wealth from rich to poor, and this was not the only way the Whitlam reforms favoured the 'haves' more than the 'have nots'. For example, scrapping tertiary fees, in the absence of wider measures to get large numbers of working class youth to university, was largely a gift to the middle and upper classes. Similar ambiguities lurked almost everywhere.

Medibank, to take Labor's most famous reform, was certainly a big advance. It ensured that the whole population was covered, while cutting administrative costs. On the other hand, it was far from being a national health scheme; it was just a universal insurance scheme within which private medicine and the power of doctors remained intact. A large portion of the government's increased health expenditure actually went to meet increased doctors' fees.

Indigenous Australians got a much better deal from the Labor government, which made extensive land rights and funding commitments, but that wasn't simply the ALP's generosity at work. Indigenous people had placed these issues firmly on the political agenda through their own struggles. Moreover, there were serious weaknesses in the policies; for example, Justice Woodward, appointed to look into land rights, made the pioneering recommendation that Aboriginal people should have the right to veto mineral exploration on their land, but then outraged them by adding the rider: 'unless in the national interest'. Black people knew that, at crucial junctures, the 'national interest' would be determined by white people.

So it was with equal pay for women, parental leave and child care. Once again, these concessions had been won in struggle; once again, a closer examination revealed ambiguities. Many of the reforms were designed to back up labour force policies for industry, and many were more limited than they seemed. Formal equal pay would probably have arrived through arbitration, with or without government backing, and Whitlam did little to address the practical inequalities that remained. As for child care, the government repeatedly announced major initiatives, then channelled the funds into preschools, which generally offered much more limited care.

Migrants generally looked with favour on the Whitlam Government, because it took some measures against discrimination. The common perception, however, that Labor replaced the White Australia policy with multiculturalism is mostly false. Previous Liberal governments had already largely scrapped White Australia under the pressure of labour shortages. Whitlam merely removed the last vestiges of open racism, while ensuring that little changed in practice. His government cut the migrant intake and put a greater emphasis on family reunion; since most migrant families already in Australia were white, this ensured that few non-whites actually came into the country. Although Labor's Al Grassby did use the term 'multicultural' in a 1973 speech, the concept remained extremely vague and was little used for several years; in reality, it was the Fraser Government which institutionalised multiculturalism, while turning it to conservative ends.[16]

An equally contradictory picture presented itself in industrial relations. The Prime Minister, who wished to 'uplift the horizons of the Australian people',[17] didn't see this in class terms, but there were ministers of a more left-wing orientation or with more direct links to organised labour, such as Jim Cairns, Tom Uren and Clyde Cameron. A stout defence of workers' interests might have been expected from them, and some of Labor's early measures did please the union movement. The government did use the public sector as something of a 'pacesetter', introducing an extra week of holidays, paid parental leave and a 17.5 percent holiday leave loading. At times, Cameron even expressed sympathy with striking workers.

On the other hand, many of these changes were either just labour market adjustments to meet the longer term needs of industry or inevitable concessions to a combative working class. The extra holidays simply brought federal government workers into line with those in the states. Clyde Cameron, despite the odd rhetorical splurge, was no class warrior. Rather, he was obsessed with industrial peace, and that desire became more urgent in 1974 as strike levels soared.

Workers were defending themselves against inflation by notching up six million strike days for the year – the highest figure since 1919. Rather than helping them, Cameron pressed harder for restraint, telling Sydney members of the Australian Workers Union (AWU) that company profits must come first. If this was not to mean cuts in living standards, productivity must rise, 'but, let me be blunt, it will depend on trade union cooperation.'[18] If that was not forthcoming, he was ready with sharper language about union 'bloody mindedness.'[19]

Moreover, even the best Labor policies served to coopt the activists. Two academics said of the welfare programs that there were 'dangers of the poor being manipulated or sidetracked into symbolic/therapeutic political activities which have no real effect.'[20] Indigenous Australians certainly understood what this meant, having elected a National Aboriginal Consultative Council which the government kept carefully limited to an advisory role. The government rebuffed militants who sought to turn it into a sort of Black parliament.

One-time agitators became tied up in delivering services, with unfortunate results. Anne Summers wrote that, by the end of 1975:

> the optimism and energy that radical groups exuded during the early years of the Whitlam Government had gradually dissipated. Many feminists were fully engaged in running the many services activities... Others had temporarily dropped out of politics, exhausted from setting up these centres, lobbying for funds.[21]

Gough Whitlam speaking at the Aboriginal Tent Embassy Canberra 8 February 1972

Wage indexation had a similar effect among trade unionists. By late 1975, Labor had hit upon a strategy to control the unions: quarterly cost-of-living adjustments (wage indexation) in exchange for ending strikes. The government's main objective was industrial peace;[22] but, because indexation rises lagged behind price movements, the system also cut real wages. However, the new system's most serious effect was to demobilise the working class rank and file. It shifted the focus of wage fixing from struggle on the shop floor to the bureaucratic process of arbitration, strengthening the weight of full-time officials within the labour movement as against the rank and file activists. Consequently, wage indexation slowed the momentum of industrial struggle. Once the unions had committed themselves to trading industrial peace for periodic pay increases, their officials were required to police the agreement, and pressure increased on shop stewards to do likewise.

So we cannot simply identify Whitlam with progress and Fraser with reaction. Whitlam's reforms were only partly progressive, and he retreated from most of them after 1974. The experience of Labor abandoning its declared principles one by one accelerated the demoralisation of movement and union activists which had begun with cooptation. In truth, the era of reaction began under Whitlam. The catalyst was economic crisis.

Labor retreats

First came runaway inflation. Contrary to conservative mythology, the cause was neither union demands nor Whitlam's spending programs, but the Vietnam war. US President Johnson tried to pay for the war by printing money. Because the US dollar was used worldwide, this caused an international price spiral. The 1973 'oil shock', when the oil producers' cartel OPEC drove up energy prices, tipped overheated economies into recession. As international recession brought commodity prices crashing down, Australia's economy crashed with them. Non-farm production shrank, unemployment reached 4 percent, and – most important of all from the capitalist point of view – profits plunged. As a percentage of Gross Domestic Product, they fell from 14 to 9 percent in the course of 1974.

Even so, the economic crisis appeared somehow unreal at first. True, it caused some panic in the corridors of power; but no one grasped its full importance. The early 1970s marked the beginning of a new era of international economic stagnation and mass unemployment. Despite a modest recovery in the late 1980s, the consequences of that era continued: even under Hawke, unemployment never fell below about 6 percent, and Keating's recession at the start of the 1990s saw it reach new heights. Ferocious attacks on the working class throughout the industrialised world have not been enough to restore the system's health. Yet, in the Whitlam years, the crisis seemed a bizarre aberration, which might be corrected if only someone could find the right policy mix.

There were two reasons for this. Firstly, everyone had grown used to stability and prosperity after years of postwar boom, and there was a widespread – although intellectually fuzzy – belief that Keynesian economists knew how to prevent depressions through government spending programs. Secondly, it took some time for business to appreciate the significance of the decline in profit rates, which was not just a cyclical phenomenon but the beginning of a long-term slump. Initially, it was hardly noticed at all, because industry was still making inflationary paper profits. Firms had not yet learned to build rapid inflation into their accounting.

Neither had governments. When inflation hit 13 percent in 1973, Labor treated it with annoyance rather than alarm. Only after the Liberals harped effectively on the issue during the 1974 election did Whitlam begin listening to Treasury calls for a 'short, sharp shock' to get prices under control. When the Treasury line ran into stiff opposition in Labor ranks, he wavered once again. The 1974 budget speech, shaped by Treasury's opponents in Cabinet, declared that 'crucial as the fight against inflation is, it cannot be made the sole objective of government policy.' Labor's 'overriding objective' was to get on with its social program.[23] This simply meant that, instead of basing the program on private sector growth, the government was now trying to push through its reforms regardless of the economy. Without mobilising his worker supporters in struggle, Whitlam had no hope of pulling this off. In fact, the pressure went back on the Labor Cabinet within weeks, when inflation briefly hit 22 percent. Gough Whitlam was forced to retreat.

As recession set in, the increasingly worried government began bailing out companies. The ALP's national conference in February 1975 promised 'reasonable returns on investment', and the government told the Prices Justification Tribunal to consider the need for higher profits. Ironically, this new and openly pro-employer policy only showed how badly Labor was lagging behind events. The handouts were popular with those who received them; but the majority of business leaders, suddenly disillusioned with Keynesianism, were turning to a new economic theory – Milton Friedman's monetarism. Friedman contended that controlling the money supply and government spending was decisive in attacking inflation, thus ultimately avoiding recession. He added that a certain amount of unemployment was also required. If few business leaders or politicians really grasped the theory, that mattered little at first; it seemed a simple panacea, one which jibed with conservative rhetoric about smaller government, with the added attraction that it might intimidate the unions. By February 1975, the Liberal Party had begun to embrace it.

Labor had a hard time adapting. When Jim Cairns sought to defend economic policy, he was all at sea. Asked in parliament whether he hoped to solve the economy's problems by 'printing money', Cairns replied:

> We might do precisely that. There are still about 250,000 persons unemployed in Australia...if by government expenditure I can ensure that any one case of these men can be put to work productively...he will not be allowed to remain in unemployment because of a shortage of money.[24]

The sentiments were admirable, but they did Cairns immense damage in the eyes of business; by the middle of 1975, Whitlam was looking for excuses to dump him. The Prime Minister found a suitable pretext in Cairns' inept handling of the 1975 'loans affair'.

Minerals and Energy Minister Rex Connor had seen in the 1973 oil crisis an opportunity to borrow large amounts of Middle Eastern 'petro-dollars', which he could use to buy out foreign-owned mining companies. This was consistent with the government's previous nationalism, but Connor and Cairns made one political blunder after another in handling it. The loans affair made the government look unstable and incompetent. As with Cairns, however, Connor's downfall was not simply caused by scandal. Increasingly, business was turning away from Labor's nationalist economic schemes as the sellers' market in commodities evaporated.

Whitlam also dumped the Labour minister, Clyde Cameron. From mid-1975, he looked increasingly to Bill Hayden and Jim McClelland to rescue the government. Hayden, a one-time leftist, became a fiscally conservative Treasurer; where Cameron had occasionally shown sympathy for union claims, McClelland brought to the Labour portfolio a consistent hostility to militant trade unionism. The new ministers were installed to sound a retreat from virtually all of Labor's original platform, and the Hayden budget hacked away at almost every program except Medibank. Whitlam hoped that this might rescue his popularity with the employing class; in reality, it only discouraged ALP supporters, while encouraging the political right to launch new attacks.

Problems at the grassroots

The confusion and demoralisation caused by Labor's retreats also accelerated a decline in the radical social movements.

The movements had lost their most important source of mass recruitment after the Liberals' 1971 decision, following the USA's lead, to begin withdrawing troops from Vietnam. While antiwar demonstrations continued, there were no more mass Moratoriums. With Whitlam poised to win power in 1972, most of those opposed to the war and concerned about social issues were drawn back to electoral politics. Moreover, the government's programs and policies succeeded in coopting and disorienting a layer of activists. Finally, recession after 1974 meant that most students suddenly became worried about their future careers and turned their attention back to their textbooks. In the Fraser years, campus struggles were relatively few, and most social movements could rely on only a comparatively small reservoir of student participants.

There was still a substantial layer of experienced radical activists, but they had little coherent politics in common. They were accustomed to talking of socialism and revolution, but what did these terms mean? Only a minority had seriously studied Marxism, and many of those had done so in the context of Stalinist, Maoist or other distorted frameworks. Revolution could mean anything from urban guerrilla warfare to changing your consciousness with drugs. Most of the time, it was not meant too seriously; in practice, the bulk of the activists aimed for reforms (sometimes far-reaching ones) within the existing society. When the movements declined, the reformism became more explicit.

Reformism, in turn, meant fragmentation. People who hoped to turn the world upside down naturally aspired to build a single movement of all the discontented. When they became reconciled to piecemeal change, they began to concentrate on defending particular interests, such as women's equality, land rights or the environment. The concept of 'autonomy' soon arrived, to give this retreat a progressive veneer.

In the early 1970s, some of the previously campus-based far left attempted to find new avenues for growth through agitation in the working class, with Maoist students seeking to build a 'Worker-Student Alliance', while others close to the CPA or influenced by Gramsci's writings on Italian factory councils sought to establish a revolutionary base in metal shops. Still others set up small rank and file groups inside unions where they had members. These efforts were valuable in giving the far left some experience of the class struggle and, occasionally, in influencing individual struggles; but the links they made were nowhere near substantial enough to sustain the social movements, and the far left's toehold in industry became harder to maintain once worker militancy declined after 1977.

Yet there were still thousands of people whose politics had been profoundly shaped by the radicalisation of the 1960s and early 1970s, and many of them resurfaced in the anti-nuclear and other social movements of the Fraser years. A major breakthrough for any of those movements might have made an important contribution to reversing the rightward drift in society and the decline of social radicalism itself, but this did not occur, for reasons to be explored.

The sagging of the social movements, in turn, removed one factor driving the class struggle forward. Workers might not always approve of demonstrating students or 'women's libbers', but the militants often did, and it was they who typically took the lead in industrial struggles. The mass antiwar movement had exposed the conservative government's political weakness, and this had encouraged trade unionists to defy it industrially. But by the mid-1970s, these factors were diminishing in importance.

The onset of economic crisis from 1974 put organised labour to a decisive test, because workers were entering a new era in which they could no longer make gains without confronting the capitalist system itself. Profits, the lifeblood of the system, were shrivelling, and the system could only restore them by ruthless restructuring – weeding out inefficient firms, sacking masses of workers and hammering unions that resisted. For workers to maintain their living standards, let alone raise them further under the new conditions, they would have to confront the system, putting the defence of their own interests ahead of Australian capitalism's survival. Mostly unintentionally, a generation of rank and file union militants suddenly found themselves in conflict with the system – and consequently in conflict with their officials, who were tied to it. At several key junctures in the Fraser era, even the mass of the members was more combative than the officials.

In the short run, the rank and file could maintain a high level of struggle on the basis of the sheer anger and bitterness provoked by Fraser's power grab and his ruthless policies and by the employers' attacks. This was the basis of huge mobilisations during the Constitutional Crisis and in defence of Medibank, fuelling the great staying power shown by some groups of workers during two long strikes discussed in Chapter 5. However, the political mobilisations were derailed by the manoeuvres of Bob Hawke and other top union leaders, while the other strikes ended in defeat because they remained isolated. After that, resistance began to decline. To sustain high levels of struggle, the militants would have needed to find new leaders, build class wide solidarity and, above all, find their way to a political analysis that pointed to fighting the system as a whole. They were ill equipped to do this. Because it had been easy to win gains from the late 1960s onwards, the politics of most militants – even those who spoke casually of socialism – remained a bit naïve.

Before 1975, elementary trade unionism had seemed to be enough. Strong groups of workers had grown used to winning gains within individual industries or individual workplaces, often fighting on a localised basis and sometimes without much reference to the wider union structures. They counted on the employers' ability to grant concessions without too much fuss. Award wages were increasingly set outside the framework of national wage cases, as groups of workers in particular industries took direct action to extract a better deal from their employers – then had the Arbitration Commission rubber stamp those deals. Whereas national wage reviews had accounted for about 85 percent of award wage increases in the early 1960s, this proportion fell to 53 percent by 1970 and to a mere 9 percent by 1974. Meanwhile, the role of 'over-award' payments agreed at the enterprise level increased dramatically after 1967. In the case of NSW metal fitters, these rose from 14 to 26 percent over the award rate between 1960 and 1974.[25]

Conditions of high unemployment and low profits (or even massive company losses) after 1974 meant that, suddenly, workers could no longer rely on such elementary and localised trade union action to defend their living standards. The balance of power had shifted back to the employers. The bosses still had too much respect for the better unionised sections of the workforce to use crude threats ('knuckle under or we'll replace you with workers from the dole queues'), but there were more subtle arguments which told workers that their jobs depended on the viability of the company. The politicians took this a step further, arguing that workers could only protect their jobs by making sacrifices to 'make ourselves competitive' as a nation.[26]

To confront the new situation and answer these arguments, workers needed an analysis of the society around them. They also needed a strategy and organisations of struggle that could unite the working class as a whole, along with all its potential allies – students, activists in social movements, the unemployed and the oppressed.

It was not that Australian workers lacked experience in mass solidarity or political struggle; there had been the general strike over Clarrie O'Shea, for example, and the BLF Green Bans. But the O'Shea strike was a one-off event, and the Green Bans were limited to one industry under peculiar conditions;

both had been relatively easy to organise in conditions of full employment. To mobilise that kind of struggle in an ongoing fashion, in the face of high unemployment, required conscious and concerted organisation among a sizeable number of militants. And, whereas the earlier struggles had been led to victory by sections of the union bureaucracy, the crisis brought a new caution to even the most left-wing officials. If they wanted to win major battles, the militants would need to push hard to force the officials to fight – and organise independently of them when they refused.

Unfortunately, the forces in Australian society which possessed even the rudiments of an alternative political strategy for the working class were too confused or too weak to put them into practice. The CPA or the ALP Socialist Left spoke of solidarity and political struggle but were too tied to the official union structures to develop a strategy or forms of organisation that went beyond the horizons of the union bureaucracy. Other, further left groups, argued for general strikes and revolution, but they had few roots in the organised labour movement. Meanwhile, a large proportion of militants, like other sections of society, saw the crisis as a temporary aberration that didn't require any change of approach; by the time they learned otherwise, worker morale was badly damaged. By default, industrial and political leadership remained with the full-time union officials and the ALP, who did not challenge the essence of the right-wing arguments, preferring to repackage them in a form suited to Labor governments and their beloved framework of 'consultation'.

So, when Fraser finally fell in 1983, it was not to an insurgent working class allied with radical protest movements, but to an ALP government devoted to securing by indirect means what Fraser had sought to force by confrontation: wage cuts, an end to militancy on the job and the subordination of workers to national economic competitiveness.

An odd hero for the right

In 1975, however, that prospect was still remote. Regarding Whitlam's policies of cooptation and class collaboration as utter failures, the Australian ruling class wanted a new government to make a frontal attack on the working class and the social movements, and Malcolm Fraser emerged in 1975 as the likely knuckleman. Accordingly, when he became Liberal leader in March, his opponents promptly began to paint him as an extremist ideologue of the radical right. To understand the complexities of his years in power, however, we must discard this picture almost entirely.

Intellectually, Fraser was a traditional conservative. He was personally opposed to legalising abortion, homosexuality and easier divorce, although he was flexible about these issues in practice. He had a strong anti-communist streak and had been a hawk on Vietnam. He voiced the traditional conservative truisms about relying on individual initiative rather than government, epitomised by the notorious statement that 'life is not meant to be easy'.[27] All this one might expect from a Victorian Western District grazier. But he had long shared the Keynesian orthodoxy in economics that marked the postwar Liberal governments. His speeches as a backbencher stressed full employment ahead of price stability; as Education Minister, he presided over a near doubling of outlays in three years.

It was Phillip Lynch and Billy Snedden who began turning the Liberal Party towards monetarism. As late as mid-1974, Snedden had only argued for slowing the growth of government spending rather than for actual cuts; but, by the end of the year, his views were shifting. In February 1975, he issued policy documents putting the party more firmly on a monetarist course. Snedden, however, was proving an ineffectual leader in parliament. For this reason, Fraser replaced him in March.

By that time, Fraser had given a few hints that he was drifting towards Friedmanite theories. In his January 1975 address to the ANZAAS conference, he said that Keynesian pump-priming had been useful in the 1930s and even after World War II, but that times had changed:

> Two things have altered. Trade union leadership is no longer fearful of large scale and continuing unemployment. They lose this fear at the very time when their own actions ought to revive it. Secondly, national governments have lost the art of restraint.

To jettison Keynesianism was easy, but what would replace it? Fraser had few answers at this stage and took refuge in traditional conservative formulas, calling for 'massive incentives for private expenditure [and] a consequential and phased cut in government expenditure'. The unions would be tamed by a 'third arm' of the conciliation and arbitration system, which would have powers to police and prosecute.[28]

The speech gave some indication of what Fraser would do in office, but it was mid-year before he used monetarism systematically to add a theoretical gloss – a process assisted, ironically, by the Labor government. Cairns began promoting the private sector as the engine of growth, then the Hayden budget cut programs amid a rhetoric of government restraint. Fraser recognised his cue and pushed for more drastic measures, calling in his budget reply speech for a 'responsible program of monetary control'.[29]

Thus, Malcolm Fraser became a 'monetarist' as part of making himself the Man of the Hour. He was simply a ruthless establishment politician who wanted to lead his party and his class against a collapsing Labor government and a disoriented working class. He offered a battle cry rather than a battle plan. He had no strategic framework. The employers expected him to discipline the unions and redistribute wealth from workers' pockets to capitalist profits, while the political right wanted the unruly social movements put in their place. He believed that he could do both by applying conservative commonsense remedies such as welfare cuts, union-bashing and appeals to traditional values – an expectation much of the ruling class naïvely seemed to share. Certainly, the nearly universal anti-Labor sentiment among the bourgeoisie, the weakened position of the unions and his huge election mandate enabled Fraser to dominate politics for several years, during which his political program seemed coherent enough.

Later, when these conditions evaporated, he floundered. Neither Fraser nor his backers understood the depth of the economic crisis or the dimensions of the social conflicts that lay ahead. The government could cut budgets and wages for a time, but that did nothing to end the economic stagnation. Workers were disoriented, and militancy ebbed over the years of recession, but the unions had strong organisation and deep roots: they would endure. The radical social movements were in gradual decline, but a reasonably large layer of experienced activists remained, along with strong political traditions – lots of people knew how to mobilise in the streets. Fraser's task would not be nearly as simple as he and his backers imagined. By 1982, 'monetary control' was a distant dream, the unions had struck back, and Fraser was politically bankrupt – and not alone in that. When the government began to falter, all the underlying disunity and confusion among the leaders of the capitalist class re-emerged. They had to turn once again to the official leadership of the working class, Bob Hawke this time, to try to get things under control.

In international terms, Malcolm Fraser was an anomaly. Amid an economic crisis that was part of an international slump, he shared the desire of ruling class politicians worldwide to impose the price of resolving it on the working class. Overseas, the methods of frontal confrontation had been largely discredited in the 1960s and early 1970s. In Britain, for example, the Heath Tory government had come unstuck in its confrontation with the miners and crashed to an electoral defeat in 1974. Fascism had collapsed on the Iberian peninsula, and military dictatorship had failed in Greece. In much of Europe, a revitalised social democracy and newly respectable 'Eurocommunist' parties were in or near power, preaching social contracts or historic compromises, with even President Jimmy Carter in the USA offering a pale counterfeit of this trend. In Australia, however, it was precisely Whitlam's ALP government and the politics of class collaboration that had failed in the face of the crisis. The rebuilding of social democracy, necessary to eventually restore control, would have to go on in opposition. In 1975, Australia's rulers were looking for the big stick, wielded by Big Mal, without quite realising all the implications.

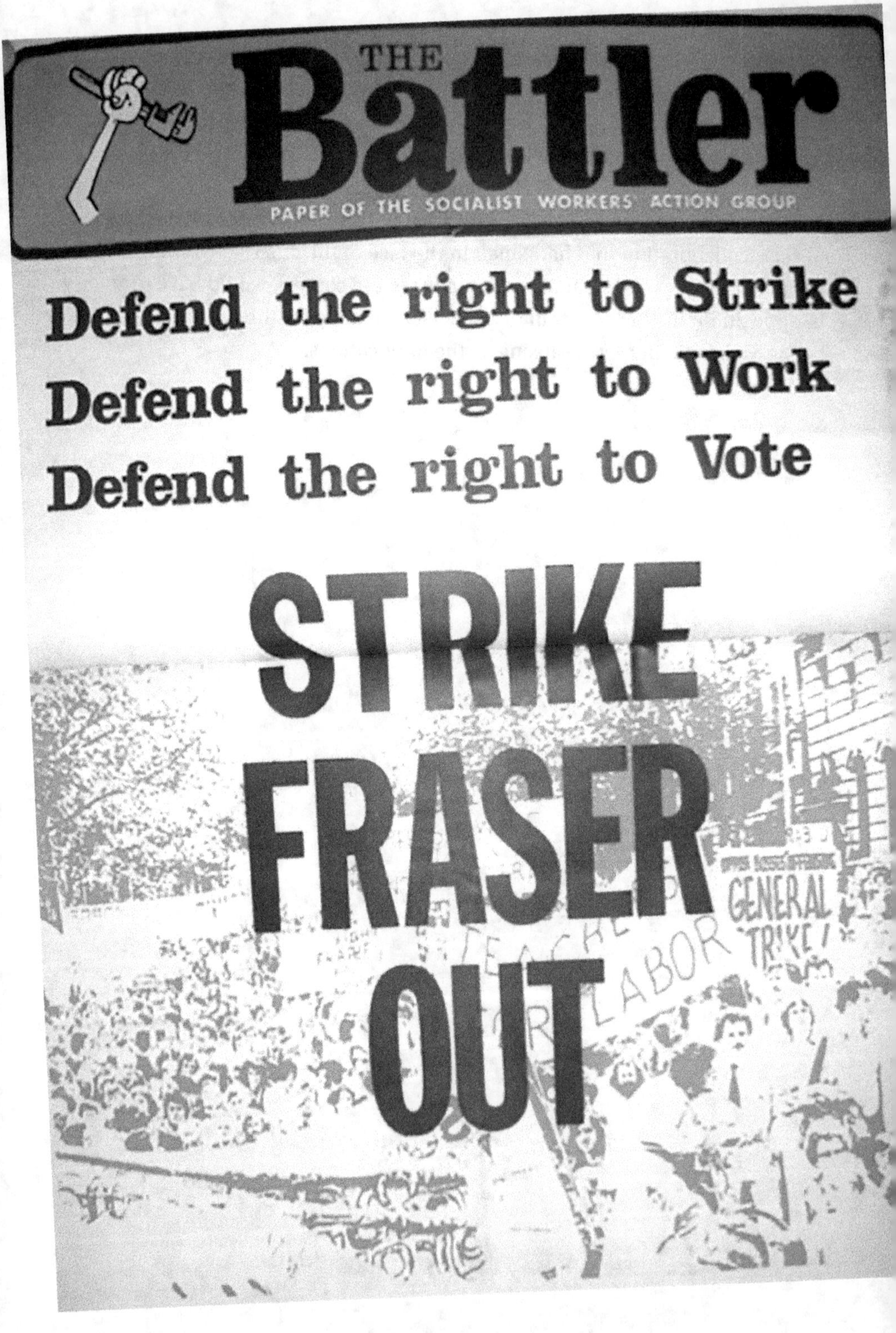

THE Battler

PAPER OF THE SOCIALIST WORKERS' ACTION GROUP

Defend the right to Strike
Defend the right to Work
Defend the right to Vote

STRIKE FRASER OUT

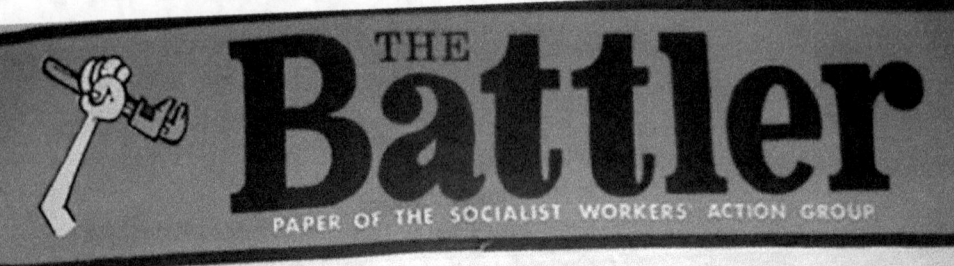

3.
Coup in Canberra

Initially, big business had accepted the Whitlam Government, although the acceptance was guarded: Whitlam's speechwriter and biographer, Graham Freudenberg, reports that the giddy pace of reform in the first weeks 'aroused uneasy suspicions' in business circles, who feared that 'when Whitlam spoke of change he might well be serious'.[1] There were some signs of a 'capital strike' almost from the start. Overseas investment fell, and profits paid overseas rose in 1973 and 1974, while the financial press complained of a 'business–government gap'.[2]

Yet, in 1973, this was not the full story. The Murdoch press continued to back Whitlam. Cairns, who had become good mates with leading industrialists on a trade mission to China, was a big hit in his economic portfolios. When he was removed from Secondary Industry, the president of the Associated Chamber of Manufacturers declared him 'worthy of high praise'.[3] The withdrawal of overseas capital was partly a response by its owners to economic deterioration in the home countries. In 1974, with the advent of economic crisis, the mood gradually turned against the government. A survey found that US firms were becoming reluctant to invest in Australia, probably owing to inflated fears of how left wing the Whitlam Government was. In rural areas, a backlash developed against the government's priority emphasis on urban development and crystallised around hostility to the removal of the superphosphate bounty. There was an anti-union march in Hobart. Peak industry bodies began to attack the government more concertedly.

Finally, in 1975, the opposition to Whitlam began to take on some features of a general mobilisation of the ruling class. Conservative governments in NSW and Queensland broke with convention to appoint non-Labor replacements for retiring ALP Senators, thus strengthening the Opposition's position in the

Police break picket lines at the Herald and Weekly Times strike August 1975

upper house. Right-wing forces were able to organise a 2,000-strong 'march against socialism' in Mt Gambier, ironically a town whose economy depended heavily on the public sector. In May, a Sydney Anglican rector asked his flock to pray for Jim Cairns' removal from the ministry; in August, he announced that 'God has answered our prayers.'[4] Emboldened by a crushing victory in the Bass by-election and the ALP's near defeat in South Australia, the federal Opposition began to scent victory and began looking for any suitable opportunity to block Supply in the Senate, which would force an election.

The Opposition's blocking of Supply (money to pay government bills) was not unprecedented. Not only had it happened at state level in the past, but Whitlam himself had asserted Labor's right to use the power of the upper house while in opposition. Even so, the conservatives' use of the Senate had a different air about it, reflecting a conviction that they and a traditional, conservative layer of the employing class – the 'Establishment', so to speak – really were born to rule. They saw Labor in office as an aberration which the voters would soon regret. Senate Opposition leader Reg Withers had said in 1973:

> because of the temporary electoral insanity of the two most populous Australian states, the Senate may well be called upon

to protect the national interest by exercising its undoubted constitutional rights and powers.⁵

Withers' contempt for the electorate was subsequently given a sharper class content by fellow Liberal Bob Ellicott, whose 1975 election advertisements ridiculed Labor's years in office as:

> Three years of so called 'working man's politicians' groping around trying to handle something they were never capable of doing: run the country. No matter how many academics they employed to compensate for their inferiority complexes, it was you who did the worrying for them.⁶

The Liberal Party ranks were in a lather by the final months of 1975, their heads filled with capitalist clichés. Peter Smark of the Melbourne *Age* described the crowd at one Fraser rally as 'slavering for action against the unions'.⁷ Donald Horne, who found himself at a Liberal branch meeting on Sydney's swanky North Shore during the election campaign, gave a memorable account of the atmosphere:

> One speaker said unemployment was caused by pampered dole bludgers who needed more discipline. Another said free enterprise must be liberated by making tariffs higher. Someone else said free enterprise would prevail only with strong government leadership… The phrase 'free enterprise' was passed from mouth to mouth like a magic charm. It was thought ridiculous to suggest that a world economic crisis affected Australia. Stimulate business confidence and all would be well.⁸

More than a few industrialists shared the mood: in late 1975, a government advisory committee reported that some manufacturers saw in Labor policy 'a socialist plot to destroy them'.⁹

Poison pens

The mass media, controlled as they are by the employers, generally reflect and propagate the views of the ruling class. Often, they do so fairly subtly, but there was little subtlety about their role in Whitlam's fall. The Murdoch press turned on Labor with a vengeance, and the media generally lined up behind Fraser, from the time of the loans affair. The bias during 1975 was unmistakable. While many of the press gallery were pro-Labor, the policies of the proprietors largely determined what appeared in print or went to air. The sensational treatment of the loans affair set the tone. To read some of the papers, you would have thought that Labor had sold the country to evil-hearted foreigners and that this betrayal had brought the economic crisis upon Australia. Irritating facts – for example, that the government had never actually borrowed any money – were virtually ignored, as a media worker complained:

> The money was never there in the first place [but] to people out there in the community, who couldn't grasp what had happened to the economy, here was something that was quite ludicrous that they could grasp onto and…provide rationalisation for saying, 'Well yes, the reason why unemployment is up is because we have got these silly people running the economy.'[10]

Union-bashing also helped set an anti-Labor tone. Industrial disputation over a $35 claim at Kurnell oil refinery in Sydney, which posed a challenge to the indexation guidelines, seems to have been the signal. The Sydney *Sun-Herald* seized on some run-of-the mill rhetoric from employer spokesmen and ran it under the heading, 'Action On Strike Chaos Demanded'. 'The cauldron is just simmering,' said the executive director of the NSW Employers' Federation. 'Unless we get some action the lid will really go off.' Amid the strained metaphors, he demanded government action, as did his fellow employer representative George Polites; the *Sun-Herald* backed them up with some evocative prose of its own about 'another grim bout of emergency conditions'.[11]

In September, the ACTU Congress gave *The Australian* an opportunity to warn of a 'Vote For Leftists At ACTU'. Readers alarmed by this new menace had to turn to the small type to learn that it consisted of four candidates who 'share the leftist views of Mr R. J. Hawke, the ACTU President'.[12]

The public sector was another handy target. In early November, the *Sun-Herald* shifted the attack to government employees, featuring a statement from an academic who claimed that the public service was 'grossly overpaid' and that the government could sack up to 100,000 public servants with little loss in productivity.[13]

During the election campaign of November–December, the media continued to hammer Whitlam. Sometimes, the methods were pretty crude. According to one source, *The Age* held over a penetrating piece on Liberal policies by its economics editor, Kenneth Davidson, bringing in the business editor to write a more acceptable commentary.[14] A different journalist voiced the frustrations of many colleagues: 'The campaign was just so depressing. I knew it didn't matter what I got, I just couldn't get it in the newspaper.'[15]

The palm for blatant 'massaging' of the news inevitably went to Rupert Murdoch's News Ltd. Murdoch, who had originally held 'high hopes' for Labor ('I still believe it was the right thing to have a change,' he later said),[16] had gone very sour on Whitlam by 1975. His Sydney tabloids used some classic tricks.

The *Daily Telegraph* city edition of 1 December was bad enough, with its claim that 'Welfare Bludgers Get $350 A Week', but the country edition went further, claiming that the total was $700. It turned out that the correct figure, $350, was for a household of four adults and six children. Then came the *Daily Mirror* front page of 26 November. Labor was proposing inexpensive rental accommodation for low income earners. The headline in one edition was 'Gough's Promise – Cheap Rents'. When someone on the staff decided that this front page was too favourable to the ALP, the story was revamped, the last edition carrying the headline, 'Gough Panics – Cheap Rents'. A new introduction made it appear that Whitlam had stolen the policy from Fraser.

The egregious examples, however, were probably less important than the weight of day-after-day reinforcement. The *Sydney Morning Herald* ran a series of relentless anti-Labor editorials, with key excerpts reprinted on page one. Reporters allowed Fraser to get away with stonewalling at his press conferences.[17] Ranald Macdonald, Chair of the Australian Newspapers Council, clearly passed a very restrained judgement on his industry when he later wrote:

> our credibility is at an all-time low. In the months leading up to the last federal election, the Labor Party didn't have a fair go.[18]

Trade unions made some efforts to combat the media onslaught. In late November, the train drivers' union placed a ban on giving news to the *Daily Mirror*, and the Cumberland NSW branch of the Amalgamated Metal Workers Union (AMWU) called for a national, one-day union ban on the daily papers. Such bans are usually ineffectual, but the South Coast Trades and Labor Council (TLC) had some success with a ban on the *Illawarra Mercury*. The *Mercury* had run a front page editorial entitled 'Our Dying Land', which attacked 'irresponsible militant union leaders' out to 'usher in an era of industrial anarchy'.[19] By imposing bans on cooperation with the paper's journalists, the

TLC won the right to reply to the editorial and to contribute a weekly column of 250–300 words.

News Ltd faced a certain amount of industrial unrest among its printing workers; at one stage, Perth unions attempted to ban newsprint supplies to the company. But the most important union action against the company's press manipulation was a strike by Murdoch journalists. Even before Governor-General John Kerr's dismissal of Whitlam, three of them had written to their boss complaining that *The Australian* had 'become a laughing stock':

> It is not so much the policy itself but the blind, biased, tunnel-visioned, ad hoc, logically-confused and relentless way in which so many people are now conceiving it to be carried out.

These writers were no radicals. They insisted: 'We make no case for a dull paper, a bleeding hearts paper, a worker-controlled paper. Our catch-word is simply: integrity.'[20] However, having concluded by 8 December that this quality was not their employer's strong suit, journalists stopped work at Murdoch publications in four cities to register their protest.

Satisfying no one

Labor's original perspective had been to reconcile and unite capital, labour and other interests. In 1975, the government found itself in direct conflict with powerful groups of companies, professionals and skilled workers; it was a sign of how unrealistic that hope was.

Concerted opposition by the insurance industry to the proposed Australian Government Insurance Corporation (AGIC) was the first of three challenges Labor had to face. The AGIC idea arose after disastrous floods in Queensland during January 1974 made large numbers of homeowners acutely aware that their insurance didn't cover flood damage. Housing Minister Les Johnson proposed a government corporation to fill the void, and the ALP made the idea part of their 1974 election platform. This set off alarm bells at the private insurance companies. They had suffered badly in the deepening economic crisis and did not wish to face a new competitor at a time of squeezed profits, particularly a government-backed flood cover they couldn't match. There was also some measure of paranoia in the industry about socialisation – apparently fed by AMP's public affairs secretary Ian O'Brien, who thought:

the demise of the industry was what [Labor] were after – and through us the whole private sector. We were the jugular vein they were trying to get.[21]

Despite their financial problems, the insurance companies had no difficulty raising funds for a political campaign reminiscent of the 1949 assault on Ben Chifley's bank nationalisation plan; in April 1975, a series of TV advertisements worth $150,000 raised the spectre of nationalisation by stealth. Around the same time, Senator Wheeldon told parliament that a prominent industry representative had threatened to 'see that everything was done to bring this government down' if it persisted with its plans. The insurance companies mobilised their staff for the campaign, giving them paid time off to attend meetings and rallies and encouraging them to sign anti-AGIC petitions. A leaked memo from one company revealed a warning to staff that 'should the legislation be enacted their future employment would be far from assured'.[22]

The Opposition didn't rush to join the campaign. While conservative frontbenchers were privately sympathetic, Fraser waited until he was convinced that the issue was a winner. He addressed a rally of 800 insurance staff in Canberra on 19 August but refused to commit himself until the Bass by-election saw a pretty strong swing to the Coalition. Then he felt confident enough to attack the government on every front, and the Opposition threw out the AGIC Bill. There was a quid pro quo, however: the insurance companies organised support for Opposition parliamentary candidates and circulated literature suggesting that a Labor victory could threaten their employees' job security.

The ALP was also facing endless headaches from the medical profession, which fought the hospital side of Medibank with grim tenacity. In exchange for substantial funding, the state governments had agreed to insist that doctors be employed for sessions, rather than on a fee-for-service basis. Overwhelming numbers of doctors refused to cooperate. In September, only emergency surgery was being performed in the standard wards of Victorian hospitals, and it was being done for free under the old honorary system. Surgeons in both NSW and Victoria threatened a complete strike, not even exempting emergency services. This resistance helped set the scene for the Medibank confrontation of 1976.

If the capitalists and the doctors were restive, so were many workers. The huge strike wave of 1974 had abated, and wage indexation was on the way, but the new wage system's birth was far from painless.

In essence, the trade union leadership had accepted Labor's wage indexation package. Most union officials believed that rank and file militancy was receding as workers became worried about unemployment. The officials seized on the illusion that indexation could maintain real wages without the risks involved in industrial action. By shifting the focus of wage fixation from industrial action at the grassroots to the chambers of the Arbitration Commission, the new system also strengthened the position of the full-time officials over the militant shop stewards and rank and file activists. This had great appeal for the union bureaucracy. At the same time, indexation also appealed to many rank and file workers who had been bruised by the previous year's industrial confrontations and who were now seeing their wage gains eaten away by inflation. They came under pressure from families and friends influenced by the 'strikes-cause-inflation' argument, and many of them liked the prospect of an easier way.

Still, the indexation system was hard to swallow whole. There were still groups of skilled workers confident of their ability to extract large wage gains, including some – such as certain metal trades workers – who believed that they had a strong case for 'catching up' with skilled workers in other areas. Even many private sector white collar workers were reluctant to accept the guidelines. Their peak union body, the Australian Council of Salaried and Professional Associations (ACSPA), threatened to reject the system until just before the conclusion of the September wage hearing.

Consequently, the ACTU executive recommended a 'two-bob-each-way' resolution to the 1975 Congress. It accepted 'the responsible role that the trade union movement must play in the present economic circumstances' and welcomed the introduction of wage indexation, but it also called for tax indexation – something that Labor, now operating within the constraints of the Hayden budget, refused to grant. The resolution continued:

> Wage increases above the minimum award rates negotiated or obtained by collective bargaining, or incorporated into voluntary agreements, are an essential part of trade union wages policy [and] this activity will be continued by affiliates where wage levels are not consistent with wage justice.[23]

A left-wing amendment rejecting any form of wage restraint was defeated.

Although the ACTU leadership didn't wish to create trouble for Whitlam, it had good reasons for keeping its options open. The executive was not sure whether it could keep the confidence of its most militant affiliates unless it gave them some room to move. In addition, Hawke suspected that the unions would be facing a conservative government long before the next Congress (two years away), and he did not want to tie their hands unnecessarily. He emphasised this point in addressing the delegates. The formulation that committed unions to playing a 'responsible role' was intended to reassure the government and the employers that there would be no generalised challenge to the indexation guidelines. However, the oil industry dispute kept this issue in the forefront.

Skilled workers in the oil industry were determined to pursue a $35 claim, which the employers insisted was outside the guidelines. The unions imposed bans at the Kurnell oil refinery in Sydney. These bans had begun to bite by 24 August, when Caltex management announced that shortages of petrol, heating oil, distillate and other petrol products were imminent. When the press began agitating for government action to end the dispute, McClelland's office responded cautiously, making it known that he was 'working behind the scenes' to resolve the conflict, but insisting that 'strong action by the government could only intensify the present problems'.[24] By September, McClelland and Whitlam had changed their tune, and the Prime Minister was warning that the claims could jeopardise indexation:

> All our efforts to protect the worker from inflation, to establish secure and stable industrial conditions, to create the right climate for a national anti-inflationary drive, will be destroyed... The strong-arm boys, by thumbing their nose at indexation, are threatening the jobs of their mates.[25]

The unionists persisted until 108 operators were stood down in October, whereupon the AWU called for national strike action. By now, the government and the media had decided that a major conspiracy was afoot, with Laurie Carmichael of the AMWU as the villain of the piece. Jim McClelland argued that the dispute would give the Liberals an excuse to bring down the government, charging that Carmichael, whose only concern was allegedly to torpedo wage indexation, 'couldn't care less'.[26] Carmichael's CPA membership provided a convenient point of attack – although, in reality, the AMWU had always had an ALP majority in their leading bodies.

In its calmer moments, the government didn't really believe that the AMWU, whose strength had been eroded by recession, was a threat to the new wages system. Whitlam and McClelland's statements represented a growing frustration with the intractability of the dispute and a desire to show the business community that the new-style Labor regime could get tough with the unions. Had they known how soon they would be appealing to those same unions to rally round them in the battle against Fraser, they might have been more cautious. Meanwhile, the government's rhetoric helped to inflame anti-union sentiment in the community, creating a climate that was a virtual gift to the Liberals.

A ruling class conspiracy?

After the Bass by-election, Fraser had taken the offensive. Following Rex Connor's resignation in October, he felt confident enough to block Supply in the Senate and bring on a constitutional crisis. At this point, according to Paul Kelly:

> Fraser spoke with senior newspaper executives from at least two of Australia's three newspaper chains... Almost without exception the press supported Fraser's decision to force an election'[27]

The powerful hostility to Labor among business was reinforced in October by pessimistic assessments of the economy. Warren Hogan, Professor of Economics at Sydney University (later a Fraser adviser), discounted government hopes of recovery in 1976 and gave its budget strategy little hope of success.[28] A bit later in the year, the experts became more optimistic; but, by that time, the business mood had hardened beyond redemption.

In the political sphere, meanwhile, the government met obstruction at every turn in trying to resolve the supply crisis. When Whitlam sought a half-Senate election, conservative state governments refused to cooperate. When he sought temporary finance from the banks, they refused to extend it – which gave John Kerr a pretext for dismissing the government. In October, Queensland Governor Colin Hannah had made a blatantly political speech attacking Whitlam, and Sir Robert Menzies joined the fray with a statement endorsing Fraser's actions. Clearly, Andrew Theophanous is right when he says that Whitlam underestimated the forces ranged against him:

> It was not just the parliamentary Liberal Party and their supporters. It was the whole corporate sector, and, by this stage, the totality of the media.[29]

Whitlam's destruction undoubtedly resulted from a general mobilisation of ruling class and conservative forces. However, the left liked to put a finer point on it. For example, the Communist paper *Tribune*, which appeared daily during the election campaign, insisted:

> The Kerr putsch was not just a Liberal Party plot. It was a class conspiracy conceived and executed by the ruling class, who saw their interests threatened by even the limited encouragement given to the working class and social liberation movements by the Labor government.[30]

This was understandable as a piece of political agitation, but untenable as analysis. A mobilisation of social forces is not the same as a conspiracy, nor was there monolithic unity in the anti-Labor camp. In fact, during the weeks before the dismissal, ruling class sentiment was fairly volatile. Shortly before Connor's resignation, the *Sydney Morning Herald* questioned Fraser's credibility: the Opposition leader had begun hinting that 'extraordinary or reprehensible' circumstances were not required to legitimise blocking Supply, and the *Herald* suggested that this new tack was itself 'reprehensible'.

After Connor's fall, the *Herald* did change its tune and declare that 'Fraser must act'.[31] Even then, he did not have an easy run. As Whitlam sought to tough out the Supply crisis, the Liberal leader had a grim battle of his own keeping control of skittish backbenchers, while the breakaway Liberal Movement condemned his actions. Sections of the media also remained nervous, with *The Age* arguing for a backdown by the Liberals and the Brisbane *Courier-Mail* pleading repeatedly for compromise. W. J. Sharp, managing director of Jennings Industries, saw the political uncertainty as bad for business confidence:

> I am in favour of passing Supply… I believe the story that the business community was urging the Opposition to stop Supply was a complete myth and ought to be scotched. If a survey of business people had been done one month ago, I am convinced that the vote would have been overwhelmingly against the Liberal Party doing what it did. My own recollection, from conversations in the last few weeks with dozens of businessmen, is that only one executive was in favour.

Another unnamed business leader expressed the fear that, if Fraser seized power, union unrest could turn him into 'another Ted Heath.'[32] Heath was the British Prime Minister driven from power by the 1974 miners' strike.

YEARS OF RAGE

This is great stuff. McClelland wants union funds to pay for his election campaign. He is prepared to accept strike action (so long as it doesn't get "out of hand") to arouse feeling against Fraser. He wants union votes to put him back into government. Yet he appeals for middle-class votes by assuring the bosses that he can attack the unions and their members better than Fraser.

Actually, he's wrong. Fraser can attack us far better than McClelland because he gets his support from the Melbourne Club and doesn't have to worry about "tantrums" from union officials. That's one of the reasons we've got to elect Labor despite McClelland.

.....but we don't want Wage Restraint

But we can have Labor without McClelland's anti-union policies. During the next three weeks, Labor politicians will be addressing factory meetings all over Australia. They are desparate for our support. This is an election in which sides have been chosen. Fraser has the bosses. Labor must have the workers.

When Labor politicians address these meetings, there are some questions we can ask them. We can ask them to repudiate McClelland's statements.... ask them whether they support holding down wages while BHP, Carlton and United Breweries, GMH and Shell petrol get the go-ahead for price rises every three or four months...... make it clear that we are electing Labor to protect us from Fraser's attacks. We are not electing them to find polite ways of carrying out the same policies.

After Fraser's coup, it might be considered divisive to ask ALP politicians "difficult" questions at public rallies, but factory gate meetings are not public rallies. They are meetings between workers and their representatives in Parliament. They should happen regularly, instead of only at election time. It is not "splitting" to attack McClelland for boasting about his ability to attack the union movement. It is McClelland who is splitting when he attacks his own supporters to suck up to the middle classes.

There are other ways of fighting for the sort of Labor government we want, rather than the sort that Hayden, McClelland and Gough Whitlam himself want us to have. Thousands of workers are joining the ALP during the current crisis. If you are one of them, make sure that you are not just used to provide funds and hand out "How to vote" cards. Handing out how-to-vote cards is necessary to win elections, but if you join the ALP, you should also be making your voice heard in branch meetings. The Victorian branch has rejected Wage Restraint in the past. McClelland and co. must be made to listen to the voice of their party, not the voices of the bosses.

Organisation

But most of all we need an active fight. Not only against Fraser and his boss, anti-union policies, but against ALL pro-boss, anti-union policies, wherever they come from. For that we need organisation.

The Socialist Workers Action Group and the Workers League are fighting organisations. We have consistently opposed Wage Restraint and attacks on the union movement. In our paper, "The Battler", we argued for a General Strike against Fraser. Had this fight been taken up through the labor movement, the elections would not be being fought on the bosses' terms. If you want to find out more about our policies for fighting Fraser and Wage Restraint, clip out coupon below.

COUP IN CANBERRA

SPECIAL CRISIS BULLETIN   Tuesday November 25th.

STOP THE CARETAKER!

WHEN Sir John Kerr tore up the rule book in his desparation to get rid of Labor, and installed Squire Fraser of the Melbourne Club as Prime Minister, A WAVE OF ANGER SWEPT AUSTRALIA FROM COAST TO COAST.

For four days, larger and larger rallies and marches cursed Fraser and Kerr and demonstrated at Liberal Party Headquarters, the bosses' exclusive Melbourne Club, the Melbourne and Sydney Stock Exchanges and the offices of News Ltd., the rabidly pro-Fraser press. The same anger and class hatred was reflected in a series of strikes. The wharfies, seamen and building workers had gone out immediately. A lot of metal shops joined them. Four hundred thousand workers in Melbourne stopped for four hours on Friday to demonstrate. Bob Hawke was appealing to workers not to force a General Strike while rnak and file unionists from Hobart to Cairns were demanding that he call one. The bosses, their tame party and their tame Governor-General were on the run.

We had the momentum up for a General Strike; a strike which would have forced the bosses to abandon Fraser and step back from their attacks on us; a strike which would have discouraged the election of a union-bashing government by making it clear to the bosses how much in lost production and lost profits they would pay for a Liberal government.

But the momentum was lost! The pressure of industrial action dropped and suddenly Fraser and his newspaper-owning mates were able to take control of the election campaign. For the first week, the issue was the sacking of Gough Whitlam, by the beginning of last week it was becoming the economy. Now it has become an argument over which party is better at attacking the unions and getting away with it.

We want Gough

There is no question that the Liberals are very talented union bashers. They had 23 years to practise last time and they managed to dig up and use an impressive array of penal powers, jail Clarrie O'Shea and generally attack our rights. This time, they've obviously been preparing. Fraser is proposing an industrial police force to physically attack us, he wants to make strikes, and especially political strikes and black bans near impossible. And he intends to open up all the bosses' laws to make it easier to charge us and sue us when we fight the bosses. They even want to intervene in our unions and sack OUR officials. More than any other reason, that's why WE MUST FIGHT FOR THE RETURN OF A LABOR GOVERNMENT.

But instead of organising and uniting the union movement against Fraser's attacks, the Labor politicians are trying other means to acheive the same thing, lower wages. Last Friday, "Diamond" Jim McClelland, the right-wing Senator who was Minister for Labor, said that wage restraint was the key
that only he could make it work. He is proud of loweri
women who elected   me time as

This reaction was understandable, given the growing social polarisation. At a Hobart rally in October, Fraser was howled down by a large hostile element in the crowd, despite powerful sound equipment. Fraser sought to play down the actions of a 'wretched rabble' he claimed amounted to no more than 100 people, but observers suggested that up to 1,500 of the crowd of 4,000 were antagonistic.[33] In Canberra, a large number of trade unionists, some of whom had stopped work and travelled from Wollongong, effectively took over a Liberal rally and shouted down Fraser with chants of 'We want Gough!'

Melbourne saw a large pro-Whitlam rally as 'hundreds of maritime unionists marched to the City Square...waterside workers stopped work until this morning, and seamen employed on tugs stopped for 24 hours.'[34] Some 2,000 workers attended a stopwork meeting in the Kwinana industrial strip south of Perth. In Darwin, about 350 workers marched through city streets. In Sydney, the port lay idle on 18 October because of a strike by 3,500 wharfies; on 24 October, students brought traffic to a standstill and later fought police while marching to an ALP rally.

These events took on added weight with Bob Hawke's impetuous suggestion that 'if they are going to withhold supply, the trade unions might very well withhold supply' from the bourgeoisie.[35] Hawke's remarks, made at a Canberra rally, were followed by extravagant statements from other union officials. Bill Landeryou of the Storemen and Packers, for example, said that it was:

> possible the trade union movement could so react that it could
> paralyse the country, as long as the servants of overseas monopolies
> use their power in the Senate to frustrate democracy.

John Halfpenny of the AMWU called for a 'massive mobilisation of workers', lest Fraser 'usher in an era of political terror.' A special meeting of 56 Victorian unions called for a national conference and indicated that they were 'prepared to mobilise union members in demonstrations and rallies immediately.'[36] By late October, some Liberals claimed to be 'stunned by the public reaction against the Opposition's bid for an early election.'[37]

In one sense, they were unnecessarily alarmed; having helped to arouse this wave of anger, the union officials quickly set about channelling it into controlled and token actions. Hawke backtracked rapidly, denying any plans for strike action: 'The only thing I was calling for is for people in their thousands to attend public meetings around Australia.'[38] A special meeting of the ACTU executive settled for some 'selective withholding of supply', and *The Age* reported:

Most sources were confident last night that union bans would not be necessary. But they warned that if action was taken it would probably be aimed at Opposition parliamentarians.[39]

This meant little, although Victorian meatworkers showed a sense of humour in banning livestock owned by Opposition MPs, an action directed at a certain Nareen grazier (Fraser).

At the official level, the union response was largely hot air. Yet the events had just as clearly demonstrated an angry mood among the rank and file. Viewed against the background of poll results showing that a large majority of the electorate favoured the passing of supply, this was a sobering prospect for business and the conservative forces, and it was hardly surprising that there was some hand-wringing in the weeks before Kerr's dismissal of Whitlam. The media held a growing belief that Fraser had missed the boat. *The Bulletin* portrayed him as the 'man in a muddle'[40] while the British *Economist* thought that blocking supply had 'begun to look like a smart tactic which went astray.'[41]

The ruling class was united in, and prepared to act upon, its political opposition to the Whitlam Government, making Whitlam's eventual destruction virtually certain; but capitalist opinion was always divided over Fraser's tactics. Important sectors feared the consequences of social unrest if a 'coup' removed Whitlam. The bourgeoisie was far from monolithic and was never to be entirely united in the following seven years. The Liberal leader, who clearly fancied himself as a tough guy, never received quite enough backing to ride roughshod over society.

Another conspiracy theory of the time raised the spectre of foreign interference. Perhaps US companies did have an economic incentive to undermine Labor; for example, a Westinghouse representative was quoted in *Nucleonics Week* as telling a US court: 'Maybe if the Labor Government is thrown out in five weeks...we can get the uranium we thought we had.' *Tribune* cited the quote under the heading, 'Uranium Grab – Why Giants Support Libs', noting that the government had banned uranium exports for a time (on nationalist, not environmental, grounds).[42] As an explanation for why some multinationals backed Fraser, such arguments were plausible – although hardly necessary, because the general trend in ruling class thinking influenced foreign firms in any case. But what of suggestions that, for either economic or security reasons, the Central Intelligence Agency had a hand in the November coup? Here, speculation was fuelled by some seemingly improbable coincidences.

It emerged that American Richard Stallings, who had established the US

SWAG members at anti-Fraser rally

communications base at Pine Gap, was a CIA agent with direct links to National Party leader Doug Anthony. Whitlam made much of these revelations, casting about as he was for any stick to beat the Opposition. The CIA was worried that the government or media might be about to blow their agents' cover or reveal sensitive information about Pine Gap, fears intensified by Whitlam's recent removal of the chiefs of two Australian security organisations, ASIS and ASIO. The CIA turned to Sir Arthur Tange, head of the Defence Department, who went to great lengths to kill the public debate.

It was easy for nationalist Labor supporters, for whom the CIA was a traditional focus of hostility, to conclude that US agents had a hand in Whitlam's fall. Subsequent analysis also found links between the CIA and US ambassador Marshall Green. Kerr himself had once been involved in intelligence work.

The theories are intriguing but unconvincing. It is unlikely that the CIA would destabilise a traditional ally so precipitately. Marshall Green's spy links are hardly remarkable for a career diplomat. There is no actual evidence that Kerr made contact with the CIA – or even considered security issues – in the period before the dismissal. Even if the CIA was somehow involved, that doesn't make its role important, let alone decisive. The Whitlam Government was destroyed by its internal contradictions, a major recession and intense social conflicts. In such a mosaic, spies could represent no more than a fragment.

COUP IN CANBERRA

**Mass demonstration City Square Melbourne
14 November 1975**

art of a huge crowd of upwards of 30,000 which gathered in the Melbourne City Square
 protest with their presence at the dismissal of the elected Whitlam Government. Their
articipation represented the exercise of a democratic right. On December 13 they will
ve the democratic right to follow through their protest at the ballot box. A further City
quare rally will be held tomorrow, Tuesday, December 2, at 12.30 pm. It will be
onsored by white collar industrial unions, and Mr Gough Whitlam, the elected Prime
inister, will be the main speaker.

YEARS OF RAGE

Members of SWAG leading the breakaway march down Burke St Melbourne 14 November 1975. Author Tom O'Lincoln can be seen with beard and glasses under the SWAG banner

Breakaway march ends with a rally outside the Melbourne stock exchange 14 November 1975

The battle is joined

Sir John Kerr dismissed Whitlam on 11 November 1975, installed Fraser as caretaker PM and called elections for 13 December, provoking immediate euphoria in much of the business world. Brokers cheered as leading share prices soared on every exchange. Among working class pensioners sunning themselves in Sydney's Martin Plaza, the mood was far more sombre; one of them, Eric O'Brien, said that Whitlam had 'done a good turn for pensioners' and that the 'workers have lost one of their best men'.[43] Why Kerr took his dramatic decision is a question which no amount of discussion seems likely to resolve fully, although Paul Kelly's reconstruction seems as plausible as any: that Kerr always entertained the possibility of dismissing Whitlam, but could not warn him for fear of being sacked himself; that Whitlam consequently defied the Senate in ignorance of the full implications; and that, as the supply crisis reached a critical point, Kerr decided that the dismissal had become inevitable. On this account, the decision was an individual one, and Kerr was nobody's puppet.[44]

If true, it does not invalidate the Marxist thesis linking political events to social forces. Kerr's options were shaped and limited by the social conflict raging around him and by his desire to preserve political stability. His ability to make the dismissal stick depended on the outcome of further social conflict. Given these provisos, we can safely grant Kerr the individual a role in the making of history. Wider social forces determine which individuals can do this, and when – a point the Marxist writer Kelvin Rowley explained very well in discussing the 'conspiracies' of 1975:

> I agree that the capitalist class is able to pursue *and realize* its class interests in ways which the working class cannot. That is, after all, what we mean when we refer to it as the dominant or ruling class in capitalist society. However, this is a function of *position* in the class structure. Between us [you] and I would be lucky to conspire to knock a beer glass off at a busy pub and get away with it, let alone topple a government. This is...because our class position is a very long way from being 'the central cog in the class machine'.[45]

The dismissal provoked a sharp initial response from the labour movement, suggesting that the fears of Fraser's capitalist critics had not been misplaced. In the following days, a major working class mobilisation began, more far reaching than Whitlam actually desired – although his own rhetoric and posturing were themselves a factor. On parliament steps, Whitlam declared that Fraser was 'Kerr's Cur' and that nothing would save the Governor-General. He urged supporters to maintain their rage. In reality, he only wanted an electoral response: 'Maintain your rage and enthusiasm. You will have a Labor Government again.'[46] But, given his tone, ALP supporters might well feel that they had a green light for more direct action.

On the day of the dismissal, angry crowds gathered in all the main cities. The Sydney demonstrators heard Joe Owens, former leader of the BLF, call for a 24-hour national stoppage. In Melbourne, 'more than 50 policemen engaged in a running battle with demonstrators' who 'clambered over the police cars, kicking and denting panels, smashing lights and brawling with uniformed and plain-clothes police.'[47] Meanwhile, trade unionists were stopping work, defying a plea from Bob Hawke to 'cool it' and donate a day's pay to the election campaign rather than strike. Militants seemed to prefer his earlier idea of 'withholding supply' from the bosses.

According to *The Australian*:

> seamen walked off the job, tying up ships around Australia, waterside workers struck for 24 hours from midnight, metalworkers in factories throughout the country held spontaneous strikes and employees in railway workshops in Sydney and Newcastle also walked off.[48]

A number of NSW coal mines stopped for 24 hours, with the Miners' Federation leadership calling for pit-top meetings nationwide. There was talk of union bans to stop ballot papers being printed for an election many saw as undemocratic.

The following day saw major rallies in Sydney and Brisbane, with workers sporting such placards as 'Give Fraser The Razor' and 'Kerr's Cur Is A Mangy Mongrel'. In Sydney, a section of the crowd invaded the Stock Exchange, and some of the speeches at the Brisbane rally suggested a radical mood:

> A union leader spoke of the futility of the parliamentary system. 'We get up after 25 years and they knock us off.'... Unionists were told: 'Everyone stop work on Friday. The capitalists understand that language – massed workers and missed profits.'[49]

A day later, on 13 November, demonstrators were back in Sydney streets. A rally initially organised by the Australian Union of Students attracted some Labor MPs and union officials. Tom Uren described Fraser's blocking of supply as a 'violent act', while Richard Walsham of the Teachers Federation argued: 'It no longer matters who you vote in. You've got to do it for yourself.' Jim McClelland's suggestion to 'turn the other cheek' was met with boos as well as cheers. Some of the crowd began chanting for a general strike. When McClelland left the platform, Linda Boland, a socialist and a militant at the Redfern Mail Exchange, confronted him. The *National Times* reported:

> Boland is taller than McClelland, and she was trembling with scarcely controlled indignation. In her view, the workers were enraged by the ruling class coup d'état, but to channel that rage back into parliamentary debate was a recipe for defeat. What was required were street demonstrations, meetings, industrial action, and if the ALP followed this course of putting the lid on people's genuine feelings, the workers would be demoralised.[50]

The crowd later marched on the offices of the Murdoch press, to be met at the front door by police. The marchers then moved quickly around to another entrance, where several hundred of them surged inside and began throwing bundles of papers off the truck, setting some ablaze.

Adelaide also saw stirring scenes after the dismissal, when striking wharfies and builders' labourers marched to Liberal headquarters, then proceeded to Parliament House to protest against the presence of armed police at their demonstration. They were impatient with Premier Don Dunstan's pleas to avoid 'riots, anarchy and strikes', and one called out hopefully: 'It's time guys like Dunstan realised the ALP doesn't run this country, the workers run it.' Two days later, the SA Labor Party attracted 7,000–8,000 to a rally at Victoria Square, which was quieter despite 'a strong nucleus of radical student-worker groups.'[51]

On the job, workers fought for their right to wear badges reading 'Shame, Fraser, Shame', despite harassment by employers. Apprentices at the NSW Public Transport Commission's Chullora College were ordered to remove them; they refused and began collecting additional badges, to ensure that everyone could put one on. The Chullora union shop committee backed them, so they were fairly safe. At Kraft Foods in Melbourne, a similar battle erupted, with unionists refusing to remove badges when ordered to do so; management claimed that the workers were violating health regulations. Back in Sydney, the

Department of Main Roads threatened to sack employees sporting the 'Shame, Fraser, Shame' insignia.

The biggest working class mobilisation was in Melbourne, where the left unions called a four-hour stoppage on Friday, 14 November; 400,000 workers walked off. Employers estimated the lost production at $10 million. Fifty thousand gathered in the City Square to hear fairly empty speeches from John Halfpenny and state Labor leader Clyde Holding. The organisers were anxious to keep the restive crowd from getting out of hand, so they led it away from the city centre to the old Treasury Building in Spring Street, where they appealed to the marchers to 'go home and make your street a street for Labor'. Keen for further action, a large section of the crowd preferred to follow the banners of a collection of revolutionaries, with about 10,000 people proceeding to Parliament House, then down Bourke Street towards the centre of town.

At the front of the march raged a battle for control between Maoists, who wished to take the crowd to the US Consulate – a considerable distance away in St Kilda Road – and the Trotskyist International Socialists (IS) who insisted on heading for the Stock Exchange. Each had a political significance: the Maoists blamed the Kerr Coup on the CIA and US imperialism, while the IS saw the struggle in class, rather than national, terms.

A combination of geography (the Stock Exchange was far closer), better organisation and superior political logic ensured victory for the IS in this tussle, while most of the 10,000 people marching behind their banner were rather less ideological in their objectives. Although they were happy to occasionally chant general strike calls, their favourite slogan was the simple, straightforward, 'We want Gough!' As one of the IS members leading the march, I remember how it tempered our exuberant mood to realise that we could only hold the huge crowd together by taking up this slogan. 'We want Gough!' cried the young socialists who had been among Whitlam's fiercest critics. When reproached by political rivals, my fellow agitator Phil Griffiths, who held the megaphone, called out blithely: 'We're reformists!' We were not, but the crowd were, and we had to face up to that reality.

Another reality awaited us at the Stock Exchange. The police had bolted the glass doors and arrayed themselves on the steps. Our small forces could not organise a successful charge on the police lines; yet, at the same time, it was impossible to make speeches over a mere megaphone and expect to command the attention of this tumultuous crowd. A young waterside worker voiced the frustration many must have felt. 'You bring us all the way here,' he told me angrily, 'then you leave us flat.' I understood his reaction but could think of nothing to do. Although we had shown some dash in leading the march, our contingent of 20 people could not hope to take the struggle any further.

After some jostling against police lines, the demonstration dispersed. Our accomplishment was to demonstrate that sizeable numbers of workers were looking for a militant lead. At the same time, it was abundantly clear that groups like the IS were too small to provide it, something which applied equally to Linda Boland and her comrades in Sydney and the 'radical student-worker groups' in Adelaide. Meanwhile, Melbourne's left union and ALP leaders, who were influential enough to lead a serious struggle, had shown their lack of enthusiasm by going home from Spring Street.

Still, in those early days, the anger and resistance clearly frightened sections of the bourgeoisie. The press eagerly seized on Hawke's call for restraint ('Keep it cool,' was the *Courier-Mail*'s front page plea) and in Melbourne, *The Age* openly confessed its fears. 'There is a very real danger that sections of the public will today feel utterly disenchanted with the whole political process,' said its first editorial, while the business pages suggested that the 'unions won't be Hawke's doves' and added: 'business leaders fear that a new Government might not be able to govern.'[52]

A determined working class campaign could have split the bourgeoisie, pushing Fraser onto the defensive, and such a campaign was entirely possible had the leaders of the ALP and trade unions fought consistently to build it. However, this was precisely the point at which the left began to falter.

Towards electoral disaster

As it became clear that Melbourne's four-hour stoppage would go ahead, *The Age* had decided that the left unions needed a stern talking-to. In an article seemingly written in consultation with the ACTU leadership ('Bob Hawke told me last night...'), Geoffrey Cleghorn warned that 'large masses of people are difficult to control,' especially with 'anarchists' and 'Trotskyists' present:

> Trade union leaders therefore bear a formidable responsibility in managing today's Melbourne rally and similar rallies and stopworks... If Mr Hawke is correct in his call for restraint – and it must be self-evident that he is – union leaders will accept that responsibility... Unionists cannot allow ideologues to manipulate the present situation and convert a crisis for democracy into a mini-revolution.

We have seen that small bands of Trotskyists couldn't really create a 'mini-revolution'. Anyway, a union leader like Halfpenny had no intention of allowing things to get out of control. In fact, he had signalled as much in a separate interview published the same day. The four-hour stoppage was consistent with Hawke's 'cool it' appeal, said Halfpenny, because the ACTU President 'had since made it clear he was opposed only to indefinite strikes.'[53] Obviously, the left officials had little stomach for them either. A few days later, when 3,000 shop stewards met at Melbourne's Festival Hall, the meeting was confined to an electoral briefing at which the stewards discussed badges, stickers and fundraising with no mention of industrial action.

Without encouragement from these union leaders – and with their critics on the revolutionary left far too weak to offer an alternative leadership – the mass struggle began to fade, giving way to the more conventional electoral contest that Hawke and Whitlam preferred. The initiative began to pass to Fraser, and Labor began to slip in the polls because, in a conventional election campaign, the ALP had little to offer.

Labor's official campaign opening, with a daytime rally in Sydney followed by an intense Festival Hall meeting in Melbourne, still aroused great fervour, as did many of the rallies in the remaining weeks before polling day. Moved by the exceptional atmosphere, Gough Whitlam even bought a copy of a radical socialist paper, *The Battler*, before entering Festival Hall. But the ferment was confined largely to those already firmly committed to the Labor Party and its leader.

The ALP's initial campaign strategy focused on constitutional issues, for fear that Labor was all too vulnerable on economics. Whitlam appealed to voters to defend democracy. As the prospect of overturning the Kerr Coup through struggle receded, however, working class voters lost interest in constitutional questions, while the bourgeoisie lost its nervousness about them. The two main classes in society began to turn their attention to the economic issues which are always the key to conventional election contests, and the middle classes and swinging voters followed suit. Labor was forced to change its emphasis. But, on economic issues, Whitlam was ensnared in dire contradictions.

To the workers, he offered a scare campaign: Fraser would cut programs, attack living standards and open up, in Hawke's words, Australia's 'most bloody and exacerbated' period of industrial relations.[54] Yet Labor had brought down the Hayden budget, and Labor Ministers had denounced 'bloody-minded unions' not long before. Despite the strong pressure to rally behind the ALP, workers often confronted Labor candidates about these issues. When former Transport Minister Charlie Jones visited Clyde railway workshops in Sydney:

COUP IN CANBERRA

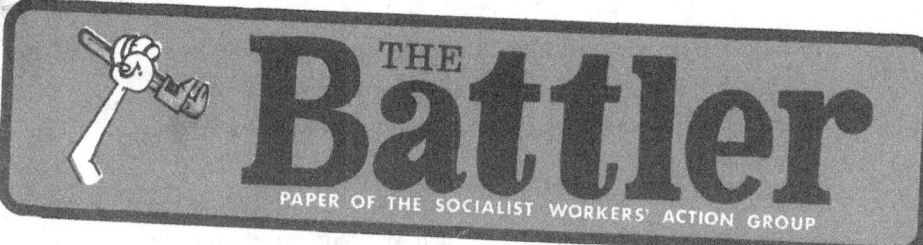

PAPER OF THE SOCIALIST WORKERS' ACTION GROUP

Number 13, November 29, 1975   10 CENTS

Defend the right to Work

HALF A MILLION UNEMPLOYED NEXT YEAR. That's the price we'll pay for a Liberal victory. One hundred thousand more jobs will be lost if Labor is kept out by the polls. Fraser is attacking Labor for causing the highest unemployment since the war, but it's Fraser who's planning the most vicious job cuts. Public spending is to be cut. That means less money for teachers, public service clerks, building industry workers and others. More than anything, he wants to control the inflation that threatens the bosses' profits. He has seen Gerald Ford cut inflation in the US by throwing 9 million workers onto the dole. If he gets away with his grab for power, he'll do it here. Stop him.

Defend the right to Strike

THE RIGHT TO STRIKE is our basic weapon of self-defence in a system we don't control. Fraser has drawn up legislation to break strikes, ban them altogether in some industries, jail union officials and outlaw picketing. If he is elected on December 13, his first act will be to pass these anti-union laws. (See page 4 for more information on Fraser's industrial policies.)

Defend the right to Vote

THE RIGHT TO VOTE is one of the few democratic rights we have in this society. Now they are trying to take that away from us. If Fraser is elected, it will mean that the Senate got away with blocking Supply and Kerr got away with sacking an elected government. It will mean that no matter how many times we elect the Government of our choice, we can no longer rely on it taking office. If that happens, we may still have elections where we write numbers on a piece of paper, but they will have no more meaning than the elections in countries like Spain and Russia, where the results are known before the election. If Fraser wins, we may have more elections, but we will have lost the right to vote.

FIGHT THE BOSSES' ATTACK...

VOTE LABOR!

the workers gave him a rough time...and raised demands as to what they wanted in the railways. The workers declared that they would support Labor, but that they wanted a better performance.[55]

So, while people kept thronging to hear Whitlam speak, this showed the enthusiasm of the faithful rather than a breakthrough into the wider electorate. And even the faithful did not seem to have much confidence in the party's election platform. Journalists on the campaign trail noticed:

the crowds are big and enthusiastic but Mr Whitlam does not seem to be getting through to them. He is lecturing, educating, defending the program. Eleven days to December 13... It's late to start telling voters what Labor's welfare programs are all about.[56]

For the employers, Whitlam had a different pitch: the Hayden budget was working. Fraser's head-kicking methods weren't required and might, indeed, be counterproductive; for, without Labor's reform program, workers would not accept wage indexation. The unions, he warned darkly, 'wouldn't wear' the abolition of the Prices Justification Tribunal.[57] This ignored unionists' own cynicism about the Tribunal, reinforced as recently as October when it had awarded BHP an 8.75 percent price rise without a hearing. The rise meant that steel prices had risen 65 percent in two years, prompting John Halfpenny to describe the Tribunal as 'little more than an arm of BHP'.[58] In any case, ruling class concerns about what the unions would or would not tolerate had been largely laid to rest by Hawke's success in ending the strikes. As for the reform programs, if Labor accepted that these had to be slashed, why not put Fraser to work slashing them properly?

A good example of the ALP's difficulties was the area of women's rights. Fraser was an easy target, given his suggestion that women should enter parliament to 'brighten the place up'[59] – embarrassing even some Liberals. Margaret Whitlam could justly point out:

Nowhere in Mr Fraser's policy speech is there an acknowledgement of women's special areas of need. In fact, the words 'woman' or 'women' are not once mentioned.[60]

However, this argument was less than compelling, given that the Whitlam policy speech had devoted just two sentences to the subject![61] While the Women's Electoral Lobby analysis of candidates found that Labor was, on balance, more sympathetic and aware, it didn't emerge unscathed. The feminist lobby group, Women's Electoral Lobby, said that both the ALP and the Coalition parties 'ignored unemployed women, child care and probate tax concessions for women.'[62] Even at a 'Women For Labor' picnic, Whitlam didn't seem very interested and ignored requests to speak. The next day, Elsie refuge, which had organised a bus load to attend, wrote to the organisers suggesting that women 'deserve more than Gough kissing babies.'[63]

Not surprisingly, the women's liberation movement response to Labor was fairly critical. In Sydney, a 200-strong special general meeting of the movement rejected a request to join 'Women for Labor', preferring to run an independent campaign against Fraser. A leaflet listed Labor's reforms but cited their limitations: 'Where are the child care centres? Whatever happened to retraining?'[64]

Unable to satisfy either its natural constituencies or the bourgeoisie, Labor staggered on to the electoral debacle that 'cooling it' was supposed to forestall. The irony is that, judging by the opinion polls, the one thing that might have raised its vote was militant class struggle. The polls had shown a revival in the party's support during the supply crisis, partly in response to Whitlam's fighting stand, and this comparatively good showing persisted for a time after 11 November. Labor's support was initially strongest in Victoria – where the level of struggle was highest – and more particularly in Melbourne, where workers were on strike and demonstrating in large numbers.

A poll taken at the end of November gave the ALP 48 percent in Victoria and nearly 50 percent in Melbourne, while the party had only 44 percent nationwide. Worker militancy was by no means alienating the Victorian electorate; on the contrary, swinging voters appeared to be impressed by the unions' show of strength. Once the struggle subsided, this picture changed rapidly. It was now Fraser and the right wing that inspired confidence. At the December 13 election, Labor's Victorian vote was nearly one percent below the national figure of 43.2 percent.[65]

In the aftermath, a bitter Jim Cairns blamed the bourgeoisie and its media. No government could stay in office if it displeased them, he said:

> This is a capitalist society. The capitalist class is the ruling class and their ideas are ruling ideas. It is all tied up with money.

It was an insightful, if belated, comment; but Cairns offered no strategy for coping with this capitalist juggernaut except that Labor should become 'more humane, idealistic, altruistic and democratic'.[66] How that could overcome the power of money, he did not explain. The fact was that the working class movement had failed in a first crucial test: it had been unable to stop the right imposing a new political leadership on the country, with a new and more openly reactionary agenda.

To win such battles, the labour movement would have needed very different politics, strategies and leadership to challenge that power. Capital was tied to the state machinery that John Kerr personified. Obviously, the working class needed a strategy to confront that state; yet Whitlam and Hawke proclaimed their loyalty to it. Capital's domination of the media ensured that workers could never win their battles by purely electoral means, but these leaders had demobilised the alternative forms of struggle in the streets and workplaces.

In the absence of a revolutionary alternative, most of the labour movement ultimately drew right-wing, rather than left-wing, conclusions from Whitlam's demise. The hard men – Neville Wran, Bob Hawke, Paul Keating – pushed for more clearly pro-business policies, and an increasing number of ALP activists saw this as the most viable course. Thus, the Whitlam debacle paved the way, not only for the Fraser years, but also for the right-wing Labor era that followed them.

4.
Fraser on the offensive

After the elections, the national mood was one of tense expectancy. Although Donald Horne (in *The Death of the Lucky Country*) believed that the Liberals might want to keep things quiet – 'They want to be left to sleep it off, like animals after the kill'[1] – Mungo MacCallum of the the *Nation Review* had voiced a more common sentiment towards the end of the campaign:

> The best thing we can all do now is go out and buy some pressure lamps, a ton or two of firewood and lots of non-perishable food in preparation for the inevitable general strike.[2]

The general populace seemed to agree. A poll found that 64 percent of Australians – the highest figure in 13 countries surveyed – expected 1976 to be 'a year of strikes and industrial disputes'. I was working in a metal shop, where the universal view was: 'now there's going to be a lot of strikes.' The question in doubt was: could the unions turn back the Fraser tide? The first half of the year was indeed pretty stormy, culminating in a national stoppage over Medibank; during these months, the unions demonstrated that they had more than enough muscle to stop Fraser in his tracks. Ironically, however, Bob Hawke and the ACTU found a way to use the biggest stoppage of all – a major national strike – to derail the growing workers' movement and hand the government its second big victory.

No sooner was Fraser in office than he began shifting rightward, breaking promises, attacking workers. Although he had promised to restore prosperity in short order, hinting at economic growth rates of 6 or 7 percent a year with unemployment falling, the Prime Minister, egged on by advisers such as

The Battler
PAPER OF THE INTERNATIONAL SOCIALISTS

Number 14, December 17, 1975 — 10 cents

post-election special

You may have won the election Squire, but

THE FIGHT'S NOT OVER YET!

FRASER, PEACOCK, ANTHONY AND THE REST of the coalition were smirking on TV on election night. So were their media henchmen. You can tell Fraser thinks he's going to treat Australian workers like peasants on his country estate. The Melbourne Club will pour more champagne and count all the money they plan to make. The Stock Exchange will start cheering again.

The Libs still think they've been born to rule. But we can wipe the sneering smile off Fraser's face.

The Labor Party has lost the election. This doesn't mean that the Australian workers are beaten. Many people voted for Fraser out of desperation over unemployment and inflation. But Fraser's so-called solutions for the economy will be to force us to make more sacrifices. Only a minority of big business parasites voted for that. And when Fraser tries to do it, he can be stopped and beaten.

Labor's defeat was a disaster, but it isn't the end of the world. We have to learn the lessons from it, and go on to build a fighting workers' movement that can turn the tide against Fraser. This issue of the Battler is mostly devoted to learning those lessons and building that movement.

WIPE THE SMILE OFF FRASER'S FACE

INSIDE: *HOW TO FIGHT FRASER* pages 4 and 5

Treasury Secretary John Stone, soon began to move in the opposite direction. The monetarist philosophy called for a longer recession to stamp out inflation. This was the notorious 'fight inflation first' strategy.

Bonds were floated to take money out of circulation. The high returns offered forced up other interest rates, and the government also put restrictions on bank lending. These measures were rather technical, and the general public didn't immediately grasp where Fraser was heading until, on 30 January, he dropped a bombshell that no one could ignore. The man who had promised to maintain wage indexation suddenly announced that he would urge the Arbitration Commission to award a rise of just half the CPI. And on what grounds? That the December quarter CPI increase of 5.6 percent was too great to be translated into a wage hike without further fuelling inflation. Workers who had seen Whitlam discount the previous CPI figure to under one percent (because Medibank removed health costs from the CPI), and then received no wage rise at all because this inflation figure was too low, now heard Fraser say that they should miss out again because 5.6 percent was too high.

The move had no chance of success. Five out of six state governments, including the conservatives ruling in key eastern states, opposed Fraser's proposal, while the ACTU responded with predictable outrage. The employers generally lacked enthusiasm for it, believing that it would lead to industrial conflict at what was an awkward time for them. Indeed, some firms in the metal trades had already negotiated full CPI rises. The Commission refused to cooperate, partly because its own prestige had grown with the success of the indexation system. To automatically accept Fraser's demands would both disrupt the system and make the Commission look like a puppet. It awarded the full wage rise demanded by the unions.

Nevertheless, the Prime Minister's wage initiative was full of implications for the future. It demonstrated the ascendancy of monetarist theories within the government. It served notice that wage-cutting would be a major objective of the Fraser regime. It was also a broken promise, the first in a long saga of what Fraser liked to call 'flexibility'. The conviction began to deepen among trade unionists that the Liberals could not be trusted.

The 'social wage' also became a target. Fraser abruptly dissolved more than 40 governmental bodies in such areas as foreign aid and assistance to deprived children. He proposed to reintroduce radio and TV licences and to abolish pensioners' funeral benefits (although he failed to carry his own back bench on these two points). The government began cutting public service staffing, raised pharmaceutical prescription fees and delayed pension increases. Crackdowns on social security benefits began, Aboriginal programs were cut back, and the government foreshadowed a tough 'mini-budget' for May.

It was said that times were tough all round. Yet there was money for a butler at the Lodge! There was money to fly 35 ASIO graduate trainees from Canberra to Melbourne on a two-day training exercise, all expenses paid. The ambitious urban development programs of the Whitlam era had to go, but there was cash to provide incentives to industry: the government offered a 40 percent special depreciation allowance to enable firms to buy capital equipment. To working class Australians, it was clear that the new government applied different standards to rich and poor, to bosses and workers.

The Liberals added a dose of insult by their attempts to capitalise on an internal Labor Party crisis over the 'Iraqi money affair'. During the election campaign, Whitlam had gone along with attempts to raise money for the party from Arab sources. This was really the ALP's business – in any case, it didn't raise a cent – but, in the aftermath of the Loans Affair, it could be made to seem sinister. Some people thought it scandalous for an Australian political party to be funded from abroad – worse still, for the funds to come from Arabs, who were targets for racist paranoia following the 1973 oil crisis.

Fraser announced an inquiry, the press carried lurid stories, there was internal turmoil inside the ALP; yet, ironically, the controversy strengthened Whitlam's position as leader of the Opposition. Although the ALP National Executive formally condemned his actions, the ranks rallied to his support, seeing the episode as a sordid manoeuvre by Labor's foes. Reflecting these pressures, the NSW branch endorsed the condemnation, but then gave Whitlam a rousing ovation.

Coming on top of the 'Kerr Coup', Fraser's actions in early 1976 aroused immense bitterness in the working class and entrenched in the popular mind the arrogant, elitist image that Fraser would never escape. It mattered little that Labor was proposing nothing very different in policy terms. In fact, Bill Hayden later described the ALP's economic policies of 1976 and 1977 as doing 'things pretty much the same, except that we will do just a little bit more on the employment side of the equation.'[3] But society had been polarised on a class basis, and those aware of Labor's political 'me-tooism' simply looked instead to the unions or to other forms of struggle outside parliament.

Preliminary skirmishes

In 1976, the economy picked up for a time, largely because Whitlam's earlier deficit spending had stimulated the private sector. Consequently, quite a few employers lacked enthusiasm for industrial confrontation. They wanted to seize the opportunity to make profits, not fight strike battles; so it seemed that Fraser's election victory had not cemented anything like an impregnable business–conservative front. The unions, finding their economic bargaining power somewhat strengthened, became more aggressive. Bob Hawke set the tone by calling Fraser's wage proposals 'an act of blatant dishonesty',[4] and even the politically conservative AWU threatened to break out of the wage-fixing system. By March, there was something of an industrial offensive underway. A strike by tug crews had immobilised 110 ships at a cost of $1 million a day; 2,500 Transport Workers Union (TWU) members were on strike at the airports; and train guards, Storemen and Packers and meatworkers were all taking action of some kind.

Some of the difficulties the government would have in cutting wages were highlighted by a wage rise paid by General Motors Holden (GMH) to its clerks, engineers and scientists. This was a flow-on from an earlier increase awarded by Arbitration to almost 90 percent of the company's employees. GMH asked the Commission to allow the flow-on and was knocked back – in a decision delivered eight months late – on the grounds that a flow-on could technically breach the wage indexation guidelines. The company paid the rise anyway, pointing out that Ford and Chrysler were already paying it. Fraser reacted with threats to cut Commonwealth purchases of Holden cars. This provoked great annoyance among business leaders and the press; the *Sydney Morning Herald* thought it not very constructive for the Prime Minister to 'attack others for breaking down wage indexation when his own government's policy means the effective end of indexation.'[5]

A similar dilemma faced the conservative government of NSW. In an effort to block 'sweetheart agreements' in which employers and unions sought to by-pass the indexation guidelines, the Lewis Government decided to challenge a $19 rise that the NSW Industrial Commission had granted to nurses. There was such widespread sympathy for the nurses that Justice Dey, who had originally awarded the rise, remarked that 'the cost of placing the salaries of nurses at a reasonable level is something which the conscience of the community must face.'[6] A mass meeting of 1,600 nurses voted for rolling stoppages along with a series of bans, then marched to Parliament House, where they sat down in the street before establishing a permanent vigil. The speaker of the Legislative Assembly later refused to allow them to take shelter from a rainstorm on the Parliament House veranda lest the next step be 'the equivalent of Aboriginal tents on [the] front lawn.'[7] This was a sign that the government was out of touch.

Pensioners delegation to Canberra February 1976

Public outrage over the NSW Government's penny pinching probably contributed to its narrow defeat at the polls in May.

The conservative forces had promised administrative measures to curb 'union power', but this would be no easier. During the election campaign, Malcolm Fraser had talked about controlling militant unions by imposing secret ballots in elections for official positions and creating a sort of industrial police force. Coalition policy declared that industrial action for 'non-industrial' purposes was illegitimate – a formulation directed against political strikes – and provided for a 'third arm' of the conciliation and arbitration machinery called the Industrial Relations Bureau (IRB). The IRB would investigate breaches of industrial law and bring them before the industrial court. The penalties (or, in Fraser's preferred terminology, the 'consequences') could include deregistration, seizure of funds, fines or assistance to people wishing to claim damages.

These proposals sounded ominous, and Victorian Meatworkers' Union secretary Wally Curran was not alone in warning that 'the government was more concerned about trying to break the power of the trade union movement than the actual state of the economy.' He added that Fraser 'wanted to pull on a confrontation as a threshold to the introduction of new industrial legislation.'[8]

Between the pay disputes, the IRB and constant speculation about the future of Medibank, the industrial temperature rose steadily. If unionists like Curran thought that Fraser was spoiling for a fight, observers on the political right made the same charges about the unions, especially those with left leaderships. *The Bulletin*'s Joe Manton wrote:

> Already the left is searching for the right issue to 'go' on. Interference with Medibank and a heavy handed portrayal of Fraser's arbitration clauses as 'penal clauses' have both been given a run over the holiday period... Sooner or later, the left can be expected to make its run, probably not until later in the year.[9]

Conspiracy theories about the trade union left had been a common theme of both Liberal and Labor politicians in the preceding year or two. They would reach a new intensity during the Medibank dispute. It was true that, while most unions expected a fight, the centre and right were less enthusiastic about the prospect than the left. Organised labour was no more monolithic than its opponents. Bob Hawke, from the start, sought to find some sort of accommodation. His election night TV comment was that, while 1976 would be a 'difficult year', the unions would accept the election result: 'The will of the people will be respected.' A day later, he said that he would meet with Fraser, 'and I would hope I could persuade him of the stupidity of some of his industrial programs.'[10]

There ensued a period of détente at peak level. On 16 January, a meeting of employers, unions and the federal government decided to set up a consultative committee and hold a special conference on the Prices Justification Tribunal. Although Fraser had vowed to scrap the PJT, he knew that the employers were no longer concerned by it; if anything, they were growing fond of it. (*The Age* would later report: 'the main push for retention of the Tribunal has swung around from the unions to employer groups.'[11]) Therefore, Industrial Relations Minister Tony Street indicated that it was now negotiable, seeing it as a relatively painless concession to make to Hawke in exchange for his help with more serious issues.

Key Trades and Labor Councils supported Hawke's conciliatory approach, but the industrial left was less impressed with the Hawke-Fraser rapprochement: the pair looked too chummy in their joint photographs. Plain-spoken Norm Gallagher of the BLF accused Hawke of 'pussy-footing'. Twenty-two Victorian Socialist Left unions issued a statement describing the government as illegitimate and the PJT as being of 'doubtful importance'. They wanted no industrial peace conferences:

> The talks for industrial peace are aimed at establishing social contracts which are little more than no strike guarantees in return for talks about wages. As well, Mr Hawke seems to have forgotten the ACTU Executive decision of November 25 which heartily condemned Liberal/National Party industrial policies.[12]

A federal caucus of left unions also took a fairly hard line, with Pat Clancy of the Building Workers' Industrial Union (BWIU) declaring: 'If the ACTU and State Labor Councils don't want to engage in industrial action...we will.'[13] Even within the left, however, there were differences. The Victorian unions were significantly more militant than the forces Clancy represented. There was also a layer of shop stewards and rank and file activists, some of them politically oriented, which was more militant still. On the industrial right, too, some unions like the Storemen and Packers were capable of very effective strikes, while others lived off crumbs from arbitration. A confrontation with Fraser would quickly expose these factional divides.

When the confrontation came, it would not be about the Industrial Relations Bureau. Although the spectre of an 'industrial police' haunted the unions for several years, it proved impractical. The 1969 Clarrie O'Shea battle had shown that this one issue could unite officials of right, left and centre unions, and Bob Hawke probably convinced Tony Street of this in their first discussions. Government members were soon telling the press: 'there are problems with the feasibility of the policy'.[14] Finally, on 23 June, Street indicated in a speech to the Economics Society that the IRB was to be indefinitely shelved; there were:

> quite severe limitations on the Commonwealth Government in this area, and we have frankly found great difficulty in defining the role which the third arm might play.[15]

The IRB was finally established in 1977 but never did much.

Fraser and Street also had trouble with their plans to regulate union elections. Fraser had admitted his hope that his proposals would get rid of communist union leaders such as Laurie Carmichael and John Halfpenny of the AMWU, arguing that low voter turnouts in this union made its leadership unrepresentative. Halfpenny retorted that Fraser was out to 'destroy the union movement as the independent voice of Australian workers'.[16]

The term widely used for the Fraser plan was 'compulsory secret ballots'; however, the *Sydney Morning Herald* reported in April:

> a wide canvas of unions this month failed to reveal any of them which elected their officials by non-secret ballots. Therefore, while some may have misgivings about the methods used, it is pointless to argue that union ballots are not secret.

The genuinely new proposal was that all ballots be conducted by the Commonwealth Electoral Office, with election rules under its administration. Waterside Workers' Federation (WWF) federal secretary Charlie Fitzgibbon, by no means a left winger, identified unions' key objection to the plan. It would:

> give complete control of trade union ballots into the hands of the government. It means the ballot will no longer be the property of the union members.

Many in the industrial movement feared that Fraser would be able to rig election results to suit his own ends.

Here too, however, the proposal was not as radical as it seemed. There were already provisions for ballots to be conducted by the Commonwealth Industrial Registrar upon a petition of 1,000 members or 10 percent of the membership, or the Commission could order a ballot in disputed cases. Moreover, there was a trend for unions to use these avenues voluntarily, because the service was free. On the other hand, in the WWF, the Fraser plan would have meant a lower return, because the WWF had long used compulsory voting at its own polling stations and achieved returns of up to 92 percent. That hadn't stopped communists from winning office. Further, the Federated Clerks' Union (FCU), whose collegiate voting systems had served to keep arch-right wingers in office, also opposed the Fraser plan.

More sophisticated voices among the bourgeoisie recognised that union militancy wasn't a simple reflex of political ideology. The *Sydney Morning Herald* said, for example:

> Anyone who believes that the ousting of Communist officials from unions will automatically stop strikes should study present industrial unrest. The three biggest disputes – in the wool industry, airlines and NSW public transport – involve unions which are not Communist controlled or influenced, or particularly left wing.[17]

Finally, there was the irritating fact, which Bob Hawke helpfully pointed out, that holding more government-run elections would increase the budget costs which Fraser was keen to cut. In May, the government retreated at last: it would merely require that all union ballots be secret. Neither the IRB nor control of union ballots could provide the spark for industrial confrontation; but other issues were not in short supply. The most emotive of them all was served up in the government's autumn mini-budget.

Storm over Medibank

When Treasurer Lynch brought down an economic statement on 20 May, Hawke startled Labor supporters by describing it as 'good in parts'. He had in mind the introduction of tax indexation. But most union militants agreed with Bill Hayden, who called it a 'horror budget in the worst Liberal tradition.'[18]

While the package did increase child endowment, reflecting a traditional conservative emphasis on the family, that was really the only positive aspect. Tax indexation was part of a wider framework which, on the government's

Medibank mass demonstration Melbourne 12 July 1976

own estimates, left 57 percent of taxpayers worse off, including large sections of the working class. Other regressive moves included taxing unemployment and sickness benefits and various pensions. Moreover, Fraser intended tax indexation to be a discipline on the public sector: by holding revenue down, he would force departments to cut programs.

These were controversial measures, but the greatest attention focused on the changes to Medibank. Lynch announced a 2.5 percent levy on taxable incomes to finance the scheme, although pensioners and low income earners would be exempt. Most importantly, people could opt out and use private health insurance; it was clear that, under the Fraser plan, a large section of the population would find it cheaper to leave Medibank. The government itself expected about half of all taxpayers to opt out. The basic principle of the Medibank scheme – universal health cover – was being undermined as an initial step towards its complete abolition.

Health policy had long been a battleground, and attempts by successive governments to get some control over doctors' fees and medical benefits had foundered in the face of powerful medical lobbies. In the postwar era, health cover had been the preserve of private funds, some controlled by doctors.

However, from the late 1950s, these funds had found an increasingly powerful critic in Gough Whitlam. Whitlam proved that the funds were wasteful, not to say irresponsible (in 1967, it emerged that a major NSW fund had bought an aeroplane for its chief executive). The Labor leader hammered the fact that a large minority of the population, many of them living in poverty, had no health cover. As Labor fine tuned its Medibank concept, Whitlam laboured tirelessly to win the public. The ALP carefully explained the policy before and during its term in government, and this painstaking preparation made the scheme harder to kill than the doctors or the Liberals anticipated.

The medical lobbies had fought the scheme with a single minded fury. Some health funds had even used contributors' money for political propaganda. In the Senate, the Opposition twice rejected Whitlam's enabling Bills; he could not implement Medibank until he called a double dissolution, won a second election, and forced the Bills through in a joint sitting. Even then, the conservatives cynically rejected his proposed 1.35 percent tax levy to fund the scheme, forcing further delays while arrangements were made to finance it from general revenue. Medibank only commenced on 1 July, only a few months before Whitlam's fall. And even then, doctors' boycotts gave it a rough passage.

Once Fraser took power, the anti-Medibank forces were anxious to wreck it as quickly as possible, for the simple reason that it was rapidly proving a success. In January 1976, the *Financial Review* outlined its achievements after only a few months, while explaining that many weaknesses were only teething problems. Medibank had:

> reduced the personal cost of health services for many Australians, as well as ensuring that all, and not just those who take out private insurance, are covered for illness. It has also led to quicker processing of medical benefit claims.

There had been some confusion in the early stages, and some abuses, but the confusion owed much to the unexpectedly high volume of claims, and the scheme's administrators were doing 'considerable legwork' to detect abuses.[19]

Even the doctors seemed to be winners. Their boycott of the hospital side of Medibank in NSW and Victoria had forced patients from public wards into private and intermediate wards, where they paid fee-for-service. Outpatients were forced to visit specialists in private consulting rooms. Meanwhile, the practice of bulk-billing was slowly gaining popularity among the medical profession.

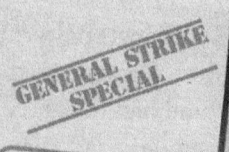

Although the doctors were doing well in the short run, their organisations feared the longer term consequences, because Medibank's universal computer files held out the prospect of full accountability by doctors to government. At the same time, bulk-billing allowed governments to control fee structures. If bulk-billing became common, the government-set rebate would virtually become the fee itself. Consequently, the doctors – and alongside them the ideological forces of free-market Liberalism – developed a sense of urgency. *Quadrant* warned that Medibank would:

> largely destroy the private practice of medicine and therefore the private doctor. Doctors will increasingly become salaried servants of the government, little stooges of the state while the Medibank bureaucrats will steadily move into the field of controlling diagnosis and treatment.[20]

On the other hand, some sections of business opposed the attacks on Medibank. Not only were there employers who saw long-term benefits in having a healthy workforce; others had gained more directly from the scheme – for example, the OPSM eye care chain, which profited from a surge of people seeking eye examinations. On the negative side, the employers were uneasily aware that the unions might press them to pay their employees' levy. The state governments – even those of conservative bent – were also less than enthusiastic about Fraser's plans, because the assault on Medibank came together with his 'new federalism', under which they were to be starved of hospital funds. Fraser was by no means assured of victory.

The unions mobilise

Many activists in both the industrial and political wings of the labour movement believed that this was a battle they could and must win. By the start of June, the union leaderships were under growing pressure from their members to do something. The Queensland TLC urged the ACTU to take 'vigorous nation-wide action' to resist any changes to Medibank, while its South Australian counterpart demanded a 24-hour stoppage. In Victoria, left officials declared that 'rank and file support was greater than in the 1969 battle for the repeal of the penal provisions',[21] and a meeting of about 30 Victorian left unions took an uncompromising stance. Under their prodding, the Victorian Trades Hall

Council (THC) announced proposals for a four-hour strike, to be presented at a shop stewards' and job delegates' meeting on 9 June.

But the workers of the NSW South Coast made the first important move. This was a militant area. Labor Council secretary Merv Nixon was a communist, while the President of the Port Kembla wharfies, Stewart West, was an ALP member who regarded the communists as too moderate. On 26 May, the South Coast TLC called for delegates' meetings as well as lunchtime meetings on the job. Delegates voted by 426 to 17 for a 24-hour stoppage, to be backed by a march and rally 'incorporating the public, pensioners, housewives, etc.' AWU delegates from the district followed up this decision the next day by visiting a meeting of the NSW TLC in Sydney, where they argued unsuccessfully for action. Meanwhile, miners' pit-top meetings not only backed the district stoppage but demanded more resolute leadership from Bob Hawke.

On 7 June, some 40,000 workers throughout the district struck for the day. Thousands assembled outside the Labour Council building, then marched to the showgrounds, where they endorsed a second delegates' meeting to 'determine further sustained industrial action in this district next week'. The only serious weakness was in the railways, where key unions had pulled out of the stoppage. Even so, engine drivers at Thirroul decided to halt more than 12 local services and three Sydney trains.

The strike showed the strength of local militancy and also had a certain impact further afield. Delegates at subsequent meetings in Melbourne showed considerable interest in the news from Wollongong. But a small district could not maintain this momentum on its own. While local officials attempted to form links with the Victorian left unions, even participating in a phone link-up with one of their meetings, developments in NSW – or rather, the lack of them – inevitably weighed more heavily on the minds of South Coast workers. The passivity of the NSW TLC, together with Bob Hawke's reluctance to back industrial action, discouraged them. They were reluctant to be 'one out' if the wider union movement was holding back.

On 16 June, fewer than 100 people turned up at a public meeting intended to revitalise the campaign. ACTU vice-president and Victorian left official Jim Roulston declared bravely from the platform: 'there can be no truces with the Fraser Government. We can't turn off the campaign to save Medibank', but there was no further industrial action on the South Coast until July.[22]

In early June, however, when Wollongong first swung into action, the industrial momentum was still growing nationally. Counter staff at post offices voted to ban literature explaining the Medibank changes, forcing the government to hunt for alternative outlets. At this time, Fraser also came under attack from another quarter, and an authoritative one: the chair of his own Health Commission, Dr Richard Scotton, slammed the government for 'loading the dice' against Medibank by ensuring that it was unable to compete against the private funds.

Scotton was not really saying anything new. A report by Dr Sidney Sax of the Medibank Review Committee had been leaked on 2 June. It began with the words: 'People are to be encouraged to insure privately. The encouragement will take the form of subsidies.'[23] However, the mounting pressure was enough to force Fraser into an embarrassing retreat: Medibank would be allowed to compete with private health funds in the sale of intermediate and private ward insurance (this was the origin of Medibank Private). The changes came only 10 days after publication of 1.4 million government pamphlets, explaining the first round of changes. These pamphlets were now waste paper.

The unions saw the changes as trivial, because the way was still open to force large numbers of people out of Medibank. But they were a sign of weakness on Fraser's part and brought down on him the wrath of the private funds, who complained of a 'blatant move to placate union pressure.'[24] Their greatest impact on the general public was to increase the already widespread confusion about just what the government intended. Fraser was stumbling on every front. While the ALP leaders had run to the ends of the earth to avoid a confrontation – Whitlam was in Scandinavia and Hayden in Japan – the organised working class was showing immense determination. At this point, a concerted union offensive seemed able to defeat the government. In *The Age*, Claude Forell declared:

> Something startling and significant happened this week in
> Australian politics and its full implications have yet to be realised.
> The trade union movement has become the effective opposition
> to a government whose authority and arrogance had seemed
> invincible.[25]

As Forell wrote, the industrial ferment was about to rise further. On 9 June, 1,500 shop stewards and job delegates packed Melbourne's Dallas Brooks Hall for a crucial meeting. By this time, it was clear to everyone that the Victorian unions would be the locomotive for any anti-Fraser offensive. Under these circumstances, the four-hour strike proposal put forward by Trades Hall appeared utterly inadequate to a large section of the meeting, but the left unions continued to back it, with John Halfpenny lining up with the conservative Council secretary, Ken Stone. A CPA leaflet distributed to arriving delegates called on them to 'vote for action' – but specified none. The four-hour proposal seemed likely to triumph by default...but there was one alternative. A leaflet signed by a collection of shop stewards and circulated by the IS demanded a 24-hour stoppage and called for weekly stoppages in every state as a move towards generalised national strike action.

When Max Costello, an IS member and Technical Teachers' delegate, got a chance to move the proposal, he won overwhelming endorsement. Few workers wanted to trifle with a four-hour stoppage when they were offered something more meaningful. 'The mood was very angry,' Costello later told me. 'Whoever got up and moved for stronger action, it was going to get carried.'[26]

The delegates returned to work, looking forward to the 24-hour strike. But there was alarm next day when workplaces learned that the Trades Hall Executive was deadlocked eight to eight on whether to proceed with it. Two days later, alarm gave way to outrage after the full Council voted to stick to the original four-hour proposal, with mass meetings of strikers to be held at Festival Hall and suburban venues.

The militants were beside themselves. The IS rushed out leaflets overnight to the doorsteps of key shop stewards. Partly because of this agitation, telephone calls began to pour into union offices. By the time the stoppage took place on 16 June, the left union leaders had recognised that the mood was hardening and that they risked being outbid by the tiny forces of the revolutionary left. They made an abrupt left turn.

Whereas John Halfpenny had been aligned with Ken Stone at the Dallas Brooks Hall meeting, he now appeared before 6,000 angry strikers at Festival Hall as the vengeful champion of the militants, taking the floor himself to demand that the 24-hour stoppage go ahead. The unions, he declared, would not allow the 'rape of Medibank and of our living standards'. Max Costello, moving a slightly different proposal, was heard respectfully, but he had suddenly become irrelevant. There was still plenty of rank and file anger, however: at one stage, a nurse snatched the microphone from Halfpenny's hand to address the crowd. The meeting's message for Bob Hawke, said *The Age*, was:

> there will be no compromise or bargaining with the government on matters of principle, and Medibank is the top priority. Mr Hawke will have to fight for the protection of the original context of the scheme – that those with greater ability to pay should foot a bigger share of the national health bill.[27]

Seeing the strong rank and file response in Victoria, some key federal unions announced their own plans for a national stoppage. However, by this stage, a combination of bureaucratic inertia and clever manoeuvring by Hawke was beginning to turn the tide against the militants at the national level.

The movement declines

Hawke had announced as early as January that some sort of Medibank levy might be acceptable, and eventually the ACTU settled on proposals for a smaller across-the-board levy similar to that envisaged by Whitlam. The ACTU plan would have preserved Medibank's universal coverage and was also more equitable, but it was a second-rate compromise just at the point when union activists wanted to charge ahead. At a time when Fraser was being attacked in the media for the confusion he had created, the ACTU had an opportunity to stand firmly on the simple principle of defending an existing and popular scheme. Instead, workers saw their leaders endorsing a new tax by the Fraser regime.

If the militants found this discouraging, they were just as unhappy about Hawke's delaying tactics. On 22 June, he persuaded the ACTU executive to postpone any decision on a national stoppage until a special unions' conference in July. By now, it was clear that Hawke's objective was to contain, and eventually suffocate, the industrial struggle. Following the executive's non-decision, many unions which had announced national actions rapidly retreated. The Victorian unions went ahead with their 24-hour stoppage, which was effective in halting production for a day: trains and trams stopped, factories closed, there were severe power cuts, and television viewing was restricted. The industrial movement had demonstrated its power to challenge the government. Yet, at this very point, Victoria's left union officials showed clear signs of waning enthusiasm.

They called no rally on the strike day. To workers and students accustomed to meetings or rallies on any such occasion, this came as a disagreeable surprise – so unexpected that hundreds of people gathered spontaneously in the City Square, looking for a demonstration. That they actually found one was due to the intervention of the same two small, rival radical groups who had initiated a breakaway march during the Constitutional Crisis. The Maoists, who had a presence in some hospitals, organised a Healthcare Action contingent with a banner, while the IS arrived with sound equipment in the expectation that a crowd would gather, and Phil Griffiths spoke to the gathering about the health needs of 'meatworkers who get their fingers chopped off'. While the IS controlled the platform, their Maoist rivals led the subsequent march along Bourke Street with a banner reading: 'Defend And Extend Medibank'.

Hawke had managed to confine the struggle largely to Victoria, along with militant enclaves such as the NSW South Coast and the maritime industry; the Victorian left officials led by Halfpenny had been inconsistent at best; still, the movement lived and breathed, and Fraser had not made enough concessions for the ACTU to end the standoff without a massive loss of face. With immense reluctance, Hawke and the more right-wing union bodies moved towards a general stoppage. The special conference, attended by 129 federal unions, set it for 12 July.

Meanwhile, the extraordinary confrontation over Medibank had sparked a furious public debate over the rights and wrongs of political strikes. *The Age* editorialised against them. John Halfpenny replied forcefully:

> On each occasion when trade unions have taken action on a political or social issue they have proved to be acting in the best interest of the majority; not always the majority in society, sometimes the majority directly concerned with a decision by government or industry. Trade union green bans have saved much of our national heritage. Union bans saved the Regent Theatre. Union involvement helped get Australia out of Vietnam... Employers make decisions and take actions in the privacy of board rooms which have a vital effect on our environment, the economy and the welfare of thousands of people. Their right to make such decisions regardless of the consequences is seldom challenged by the politicians, employers or the media.[28]

The capitalists replied, but mostly in ringing clichés. Ian Spicer of the Victorian Employers' Federation asked: 'Who Runs The Country?' and cited a long list of recent political strikes – as though you could discredit a tactic by proving that it was used a lot. Spicer did identify the fears haunting the employing class: that a state of affairs might arise where:

> it would be necessary for a government to seek trade union approval before being able to implement the policies on which they were elected. Obviously that system could not be tolerated.[29]

YEARS OF RAGE

Police batter a way through for Kerr's car when demonstrators block entry to dinner at Leonda Restaurant Hawthorn (Melbourne) 23 June 1976

Police attack protesters outside Royal Commonwealth Society dinner for Kerr in Melbourne, 9 June 1976

This prospect did not seem so intolerable to unionists, however, particularly to those who recalled that Fraser had been elected on a policy of preserving Medibank.

The unions' critics may have believed that they didn't need sophisticated arguments, because they were virtually assured of dominating debate in the press. Apart from the fulminations of the Murdoch tabloids (culminating in the *Daily Mirror*'s classic 'Killed By Medibank' front page of 19 July) and talk of 'union fascism' in *The Bulletin*,[30] the anti-strike agitation dominated the letters pages of the 'quality' dailies.

There were initial calls for workers to 'tell their union leaders that they want no part of political strikes', but such appeals seemed to be falling on deaf ears as more and more unions announced their support for a national stoppage. The letter writers then offered a range of explanations. They castigated the efforts of union leaders to 'make union members strike when they do not wish to strike', but also the sloth of the rank and file, who went on strike to get 'another long lazy week-end' and who were anyway so stupid as to be 'led unthinkingly and sheep-like to yet another economic precipice in order to force a purely political issue.' This oafishness was alarming, because a long lazy weekend would apparently 'precipitate economic chaos'; indeed, 'possibly death could occur'. To forestall disaster, one man fortunately had the perfect solution: 'For their next training exercise some Israeli commandos should make a raid on July 11 on the communist terrorist offices of the ACTU.'[31]

Actually, there was considerable debate within the union movement, resulting in some major divisions. For reasons never satisfactorily explained, the NSW branch of the AWU held its own, separate 24-hour strike on a different day, during which branch Secretary Charlie Oliver, the classic right-wing machine man, told a small indoor rally that Bob Hawke wasn't militant enough. A general meeting of the Tasmanian Shop Assistants' Union adopted a more typical right-wing stance, voting to reject 'attempts by the extreme left-wing elements in the trade union movement to enter into bans, limitations and stoppages on political issues'. Under pressure from the 'Shoppies', the state's right-wing Labor Council decided to limit its Medibank action to 'cooperation with the dissemination of literature.'[32]

Nonetheless, about 25 Tasmanian unions joined the national strike and shut down much of basic industry. Meanwhile, the white collar unions' national peak body, ACSPA, unanimously recommended that its 37 affiliates join the national stoppage. The great majority of active unionists around the country backed the strike, so that it was exceptionally empty rhetoric for Tony Street to

Student protesters at Monash University force Fraser to leave from rear exit, August 1976

blame the unrest on 'extremists' and to claim that 'hundreds of thousands of workers are bitterly resentful at being forced to strike for political purposes'.[33] Even the most apathetic strikers were unlikely to be resentful, both because of overwhelming support for Medibank itself and because the national strike was only for one day – on a Monday, in fact, creating what did amount to a 'long lazy week-end'.

This holiday atmosphere was the ultimate Hawke tactic. Unable to prevent union militants from winning mass support for the idea of a general strike, the ACTU leadership chose to embrace it, then gut it of all political content. Most of the officials were prepared to go along with this. A group of health workers complained that:

> when the general strike was called, they seized on the exemption of medical services and directives were given not to strike. No meetings were called before or on the day...except where job delegates took their own initiatives.[34]

In the days immediately before the stoppage, as unionists began to grasp the bureaucratic nature of the exercise, a general air of passivity spread through union ranks. An AMWU delegates' meeting I attended in Sydney captured the mood very well. Delegates complained that the national stoppage had been called and run bureaucratically; they supported the strike but saw it as an unnecessarily top-down affair. When Janey Stone, a socialist and shop steward at a Sydney metal factory, called for a rally on the strike day, the officials simply replied that it would be 'a flop'. The delegates, believing that this assessment was all too accurate, showed little interest in a rally. This helps to explain why, despite the small demonstrations in capital cities, involving mostly students, Hawke had little difficulty ensuring that no significant gatherings of workers occurred.

So, in place of the scenes of angry strikers we might have expected, the television coverage of the event showed no workers at all. The rank and file had become invisible. Rather, there were endless shots of Bob Hawke playing tennis. Hawke told the media that further strikes were unlikely, and few doubted that this was true. The historic event had been turned into a huge, yet harmless, safety valve. For the second time in seven months, Hawke's foot dragging and sabotage, combined with the fatal caution of Victoria's left union leaders, had succeeded in dissipating a challenge to Malcolm Fraser and the employing class.

This experience began to bring home to a wider layer of union activists what a small number had always suspected: for all his bluster, when it came to fundamentals, Bob Hawke was an ally of the Fraser Government. In his book on Fraser in power, *War Without Blood*, Russell Schneider later described their relationship:

> Fraser relied on Hawke's influence and later on his political ambitions to prevent industrial chaos in the country. Their close contact began through Ian Macphee at a time when Fraser was campaigning for the Liberal leadership and Hawke was becoming disillusioned with Whitlam... The honeymoon was public: they could be seen talking together for hours about the state of the nation at the Victorian Football League finals.[35]

Medibank's defenders fought a rearguard action through August and into September. The Federal Union Conference of 5–6 July had asked the ACTU leadership to persist with the campaign after the national stoppage; while the statement mentioned only 'the use of pamphlets and the media',[36] it did offer some scope for a minority of union leaders and activists to continue agitating. Plans for further rolling strikes came to nothing, because no union was prepared to act independently of the ACTU, but rallies and demonstrations persisted.

About 1,800 members of 10 Melbourne ethnic groups assembled at Collingwood Town Hall in August, where Gough Whitlam called on them to 'let the Fraser Government know the strength of our anger, the depth of our indignation, at their deception and incompetence.' Bob Hawke was there too, denouncing Fraser's 'undemocratic piece of bastardry', although his only action proposal was to 'extend pressure on members of parliament.'[37] In September, again in Melbourne, 3,000 people joined a 'Medibank moratorium' march, including some builders' labourers and waterside workers who had walked off the job. Even towards the end of the year, a workers' meeting in Wollongong challenged Hawke over his acceptance of a Medibank levy.

The example of workers taking national strike action also had a flow-on effect on campuses, where support grew steadily in September for a national strike called by the Australian Union of Students (AUS) against education funding cuts and Fraser's decision to freeze benefits under the Tertiary Education Assistance Scheme. The AUS call followed a successful city-wide campus strike in Brisbane in July. All the campuses were polled; 52 endorsed the national stoppage, with four against and 18 abstaining. Unlike the ACTU, the students organised well-attended rallies on the strike day. AUS education research officer Mike Gallagher called them the 'biggest student demonstrations since the Vietnam moratoriums.'[38] Moreover, the actions achieved some tangible results. Six days later, Senator Carrick, the Education Minister, announced that tertiary allowances would be raised. He also made a number of other concessions.

If a failed working class mobilisation could engender such a sequel, we can surmise that a victorious Medibank campaign would have had a much more sensational impact on public consciousness. The fact remained, however: having defeated the unions at the end of 1975 on the explicitly political issue of who would govern, Fraser had routed them seven months later on the social issue closest to workers' hearts. The danger now was that a debilitating pattern of defeat would become established.

Chasing John and Mal

Nonetheless, resistance continued. Although confrontations between the 'big battalions' of capital and labour over wages and Medibank began to subside, a guerrilla war of sorts continued to rage at stage left – for, virtually everywhere they went, Sir John Kerr and Malcolm Fraser faced rowdy demonstrations.

The fun had begun in Adelaide back in March, when 200 students jeered and heckled the Governor-General as he opened a new college. They occupied the upper levels of the amphitheatre, making such a racket that, at times, Kerr could only be heard in the front rows. Numerous invited guests had declined to attend, forcing the administration to invite all the staff – most of whom likewise declined. Kerr said that he would not be deterred by the demonstrators' 'illiterate stupidity', but he was reportedly very shaken.[39]

A week later, 600 students appeared when the Governor-General arrived for a dinner at the Australian National University in Canberra. They blocked the front entrance, obliging Sir John and Lady Kerr to enter through a side door. The dining room had one wall made of plate glass windows, so the guests had to eat in full view of the protesters, who pounded on the glass until forced back by police. The protesters, 'some drinking beer, said they were not to be outdone by the demonstration by Adelaide students last week.'[40] In May, a crowd forced the Kerrs to enter Perth's Parmelia Hotel through the back door, while Senator Peter Walsh jumped onto his car to call the Queen's representative 'a megalomaniac'.

By June, Kerr-baiting had become something of a national sport. His popularity among the labour movement had not been enhanced by reports that the extreme right-wing League of Rights was campaigning in his defence. When he arrived at a Royal Commonwealth Society function in Melbourne, 700 people blocked his car despite efforts by mounted police to clear a path:

> Suddenly a young man jumps on the roof of the Rolls-Royce [and] starts banging the windscreen with a loudhailer. The noise he makes is deafening. A moment later he's lifted from the car roof and appears to vanish in the crowd. Several others throw themselves on the car bonnet.

Two weeks later, a 1,000-strong crowd awaited Kerr at Leonda Receptions, also in Melbourne. Although a huge police presence kept things more or less under control, guests were harassed on arrival. Even in Bendigo, there were angry crowd scenes when the vice-regal Rolls Royce, 'still battered and with heavily taped windows from Melbourne,' arrived at a pottery industry function.

Some protests were more genteel, as when Canberra concertgoers hissed the Kerrs twice in one evening, or a group called Society for Asserting the Constitution over Kerr (SACK) appealed for 15 cent donations towards Sir John's 'Early Retirement Fund'; but, inevitably, the demonstrations got more attention. Fears were raised about incidents when the Queen visited in 1977 ('They'll have to round up half the population of Australia to make sure no one is going to throw a stink bomb.') Two Archbishops warned that the unrest could lead to social divisions like those in Northern Ireland. A public opinion poll showed that 53 percent of people thought that the Governor-General should not resign, but a respectable 39 percent thought that he should. 'If two out of every five people think you're a bastard,' wrote Mungo MacCallum, 'it's a bit hard to claim the overwhelming support of the silent majority.'[41]

If Kerr was having a hard time, Fraser fared no better. When he came to open the Krongold Centre for Exceptional Children at Monash University, 1,500 students showed some exceptional talent of their own, sealing off all exits to the Alexander Theatre and forcing the PM to take shelter in the manager's basement office for 80 minutes. Finally, flanked by a column of uniformed and plain-clothes officers, Fraser dashed to a waiting police car, which raced from the scene.

The conservatives sought to use the tumultuous protests to put ALP leaders on the spot with a motion to the June Premiers' Conference 'deploring violence'. But so strong was the anti-Kerr and anti-Fraser mood among Labor supporters that the three ALP premiers refused to support the motion, although Bob Hawke and Jim McClelland did call on demonstrators to protest peacefully.

The Kerr issue persisted for years, partly through the man's own doing, as with his 'tired and emotional' performance while presenting the Melbourne Cup in 1977. It faded with his eventual departure from the job and the country, but rowdy protests remained a constant feature of the Fraser years, evidence of a country deeply divided. The pleasure of harassing the two individuals might be poor compensation for defeat in more important battles; but, at the same time, it was a warning that Fraser's enemies were by no means cowed. They hurled flamboyant insults at him: his policies were 'Mal-Practice', his government was 'Mal-Functioning', his promises were (in John Halfpenny's words) 'Empty Phrasers'. He was the 'Crazy Grazier' and 'Mal the Knife'. Eric Bogle sang:

> *He's our buddy, he's our mate, he's our pal, pal, pal*
> *Ain't we all so lucky to have Mal!*

And if Bogle's irony was too gentle for you, you could always join the young demonstrators in the street, chanting: 'One more cut – Fraser's throat!'

5.
In the trenches

Having fatally wounded Medibank, Fraser and his supporters gained immensely in confidence. Even so, there were many on both sides of the class divide who recognised that there had still been no decisive test of strength. During the Constitutional Crisis, and again over Medibank, there had been short political strikes and much agitation, but the ALP leaders and the union officials had headed off a real confrontation in both cases. Union militants felt that neither they nor their opponents had really been tested. Perhaps political strikes were hard to sustain; but what would happen if an entrenched, well-organised group of workers took on the bosses or the government in a traditional economic 'stoush'?

Over the following year or so, two traditionally strong groups of workers made the attempt. However, both the Fairfax printers in Sydney and the Latrobe Valley power workers were to learn that major economic struggles were also political and were harder to win in the new industrial climate. They were comprehensively defeated, leading many observers to conclude that their strikes had been more or less unwinnable. Leonie Sandercock, for example, wrote that the Latrobe Valley dispute:

> demonstrated the dangers inherent in an isolated action...in which those directly concerned lacked the industrial strength to win their demands but were unable to call on other unions for the measure of support which might have ensured their success.[1]

Was it really so hopeless? Or could both strikes have been won with different strike organisation, politics and leadership?

Showdown at Fairfax

The 1970s brought a technological revolution to the newspaper industry, with Australian trends following those overseas. New techniques had already restored profitability to the US newspaper industry, and Australian firms such as Fairfax were anxious to follow their lead.[2] The company's printing workers were naturally concerned that the changes might jeopardise their jobs. After some exchanges before the Arbitration Commission during 1976, the Printing and Kindred Industries Union (PKIU) concluded that, despite some vague assurances from Fairfax management, there was a real threat to employment. The union had clear grounds for concern, given that a company booklet entitled *Automation Plan* stated:

> PKIU employees in redundancy areas will be invited to apply for transfer to new duties created or to other vacancies in the company *provided they are, in the opinion of the company, competent to be retrained.*'[3]

This was hardly a firm guarantee of job security.

The Fairfax printing workers began to demand better guarantees but found the company unwilling to provide them. PKIU State Secretary Frank Kelly complained: 'we've had 14 meetings with management and been faced with the repudiation of existing agreements which were 18 months old.' He reported Fairfax's estimate that it would need 300 fewer printers, and 'we know what that means'.[4] A fight would be required.

Fortunately, by August 1976, management was facing more than the PKIU. A Combined Unions Committee (CUC) established at Fairfax brought together not only the printers and the traditionally militant metal workers, but a number of other unions, including carpenters. In the interest of unity, the PKIU allowed itself to be underrepresented on the committee. While it accounted for some 1,100 out of 1,500 printing workers, it had only three people on the CUC: two workers and one official. The six other unions were represented by one worker and one official each.

The printers' job organisation was strong and steeped in tradition. Delegates existed in all sections, and the quaintly named Father of the Chapel was free to do union work at any time, making him virtually a full-time officer. The formation of the CUC followed an important change in the Chapel leadership in July, when the old, conservative leadership of Leo Sommer was replaced by a militant team. The new Chapel Father was a thoughtful, left-leaning man named Don Paget, his deputy a spirited young activist named Ian Joliffe. From August onwards, the new rank and file leaders began preparing for a showdown, gradually building up commitment and unity in a series of mass meetings, go-slows and short stoppages.

The company also began to prepare, counting on the large number of non-union 'staff' maintained beyond normal production needs. In addition, the journalists were willing to work during a strike. In earlier years, journalists had fought together with the printers more than once, taking joint strike action and publishing their own newspapers; but, in the 1970s, management had convinced the Australian Journalists' Association that they would get most, if not all, of the work on the new equipment – and, conversely, that journalists' jobs might suffer if the printers won. Offers by the blue collar unions of solidarity if journalists were sacked failed to win them over. Advertising staff, represented by the conservative FCU, were likewise prepared to work during strikes.

Following some minor stoppages in September and October, Fairfax management decided to take the offensive during one walkout. They secured an order from Justice Cahill of the NSW Industrial Commission instructing the unions to desist from striking. The company then announced that, on their return to work, PKIU members would have to handle work done by staff during the strike. They refused and began organising mass picketing. What had started as a one-day stoppage now became an indefinite strike for the unions' log of claims.

The claims were for a 35-hour week, to result from reduced workloads as new technology was introduced; a company guarantee that no redundancies would occur as a result of technological change; payment of Medibank levies by the company; and a $20 rise. While the media made much of the other three claims, declaring at every opportunity that they were outside the indexation guidelines, the strikers' attention was riveted on the call for job security. The company insisted that its ambiguous statements satisfied this demand, putting the union's alleged obstinacy down to the irresponsibility of a disruptive minority – occasionally hinting at connections between Don Paget and the Communist Party.[5]

At the outset, few of the unionists expected a really prolonged dispute. Militants told me that, had anyone proposed an eight-week stoppage in October, it would have been overwhelmingly rejected. Ian Joliffe joked that, initially, 'I said we'd last about a week.' But, once underway, the strike gained momentum.

The mass pickets, held daily between 10 am and 1 pm in an attempt to disrupt distribution of the mass circulation *Sun*, became the heart of the strike. Picket

lines are normally carried by a minority; by conventional standards, the roll-up outside the Fairfax building was usually quite respectable. At its height, more than 300 workers were present, while others were engaged in raising money or organising solidarity elsewhere. The gatherings provided a daily rallying point, offering an opportunity for discussions of issues and tactics. On the other hand, as the Fairfax workers gradually began to realise, this would be an exceptionally difficult dispute to win.

The strike organisation was not entirely adequate to the task. The CUC leaders had an organised base in the rank and file, but it was too thin; they had links in the wider labour movement, but these were underdeveloped compared to the magnitude of the task they would face; they had considerable political nous, but still they placed too much faith in union officials and in the state Labor government.

A picket committee elected from among volunteers turned out to have little idea what to do, and a new committee had to be assembled on the spot. Even then, the picket line seemed only to be effective when union officials or Chapel leaders were present. When they had to be somewhere else, workers often hung about the front of the building idly, waiting for lunch and scarcely harassing strike breakers who came in and out. Even at crucial moments, the picket line could be indecisive; for example, the strikers periodically rocked delivery vehicles back and forth, but the effect was purely theatrical. Had a dozen people been organised to tip over one or two delivery vans, the picketing workers could have gained a psychological advantage. Instead, the initiative on the street gradually shifted into the hands of the company and the police.

The CUC seemed to be in constant session, its members increasingly overworked. Not only did it have to leave the picket line leaderless far too often; it never addressed some important tasks. At one meeting, a printer insisted that they needed 'a street full of wives', and a few wives of strikers came down to join them outside the Fairfax building in Jones Street, but nothing was ever done to organise them. Don Paget later conceded that it would have been valuable, admitting that the CUC lacked an experienced person to do it.

The picket line was also the focus for solidarity action from other workers and radical students, who swelled the numbers and got a firm grasp of the issues, enabling them to take the arguments back to their workplaces or to nearby Sydney University. Delegates from the CUC toured industry. Printers who had previously taken a dim view of militant watersiders found themselves receiving a rousing reception on the wharves. The Fairfax metal workers, trading on their union contacts and organisation, raised money by visiting factories. PKIU

Chapels at newspapers throughout NSW and in Melbourne also raised many thousands of dollars. By the end of the struggle, $114,000 had been collected – hardly a fortune, but enough for the CUC to pay up to $65 a week to strikers who were actively involved in the strike.

When they visited workplaces, the Fairfax strikers took along copies of their strike paper, *The Fair Facts*, of which four issues appeared with a total distribution of hundreds of thousands. One issue was called the *Sin* in parody of the the *Sun*. As a result, there was a slow but steady growth in support for the Fairfax workers. It was a good start, but it would not be enough to win this dispute.

Uncertain solidarity

On 27 October, Sir Warwick Fairfax told his Annual Meeting:

> We shall fight it to the finish, and we do it in defence of the press itself, of the Industrial Commission, and of all the citizens of this country.[6]

On the following day, postal workers escalated the struggle to a new level by placing a total ban on mail to the Fairfax newspapers – an anonymous editorial punster called it a case of 'black mail'. The CUC had requested this ban by the Australian Postal and Telecommunications Union (APTU). At the same time, members of the Australian Telecommunications Employees' Association (ATEA) banned repairs to phones and teleprinters. Earlier, printers at *The Land* newspaper had stopped work over the transfer of printing material to the Fairfax plant, because it would be handled by non-union labour. The solidarity actions, and the mail ban in particular, made the struggle a national issue and stung the federal Liberals into responding.

On 3 November, Supreme Court Justice Taylor ordered the APTU to lift its mail ban. At that stage, 28,600 items were being held, including 3,500 intended for the *Sun*'s Abba Fan Club. Next day, Liberal backbencher Billy Wentworth told federal parliament that the strikers were using 'strong arm operations...to hold the community to ransom.' If this situation continued, he said, Australia could become a 'totalitarian dictatorship. It's a rehearsal for revolution.' Although Wentworth was a buffoon, his jibe showed how political the dispute had become. The strikers were up against politicians as well as the Fairfax management.

The unions defied the court order, leaving the next move up to Malcolm Fraser. Milton Stevens, state manager of Australia Post, urged the government to keep cool and told Fairfax, in response to their persistent public demands, that if he personally handed over their mail, 'I would cause a riot.' But the politicians were determined to intervene. On 11 November, federal Cabinet authorised minister Eric Robinson to suspend workers if they refused to lift the ban; the following day, Australia Post management stood down four employees. This was a major test for the APTU. Management was terrified that the union would respond by stopping mail distribution on a wider scale. However, George Slater, the union's federal leader and also a Postal Commissioner, signalled that this was not on the cards. He told Australian Broadcasting Commission (ABC) radio:

> I advised the NSW branch that if members were suspended or dismissed they should remain at work – and not be placed in a position by Malcolm Fraser where the people of NSW are going to be deprived of their mail service.

The seemingly defiant rhetoric was really a signal that the dispute would not be widened – indeed, the suspended employees would work for nothing to ensure that the mail got through. The strikers' federal union officials were working against them as surely as was Eric Robinson. Encouraged by Slater's statement, management suspended six more postal workers over the next few days.

During this same week, the CUC at Fairfax had a visit from the NSW APTU leaders, who told the CUC in no uncertain terms that the ban must be lifted. To defend the suspended workers would require a national strike, for which Slater had no enthusiasm. In any case, the postal workers themselves would probably vote to lift the ban. The CUC had relied on the APTU leadership, not only to slap on the ban, but to explain it to their rank and file. This turned out to be a grave error. No meetings had been held at the Redfern Mail Exchange. CUC circulars explaining the issue were still sitting in the union office when the Redfern posties finally met on 15 November.

At that meeting, the officials arrived with a face-saving 'request' from the Fairfax unions to lift the ban. While this saved them from losing a formal vote, they did not escape a backlash from the membership. Militants and leftists were well represented at Redfern but were on the defensive that day, as one right winger after another rose to attack militant trade unionism and solidarity actions. The left was reduced to making an elementary defence of basic trade union principles. At a time when the Fairfax workers and their allies needed to develop a higher level of political awareness in the labour movement about the nature of the struggle, they were actually pushed backwards. Later, the APTU officials had to face the media with red faces. When challenged by ABC radio about his failure to consult members earlier about the ban, the union's state president Alex Saint replied lamely:

> Well, that is correct. But...where the livelihood of trade union members who are on strike is threatened, then sometimes you have to take quick action without reference to the members. We have done it in the past, we have been chastised for it, and we take the chastisement.

The excuses were transparent. The APTU officials had had well over a fortnight to explain the issues to their members. The CUC's mistake lay in relying on them to do so, rather than establishing direct links with militants at Redfern, which would not have been at all difficult. Their failure to build these links ensured that their greatest single source of industrial leverage was not only squandered, but was transformed into a propaganda victory for the employers.

Meanwhile, the strikers were taking something of a battering on the picket line. Initially, the police had been rather restrained, even when the picketers rocked trucks from side to side. Sometimes they marched along lines of vehicles, harassing the drivers; on one occasion, a cop was obliged to climb in with a frightened driver and comfort him. As it became clear that the picket line was having an effect, however, the police grew more aggressive. Their change in attitude seemed to coincide with a charge by Liberal leader Eric Willis that Neville Wran had instructed police not to prosecute picketers 'when they commit such offences as assault, theft, offensive behaviour...and lighting fires in public places.' When Wran failed to defend the rights of union picketers, the police apparently took it as encouragement to crack down.

One of the more effective picket line tactics involved the use of loudhailers to harass strikebreakers, who were informed by the relentless voice of Ian Joliffe that they were 'nothing but a foul scab, the lowest form of life, the foul scrapings of the human barrel.' By mid-November, several additional loudhailers had appeared, and Editorial Manager Graeme Wilkinson found himself surrounded one day by four unionists dinning 'scab!' into his ears as he directed cars into the loading bays. A *Sydney Morning Herald* editorial virtually ordered the police to act. They hastened to do so, banning loudhailers and prohibiting use of the word 'scab'. This became a test case.

The printing workers, although flummoxed at first, soon decided to force the issue. One hundred and fifty picketers marched in a circle chanting the word in unison. The police looked sheepish, and were able to make only one arrest. The picketers began singing: 'Scabs are working at the *Herald*' to the tune of *Solidarity Forever*, insolent grins on their faces. They then held another meeting, flushed with victory. At this stage, the union officials could have defied the ban on loudhailers, as rank and filers called repeatedly for someone to do, but the officials were too timid and the rank and file too disorganised to take the initiative. In itself a minor issue, this still highlighted a weakness in the strike: if the officials wavered, the militants were not capable of independent action. In fact, their position weakened as the strike went on, partly because of growing police repression.

Some arrests involved students, as the authorities played the 'outside agitator' card. The CUC boldly told the media that they supported the students. More important in their impact were the arrests of unionists, because the militants were singled out and, once arrested, were reluctant to return to the picket line. As the numbers of arrested activists grew, there was an increasing vacuum of leadership in Jones Street. By the final weeks of the dispute, the picket line had deteriorated. The CUC tried morale-building exercises, such as a demonstration outside the company's Hunter Street offices, but the trend was irreversible. Demoralisation on the picket line, the heart of the strike, translated itself into discouragement among the general body of unionists.

As the strikers weakened, NSW TLC secretary John Ducker appeared on the scene. The CUC had anticipated involving the TLC in final negotiations, but Ducker's role was to be much greater than they wished. When he contacted management in early December, the bosses asked to see him alone. Knowing that the strikers would never accept this, he insisted that officials from each union go along, but no rank and filers were allowed to attend – even the day-to-day leaders of the dispute. The CUC was hardly pleased, and a crowd of strikers assembled at the Fairfax building when Ducker's delegation arrived, yelling 'no sell-outs!'

Ducker couldn't end the dispute, but he could sway the union officials. In exchange for a company offer to withdraw deregistration proceedings (initiated by the employers precisely to create a bargaining chip), the officials agreed to raise with the CUC the idea of a return to work. Accounts differed on this agreement: while Fairfax claimed that PKIU secretary Frank Kelly had agreed to recommend a return to work, Kelly more or less denied it later in a waffly speech. However, Ducker probably believed at this stage that the dispute was under control.

He was mistaken. The CUC angrily rejected any return to work. Its recommendation to stay out was carried at the next mass meeting by a margin of three or four to one. However, the vote was rather closer than the 10-to-one margin at a previous mass meeting the fortnight before; and, for the first time, a back-to-work movement appeared, with some 60 workers organised to sit in front of the microphones and cheer for right-wing speakers. One of these complained that he saw:

> the company getting stronger and stronger, and us getting hungrier and hungrier. I can see new technology coming in, and we are not going to get a chance to learn that new technology.

It was now mid-December. Like other unionists, he saw Christmas looming. It is not easy to sustain a strike over the Australian summer holidays.

Ducker prepared to intervene again. He knew that Kelly and most other officials in the CUC were wavering, plus he had a new angle: the mass meeting had called for a total union black ban on Fairfax, something only the Labor Council could officially impose. Ducker used this to bring himself into the centre of the dispute.

He could be confident that morale was still weakening. Led by former Chapel Father Leo Sommer, a group that had played no role on the picket line suddenly appeared with a petition demanding a return to work, and arguments were underway behind the scenes. Ducker set out to manipulate the demoralisation. He wrote letters to the unions still working at Fairfax, knowing that these would show no interest in black bans, then took a stack of discouraging replies to the next mass meeting on 16 December. He could also point to one minor concession: the company's commitments on job security had originally applied only to employees hired before a certain date, but Fairfax now agreed to extend them to all employees. It was small potatoes, but Ducker reckoned that the demoralised workers would seize on it as a rationalisation for ending the strike.

He told the meeting that a total black ban was 'just not on'. The other unions would not participate, and it would be undemocratic to force them. There were 'not a lot of people rushing to get into a dispute seven days before Christmas'. The concession on job security was an 'important victory to be recognised and built on, and shoved down the throat of every boss'. Frank Kelly added to the gloom: Ducker had done a wonderful job and got all that he could get for the workers. The settlement Kelly had rejected eight days earlier was now portrayed as a major achievement.

Faced with the collapse of their officials and Ducker's manoeuvres, the printing workers lost heart. Militants were jeered for suggesting that the strike could still be won, and the vote to end it was overwhelming. Gloomy CUC members met briefly, then went off to negotiate a return to work.

Over the following weeks, their spirits lifted. Don Paget remarked:

> we didn't gain what we hoped, but the company didn't gain anything at all. They spent millions to break us, but our organisation is as strong as ever.

In fact, the CUC did seem to enjoy greater prestige at Fairfax than before the strike. The workers' view of the world was also greatly changed. They had become used to mixing with radical students and to meeting other unionists with different politics. Ernie Fairbrother, who had collected money on the wharves, told one mass meeting: 'A lot of us…used to talk about the wharfies as stirrers and commos. Now I see things differently.'

Still, their defeat was undeniable. They had not budged the company, despite strong union organisation and a long strike. To win would have required a better understanding of the vacillating, relatively conservative nature of full-time union officials, along with stronger organisation by the militants to counteract it. It would probably also have required more daring tactics, such as an occupation of the building to stop production. There had been a brief occupation of sorts a year earlier, when unionists had been declared 'on strike' by management but had refused to go home. However, the CUC did not attempt to build on that experience.

The employers' tenacity came as an unnerving shock to unionists grown used to easier victories during the prosperous postwar years. In the new climate of high unemployment and low profits, with an aggressively anti-union government in Canberra, employers were harder to beat. Something resembling a 'rehearsal for revolution' was required: stronger and more political organisation by rank and file workers, across union lines. Victorian power workers were also to learn this the hard way.

The Latrobe Valley strike

By early 1977, the Fraser Government seemed to have won its initial battles fairly easily. Ironically, some observers suggested that this might cause it a few headaches. After 18 months of austerity under the Liberals, the economy was still performing badly. Without some major industrial dispute to serve as a scapegoat, it might be hard for Fraser to avoid shouldering some of the blame.

Consequently, the *National Times* suggested: 'the Government may be looking for a test of strength with the unions by April or May next year.'[7]

They needn't have worried; the unions were proving resilient. In the middle of the year, the conservatives had several disputes to choose from. Twenty TWU members were jailed in Fremantle after picketing a Golden Fleece terminal, and the TWU threatened a national stoppage. Pilots' strikes grounded the major domestic airlines, and mail drivers walked off the job in Melbourne. In early August, the postal workers held a national 24-hour strike, as did Melbourne's transport unions; Victoria was again emerging as the main centre of industrial militancy. On 4 August, *The Age* reported strikes in pubs, the Gas and Fuel Corporation, Telecom and the state's high schools.

Occasionally, the papers mentioned a small dispute in the Latrobe Valley east of Melbourne, where maintenance workers with the State Electricity Commission (SEC) were seeking wage parity with their NSW equivalents. Not until September or October did the public – and the strikers – begin to realise that Victoria's Liberal Premier Rupert Hamer had chosen the SEC for the crucial industrial confrontation of the year. The Victorian government led the attack on the unions, although the federal government stuck its oar in wherever possible. One of Premier Hamer's objectives was to distract attention from scandals over land sales. Hamer, however, played the role of a relative moderate in the dispute, compared to hardliners in his Cabinet who welcomed a long, bitter conflict as a means of thoroughly crushing militancy in the SEC.

The origins of the dispute went back to 1972, when the SEC joined the State Incremental Payments Scheme, and the Commission's maintenance workers lost a 'special payment'. This payment was absorbed into a statewide over-award, and the maintenance workers gained a net pay rise, but they lost ground relative to other public employees. By 1977, they reckoned that they were $27.50 behind their rightful wage level, and this was the 'real' demand behind their $40 'ambit' claim.[8]

In March 1977, the Central Gippsland Trades and Labour Council served an 11-point log of claims on the SEC on behalf of its maintenance workers. The key components were a $40 rise and a 35-hour week. They also sought increased overtime payments and meal allowances, a holiday for Easter Tuesday and increases in penalty rates. They argued that electricity commission workers in other states, particularly NSW, were earning $15–20 more. Union surveys also showed that SEC workers had fallen well behind plumbers at the State Gas and Fuel Corporation and metal trades workers elsewhere in Victoria. They were also angry at being paid significantly less than maintenance workers employed by private contractors, who were doing the same work right alongside them. Finally, the unions argued productivity: in 1967, generating capacity had been 0.143 megawatts per employee; by 1976, the figure had risen to 0.255.

The state government took an intransigent line. It was aware that the SEC had managed to divide its workforce by giving preferential treatment to white collar technicians (members of the Municipal Officers Association – MOA) and to coal-dredge operators (members of the Federated Engine Drivers and Firemen's Association – FEDFA). These unions stood largely aloof throughout the strike. Consequently, SEC management was instructed to give no ground. Its industrial advocate challenged numerous details in the union claim, but the crucial sticking point was the litany trade unionists had been hearing for nearly two years, that no wage claims could be allowed outside the indexation guidelines.

In the dispute's early months, the initiative remained with the shop stewards. When the SEC told them that only the union officials in Melbourne could make claims for a new state Award, the stewards ignored the argument. Angered by management intransigence, they called a mass meeting in Morwell on 15 June, at which 2,300 maintenance workers voted to impose overtime and availability bans.

June was also the month when Acting Premier Lindsay Thompson first hinted that the SEC maintenance workers' campaign would become a political football, suggesting that it might be a case for the Industrial Relations Bureau which was being established at the time. Showing a rare command of the industrial relations cliché, Thompson called on the power workers to 'accept the umpire's decision' after arbitration, warning that he would be 'standing up for the people of Victoria' if they didn't, because 'Communists, left-wingers and anarchists' were trying to 'put this country out of business' by 'holding the country to ransom', and something must be done 'before the unions wreck Australia'. Thompson denied that he was union-bashing. Electrical Trades Union (ETU) state secretary Charlie Faure retorted: 'we don't take much notice of what Mr Thompson says', but this was a mistake, because the government meant business.[9]

Meanwhile, the conflict between the SEC and the unions escalated, with another mass meeting at Morwell Oval voting to strike for a week. One week later, the workers voted to remain out until Commissioner Vosti heard the ETU's claim on 23 August. Management remained confident that the power stations were in good shape, however, and Vosti decided that the hearing would not proceed until the men returned to work. They were persuaded to do so, but not for long. The Commission met on 24 August but then adjourned. Feeling cheated, about 1,000 workers were back on strike within 48 hours; Charlie Faure said that they had 'just drifted off the job' in protest at the delays.[10] Strikes continued into the following month. In mid-September, they spread briefly to Melbourne, where a mass meeting at Dallas Brooks Hall endorsed a 48-hour stoppage. For the first time, too, SEC management conceded that power generation levels were deteriorating, making shortages likely.

When the last days of September finally brought power restrictions, the strike came to dominate life in Melbourne almost as much as in the Valley itself. Industry had virtually no power, so around 500,000 workers were stood down; tram and train services were cut in half; heating and lighting were radically reduced. You could only watch television from 3 to 11 pm. At one point, even TV coverage of the Australian Rules Grand Final was in doubt – although, given the small amount of power drawn by television sets, this may have been a deliberate government tactic to turn public opinion against the strikers.

All sides became more aggressive. Commissioner Vosti 'ordered' the unions to hold a meeting within 48 hours, which the unions promptly announced was impossible – the shop stewards must meet first. There were picket line clashes at Yallourn. The press grew more rabid, with *The Age* one day appealing to the rank and file to rebel against the 'belligerence and intransigence' of the shop stewards, and the next day describing the rank and file themselves as 'cynical and callous'.[11]

The Age also warned:

> if the trade union movement will not act to curb this madness then the community, through its elected governments, will have to take emergency measures to defend itself.[12]

The paper seemed to know Hamer's intentions, because – on that same day – the premier threatened to declare a State of Emergency, using the *Essential Services Act* which provided for fines and jailing of unionists. His tone was similar to the editorial:

> It's time for responsible unionists to take over. I include the Trades Hall Council, which so far has stood aside and allowed the dispute to be conducted by shop stewards in the Latrobe Valley.[13]

It was an unusual line of argument for Hamer, who, like all conservative politicians, normally blamed union officials for dragging reluctant members into strikes. Now he was demanding that Trades Hall intervene to stifle the most

Victorian Premier Dick Hamer has declared a State of Emergency to try and break the State power strike. This enables him to fine and jail the unionists involved — just like the old penal powers which sent Clarrie O'Shea to jail and which we crushed in 1969.

SUPPORT THE VIC POWER WORKERS!

WHY ARE VICTORIAN POWER WORKERS STRIKING?

■ for a fairer deal on wages. Victoria's State Electricity Commission maintenance workers are way behind people doing similar work for other employers. A fitter who has worked with the SEC for two years gets $167 a week; in the NSW power industry he would get around $190 a week; in most Victorian industries he would get $185-210 a week. Working with private contractors employed by the SEC he would get up to $250.

■ for a fairer deal on conditions. For example, if a fitter and a boilermaker work overtime on a Saturday, they will only get doubletime after three hours. Yet the cranedriver they are working next to will get doubletime after two hours.

WHY ARE THEY STRIKING INSTEAD OF NEGOTIATING? WHY DON'T THEY GO BACK TO WORK LIKE COMMISSIONER VOST! ORDERED THEM TO, AND ACCEPT ANY DECISION HE MAKES?

■ The unions have *tried* to negotiate. But the SEC delayed talks for five months by haggling over how negotiations should take place. And their idea of "negotiating" has been to say "No!" to everything. Last year when the unions negotiated a log of claims with the SEC, they put in 36 claims — and were granted tea and sugar at the morning smoko!

■ The power workers have *already* gone back once to allow Commissioner Vosti to arbitrate. The SEC then turned around and said it would not accept any increase Vosti granted and would appeal. In the two days that they were back at work, the SEC got enough work done to last out three weeks of any ensuing strike. SEC workers are not prepared to be tricked like this again.

■ Why should SEC workers trust in Arbitration anyway? Arbitration claims to be a "neutral umpire" —

but in the last 2½ years they have only granted full wage indexation once. Wages have fallen behind the cost of living by at least 7 per cent. Meanwhile company profits rose last year by about 30%. This is the sort of "neutral umpire" that SEC workers are being asked to place their trust in.

AREN'T THE SEC WORKERS BEING SELFISH BY STRIKING WHEN IT CAUSES WIDESPREAD STAND-DOWNS?

■ This is thrown at SEC workers every time they strike. Are SEC workers supposed to accept lousy pay forever rather than strike? The SEC could easily bring the stand-downs to an end — by granting power workers' claim to wage jus[tice]

■ The SEC is banning use of po[wer] for industrial machinery — allowing power for television! SEC is deliberately causing st[and] downs to turn other workers ag[ainst] the power industry strikers.

■ Who does the standing down way? Companies that are only happy to keep their profits to selves when things go well immediately put the burden o[n] workers when they look like money due to power cuts.

■ If the SEC workers win, it [is] a major defeat for Fraser's cutting strategy — and th[is] benefit *all* workers.

If Hamer tries to fine or j[ail] torian SEC unionists for figh[ting] a decent wage, our answer sh[ould be] the same as in 1969 — a [General] General Strike.
If Hamer gets away with [these] jailings, it will be open sla[ther for] *every* boss, *every* Liberal Pre[mier,] Malcolm Fraser himself to [do the] same to any Australian trade [unionist] who takes industrial action. For the sake of trade uni[ons] Hamer must be stopped.

SEC Latrobe Valley strike support leaflet

democratically run strike in years – not that the Trades Hall officials were averse to trying. They did want the strike ended, but they knew that the government did not; hence, both state ALP leader Frank Wilkes and Trades Hall secretary Ken Stone found themselves making curious criticisms of the premier. Wilkes said that Hamer: 'should have waited until today's [mass] meeting before saying anything about invoking the *Essential Services Act*.' (Thereafter, it would apparently be all right.) Stone similarly called Hamer's threats 'provocative and ill-timed'.[14] He feared that they would only strengthen the strikers' resolve; and so it proved, when a Yallourn mass meeting voted by 2,000 to 30 to stay out until substantial progress was made. The government responded by rushing through amendments to the *Essential Services Act* to tailor it to the power strike, as well as considering moves to deregister the unions.

Although there was talk of the government sending in troops, the power workers were by no means cowed. They pointed out that only one army unit was capable of operating a power station – a unit made up of SEC maintenance workers. George Wragg told the media: 'if we had to we could take to the hills – there's 10,000 square miles of country round here,' adding that Hamer would get nowhere fining unionists because they didn't have $2,000 to pay the fines:

> They have not got 2,000 cents. It would be like trying to get blood out of a stone… I can't see them taking 2,300 of us away to jail.[15]

FEDFA secretary Stan Williams warned that punitive action against the maintenance workers or their unions would bring his organisation into the fray. This last point was the crucial one.

If the SEC workers were better prepared to confront the repressive forces of the state than those at Fairfax, this had less to do with the local landscape than with political traditions. Victorian unionists had led the fight to release Clarrie O'Shea only eight years earlier. If a similar fight were needed this time, a layer of militants statewide could be relied on to respond. Knowing this, the government was obliged to tread cautiously. Unfortunately, the failure of the union leaders to actively mobilise the wider community of militants in any way during the whole dispute contributed to this layer's demoralisation and long-term decline.

The main consequence of Hamer's action was that Justice (Sir John) Moore intervened to announce that a Full Bench would hear the dispute. Hamer promptly deferred use of the Act to allow hearings to proceed, but the Full Bench offered the strikers no satisfaction whatsoever. It declared that their

George Wragg, AEU shop steward at the SEC Latrobe Valley

...tory to the
...r Strike

demands for 'money in the hand' before a return to work would contravene the Commission's wage principles, that the indexation guidelines were inviolate, and that existing offers by the SEC should be accepted.[16] By this time, the power workers were growing increasingly angry and ignored suggestions from Halfpenny that they return to work, raising the spectre of confrontation. Then, at the critical moment, Bob Hawke entered stage right to tell a delegation of shop stewards that 'he could fix it'. *The Bulletin* wrote:

> He would get the Trades Hall Council and the rest of the union movement on side with them. Hamer would come to the party. He intimated he was on good terms with Sir John Moore and that a way out would be found. They would get an anomalies case together. It would work. If they went back he could virtually assure them of something to take back to the Valley.[17]

Hawke insisted that widespread standdowns would turn other workers against the strikers. A majority of the stewards reluctantly agreed to recommend a return to work, and a mass meeting reluctantly complied on 13 October, despite resistance from the militants who believed that an anomalies case would achieve little. Meanwhile, the ACTU rushed to prepare a new case based on anomalies within the SEC. The case wasn't very coherent, but Hawke apparently expected the Full Bench to allow token wage rises now that his own prestige was on the line. The Full Bench, however, declared bluntly that 'on the material put before us, we are unable to find any grounds which would justify granting the unions' claim.'[18]

The embarrassed ACTU leader responded with a display of rage which, whether genuine or synthetic, was his only means of retaining credibility with the SEC workers. The decision, ranted Hawke, was 'totally absurd'. Even if the claim was incoherent, 'those bastards' the Commissioners were paid 'enough bloody money' to settle the dispute with a compromise.[19]

The government was delighted with the decision, which it saw as a green light allowing it to take deregistration action against four unions as well as threatening 2,300 striking workers with dismissal. The SEC began advertising for non-union labour, but it soon became clear that they had overreached themselves. The MOA and FEDFA branches in the Valley announced that they would stop work if strike breakers were used. Said local MOA secretary Doug Gregory: 'What the SEC is trying to do is gather scab labour. We won't tolerate this.'[20]

THE STRIKE

The strikers in the Latrobe Valley are engaged in a battle that involves all Australian workers. Their 10-week strike over a pay claim is not only a fight with the traditionally unreasonable S.E.C., but also with the so-called "wage indexation guidelines". The Latrobe Valley strikers are fighting on behalf of all of us to break the "wage freeze"(otherwise known as the "indexation guidelines").

what do strikers want?

The maintenance workers in the Latrobe Valley are asking for a pay rise of $40 per week (though they have indicated a willingness to negotiate about the amount).

Private contractors employed by the S.E.C. employ tradesmen with the same skills as the maintenance workers but pay them $40 - $45 per week more. Maintenance workers in similar positions in N.S.W. also get paid a lot more.

For 6 months the maintenance workers asked for wage justice - for 6 months the S.E.C. lied, stalled obstructed, and suspended workers. Only after 9 weeks of striking did the S.E.C. and the Government begin to take notice.

WHY WEREN'T THEY GIVEN A RISE?

Earlier this year the S.E.C. big whigs gave themselves a fat rise. Recently Mr. Hamer and his fellow politicians gave themselves another $50 per week, backdated to June 1st. What happened to the "indexation guidelines" here?

Wage indexation is really a way of taking money from the workers. Living standards are being attacked in many ways - price increases, increases in indirect taxes, cuts in hospital and education services, cuts in Medibank, to name just a few. Wage indexation is a political stunt to try and bluff workers into accepting these reductions in living standards.

Indexation is based on the "Consumer Price Index" which is a very conservative and inadequate measure of living standards. Even if workers obtained full indexation they would fall further behind. But we don't get full indexation anyway, so we end up losing money all the time.

The Government, on behalf of the employers, wants to increase profitability - in other words, they want to reduce the workers' share of the cake and give it to the employers. That is what indexation and Government cuts in spending are all about. As the economic crisis worsens the Government will take an increasingly more repressive line. And as the economic crisis in the U.S. worsens the U.S. multinationals will want to take an even greater share of the cake back to the U.S. - and they will pressure the Government to repress any opposition.

This is why the Government is seeking a confrontation - it wants to show the workers that they either accept a drop in living standards or face fines and gaol. This is why the S.E.C. was told not to negotiate, why the Arbitration Court fully supported the Government, and why the scabs and police are being brought in.

SEC Latrobe Valley strike leaflet explaining their demands

Bob Hawke, keen to repair his image, warned that scabbing would be 'totally opposed by the trade union movement',[21] while John Halfpenny refused to rule out a general strike, and Hamer's demands that the THC should 'take control' of the dispute[22] also backfired. The Council had avoided meeting for weeks, citing a trip to Sydney for the ACTU Congress, the Show Day holiday and power restrictions due to the strike![23] This allowed Ken Stone to dodge any responsibility, but it also left time for pro-strike sentiment to build up throughout the Victorian union movement.

When the Council finally assembled on 20 October, the left had mobilised. Pat Clancy moved to support the strikers' 'fully justified' claims. Ken Stone managed to water down the motion and block calls for financial assistance, but it was clear that the union mood was hardening.[24] Meanwhile, in the Valley, Sam Armstrong announced plans for anti-eviction and anti-repossession squads to keep landlords and finance companies from the door. In the face of this response, the government again backed away from confrontation. The SEC deferred any sackings until Monday 24 October; they were then deferred again.

Appeals for strikebreakers had flopped, in any case. After announcing plans on 18 October to bring bus loads of them to the Valley, the SEC could only say a day later that 'several' people had applied for jobs. The Melbourne *Herald* reported that two hours after the employment office opened, exactly two had applied, with one then backing out.[25] The printers' union announced that it would ban SEC ads seeking strikebreakers.

Had Hawke, the THC or the left union leaders wanted to win the dispute, now was the time. The strikers were still solid, although suffering great financial hardship; government attacks on them had angered unionists across Victoria and even interstate; the MOA and FEDFA would probably have followed a lead from Halfpenny, or at least from Hawke or the THC; and no one doubted that they had the muscle to decide the issue. In fact, according to the *Latrobe Valley Express*:

> had the FEDFA members supported the strike it would have been over in one day, or a few at the worst... Victoria would have been plunged into darkness and brought to a standstill.[26]

The trouble was that the union officials wished only to get back to arbitration with the greatest possible speed. Seizing on a Full Bench suggestion that a 'review of work and pay within the SEC' might resolve 'relativity problems',[27]

Bob Hawke asked for a hearing before Commissioner Mansini. By the following Monday, he had arranged a work value inquiry, convincing a majority of the shop stewards to go along with it.

On the picket line

While arbitration dragged on, the strikers were entangled in the fight of their lives. They returned to work more than once, hoping to bring a settlement, only to find that management seized the opportunity to make crucial repairs while giving no ground on the issues. When they were on strike, they faced assaults on their picket lines. On 27 September, after breakdowns had radically reduced the movement of coal by rail, six SEC trucks raced from the Yallourn open cut mine to the briquette factory, then returned to find their way blocked by picketers, who halted five of them by sitting down on the road. After 10 minutes of argument, the police arrived and cleared a way for the trucks.

Later in the evening, the strikers booed and jeered as police escorted another convoy through. The following day, a further 20 trucks made the trip, despite picketers throwing a barrage of rocks and eggs and placing nails on the road. Ordered to stop throwing rocks, some of the unionists stole onto SEC land to splash paint over the windscreen of one of the trucks.

The problem lay with the TWU officials, who had no enthusiasm for the strike, and with the Yallourn branch of that union, who usually drove buses but had been drafted as truck drivers for this exercise. They were used after the Morwell branch of the TWU voted unanimously not to move the coal. Five days later, the Morwell TWU also voted to dissociate themselves from the Yallourn branch, declaring: 'To those members who have been conveying coal by road, we say this: it's on your conscience, not ours.'[28] TWU organiser Aub Reeve, who sought to overturn the Morwell decision, was declared a 'non-person' after the picket line was breached. The events were such an embarrassment for the union that, by the end of the week, its state secretary Jim Davis had travelled to the Valley. The Yallourn drivers agreed to stop crossing the lines, ostensibly because it was too dangerous.

The maintenance workers and their families showed great tenacity. On 30 September, cheers greeted Bruce Ferguson at Morwell Oval when he told a mass meeting: 'I've been out seven bloody weeks and I'm not prepared to go back with nothing.'[29] By this time, the prolonged dispute was bringing hardship to the Valley, but the strikers and their supporters in the local community sustained themselves with a deeply rooted solidarity.

SUPPORT LATROBE VALLEY WORKERS AND FAMILIES

CAR CAVALCADE — MASS PICNIC & RALLY

SUNDAY OCTOBER 30, 1977

* Financial hardship is being used as a political weapon.

* Attacks on trade unions are a threat to our democratic rights.

> "When Hitler persecuted the Jews I did nothing; when the communists were put in prison I did nothing; when the trade unions were attacked I did nothing .... I only spoke out when the Church was attacked, but by then it was too late."
> — Pastor Niemoller, leader of the Protestant Church, Germany, late 1930's.

* Meanwhile, attention is diverted from:
  - the Government's economic mismanagement;
  - Fraser's uranium sell-out;
  - U.S. Omega war base planned for Gippsland.

ASSEMBLE: 9 am at Dandenong Town Hall, Princes Hwy.

BRING: MONEY for the "Strike Fund". BAR-B-Q FOOD for yourself and a striker's family. FOODSTUFFS — tins, fruit, vegetables, meat, bread, etc for distribution to families.

Organized by the Congress for International Co-operation and Disarmament. 208 Little Lonsdale Street., Melbourne Ph. (03) 663.3677.

SEC Latrobe Valley strike leaflet advertising support rally and picnic

A worker, Lee Martin, told the press that he had only been working with the SEC for five days when the strike began; he had not even had time to join the union. He had just completed 18 months on the dole and now had just one week's pay to sustain him through the long dispute, yet he promptly signed up with the AMWU. He and his wife slammed the SEC and the government. Helma Martin said:

> The SEC has been asking for trouble in the Valley for a long, long time. Now they have got it, and we are not going to back down without getting what we want.[30]

Local Labor MP Derek Amos said:

> people in Melbourne don't understand the sense of solidarity which operates in an isolated industrial community like the Valley. They're like a people who feel they're at war.[31]

While the union fighting fund depended mainly on donations from outside the Valley, local people also dug deep. The *Latrobe Valley Express* reported that one anonymous man had donated more than $1,000 – his entire wages during the strike – and that the maintenance workers themselves were donating money for the most needy when the bucket went around at mass meetings.[32] It was hard to discern in these ragged trousered philanthropists the people Hamer had charged with a 'complete lack of humanity'.[33]

The strikers' wives were solid in support, despite attempts to turn them against the union. From the comfort of Melbourne's affluent suburb of Malvern, one Pauline Mitchell sent a letter to the *Latrobe Valley Express*: 'Women of Morwell, where are you? Stand up and be heard!... I would not let my husband cause this foolishness.'[34] But such calls had little impact, not because all the wives had spontaneously favoured the strike, but because of pro-union forces' organising and government statements that had polarised the situation. One local woman later recalled arguing with some wives who disliked the strike:

> Three days later, Hamer made this bloody lousy statement about it. And...one of them came flying down to me and she said, 'we've got to do something. I don't want this strike but they're not going to use my man like that'.[35]

'They are not only supporting their men, they are urging them to stay out,' remarked Derek Amos. 'All the wives I have spoken to don't want their husbands to go back to work without some real concessions.'[36] The media, which would doubtless have seized on any counter-examples, were forced to confirm his observations. An *Age* headline in early October: 'Strikers' Wife: I'll Beg Before Surrender' was matched by a later *Herald* report that wives of unionists would meet at the home of Maggie Carnduff. All the women were 'right behind the men,' said Mrs Carnduff, 'make no mistake about that.'[37] In the anti-union *Sunday Observer*, columnist Jill Fraser suggested that wives be allowed to vote on the dispute, but carefully stopped short of discussing how they would vote, for the answer was all too obvious.[38]

But no unity is impregnable. Every long dispute eventually brings a debate over whether it can be won and whether to persist. Employer claims that a strike is 'pointless' or will 'achieve nothing' are designed to exploit these rifts, and incipient back-to-work movements arise among those workers who see lost pay and other hardships as outweighing any likely benefits. It took six or seven weeks for such a debate to break out in the Latrobe Valley dispute.

The maintenance men remained very united, partly because their solidarity was that of a somewhat isolated community. Most of the people urging them to return to work came from outside the Valley – a point illustrated when ABC television's Peter Couchman staged a live debate in Morwell. No conservative politicians were game to appear. When Couchman himself, perhaps seeking to fill the vacuum, suggested that the maintenance workers were 'motivated by self-interest', the barrage of boos 'out-decibelled the Grand Final'.[39] The unionists were not always much better disposed towards their own Melbourne-based officials; they frequently booed Halfpenny at mass meetings, while cheering stewards' Chair Sam Armstrong.

By the seventh week, however, the strikers were becoming increasingly aware that powerful forces were ranged against them; their local dispute was assuming statewide and even national importance. A bread-and-butter claim had become a political cause célèbre. To win it would require widespread solidarity outside the Valley, built through political as well as economic struggle.

Unfortunately, the SEC workers were poorly prepared for these tasks. They had a stronger rank and file organisation than the Fairfax workers but were geographically isolated and somewhat provincial in their outlook. Lacking direct links to militants in Melbourne, they found themselves largely dependent on the very union officials they so distrusted. They also lacked anything resembling a political strategy – oddly, it might seem, given Sam Armstrong's membership of the Communist Party. So they were saddled, by default, with their officials' political approach, which was dominated by fears that Fraser would make political capital out of the strike. Just at the point where it was essential to escalate the struggle, therefore, the initiative passed to forces that were increasingly keen to end it.

Setting a course for defeat

John Halfpenny and Sam Armstrong were key figures in the debate. While they represented different constituencies, they also had much in common as CPA members, and Armstrong was Halfpenny's most likely ally among the strikers. The shop stewards' Chair, so often portrayed as a fire-breathing radical, was really a moderate. 'About 25 years ago,' commented *The Australian* in an interview, 'he would have described himself as an industrial militant, but the world has changed since then, he claims.'[40]

Earlier in the dispute, Armstrong and all the other shop stewards had differed with Halfpenny and with the CPA leaders in his desire to pursue the struggle to a successful conclusion. By early October, however, the stewards were under increasing pressure. Halfpenny told them that they lacked support outside the Valley. He found an ideal tactic for wearing down their resolve: the apparently democratic practice of taking them to attend arbitration hearings, which detached them from their rank and file base while they spent hours travelling to Melbourne – not to promote solidarity, but to sit through tedious hearings.

A minority among the activists were more fortunate. George Wragg, Max Strong and Luke Van Der Meulen became involved in speaking to worker and student meetings in Melbourne, where they discovered that the strike enjoyed considerable public sympathy. Wragg, for example, got a friendly reception from wharfies at Seatainer Terminal and tramway workers at Preston Depot, while Strong and Van Der Meulen received substantial support at the West Gate Bridge construction site, at BHP Hastings and on two campuses. Buoyed by their experiences, these three opposed a return to work at all times. Two other unionists toured Newcastle and Wollongong, including one who had previously voted to return to work; the two sent a telegram to the final mass meeting saying support was excellent, and the strike should continue. Had all the activists been offered such experiences, the strike might have been built up rather than run down.

Instead, the stewards' mood shifted gradually towards capitulation. As early as 30 September, when militants moved to extend the strike indefinitely, Sam

THE POWER DISPUTE

We did it their way

GO TO ARBITRATION

This was the cry from the media, the Liberal Government, and the S.E.C. Against our better judgement, Latrobe Valley maintenance workers did decide once more to return to work to allow the Arbitration Commission to hear our claims.

WHAT HAS HAPPENED?

After presenting a case that was among the best ever put to the Arbitration Commission, our claims have been flatly rejected. The fact that anomalies exist within the S.E.C. cannot be denied. When a tradesman, after completing his apprenticeship, starts on a base rate of $162.40 per week and a storeman with three months' experience receives $161.70 per week, discontent is inevitable.

Also a tradesman's assistant receives $134.20 per week, while a truck driver's assistant working alongside him gets $146.50 per week. Then a tradesman with the same skills working for a private contractor on S.E.C. work in the Valley is paid $40.00 per week more than S.E.C. maintenance workers.

If this is not an anomaly, what is?

SEC Latrobe Valley strike leaflet after arbitration failed

Armstrong was counselling a more cautious course (although it was dressed up in pugnacious boxing jargon):

> Don't throw the initiative away and turn the tables by putting us into a fixed position. Allow us to go back into the ring and fight the fifteenth round, because that's where we are.[41]

Throughout October, Armstrong and Halfpenny pushed the stewards towards ending the struggle. By the time Hawke and Moore had arranged a work value inquiry, they were in a position to win the vote inside the shop stewards' committee. When the maintenance men met at Yallourn on 25 October, the mood was bleak. Sam Armstrong told them that a return to work was 'the only way at this particular time,' because to box on would provoke 'the biggest political fight Victoria has faced in its history.'[42]

Here, he was addressing an absolutely decisive question. Halfpenny and Armstrong had always talked about keeping politics out of the campaign, with the latter telling a meeting in October:

> We are not prepared to be a political football in this dispute. We began this strike seeking only comparable wages and conditions. Politics were not involved.[43]

Of course, such rhetoric could not keep politics out of the struggle, but it could help to ensure that, at the final turning point, the prospect of a political battle frightened most of the rank and file.

Opposing the return to work, George Wragg warned that they would gain little from the work value inquiry. 'If you accept this resolution,' he argued:

> you'll be where you were before the strike started, and it's where you'll be at the end of the work value case. We're already bloodied by the battle. It's better to have the confrontation now.[44]

By this time, however, it was too late for such arguments. Although many shared Wragg's scepticism, most strikers were now too discouraged to continue, and it was tempting to hope that arbitration might still yield results. Moreover, the CPA paper *Tribune* was dismissive of suggestions to the contrary:

Some commentators see the return to work in Victoria's power dispute as a total defeat for the workers. Some suggest that arbitration as the final umpire is the kiss of defeat.[45]

Tribune thought the 'commentators' stupid; unfortunately, the commentators were proved correct. Without the pressure of industrial action, the Commission had no incentive to meet the workers' claims. The decision four months later gave them pitiful rises of $2 to $5, with some 30 percent getting nothing at all. This result prompted no rethinking among the union leaders; the AMWU's Max Ogden drew only trivial lessons from it, and he went so far as to describe Bob Hawke's role as 'constructive and positive'. Ogden believed that little more could have been achieved, mainly because public support would have declined through growing hardship:

> It was generally discussed that if it went much longer, the public position would have changed. It was amazing how well it was maintained as it was. People simply can't cop it forever.[46]

Of course, popular support may decline if you don't mobilise it, but that was never systematically tried. While Halfpenny had declared that 'all the Australian trade union movement must come to the aid of these power workers,'[47] the AMWU organisation outside the Valley had done relatively little to put the sentiment into practice. Yet, the potential was considerable. The *Latrobe Valley Express* reported that outside support was growing at the end of the strike:

> A heck of a lot of money is beginning to pour into the SEC maintenance workers' distress fund... Unionists elsewhere now see this 'small strike' by 2,300 workers in a new perspective. If they win, everyone else will.

The *Express* went on to quote Dave Pollock, shop stewards' chair at GMH Elizabeth (South Australia), who had been stood down because of the power strike, as saying: 'We are looking to the strikers to carry through because it means a lot to all workers in Australia.'[48]

The AMWU officials and the CPA were particularly fearful that the strike might damage the ALP electorally. Here, too, their judgement was astray. Fraser was careful not to announce an election until just after the strike ended. Had he seen the dispute as electorally useful, surely he would have gone to the polls earlier. And a Victorian by-election at Greensborough on 5 November also suggested that, if anything, the strike had damaged the Liberals. After the Liberal candidate declared it a 'hot issue' in the campaign, he suffered a 19 percent swing. Labor's Pauline Toner won the seat.[49]

Contrary to Leonie Sandercock's view, the dispute was by no means unwinnable. The strikers were united until almost the very end; they enjoyed immense sympathy among Victorian trade unionists generally; and the Greensborough by-election showed that they were not politically vulnerable. To win the strike, however, would have required a different kind of organisation and leadership: one that set out to build direct links to workers outside the Valley, to mobilise those workers in solidarity action and to face the political issues and educate workers about them, rather than running away. These tasks called for a revolutionary or at least a militant political organisation of working class activists – something the CPA sometimes still claimed to be but, unfortunately, was not. Those forces in the Valley and in Melbourne who did fight for such a perspective were too weak to influence events.

The Liberals, led by Fraser and Hamer, had won a sort of trifecta: defeats for the unions in the sphere of politics and social programs were now succeeded by defeats in the purely economic sphere, in strikes that had been watched with great interest by large numbers of workers. Under such circumstances, working class militants had a hard time maintaining any sort of morale. In the aftermath of the Latrobe Valley strike, levels of disputation in Victoria, which had been the highest in the country, plunged dramatically.

Industrial militancy would not revive until later in the decade. When it did, it sealed Malcolm Fraser's fate, and that drama occupies the concluding chapters of this history. Before discussing that, we turn in the next chapters to a consideration of the social movements of the time, the distinctive conflicts in Joh Bjelke-Petersen's Queensland and some debates on the Australian left.

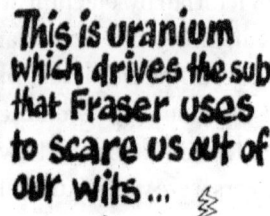

6.
Workers, peace and the environment

In recent times, millions of people have fought to protect the planet from nuclear power, nuclear war and a vast array of environmental disasters. Marxists have been among the campaigners, raising the controversial argument that only organised labour has the social power to banish these threats. From this perspective, the Fraser years assume particular importance, because the 1970s were the decade when Australia's class and environmental issues converged in two major campaigns: the fight against construction of a power station at Newport, Victoria; and the national struggle to stop uranium mining. Two other campaigns in Fraser's last years, around disarmament and the Franklin River, unfortunately saw these strands drawing apart once more.

In 1967, the SEC of Victoria began planning to build a power station at Newport in Melbourne's working class western suburbs, opting for natural gas as the cheapest fuel. By 1971, however, Williamstown residents had become worried about pollution, and the local Conservation and Planning Society began holding public meetings. By 1972, they had convinced some unions to ban construction until an independent inquiry was held. Trades Hall banned the project in 1974 amid concerns that it would waste the state's natural gas reserves.

Although new development projects were supposed to face environmental tests, no assessment of Newport was even considered until community opposition had built up. Even then, the Environmental Protection Authority's (EPA) terms of reference were limited, and its chair said that some important issues had been ignored, including the desirability of siting the power station at Newport and of using natural gas. Critics in the community demanded an unrestricted inquiry by the Parliamentary Public Works Committee, but the government turned a deaf ear. Finally, in October 1974, after Premier Hamer had read a long reply to questions, Federated Engine Drivers' secretary Stan Williams exploded:

> Look, we're sick of all your talk... The fact is that we're not going to build it at Newport – and that's final. Whatever you say, it's not going to make any difference.[1]

When other union leaders agreed, Hamer was taken aback: 'We cannot physically take a man and make him build a power station. We have just got to reconsider the matter.'[2] At this stage, the premier was not at all confident. Still, there were those in Cabinet who believed that they *could* 'take a man and make him build a power station'; within days, they had reaffirmed the Newport site.

The issue subsided during the upheavals of 1975, reviving in April 1976, when the industrial climate had changed. Recession had weakened the unions, and an anti-union government was in power federally. The Trades Hall right wing, led by Ken Stone, began looking for a way to dump the bans. While he had declared on 9 March that the bans would stay,[3] *The Age* of 3 April published a 10-point compromise plan agreed by the government and the Trades Hall Executive. The state government undertook not to build any more metropolitan power stations, to confine Newport's operation to meeting peak load requirements and to consult more in future – along with various other concessions. Construction would still proceed, so the deal was far from acceptable. Even so, the element of compromise was a second indication that sections of the government lacked resolve; a determined union stand might be able to stop the whole project.

Newport dominated the Trades Hall meeting on 8 April. Demonstrators warned the delegates that Hamer could not be trusted. Stan Williams, along with Charlie Faure of the Electrical Trades Union, declared that they'd known nothing of this deal, despite being on a committee appointed to negotiate. The Plumbers also came out against the compromise, but John Halfpenny remained noticeably silent. Trades Hall postponed the vote until 6 May.

Far from seeing the government's proposals as a sign of weakness, Halfpenny's CPA backers now began outlining a rationale for accepting them, with *Tribune* saying: 'disappointment at the latest turn of events should not blind people to the new possibilities'. *Tribune* remained rather vague about these possibilities, suggesting only a campaign around urban planning, which

WORKERS, PEACE AND THE ENVIRONMENT

Police at Omega protest site 8 July 1978

would apparently be more effective because the 10-point plan had established 'the right of the union movement and other movements to actively intervene in environmental issues'.[4] This was a curious argument to advance in favour of *ending* an actual intervention. It was widely believed that Halfpenny was the author of the 10-point plan,[5] although he had been obliged to back away from it by the AMWU State Council.

A group of left unions fought the deal and won reaffirmation of the original ban by 152 votes to 94, but neither Stone nor the government could accept this defeat. In early September, Hamer released a letter from him to Stone. The Trades Hall secretary then quietly organised a meeting of selected unions, hoping to put together a majority for compromise. Several left officials who heard about the meeting turned up at the door to protest, and the meeting decided nothing. In November, the compromise was again rejected, 179 to 175.

Hamer was furious. Within 24 hours, he announced that no new public works projects would begin until the Newport dispute was settled; the government would defer some existing projects. A new law would require secret ballots for bans of the Newport type, on pain of deregistration. In November, he announced suspension of nearly 300 projects.

Direct Action Newport Forum leaflet

Bob Hawke called the legislation 'the most repressive in Australia's history', while Ken Stone warned darkly that a general strike was 'not beyond the realms of possibility,'[6] but the defiance was merely a pose. The Trades Hall right again began pushing for compromise, and some of Newport's opponents became nervous. The union officials, who had never campaigned systematically around the issue among their membership, feared that these members – influenced by rising unemployment – might dislike a ban that was costing hundreds of jobs. Some were intimidated by the government's sabre-rattling and Hamer's largely empty threats, although a number of the projects were not very labour intensive, and the government was simply making expected budget cuts to some extent. The legislation would also be hard to enforce.

In any case, the balance of sentiment was shifting at Trades Hall. The State Labor Advisory Council (ALP and Trades Hall) now called for an inquiry, and the THC voted again on 25 November. Ken Carr of the Furnishing Trades moved an amendment accepting an inquiry but ruling out the Newport site as an option, but he was unsuccessful. For the first time, Newport's opponents lost a vote – and convincingly, by 145 to 77. The left had split, and John Halfpenny had declared himself at last, voting along with the rest of the AMWU against Carr and for compromise.

Hamer attacks

After initially rejecting the Trades Hall proposal, Hamer negotiated with Stone. He established a review panel featuring Sir Louis Matheson, former Vice Chancellor of Monash University – known for his feuds with radical students. Unionists believed that he was unlikely to favour the anti-Newport cause. With representatives of the Gas and Fuel Corporation and the EPA (which had already approved Newport) on the panel, it was clearly designed to rubber stamp the project, although THC president Jack Ellis was also included. Trades Hall endorsed it by an overwhelming vote on 21 December, giving the first public indication that it might not be entirely serious about opposing Newport. Concerned by this, demonstrators from the Western Suburbs Campaign Against Newport picketed a February meeting of the THC, demanding that it stand firm.

The panel reported twice. Its 'interim' report indicated that even a half-sized, 500-megawatt power station at Newport would do considerable environmental damage. Accordingly, the THC unanimously rejected Newport as a site, and acting secretary Tony Vella called the project a 'dead duck'.[7]

So the unions were startled when the final report opted, after all, for Newport, although for a smaller station. The critics lashed out. Jack Ellis had dissented from the finding. The final report was poorly argued; for example, a site at Hazlewood in the Latrobe Valley was unacceptable because of potential pollution – so why was Newport OK? Ellis released documents showing that the panel had rejected the Newport site by a three to one majority only 12 days before reporting to the government, adding that two members had changed their vote under political pressure. *Scope,* the left unions' newspaper, referred acerbically to:

> [the] iron rule of politics, that governments only set up commissions and inquiries when they can be assured that the result will confirm their policies and intentions.[8]

Trades Hall reaffirmed the ban, while the government prepared to start construction. 'What the consequences will be we hardly dare to contemplate,' said *The Age*.[9] What few expected, perhaps, was that the unions would make almost no fight at all.

When the government advertised for building workers, Norm Gallagher radiated confidence. 'They'll probably clean the joint up, that's all,' said Gallagher. '[Lindsay] Thompson has apparently got the barrow...he'll have to push it.' John Halfpenny was equally cocky. 'Maybe they can get some people to chip some grass, turn a few sods or build a path.'[10]

Three weeks later, Halfpenny was less dismissive, warning against attempts 'to bust union opposition by the use of scab labour'.[11] Alas, by now, it was not just random scabs: seven unions, observing that Trades Hall wasn't serious, had allowed members to work at the site.

By late June, with 150 people working there, some left unions finally stirred themselves. Officials of five organisations visited to warn the scabs that they risked blacklisting if they didn't leave. Only about a dozen responded; yet Trades Hall remained complacent. True, some unions issued warnings to subcontractors. Postal and telecommunications employees refused to connect phones to the site. But these were token actions. Newport, many officials continued to insist, could never be built without union labour.

Local citizens and radical activists thought differently. As early as April, a group of protesters had invaded a Trades Hall Council meeting with signs reading: 'Does the THC support scabs? If not, then do something about Newport.'[12] The deepening concern was reflected in a 300-strong public meeting at Williamstown in June and in periodic pickets and rallies outside the site. In August, 200 demonstrators mixed it with police, who used considerable force to drive back the crowd. These events were followed a week later by a two-day vigil. Harry Van Moorst of the Anti-Newport Co-ordinating Committee announced 'an immediate campaign to boycott contractors who are working on the Newport site.'[13]

Such calls were largely bravado, given the unions' failure to act. Van Moorst's comrades could engage in minor harassment, but stopping the scabs would require mass picketing and industrial action to pressure Hamer into backing off. Some union officials, most notably Charlie Faure, joined demonstrations and brought a few shop stewards with them, but they did little to mobilise their rank and file; the nearby Williamstown Dockyards could have provided the forces for a serious mass picket. The original excuse that Hamer would 'never get the labour' now gave way to a second: that it was too late to stop the project. By September, construction was ahead of schedule. A year later, *The Age* wrote smugly that the station was 'settling into the skyline.'[14] In March 1979, the paper claimed:

> It seems certain that the $160 million project will be completed on schedule, and at an insignificant additional cost, thanks to Trades Hall Council bans... Since work started...there has been virtually no industrial disruption, productivity has been high and pay rates have been lower than those paid to workers on other comparable sites.[15]

Sections of the ALP left fought to maintain formal opposition to the project, but it was futile. Food Preservers' Union (FPU) secretary Tom Ryan might tell Labor leader Frank Wilkes that it was 'suicide' to accept Newport, but the state Labor conference, including most of the Socialist Left, thought otherwise. Bob Hawke could dismiss the diehards as a 'phone-box minority'.[16] In 1980, Trades Hall lifted its bans. It helped the ETU's Ron Luckman little to complain that some unions had 'sold their soul', because Ken Stone had a more practical argument: lifting the ban made possible a redundancy agreement for workers at the old Newport power station.[17]

Given Trades Hall's dithering, were the Newport bans an artificial exercise? Many union officials seemed to doubt the reliability of their rank and file members, probably because they had made no serious effort to mobilise them. Yet, there was evidence that the issue struck a chord among ordinary workers. Unionists at Williamstown later drove a man out of the dockyards on discovering that he had worked at Newport; and Max Costello recalls customers at a western suburbs rock music shop watching anti-Newport demonstrators

Public Servants Against Uranium Mining at MAUM march Melbourne 3 August 1981

walk by and commenting sympathetically that 'they wouldn't build the power station in [affluent] Toorak, would they?'[18] The issue had the *potential* for an effective industrial struggle, but there was no credible force willing to lead it.

The movement against uranium mining

The anti-uranium campaign reached its height around the time that a pattern of defeat began to emerge for the labour movement generally. Ironically, this did not make the campaign harder to build at first. While the majority of workers had lost confidence in their ability to win large, set-piece struggles, a minority turned to uranium as a different sort of issue, a new terrain on which to keep fighting. Large sections of the population opposed uranium mining and sympathised with the idea of union action. The issue also appeared to continue the traditions of the Vietnam-era antiwar movement to some degree. The new campaign offered a possibility of revitalising the class struggle.

Uranium had been controversial under Whitlam, but the main issue initially had been economic nationalism. Rex Connor had held up approval of new contracts for Conzinc Riotinto of Australia's (CRA)'s Mary Kathleen Uranium mine (MKU) until his patriotic resources policy was in place. At the same time, CRA needed additional capital to fulfil existing contracts, so the Labor government underwrote a $17 million share issue to ensure 100 percent Australian ownership, appointing two directors: Treasury Secretary Lenox Hewitt and Queensland union leader Jack Egerton. The pause imposed by Labor, which continued into the early Fraser years, was important: it allowed time for environmentalists to develop a strong anti-nuclear case and win over a chunk of public opinion – including much of the trade union movement. The 1975 ACTU Congress called for a halt to mining, pending a full inquiry.

This foreshadowed a brawl with Fraser, who, from the time he seized power, pursued two objectives fairly single mindedly: to get a green light for uranium mining, by hook or by crook, and to break the back of the Aboriginal land rights struggle. The two were linked because key uranium deposits were on Aboriginal land.

Conflict first erupted on the union front in May 1976, when Townsville railway shunting supervisor Jim Assenbruck refused to couple trucks headed for Mary Kathleen. Assenbruck was sacked; his workmates struck; and industrial action halted all rail traffic in North Queensland. While top union leaders had little enthusiasm for the dispute (Queensland TLC secretary Fred Whitby called it 'absurd'),[19] they were bound to defend a member sacked for implementing union policy. Ultimately, a 24-hour national rail strike won a compromise, with Assenbruck keeping his job but agreeing not to block shipments. Although the attempt to enforce union bans had failed, it was a political bombshell. While conservative politicians attacked the rail strike, Geoff Mosley, Australian Conservation Foundation director, praised it: 'This strike is over the most important environmental and social question facing today's society for its future.'[20]

A national union meeting, under the influence of AWU claims that 300 jobs were at stake, decided early in June that mining could proceed at Mary Kathleen pending the forthcoming Ranger Inquiry. However, the same unions voted a few weeks later to ban exports of uranium from MKU. Journalists travelled to Mary Kathleen to quote people such as the local garage proprietor, who thought: 'any bloke who says that uranium should stay in the ground is so silly they ought to take him out and shoot him.'[21] But such silliness was on the increase: an *Age* poll found that 57 percent were concerned about the dangers posed by nuclear power, only 24 percent trusted scientists to solve the problems, and 76 percent wanted alternative energy sources 'even if it costs a lot more.'[22]

The experts were also divided. One prominent scientist, pro-nuclear hawk Ernest Titterton, argued: 'unless we are prepared to have an energyless,

MAUM demonstration Melbourne 3 August 1978

caveman style of society, mankind must have a new and very large energy source'; only nuclear power could fit the bill.[23] Another, Macfarlane Burnet, responded by warning that nuclear facilities brought with them the capacity to produce nuclear weapons.[24]

Making much of the initial political running for the opposing camps were the environmentalists and the mining companies. 'Moderate' environmentalists looked to the Australian Conservation Foundation (ACF), while their more radical colleagues backed the activist Friends of the Earth (FOE). Right-wing attacks on the 'Friends of the Dirt', as Queensland Premier Joh Bjelke-Petersen termed them, led to occasional ACF attempts to distance themselves from the radicals. The ACF was particularly embarrassed when FOE unearthed a document quoting ACF public relations officer Bob Howard and an MKU scientist as apparently agreeing that FOE activists were 'entirely destructive, naïve and too dreadful for words'.[25]

Their opponents were the Uranium Producers' Forum, which spent large sums on efforts to rescue the industry's deteriorating public image. Spokesperson George Mackay said in 1977: 'As the opposition forces have become more aggressive, we have taken up the same position.'[26] He was referring mainly to protest actions by the umbrella organisation Movement Against Uranium Mining (MAUM), whose demonstrations the Forum monitored closely. The industry was also shaken in 1976 by FOE's disclosure of leaked documents in which CRA head Rod Carnegie acknowledged 'the possibility of terrorists getting hold of materials from which bombs could be made' and admitted that radioactive waste disposal 'could not be proved to be safe'.[27]

The debate focused increasingly on the Ranger Inquiry charged with reporting on mining in the Northern Territory, where the key deposits lay. Justice Fox released his first report in October, but it resolved nothing, because the contending factions each seized on sections that suited them. The government and the Uranium Producers' Forum cited the first two recommendations, which said that the hazards of uranium and nuclear power were not grounds to ban mining, milling or power stations 'if those operations are properly regulated and controlled'.[28] The mining companies promptly declared the issue resolved.

However, critics soon pointed out that other recommendations placed stringent and probably unachievable conditions: the government must be able to stop it at any stage (presumably by nullifying contracts); overseas customers must adopt unprecedented safeguards; and the government, rather than the mining companies, should control the whole process. When you added the Commissioners' obvious fears about nuclear weapons and their reported

Rivna Green, Indigenous activist, speaking at the MAUM demonstration Melbourne 3 August 1978

unhappiness with the government's 'green-light' interpretation, the report could be read as a case for uranium bans. The second report, in May 1977, was equally inconclusive. Fox himself said that it did 'not lend itself to green and red light reporting any more than did the first.'[29]

The Fox Commission was a turning point for the anti-nuclear forces, who concluded that lobbying and making submissions wouldn't be enough to stop uranium mining. After the release of the first report, FOE, MAUM, the ACTU and the Australian Railways Union (ARU) held a joint press conference to announce the launch of a struggle 'comparable to the campaign against the war in Vietnam.'[30] The next few years saw repeated mass demonstrations across the country demanding a ban on mining and export. The first round of 1977 set the tone. The largest mobilisation was in Melbourne, where MAUM was developing a sizeable network of local groups, some led by veterans of the Vietnam protest era. Local rallies took place in the suburbs, culminating in a major event in the Melbourne Town Hall on 30 March. On 1 April, 10,000 rallied in the City Square. Speakers at the rallies around the country included ALP left personalities Joan Coxsedge and Tom Uren and Aboriginal leaders Gary Foley and Marcia Langton. The importance of Indigenous speakers was later emphasised by Brisbane activist Ross Watson: 'If blacks got land rights, real land rights, then there would be a lot less uranium going out of this country.'[31] A second round of rallies took place in August in conjunction with Hiroshima Day.

These large, peaceful 'uranium moratoriums' became a feature of the late 1970s, but there were also smaller and more radical actions, including confrontations on the wharves of Sydney and Melbourne. In June, demonstrators tussled with the cops for hours at Sydney's Glebe Island container terminal in a vain attempt to prevent yellowcake (uranium ore) being loaded on a ship. At the start of July, Melbourne activists won a victory at Swanson Dock.

Focus on the unions

The ship *Columbus Australia*, with yellowcake bound for Britain and Japan, arrived on 2 July in what MAUM convenor Jim Falk called a 'try-on by the Fraser Government to make the export of uranium an established fact.'[32] Melbourne members of the WWF black banned the ship, only to be overruled by their federal executive because of its policy of fulfilling existing contracts. Hundreds of demonstrators then assembled on the dock, causing the ship's captain to raise the gangplank. That violated union safety rules, and the wharfies stopped work. Finally, police attacked the demonstrators, arresting about 30 of them;

this move only provoked the wharfies to ban the ship again.

Two days later, a mass meeting made the ban permanent. The *Columbus Australia* departed, leaving behind a $1 million cargo. Although WWF federal secretary Norman Docker sought to distance his union from the anti-uranium movement ('we can have no sympathy for people who invade our work areas'),[33] the rank and file wharfies saw it differently. A job delegate doffed his cap to the demonstrators, saying: 'We reckon you're lovely.'[34] It was an example of the kind of unity in struggle between environmentalists and unionists at the grassroots level which, if generalised, could have stopped the nuclear industry in its tracks. It had been achieved, not through negotiations with officials, but through direct action.

As always, such confrontations raised fears that militancy would alienate public opinion, but the main effect was a dramatic increase in public interest. *The Age* was full of letters, including attacks on both the 'greed-crazed exploiters' of the uranium industry and the 'communist parties' among the demonstrators. Assertions that nuclear power was 'a great step forward in the conservation battle' jostled with warnings of dangers to 'not just this generation but those of the next 500,000 years'. Similarly, a call for mining in the 'interests...of the free world' stood alongside the blunt challenge: 'Pro-uranium supporters should ask themselves if they would be happy to have a nuclear reactor on the block next door.'[35]

The wharfies' actions had also shown the power of organised workers to stop uranium. The movement began looking forward to the ACTU Congress in September, which was to see the first major debate among top union leaders.

Bob Hawke had been commenting for some time. In mid-July, he said that, despite wishing 'the bloody stuff had never been found or heard of', he was for mining it eventually, after a wider debate. A few weeks later, he accused nearly everyone else in the debate of 'total dishonesty': one side thought only 'of what will put a dollar in their pocket' but pretended to speak for the national interest; while the other leapt from pointing out the dangers of nuclear power to the 'illogical' conclusion that these could be avoided by leaving Australian uranium in the ground. Such statements angered the activists, and he was heckled at an anti-Fraser rally in Sydney. Hawke stalked off the platform, branding the hecklers as 'enemies of the working class'.[36]

Hawke's attempt to steer a middle course was rendered more difficult on 25 August, when the Fraser Government approved full scale mining and export. The policy was carefully crafted to conform as much as possible to the Fox recommendations: sales only to countries which agreed to use uranium for peaceful purposes; traditional owners to get royalties and the right to negotiate directly with mining companies. None of these measures came close to satisfying the protest movement. The next day, seven of Australia's 10 largest unions declared their total opposition, then began rallying their forces for the ACTU Congress.

Almost the entire fourth day of the Congress was devoted to the debate. The executive motion called for a referendum and threatened that, without it, the union movement would ban the mining and transport of uranium. A left-wing amendment, moved by Ralph Taylor of the ARU and seconded by the AMWU's Jim Roulston, proposed a meeting of unions involved in uranium mining, to endorse a ban on fulfilling existing contracts from Mary Kathleen. It was an occasion for fiery speeches, with Hawke stressing the referendum issue and challenging his opponents to concentrate on that ('tell the Australian people why you don't trust them'). Taylor rejected this focus and addressed issues such as waste disposal, before calling on unions to prepare for a 'confrontation on our terms'. As for a referendum, he said, unions shouldn't abdicate their 'social responsibility'.

Jim Roulston cited the effects on Aboriginal communities while warning that a referendum would be rigged, because uranium supporters controlled the media. John Halfpenny followed with a passionate speech, recalling that the unions hadn't called for a referendum on issues such as Vietnam: 'we set about persuading people, and took a stand.' Hawke responded with a 49 minute oration. 'It was a speech that drew jeers as well as applause,' wrote one observer. 'It also drew blood in unusual quantity.'[37]

The amendment failed by 493 votes to 371, meaning that MKU could proceed. The referendum demand was the ACTU's only real policy. Fraser would steadfastly ignore it.

Despite the ACTU's conservatism, public opinion continued to shift against uranium mining (an *Age* poll found that opposition had risen from 34 percent in June to 42 percent in September). The October round of protest marches was the largest yet, with 15–20,000 marching in Melbourne and Sydney; 1977 had been a year of advances for the movement. So great was the pressure on the ALP that South Australian Premier Don Dunstan campaigned for re-election on an anti-nuclear theme of 'play it safe' – although he kept his Uranium Enrichment Advisory Committee going, just in case the wind changed.

By comparison, 1978 was, at best, a year of consolidation. Revelations that British nuclear waste had been dumped at Maralinga in South Australia during the 1950s and 1960s heightened public concern. Students Against Uranium Mining, which had sprung up in 1977, leafleted numerous Sydney schools in March 1978 before a mass rally. In Melbourne, the environmental group INSPECT had branches in a number of high schools. On the other hand, some local groups declined or collapsed; St Kilda MAUM in Melbourne, which had mobilised scores of people in 1977, had to be set up again from scratch in the following year.

Although sometimes compared with the movement against the Vietnam war, the anti-uranium struggle proved to be less dynamic. It never dominated the public mood in the same way, and it did not draw as many new people into activity – rather relying to a considerable degree on veterans of the earlier movement. Moreover, it didn't have the same *radicalising* impact. Socialists were involved, but the anti-uranium campaign did not generate any significant layer of new revolutionary activists. This was partly because, by 1978, it was showing all the signs of ending in the same disappointing fashion as other mass struggles against Fraser, suffocated by the foot dragging of the official union leaders. It was also partly because a majority of the left was starting to draw pessimistic conclusions and drift rightward. This was not an easy climate for even a significant minority to move to the left. The activists were more likely to be attracted to a narrow focus on environmental issues or to moralistic politics such as pacifism.

Meanwhile, Fraser pressed ahead, making a deal with the Philippines dictatorship to build a reactor on a site widely believed to be unsafe (and the Aquino Government later did abandon the site, which was located on a fault line). Next, he imposed a deal on the Aboriginal Northern Lands Council to develop not only Ranger, but also a second mine at Nabarlek.

The trend was the same at state level, with WA Liberal Premier Charles Court proposing to build a nuclear reactor within 100 kilometres of Perth. Even Don Dunstan no longer wished to 'play it safe'. Encouraged by his adviser Ben Dickinson, a prominent mining industry figure, Dunstan went overseas on a fact-finding tour clearly intended to lay the basis for developing uranium deposits at Roxby Downs. Only his resignation because of illness forestalled a change of policy.

In the industrial sphere, a meeting of 12 key unions in March 1979, in what one unnamed official called 'a gutless and disgraceful performance',[38] gave in to pressure from Hawke and effectively decided that uranium could not be stopped. The pro-mining forces now seemed to be clearly ascendant.

Then, on 30 March, a small story appeared in the press about an accident in a US nuclear plant. Authorities played it down, saying that 'nothing critical had failed', but 24 hours later came front page headlines about 'US Nuclear Terror'.[39]

Ernest Titterton sought to reassure us: 'Even if this situation did happen in Australia, what of it? Nobody has been hurt. In short, there is no problem.'[40] Nevertheless, the disaster at Three Mile Island, Pennsylvania, immediately revitalised the anti-nuclear movement. The demonstrators were back in the streets, and the issue stayed alive in the union movement until the early 1980s.

Lost opportunities

Unfortunately, the unions also remained divided. The AWU, which had members in the mines, wanted no part of uranium bans; nor did the right-wing FIA and FCU. The Miscellaneous Workers' Union (MWU), despite having an anti-nuclear policy on the books, was recruiting members in the mines to avoid losing ground to rival organisations. Other unions called for bans but were reluctant to impose them where they really mattered, as with the WWF. *The Bulletin* reported late in 1979:

> On September 26 the 100 delegates at the all-ports conference of the WWF carried a policy statement [which] pointed out that staunchly anti-uranium railways unions were engaged in transporting supplies to Mary Kathleen and moving supplies and equipment destined for Nabarlek and Ranger. It added: 'All postal and telegraphic services have been provided to these undertakings and the WA uranium mine at Yeelirrie has been allowed to be developed without any effective hindrance by the WA trade unions.' Quite cleverly the WWF declared that it would ban all uranium cargoes from December 1, 1979 *if* all 25 unions engaged in uranium agreed to do so the same. Given the attitudes of the MWU, FIA and AWU, there is no chance of that kind of agreement. The WWF was saying, in effect, 'Count us out.'[41]

Bob Hawke was now able to call the anti-uranium cause 'an exercise in futility', arguing with considerable logic:

> I've flown over Nabarlek, I've seen it, and by the end of this year... the operation will have finished. Now there weren't phantoms there mining...they were all members of the Australian trade union movement, serviced by Australian trade unions.

The ACTU was risking 'a national Newport.'[42] Hawke knew how little the left officials had done to mobilise the rank and file in action behind their policies. As with Newport, they had relied on resolution-mongering; by 1982, a union working party revealed just how impotent the resolutions had been: in the five years since the unions had formally adopted a hard-line anti-uranium policy, there had been 102 shipments of yellowcake out of Australia.

This dismal result was not inevitable. Anti-uranium sentiment was actually fairly strong in the union rank and file. Unionists had established workplace groups at militant sites such as the Williamstown Dockyards and Adelaide's Islington Railway Workshops. The Williamstown group opened a weekly 'Keep it in the ground shop' at lunchtime and held meetings in a nearby hotel, and their members were also involved in establishing locality groups at Williamstown and Altona. A Public Servants Against Uranium Mining group sprang up in Victoria.

MAUM sponsored a national tour by Mt Isa miner John Boyd, who was well received on ships, on the wharves and by local Labor Councils. After he addressed construction workers at a Geelong oil refinery, they walked off the job as a protest against uranium mining. In November 1979, 150 shop stewards signed a national open letter to a special unions conference demanding action. In Brisbane, the Workers Against Uranium Mining group successfully agitated for a job delegates' meeting, which in turn demanded action from the ACTU and the Queensland TLC. Shortly afterwards, the ETU announced that they were instructing their members to withdraw from the MKU mine. This was a token action, disregarded by the members on the job, but it showed that the rank and file in Brisbane were exerting pressure on officials.

Given the chance, many of the rank and file were also willing to act – even without much official backing. After Sargeants/ANI won a contract for 4,000 tons of steel for the Ranger mine, AMWU members there voted to ban it. When management tried to subcontract the work out to smaller engineering shops, workers at Evans Deakin voted to take the same anti-uranium stand, despite the risk of losing 20 jobs. Bernie Mendis, AMWU shop steward at Sargeants, pleaded for wider action: 'If other stewards and unions start pulling their weight, we won't be isolated.'[43] Unfortunately, although similar bans were in place at Johns and Waygood in Victoria, the movement never achieved the *generalised* solidarity required.

Industrial action continued, however. As late as 1981, the maritime unions were still making it difficult to export yellowcake. In May, the *Parella* did manage to get around bans by the Seamen's Union when waterside workers agreed

Anti-uranium picket of rail shipment of uranium at Hamilton wharf (Brisbane) 1978

to load it. The ship then left without tugs. Protest demonstrations greeted it in Canada. Meanwhile, in Darwin, the two key maritime unions were more united and managed to hold up 20 containers of yellowcake for several months before they were spirited out using non-union labour. Almost immediately, they managed to ban another seven containers, holding up an equal number of vessels until threats of government legal action forced them to retreat.

Protest actions also continued, for example, in South Australia where the new Liberal government was proceeding with mining at Honeymoon and Roxby Downs. Demonstrators occupied the Honeymoon site in May, raising the land rights flag and pulling down a fence. In October, they were back to set up a peace camp nearby. In August–September 1983, people came from all over Australia to blockade Roxby Downs.

But, while the movement had slowed the development of the nuclear industry – and probably prevented the building of atomic reactors in Australia – mining and export went ahead, with workers on the mining sites suffering the most immediate consequences. In 1981, 180 employees at the Ranger mine struck for two weeks over safety issues. Again in October 1983, Ranger workers went on strike after discovering that their drinking water was contaminated with radioactive material.

Marching for disarmament

The anti-uranium cause was linked to strong antiwar traditions in the labour movement and the left. Many of the activists came from the Vietnam era or from campaigns against nuclear weapons in the 1950s and 1960s. In the 1970s, Victoria had seen a battle over construction of the US communications base Omega. Then, just as the movement against uranium mining declined at the start of the 1980s, public concern began to grow about a new surge in the global arms race.

For decades, the US–Russia arms race had been governed by the doctrine of 'Mutually Assured Destruction'. However, under the Reagan presidency, US military strategists began thinking about 'winnable' nuclear war, an alarming development which accompanied a sharp polarisation between the two great powers. In response, mass movements arose around the globe, demanding peace. In Australia, many of the people who had sustained the anti-uranium campaign now reappeared in groups such as People for Nuclear Disarmament (PND). They were joined in the streets by huge crowds, whose fears about the 'new cold war' were by no means irrational: the Office of National Assessments,

Rallly at Honeymoon uranium mine 19 May 1982

Australia's intelligence coordinating body, estimated that there was a 50 percent chance of nuclear war.[44]

Smaller actions complemented the big marches. People were prepared to travel immense distances to camp outside the US communication bases at places like Pine Gap near Alice Springs, where they staged generally non-violent but defiant blockades accompanied by token invasions. When the US warship *Goldsborough* visited Australia in late 1982, demonstrators met it with pickets in Brisbane, then with a full mobilisation in Melbourne.

Students and some of the more left-wing off-campus activists set up a tent village on the beach near Station Pier. They skirmished with police guarding the ship; watersiders walked off the job; the ARU banned freight shipments in the area; and the AMWU banned repairs. Despite a split in the peace movement, reflecting the more right-wing central organisers' hostility to the student and left forces, Students for Nuclear Disarmament were able to rally 2,000 people in the City Square. The crowd marched to Flinders Street station, poured onto trains and arrived at the pier – just in time to rescue the central organisers, whose rival rally at the pier (called for the same time to undermine the students) had been a dismal flop.

In Perth, where visits by US warships (all with tactical nuclear weapons capacity) had a long history, large mobilisations against them continued as part of the new peace movement. Up to 50,000 US naval personnel visited the city in 1982, and demonstrators were on hand. The local anti-nuclear movement explained:

> The American sailors should be accepted in their private capacity. But as representatives of a nuclear war machine which threatens our population, there is no way that their presence should be tolerated.[45]

The anti-uranium movement seemed to have revived in a new guise, given the overlap of issues and activists; but there were important differences. Organisations like PND had not simply followed on from the anti-uranium movement. In some ways, they had arisen out of its defeat. The attempt to stop uranium mining through aggressive political campaigns and, above all, through working class action had failed, and both the make up and the style of the subsequent peace campaigns reflected the fact: they were far more middle class. It was true that most people marching in the streets were still workers, but they were generally present as individuals, not as trade unionists. While various unions were affiliated to the peace organisations, there were no workplace groups, no industrial actions, no riveting ACTU debates.

To a degree, this situation resulted from circumstances beyond the peace movement's control, because there was much less focus for industrial action. What could the average factory worker black ban? It was also true that the union militants had lost confidence after the Newport and uranium defeats and would have been hard to revitalise. But at the start of the 1980s, the most prominent anti-nuclear leaders did more than register this fact. They positively welcomed it, seeing in it an opportunity to embrace more mild-mannered tactics, to give more weight to the churches and the more conservative outer-suburban locality groups. Key people in Melbourne PND argued explicitly that, if the movement became more middle class, this would bring greater influence, and even a supposedly Marxist PND leader such as Belinda Probert could suggest in all seriousness that 'today socialists need the Christians to extend and deepen the ethical arguments for socialism' within the movement.[46] Under these circumstances, it was not surprising that the main disarmament rallies were exceptionally bland affairs.

Inevitably, a variety of middle-class political ideas gained in influence. The anti-uranium movement had already included pacifist currents who regarded non-violence as an absolute principle. These now grew considerably in strength and argued against proposals for militant action. We also heard more from those people, also present in the earlier campaigns but restrained by the strong union presence, who thought that the nuclear menace transcended class. Since the bomb threatened to wipe out the human race, some argued, capitalists could be mobilised against it just as effectively as workers. The main leaders of the movement – who were drawn from the right wing of MAUM, the stodgy traditional disarmament group Campaign for International Cooperation and Disarmament[47], sections of the ALP and the remnants of the CPA – seized on these arguments with alacrity, thinking to widen the movement's appeal.

Superficially, it seemed to work. The crowds in the streets were bigger than the anti-uranium marches had ever been. But these crowds had remarkably little impact. When Fraser and (later) Prime Minister Bob Hawke made trivial gestures in the direction of promoting disarmament, this was generally enough to get them off the hook. Although the anti-uranium movement had been able to make a major impact on the national political agenda for several years, the disarmament campaign had no comparable effect.

It was far too insipid. No government was going to be overawed by people who marched on Palm Sunday, led by Christians with palm leaves; no militarist

Anti-uranium demonstration Brisbane October 1977

was going to lose any sleep over the Gardeners for Peace ('There are three principles of peacemaking which I see operating in our garden'[48]). The movement's internal life was so flat that, in most cities, its organising committees were bureaucratic shells. Only in Melbourne were there large general meetings or strong networks of local groups. Even in Melbourne, this was more a hangover from previous campaigns than a sign of real vitality.

There *was* one rather positive aspect of the peace movement's internal life: it confronted different and more diverse political issues, making it more interesting than MAUM. The leftists within it had to address the issue of Soviet[49] nuclear weapons, leading to sharp debates between older, pro-Soviet elements who had joined the movement in response to the disarmament slogan (an icon of Russian propaganda), and newer elements unwilling to swallow claims that Soviet weapons were 'defensive'. The movement in Melbourne eventually decided, over stiff opposition, to condemn the arsenals of both superpowers.

A second issue concerned 'multilateral' versus 'unilateral' disarmament, a debate harking back to the British peace movement of the 1960s. The multilateralists looked to superpower negotiations to end the arms race; the unilateralists considered that they had a particular responsibility to confront the militarism of their own rulers, an approach PND leader Joe Camilleri explained by citing a Dutch slogan: 'Let all Europe disarm but let it happen in Holland first.'[50] Translated into the framework of the two imperialist blocs, this meant concentrating on disarming the Western powers. Odd as it might seem, most of the pro-Soviet elements disliked this approach. They generally preferred multilateralism because it conformed to the Kremlin's foreign policy. It was mostly newer, more radical activists who were both critical of the USSR and prepared to adopt the more trenchant unilateralist standpoint. This included revolutionaries who adhered to the socialist slogan that 'the main enemy is at home'.

Unfortunately, the political debates didn't lead to many useful practical conclusions. Unilateral disarmament mostly meant calls for the USA to disarm before the Russians, and even this emphasis tended to disappear in the mass marches which simply promoted peace in its most general sense. Attempts by the left within the movement to focus attention on the US communication bases in *Australia* – sites which offered targets for militant action – had only limited success. In some cases, the debates led to dead ends, as with certain arguments about feminism. Encouraged by a women's peace camp at the Greenham Common missile base in Britain, a number of activists began arguing that women were naturally more peaceful, hence better suited to wage the struggle against war. A series of women-only or women-led actions followed. Since the later stages of the anti-uranium movement, feminists had been suggesting that women could achieve a new consciousness that would more effectively challenge the nuclear industry:

> Women are finding out that in developing an awareness of how we relate to our bodies, to each other and to the world, that a non-hierarchical collectivist consciousness develops. Alternative energy systems, or soft energy (e.g., solar, wind, methane, etc.) provide a flexibility of approach which is aligned with these discoveries.[51]

Such arguments had considerable appeal in the later stages of the disarmament campaign, when the movement began to sense that it was achieving little. 'Peace feminism' became a fad for a time in the early 1980s, yet it could not solve the movement's difficulties. Firstly, apart from a certain novelty value, it was not clear what staging women-only actions achieved *concretely* – apart from limiting the numbers who could participate. Secondly, there was the nagging reality that women were participating on *both* sides of the battle over nuclear energy. For example, Eileen Ekblom and Joy Baluch, the female mayors of Whyalla and Port Augusta, both supported uranium mining at Roxby Downs. The supposed links between feminist consciousness and alternative energy systems found no practical application; nor could they. The strength of 'peace feminism' was essentially a reflection of the middle-class nature of the movement, a sign of its underlying weakness rather than a source of strength.

To save the Franklin

What the uranium miners were to the Northern Territory, the Hydro-Electric Commission (HEC) was to Tasmania. By the end of the 1970s, the HEC had succeeded in sacrificing Lake Pedder to its endless appetite, before proceeding to destroy the Pieman River system. Next, they intended to dam the Franklin River. But Labor Premier Doug Lowe announced in 1980 that he would rescue the state's last great unspoilt river by making it a national park, proposing a smaller dam on the Gordon River to replace the Franklin Dam. Lowe was responding to a strong campaign by environmentalists.

The HEC immediately counterattacked, mobilising allies on both sides of parliament, and the upper house rejected Lowe's plan. When he tried to hold a referendum which included the option of 'no dams', he was rolled again and forced to limit the referendum to his compromise proposal alongside the HEC

Protesters at the Franklin Dam site Tasmania 17 December 1982

plan. In November, the party dumped him as leader. But the referendum itself brought a dramatic result: 47 percent for the HEC scheme, 8 percent for Lowe's compromise, and a remarkable 45 percent voting informal – most of them writing 'no dams' on the ballot. The electorate was effectively divided in two. When Labor lost office in 1982, Robin Gray's Liberals took office, determined to dam the Franklin.

The 'no dams' vote showed that opposition was growing, as was the Tasmanian Wilderness Society (TWS). These environmentalists had compelling arguments. The region was magnificent. *The Age* called it:

> a land of grand river valleys as unspoilt as the first Eden, and still remote enough to evoke that sense of wonder that the first explorers might have felt.[52]

There were caves along the Franklin sacred to Aboriginal owners and of immense archaeological importance. If the HEC got its way, more dams were likely, because the Commission had three more big projects in mind for the area. To claims that the scheme was needed to create jobs, the TWS's Bob Brown responded by citing the historical record: 'Through hydro industrialisation we have got 13 industries using 66 percent of the State's power and providing 6 percent of the State's jobs.'[53]

Buoyed by a 14,000-strong anti-dam march in Melbourne, the TWS launched a write-in campaign for the December 1982 Flinders by-election. Once again, they triumphed, when 41 percent wrote 'no dams' on their ballot papers. Next, they organised a blockade of the construction sites. Scores of people camped in the vicinity while a $37,000-a-day police force assembled to confront them. The protesters set out in dinghies to obstruct the work, whereupon the cops systematically arrested them. Despite Robin Gray's description of the activists as 'fanatics',[54] the only violence occurred when a group of pro-dams young men invaded the TWS's Strahan headquarters, threw furniture about and assaulted one of the environmentalists.

Within days, authorities had jailed 100 people. On 22 December, 3,000 people rallied in Hobart to counter Robin Gray's claims that most Tasmanians favoured the dam. The following day, four Aboriginal activists visited Kutikina ('spirit') Cave, also called Fraser Cave, where Michael Mansell told the press:

> Every race of people strives to respect and preserve its heritage, not destroy it. Can't they see this is a beautiful place? If anything in Tasmania is a sacred site, this is it.[55]

After 10 days and hundreds of arrests, the blockaders stopped to rest over Christmas, but the debate raged on. There was little hope that Robin Gray would relent, so attention focused on Canberra. The federal government tried to dodge the conflict on the grounds that it was a state issue, but Fraser came under increasing pressure as the clamour mounted. The 'states' rights' argument was weak to start with: the same federal government had stepped in to stop the export of mineral sands from Fraser Island, despite complaints by the Queensland Premier; it became weaker after the World Heritage Committee listed the Southwest Tasmanian Wilderness Area, on the Fraser Government's own recommendation. Surely Fraser was now obliged to protect the Franklin? The PM finally offered the Tasmanian Government $500 million to build and subsidise an alternative, coal-fired facility – an offer that Gray contemptuously refused.

By now, the federal Liberals had begun to crack. Four government senators crossed the floor on the issue; about 20 backbenchers met top Coalition leaders to discuss it; and the president of the Young Liberals foreshadowed an anti-dams motion at their national convention. Three ministers were wavering.

Protesters at Franklin Dam rally Sydney February 1983

Franklin rally Sydney March 1983

The unease in the Coalition grew further when a poll showed that large numbers of swinging voters were concerned about the issue.

Early January brought a new round of protests and arrests. In Strahan, Aboriginal protesters set up a tent embassy and announced plans to visit archaeological sites, for which Michael Mansell said they had not sought permission: 'We consider it to be our land, and the white man's trespass laws do not apply to us.'[56] Then, at the start of February, Malcolm Fraser called a general election; the movement shifted gears, calling a mass 'Rally for Reason' that brought 12,000 or more into Hobart streets. The turnout, said the local *Mercury* newspaper, 'stunned most people':

> The no-dammers were still leaving Franklin Square when the first of the protesters arrived back after wending their way along Elizabeth, Collins, Argyle, Liverpool and Murray Streets... The best ear muffs wouldn't have stopped the HEC Commissioner, Mr Ashton or the Premier, Mr Gray, from hearing the chants: *Jobs not dams*.[57]

The first day of March was set as 'Green Day', to be the occasion for further direct action. Again, Robin Gray and the *Mercury*[58] issued dire warnings of violence, which again proved utterly baseless, although police arrested 228 protesters on the river. (The closest thing to violence occurred when pro-dam elements threw washing powder and nuts at conservationists in the Strahan TWS shop.) Greenies in Hobart hoisted a 'No Dams' flag atop the HEC building, while others welded themselves into a steel cage outside.

The direct action made the TWS campaign rather exciting, which somewhat obscured the fact that it continued – and perhaps accelerated – the rightward trend in Australia's environmental movements. Where the Newport and uranium campaigns had a strong working class content, and the disarmament movement had still relied primarily on ordinary people, the Franklin campaigners depended much more heavily on backing by liberal sections of the ruling class, who did not see the need to further develop Tasmania's already huge power generation systems, given the environmental cost. A group of 60 Tasmanian businesspeople commissioned a report which concluded that money should be spent on job creation schemes rather than hydro-electric power, and the protesters near Strahan arrived on a cruise boat provided by a tourist firm and camped on a 10-acre site provided by a local landlord. Electronics entrepreneur Dick Smith helped to fund the campaign. When English botanist and environmental campaigner David Bellamy arrived to join the protests, he made a point of affirming his admiration for Malcolm Fraser as well as his support for the royal family – and, indeed, both the Prince of Wales and the Duke of Edinburgh were backing the no-dams campaigners.

The TWS had financial resources other protest movements could only dream of. Dick Smith made a generous donation, and a fund appeal in late 1982 had prompted 100 people to send $1,000 or more. One informed estimate put the TWS's annual turnover at around $1 million, compared to about $200,000 for the anti-uranium movement, and the society could afford the services of a market research company and an advertising agency.

Moreover, the TWS's politics were middle class in the most literal sense. 'Dr Brown's vision,' reported *The Age*, 'is of Tasmania as a much more highly decentralised tourist resort with many more small, labour-intensive and preferably locally owned industries.'[59] Brown himself, according to historian Verity Burgmann, 'conformed absolutely to middle class notions of respectability.'[60] It was hardly surprising, then, that the 'no-dams' write-in effort during the Flinders by-election was supported by 32 percent of Liberal voters, or that the Young Liberals and various government MPs supported the TWS campaign.

While trade unions on the mainland were often sympathetic, the TWS did not make much of an effort to win over unionists in their own state. The main reason trade unionists were sceptical about the no-dams campaign was that unemployment was particularly high in Tasmania – but, notwithstanding the 'Jobs Not Dams' chants at the Hobart rally, the TWS never made a serious effort to discuss the unemployment issue with unionists. When pressed by a socialist interviewer, Bob Brown admitted in early 1982:

> There's been a definite failing of the conservation movement and the unions to get together in Tasmania. We've failed in that, after a couple of attempts, we've largely given up... The unions have failed in that, with one or two exceptions such as the AMWU, they have made no approach to us whatever. They've simply seen us as a threat.[61]

Brown was careful to add: 'I don't mean the members of unions, I mean the officers,' noting that many of the rank and file were sympathetic. But the movement had never attempted to organise this rank and file *as workers* the way sections of the anti-uranium movement had done. The TWS' approaches to the union movement consisted of formal appeals to union bureaucrats.

The anti-uranium experience of building links with workers on the job had been lost.

The limitations of the movement were equally clear in two other, apparently unconnected, aspects of the campaign. The demonstrators on the river were a select band, who had all been through special non-violence training. They had to do the training to join the actions and to take a two-day refresher course if they'd been away for a while. By definition, this precluded rapid mobilisation of large numbers of ordinary working people. That was why, although some people in the uranium and disarmament campaigns had also argued for non-violence training, they had generally remained isolated, because these movements relied on getting large numbers into the streets. The TWS campaign, however, relied mainly on assembling smaller numbers in a remote area for prolonged periods, during which they were cast in the role of a heroic elite, a status the non-violence training reinforced. True, there were also mass rallies in the cities, but those who joined them had been assigned a supporting part.

One reason for the special training, according to a non-violence instructor at Strahan, was that: 'we have to look to our public image, and our course has been worked out partly according to how we think the public would respond.'[62] This reflected the fact that, for all the direct action and demonstrations, the TWS leadership was primarily interested in the electoral and parliamentary sphere. They had set up branches in several marginal federal electorates as early as May 1982. In early March 1983, as it became clear that Labor would win the election, the TWS called off the direct action and reduced its presence on the west coast to a watchdog camp. The battle, they said, was 'all but won.'[63] In fact, Bob Brown had predicted in late January that 'the Franklin will be saved by an election campaign, not by a blockade.'[64]

After winning the election, Bob Hawke did intervene to preserve the Franklin River. It was an encouraging victory after so many defeats on the environmental front, but it was also partly a damaging one for the left, because it spawned dangerous illusions. At a time when the class struggle and social movements were in decline, it gave environmentalists an illusory feeling of power, and much of the left spent the following decade in futile efforts to rebuild itself by tailing after 'green politics'. The victory also gave an artificial boost to advocates of 'non-violent action' and electoral tactics, because these appeared to have worked so well. The reality – that victory came so easily only because important sections of the bourgeoisie had opposed the dams – could be brushed aside.

The no-dams struggle of 1983 showed how much the political climate had changed in less than a decade. Socialists, who had been conspicuous in earlier campaigns, had trouble even selling a paper or two at no-dams rallies. Working class struggle, so important in the uranium movement, had been sidelined by the disarmament campaign, and most people working to save the Franklin did not even think about it. Bob Hawke, who had betrayed the struggle against uranium mining, could make hay out of the no-dams issue. That Fraser could not cope with it simply showed that he had lost control of Australian politics generally by 1982, including forfeiting the confidence of his own supporters.

7.
'Work or riot':
the unemployment crisis

During the 1970s, poverty and unemployment ceased to be issues at the fringes of society and began to invade its core, in previously comfortable middle-class areas as well as among the working class. At the start of the decade, it was believed that no government could survive unemployment higher than 2 or 3 percent, and jobless figures of 4 percent had played a part in Whitlam's fall. Malcolm Fraser, however, was able to survive much higher unemployment levels. His government had the dubious distinction of establishing, in a population used to relative prosperity, a grudging acceptance that mass unemployment was 'normal'. He did this partly by taking the offensive.

In the monetarist framework, unemployment became a tool of policy, helping the government to 'fight inflation first' by reducing consumer demand and by discouraging industrial militancy. Of course, if put this baldly, Fraser's methods would have aroused public outrage; instead, he resorted to stratagems aimed at deflecting public blame away from himself and onto the victims.

The Whitlam Government originally contributed the myth of the 'dole bludger' to Australian folklore, but it was fully developed and enriched in the middle to late 1970s. Victorian Liberal MLA Jeff Kennett set the tone magnificently in July 1977 with his claim that only about 17 percent of people on the dole were really unable to find work – estimates he supposedly derived from 'commonsense evaluations'.[1] The media backed up efforts of opportunist politicians like Kennett: for example, the *Daily Mirror* portrayed the jobless as 'bludging on beaches' while 'being paid for doing absolutely nothing'.[2]

Fraser had taken office pledging to crack down on this supposed abuse, and his successive moves to tighten the rules brought applause from not only the media but also a large proportion of ordinary people. Partly, this resulted from media manipulation. For example, *The Australian* reported in 1976 that the:

> number of people prosecuted for abusing unemployment benefits doubled in the first six months of 1976 compared with the previous half year. Figures compiled by the Department of Social Security show 47,000 people had their benefits ended in the last year after investigation by the Department's field officers.[3]

Casual readers might assume that 47,000 people had been prosecuted, although the small print revealed that the total was 115. The Department had stopped benefits to most of the 47,000 for reasons far removed from 'dole bludging'.[4]

Media hype alone could not fully explain the pervasiveness of the 'bludger' myth. Large numbers of people seemed remarkably anxious to embrace it. Working in a sheet metal factory at the end of 1975, I was astonished by my fellow workers' angry demands to 'get the bludgers off the dole'. When I pointed out that unemployment had soared in the previous year, asking whether an epidemic of laziness had suddenly hit the country, I was met with belligerent assent. These were well meaning people with no apparent reason to attack the unemployed, but they were also poorly paid and trapped in a dirty, oppressive workplace, making them prime candidates for a syndrome Keith Windschuttle (then a leftist) explained very well:

> For most people, work time and labour are given grudgingly... Often the worker doubts the fairness of his rewards. There exists widespread suspicion that the sacrifices are not worth the rewards received. Under these circumstances, the person who demonstrates how to get the rewards without making the sacrifices is a subversive... This provides the basis for a dual response by the mass media. On the one hand, the reader is fascinated by the concept of breaking the rules, of rejecting the socially approved goals and the socially-sanctioned means towards them. But on the other hand, the reader feels such breaches are not possible for him. He is encouraged by the media to feel strong moral indignation towards those who achieve that freedom, particularly if he believes their indulgence is at his expense.[5]

As the jobless levels rose higher and time passed, more workers began to see through the myth – if only because people they knew, often their own children, were unable to find jobs. Under such circumstances, the hostility could give way to solidarity and a consequent public backlash against the government; therefore, from the start, Fraser sought ways to distract attention from the problem, or fiddle the statistics or force people off the dole. The very first full Cabinet meeting in January 1976 decided on stern measures. The government would deny unemployment benefit to people who moved to areas with few jobs, as well as those who made themselves unacceptable to employers by their dress or appearance. It would allow the Department of Social Security (DSS) to postpone benefits if you were 'voluntarily' unemployed or were sacked for 'misconduct'.[6]

Two months later, they tightened the eligibility criteria further: school leavers couldn't get benefits until the next school year began; skilled workers had to take unskilled jobs; 'voluntary' unemployed had to wait six weeks before benefits started; and income statements had to be lodged in person rather than posted. None of these measures created any jobs (except, perhaps, behind the counter at DSS and Commonwealth Employment Service (CES) offices), but they helped to keep down the numbers on benefits.

Fraser's next step was to cut back on the benefits. In January 1977, he made them taxable. In March 1977, he abandoned the Whitlam Government's plans to gradually increase them in real terms, announcing that they would be indexed to the CPI. The August 1977 budget announced that they would be paid two weeks in arrears. The effect of these decisions was to drive increasing numbers of people into the arms of private charities, because many of the jobless had scant resources of their own. In fact, an October 1975 survey had found that 40 percent of people registered with CES had no savings at all.[7] The attacks continued off and on throughout the Fraser years, concluding with an unsuccessful attempt in 1981 to eliminate benefits for under-18s.

Although harassing the jobless served no socially useful purpose, the government persisted for political reasons. In March 1979, *The Bulletin* reported that senior officers in DSS 'argue that application of the work test is futile' but that Employment Minister Ian Viner thought that aspects of it might need to be tightened.[8] Of course, there were those advocating more drastic measures. The national president of the Returned and Services League (RSL), for example, suggested conscription of all young men for two years at the age of 18.[9]

As the Fraser years wore on, the dimensions of human suffering became clearer. Most attention focused on youth. As in most Western countries, youth

HOW CAN TRADE UNIONS FIGHT UNEMPLOYMENT

A Right to Work Leaflet

unemployment had been rising more rapidly than the adult jobless totals since the mid-1960s, a problem which the economic recession simply brought to crisis point. In August 1976, Peter Kirby of the Department of Employment and Youth Affairs (DEYA) told a conference that about 35 young people were registered as unemployed for every vacancy listed with the CES and that the national average concealed 'such alarming ratios' as 600:1 for unskilled junior males in some country areas. By the time Kirby spoke, nearly 20 percent of unemployed youth had been out of work for over six months.[10]

The 'dole bludger' myth ensured that many of these unemployed young people blamed themselves or faced harassment from their parents. A 17-year-old told journalist Anne Summers:

> I keep getting hassled at home, with Mum saying, 'Why don't you practise [typing]?' But I keep going for interviews and keep getting knocked back and I just feel so useless.[11]

More sophisticated blame-the-victim arguments suggested that rising youth wages had priced young people out of the job market, but calculations by economist Peter Sheehan showed that the wage relativities between juniors and adults had not changed much at all; if anything, wages for young women had deteriorated, relative to those for adults, while their unemployment levels had shown a long-term increase.[12]

Unemployment benefit was lower for under-18s than for adults. Parents were supposed to be taking care of their kids; in reality, nearly one-third of them had to survive on their own, and many were homeless. Inevitably, some of them turned to illegal forms of work, as in Sydney's King's Cross, where a floating population of up to 4,000 teenagers survived through prostitution and drug deals, living in fear of the police. A visiting journalist spoke to one young man working as a prostitute: 'I asked Ivan if he would call himself basically gay or bisexual. He shrugged his shoulders and replied, "basically broke".'[13]

It became harder and harder to deny that young people were the innocent victims of the unemployment crisis. Gradually, the government and the experts became alarmed by the dimensions of the problem. A 1978 submission from DEYA announced that 'the trend towards an increasingly higher level of unemployment shows no signs of abating' and warned that, for the foreseeable future, unskilled school leavers would find jobs very scarce.[14] Fears mounted that an entire generation of workers was being traumatised. A number of riots among young people accentuated these fears.

The most spectacular took place in September 1979 at Newcastle's Star Hotel, a favourite venue for unemployed and poorly paid young workers. When the owners made a commercial decision to close the pub, a crowd of 2,000 gathered on the final night. Stimulated by alcohol and probably also by the band's last number, which featured the lyrics: 'I want action, I want fighting in the streets', hundreds responded to a police car driving into the crowd by hurling bottles and abuse at the cops. Other pitched battles occurred during the 1982 recession at beach locations in South Australia and Victoria.

The Fraser Government responded to this generational crisis with an array of training schemes. Most important was the Special Youth Employment Training Program, which subsidised employers to hire young people. Critics pointed out that employers often simply used the scheme as a source of cheap labour, letting kids go when the grant expired and replacing them with new, subsidised trainees. Often, the 'training' was a myth, with jobs restricted to stocking shelves and running messages. Other schemes included rebates for apprenticeship training (which aroused little interest among employers pessimistic about the future) and the Community Youth Support Scheme (CYSS). CYSS funded a rag-bag of activities, ranging from community work to letter writing. None of the schemes seriously addressed the youth unemployment problem; at best, they recycled it, because those who got jobs through them did so at others' expense.

Stress and scapegoats

If the youth got only bandaids, unemployed people at the other end of the age scale did little better. By 1982, almost half of people aged 55 to 59 were outside the workforce. For many of them, 'early retirement' was an unexpected, deeply resented descent into poverty. Metal worker Dulcie Howard was one of 700 who 'retired' from Sunbeam in Campsie, NSW in 1982. She reported that the company had put great pressure on older workers to 'get out voluntarily':

> They pushed this supervisor that had worked at Sunbeam for 40 years. He had started as a young boy in the tool room and worked his way up, as they did then. He was easily 57 or 58. They pushed him off to where he didn't know anything. We were shocked because he was the sort that had made Sunbeams his life, that Sunbeams always came first with him. I thought, 'Well, that didn't get him anywhere.'[15]

Many older unemployed were confronted with a particularly cruel irony: steady long-term work for one company had left them too narrowly skilled to find other jobs. A survey of migrant women retrenched from the clothing industry found that some could sew only dresses, others only shirts.

Unemployment meant stress, bringing serious medical consequences. Two academic studies during the 1970s found that Melbourne suburbs with high jobless rates also had higher death rates; in Adelaide, the unemployed were more likely than other people to report heart trouble. The economic crisis was a killer.[16] But the emotional damage that unemployment and the 'dole bludger' stigma could do was illustrated in more spectacular fashion in April 1979, after 34-year-old cabinet maker Domenico Speranza became Australia's first international hijacker. Police shot Speranza dead when he tried to seize an aeroplane at Sydney airport. His family revealed that he had been deeply unhappy, and neighbours had ridiculed him for being out of work.[17]

Women were often hard hit. Early fears that females would be driven back into the home in large numbers proved unfounded, but some other consequences were drastic enough. The number of homeless women grew, while those looking for work became particularly vulnerable to abuse, as one teenager recalled:

> My sister...went for a job in advertising, and the bloke said we need photos of you just for identification and she said fair enough, and he said, 'drop your clothes', and she said, 'what?' And he said, 'do you want to work here?' and she desperately wanted to work there, and...she got done. She got raped – by all these high class blokes who worked in the place.[18]

In addition to those identified as jobless, there were huge numbers of hidden unemployed. Polls and surveys in 1973 and 1974 showed that 24–32 percent of women would work if convenient child care was available. Applying these results to the 1978 jobless figures, Keith Windschuttle estimated that over 800,000 women could be considered hidden unemployed.[19]

The female workforce also became a scapegoat for the economic problems of the time. Popular prejudice had it that married women were stealing jobs from men. The *Weekend Australian* embraced this proposition with a 1978 feature article headlined: 'If Mum Quit Work There'd Be Jobs For The Boys (And Girls)'. Apparently, greedy mums were victimising not only men, but also single women! Agitation of this sort had a considerable impact, particularly in regional centres dependent on hard-hit traditional 'male' industries such as steel or shipbuilding. In Wollongong during the 1982–83 recession, Meg Fowler of the Lake Heights Community Centre reported:

> I had so many people ringing up and saying it was the fault of those women in David Jones behind the counters, with all their rings on their fingers. I was so shaken up I took my rings off for a few weeks.[20]

Several federal ministers sought to manipulate this irrational reaction in order to distract people's attention from the government's economic failures. Ian Viner, Ralph Hunt and Eric Robinson all accused women of taking jobs from men and school leavers. Hunt went one better, arguing that married females were causing unemployment by having abortions![21]

If these arguments ran out of legs, there was a handy alternative: in 1977, Ian Viner suggested that the rapid introduction of equal pay was to blame. It should, he said, have been brought in more slowly and paid for by cutting men's wages. On the same day, Claude Forell declared that there was 'no doubt' equal pay had increased unemployment.[22] The fact that wage equality *had* been introduced by gradual stages – insofar as real equality was achieved at all – apparently cut no ice with Viner or Forell. Such inane reasoning naturally provoked replies, one of the most sophisticated coming from Joy Selby-Smith of the Australian National University. Smith published research in 1979 showing that, while women were continuing to join the workforce, many were not taking jobs to which men aspired. If anything, men were moving into so-called 'women's jobs': an additional 54,200 males had been employed in teaching, caretaking and cleaning between 1972 and 1977.[23]

There were occasional attempts to enlist public sympathy for retrenched managers; and, no doubt, some middle-level executives and their families did suffer severe blows. But working class people generally saw a double standard at work: for example, in February, 1979, Ian Viner announced that anyone refusing to travel to seasonal work such as fruit picking could lose their benefit. Days later, it emerged that a top public servant was being paid $860 a week to stay on his farm while a suitable post was found for him, prompting several letters to the press suggesting he be redeployed to the orchards.[24] After the closure of GMH's Pagewood plant in 1980, 60 employees out of 12,000 saved their jobs by transferring interstate. Details of the conditions offered to the managers and to the rest of the workforce varied greatly – a 'perfectly natural' arrangement, according to the company's public relations manager.[25] Others saw it as a class system.

While unemployment was the dominant issue, the Liberals' small-government agenda caused them to attack social welfare of all kinds, and the attacks left great bitterness in their wake. In 1979, the Director General of DSS decided to 'clarify' the law on invalid pensions. Previously, doctors assessing people's eligibility had been allowed to consider educational, psychological, social and environmental factors in borderline cases. The new ruling eliminated this option. In early 1980, the Health Department's NSW Division tightened requirements further, telling Commonwealth Medical Officers that a person's incapacity to work related to *any* useful work, not just what they were accustomed to. The implications could be horrific:

> A rehabilitation worker told the *National Times* that under the new guidelines a person in an iron lung might not be considered 85 percent incapacitated since there was undoubtedly some small job he could do even though no employer would hire him.[26]

The new approach was used to withdraw pensions from borderline cases, who were then told to apply for sickness or unemployment benefits, losing $9.55 a week in pension income as well as a range of other entitlements. The *National Times* reported:

> One man who lost his pension is a spinal injury victim whose disability makes it impossible to drive, lift heavy objects or sit at a desk for long without suffering crippling spasms that last up to three days.[27]

In 1981, the government launched yet another assault on welfare programs, as part of a 'Review of Commonwealth Functions' – better known by its nickname, 'the Razor Gang'. Nevertheless, despite the meanness which millions felt characterised Fraser's every step, welfare expenditure actually rose slightly from 26.4 percent of budget outlays in 1976 to 27.8 percent in 1981.[28] This reflected the levels of unemployment benefits and an increased number of aged pensioners. The irony, however, to many of the government's establishment supporters, was that Fraser was managing to sow immense social bitterness without delivering the smaller government he had promised. Further, the diversity of the attacks on social welfare created a greater potential for his opponents to form alliances and develop a general critique, both of Fraser's policies and of the capitalist society that spawned them.

Into the streets

The economic crisis gave birth to a host of activist groups fighting on welfare issues, including the Unemployed Workers' Union (UWU), the Coalition Against Poverty and Unemployment and the Right to Work Campaign. These were generally initiated by one or another radical left grouping, but they had a wider resonance because they stood on firm ground ideologically. Initially, very few Australians were prepared to accept mass unemployment. However, because there was no coherent political and consistent movement with the determination and the social weight to mobilise large numbers of people, in and out of work, the labour movement ultimately failed to defend this ideological terrain.

In Sydney, the Right to Work Campaign began operations in February 1977 with a picket at the Dunlop factory in Drummoyne, protesting against the retrenchment of 600 employees. They leafleted two shifts with multilingual literature, brandishing placards calling for a 35-hour week and nationalisation of Dunlop. A member of the Socialist Workers' Party, which was heavily involved in the group, wrote:

> Last year Dunlop raked in a tidy $26 million [profit]... What [the rubber] companies are doing is taking advantage of this period of economic crisis when the labour movement is on the defensive... to 'rationalise' their operations – to close down the more inefficient plants, transfer operations overseas where labour is cheaper, effect speed-ups and so on. And if they're lucky, they may even receive government compensation and subsidies to assist this reorganisation.[29]

Two months later, a Demand for Work Campaign in Melbourne drew 1,000 people, largely migrants, to hear Gough Whitlam speak at Collingwood Town Hall. The meeting was partly a manoeuvre by pro-Whitlam forces in the ALP leadership tussle then in progress, but it showed the depth of working class concern about unemployment. There were plenty more smaller rallies and actions around the country over the following year or two, some of them respectable events addressed by Labor politicians but others a bit more aggressive. In Melbourne, Virginia Kane, tired of trying to extract a dole cheque from DSS,

Protesters in front of a nursing home force Fraser to leave through a back door, 30 March 1980

chained herself to a desk at the Department's main headquarters. She got her cheque but refused to budge until police arrived. 'There were people there in worse situations than I was,' she said. 'I wanted to show them that if they stood up for themselves they could get somewhere.'[30]

Fraser himself was an inviting target for angry young agitators. When the Prime Minister arrived to open the Harold McCracken nursing home in Fitzroy (Melbourne) in March 1979, he was met by a 1,000-strong hostile crowd, whereupon:

> there was a mad scramble to move the 600 official guests into the church... They did it just in time for the Prime Minister to enter the church through a barrage of eggs and tomatoes.[31]

Some of the eggs found their mark. (A demonstrator subsequently remarked that 'lots of people are now heavily into throwing food.') Confrontations with police led to nine arrests, and the subsequent march to Russell Street police station to demand their release sparked the formation of a Coalition Against the Fraser Government, which organised further demonstrations.

Protesters outside meeting addressed by Malcolm Fraser at Essendon Town Hall (Melbourne) during 1977 federal election campaign. To the right of the central policeman: Dave Nadel, Jeff Goldhar, Pauline Meaney

Student protest about CYSS Sydney 1981

UWU 'soup kitchen' outside the National Gallery of Victoria (Melbourne) 12 December 1978. The UWU was outraged at the hypocrisy of an opulent banquet in the gallery after a conference on poverty attended by the ALP, trade unions, church groups and welfare organisations. The photographer (John Ellis) and several others sneaked inside but got caught. 'What followed would make a good movie scene... One of the bouncers picked up one of the young women and threw her at a refrigerator. We were more intent then on getting him and by that time the coppers had arrived.' Some protesters were convicted but the fines were never collected

In November 1982, Melbourne's Coalition Against Poverty and Unemployment announced a 'March To Stop The City', winning endorsement from 28 trade unions, the ALP State Executive and various social welfare groups. The state Labor government got a hint of what was in store during parliamentary question time, when six women and four men unfurled a protest banner in the public gallery and shouted 'join us to stop the city' as they were being escorted out.[32] Three days later, a large crowd gathered in the City Square, where one banner read: 'Work Or Riot'. They heard former Maoist union leader Clarrie O'Shea call for a 'revolution to overthrow this rotten system,'[33] then marched to the Stock Exchange, where they hauled down and burned Australian and Stock Exchange flags before sending red and Eureka flags aloft. The marchers then headed up Collins Street to the Melbourne Club, symbolic home of the Establishment.

The crowd hurled bricks through windows and surged against the doors, taking police by surprise. The doors caved in, allowing a crowd of demonstrators to enter the building, where they caused havoc while staff hurriedly snatched paintings off the walls. The cops detained 15 people, but the crowd outside demanded their release so vociferously that only three were eventually taken off to Russell Street police station to be charged; a section of the crowd marched to Russell Street to demand their release. One of the 15 who had invaded the building later declared: 'We want to let them know that we are very angry. That is the ruling class in there, that's the tax evaders.'[34]

While the unrest was valuable in keeping the issues alive, the unemployed won few actual victories. Squatters sometimes won the right to live in unused public housing. The UWU did force the Victorian Government to provide free travel on public transport for people going to seek work, but the travel vouchers were accompanied by too much red tape to be very useful and were no help in getting the job when you arrived. Probably the most important win concerned the CYSS, which the 1981 federal budget sought to abolish.

Although CYSS was really just a bandaid measure, it did create drop-in centres, some of which had become organising centres for the more political unemployed, so there were people ready to defend the scheme. Following the budget, 60 of them occupied Liberal Party headquarters in Canberra; 500 people yelled 'No jobs, no money, no CYSS, no future' as they marched through Sydney; and an even bigger crowd packed Brisbane's town hall, where they shouted down Liberal MP Don Cameron. In September, there was a demonstration in Melbourne. Protest groups began to proliferate and ultimately forced Fraser to extend the scheme.

In general, however, the activist groups could make little lasting impact. They were simply unable to mobilise most of their potential constituency. Most of the unemployed were too preoccupied by the struggle for survival or too demoralised by their circumstances to take readily to the streets on the instigation of a minority of agitators – or, if they did, they had little staying power. Only a wider social movement could have mobilised them effectively. The unemployed groups did periodically call for unity between employed trade unionists and the unemployed, pensioners and the poor – and rightly, because only the organised labour movement could have provided the necessary leadership. But, given the politics of the existing union leaderships, such an alliance was almost impossible to build.

YEARS OF RAGE

FIGHT UNEMPLOYMENT

JOIN IN
THE CAMPAIGN FOR THE DEMAND TO WORK

- SHORTER WORKING WEEK – NO LOSS OF PAY
- COUNTER DOLE BLUDGERS IMAGE AND PUT ONUS BACK ON GOVERNMENT
- DEMAND EXTENSION OF WORK OPPORTUNITIES
- DEMAND FOR THE RIGHTS OF UNEMPLOYED TO BE IMPLEMENTED
- ALL UNEMPLOYED PEOPLE TO HAVE THE RIGHT TO UNEMPLOYMENT BENEFITS

SUPPORT THESE DEMANDS

- MORE JOBS
- JOB SECURITY
- GOVERNMENT POLICIES TO MEET THE PEOPLE'S NEEDS

ATTEND

THE PUBLIC MEETING AT THE COLLINGWOOD TOWN HALL

2pm   Sunday 3rd April, 1977   2pm

HEAR **GOUGH WHITLAM
TED INNES
JOHN HALFPENNY**

AND

March with the Unemployed on Friday 15th April, 197[7]

Leaflet for mass meeting at Collingwood Town Hall (Melbourne) and subsequent march, April 1977

Some responsibility lay with the more ultra left activists, such as those who portrayed staff in DSS as repressive agents of the state and abused them during demonstrations at DSS offices. While some DSS clerks might be guilty of the charge, far more of them were sympathetic to the unemployed. Their unions might have done more to help, had they been approached constructively; for example, DSS clerks in Victoria banned a new set of work test guidelines in September 1979, demanding more staff and training. While they didn't spell it out, some of them also wanted to prevent crackdowns on the unemployed.

A greater responsibility rested with the union officialdom, whose support for the poor and jobless seldom extended beyond rhetoric, and who almost never actively mobilised their members in struggle around the issue. The unions never even seriously attempted to ban overtime in order to create more jobs. Building an unemployed movement would have required an alternative leadership in the working class. Many of the activists looked to the unemployed campaigns of the Depression years as a model; but those campaigns had been built by a rapidly growing CPA, which still embodied some revolutionary impulses, despite the impact of Stalinism. Nothing similar existed in the Fraser years.

Resisting the sack

The closest the ACTU came to seriously tackling the jobs issue was in the area of new technology. The arrival of the microchip had caused great foreboding in much of the Australian workforce. The Myers report on technology estimated that the number of word processors in Australian offices could rise from 9,500 in 1979 to 80,000 by 1985,[35] and automated tellers seemed set to slash employment levels in banks. Robots, already at work on Japanese assembly lines, would inevitably make their appearance in Australian car plants. A labour movement already beset by double-digit jobless figures wondered whether far, far worse was on the way. And how believable were the assurances of the computer companies that their technology would also *create* jobs?

In 1979, the ACTU adopted a 13-point resolution about technological change, demanding six months' notice of retrenchment, improved severance pay, portable long-service leave, assistance in finding other employment and various forms of compensation. These were worthy objectives, but the resolution suggested no means of fighting to *save* jobs. By this time, a campaign for the 35-hour week was also underway, and nominally, the shorter working week was conceived as a means of creating employment. In reality, however, the campaign was part of the 1979-81 'wage push', with the job creation issue mostly peripheral to it. Some left unions did seriously try to link the two issues. But the ACTU Congress made only a token response to proposals from the AMWU and the printing union PKIU to ban overtime in an effort to save jobs. Similarly the impressive 1978 campaign by telecommunications workers to assert union control over the pace of technological change (discussed in Chapter 11) remained largely distinct from the more direct struggles over unemployment.

The unions did resist retrenchments, and there was often a major public uproar when large enterprises closed or cut back, with furious posturing by union leaders. The rank and file were sometimes prepared to put up a stiff fight. At Chrysler's Tonsley Park plant in South Australia, car workers pelted union officials with fruit when they argued for acceptance of a four-day week in July 1977. When the union official chairing the mass meeting, Robert Walker, moved to close it, he was roughed up. A virtual riot greeted retrenchments a few days later. The militants were led by a Maoist-influenced rank and file group in the plant. Their resistance ended when Chrysler used the sackings to weed out the rank and file leaders, with the acquiescence (if not complicity) of union officials, who had denounced them as 'a violent rabble'.[36]

Clearly, the union officials weren't always your best allies in fighting the sack. Labor Party leaders were even less reliable, as two struggles centred in NSW demonstrated.

Australian dockyard workers discovered in August 1976 that their jobs were at risk, when the federal government pre-empted an Industries Assistance Commission report by announcing that shipowners could place orders overseas for four 15,000-tonne bulk carriers. Australian shipbuilders had been counting on increased government assistance, so they could build the vessels profitably, but the government refused to change existing subsidy levels. A planned graving dock was to be scrapped. In practice, this was the death knell for the construction of big ships in Australia; 2,000 jobs were now on the line at Newcastle, along with many more across the country, including at Whyalla in South Australia. The NSW Government said that it would consider buying a floating dock for Newcastle, so smaller scale work could continue. That, however, couldn't solve the basic problem: Australian shipbuilding was uncompetitive, even with the 35 percent subsidy that had applied for some years. To save these jobs required huge outlays from somewhere. To get them from the public purse – let alone make the rest of the employing class pay the price – was something the Labor leaders never contemplated.

Premiers Don Dunstan and Neville Wran and the federal Labor Opposition naturally denounced Canberra. Wran pronounced himself 'dismayed, shocked and disgusted,' alleging that Malcolm Fraser had 'declared economic war on NSW,' while Tom Uren called it 'sabotage of the Australian shipbuilding industry and its workers'. Neither criticism had much credibility, however. Since the policy change affected Whyalla in South Australia as much as Newcastle, it could hardly represent an attempt to victimise NSW. As for federal Labor's complaints, Transport Minister Nixon had only to reply that the 35 percent subsidy had prevailed throughout the life of the Whitlam Government; the Coalition was just adhering to it. Workers who might initially see Wran as their champion against Fraser were quickly disappointed when the premier capitulated to Fraser's demagogic attempt to blame the workers for the industry's troubles, saying: 'I acknowledge that the industrial record at the dockyard is bad.'[37]

In reality, there were other factors at work. As the generally anti-union Melbourne *Herald* reported, overseas countries made finance available to their shipbuilders on far more favourable terms than the Australian Government, while the small Australian industry could achieve no economies of scale because it was repeatedly obliged to construct one-off, custom-made ships.[38]

The government pressed rapidly ahead, announcing on 18 August that at least 1,800 workers, including more than 200 apprentices, would be dismissed at Newcastle within weeks. The dockyard workforce would be halved. Similar consequences were foreseen for Whyalla, where the overall consequences would be more serious, given the town's isolation. The ACTU warned of 'catastrophic' implications but, in practice, never played more than a mediating role.

The response from shipbuilding unions was more serious. At the initiative of the AMWU, dockyard workers in most major centres held a 24-hour stoppage on 26 August. When Don Dunstan called their action 'counter-productive' because only the state government would be economically affected, the secretary of the Whyalla Combined Union Council replied sharply:

> Every time the workers want to do any sort of strike action we get people saying it is counterproductive... It is not a strike in the normal sense... It is a political strike against the decision of the Federal Government.[39]

In Newcastle, wharfies, seamen and firemen and deckhands joined the stoppage. On the day of the strike, about 150 unionists staged a sit-in inside the NSW parliament, with some shouting at MPs from the public gallery. Their determination forced Fraser to resort to some fancy footwork.

Fraser offered to have some ships built in Australia after all - *if* the unions would ban strikes and accept a wage freeze for a year. The proposition was unrealistic, both because it clashed with the wage indexation system and because the union movement was not prepared to allow the precedent of a no-strike agreement. Even NSW Liberal leader Eric Willis thought the wage freeze idea unreasonable, suggesting a six-month rather than 12-month time span for any exercise in union restraint; but, from Fraser's point of view, the proposal had the great political merit of putting all the pressure back on his critics. The workers would have to decide, with the Labor premiers assigned the task of trying to sell the deal. 'I am not asking (and neither is Mr Fraser) the dockworkers to do anything,' said Minister Nixon smugly. 'Mr Wran will be doing the asking.'[40]

Mass meetings of dockyard workers voted overwhelmingly to reject the plan, denouncing the 'harsh and excessive demands to exploit the threat of unemployment.'[41] This was a principled stand but, in itself, entirely negative, and the unions seemed to lose direction from here on. Another contingent invaded NSW state parliament at the end of September, carrying signs reading: 'Four destroyers: Fraser, Lynch, Nixon, Cotton', while a strike around the same time won the temporary withdrawal of 373 dismissal notices at the NSW State Dockyard; however, these were all rearguard actions. Unionists' increasing desperation was reflected in a rash of occupations of Japanese ships; unable to defeat their domestic foe, the workers, who had earlier sent telegrams to Japanese unions seeking solidarity action, now began to see Japan rather than Australian bosses as the enemy. This was sadly misguided. Although a Japanese firm had won the tenders for building the Australian ships, shipyard workers in that country were hardly facing a jobs bonanza. Their industry was itself in a severe slump, with 20,000 laid off and cutbacks underway which would reduce it to 65 percent of its previous capacity.

In October, the dismissals began to flow at Newcastle and Whyalla. By April 1977, as the NSW State Dockyard launched the 25,000 tonne bulk carrier *Selwyn Range*, there were signs around Newcastle reading: 'Drive carefully - there are over 17,000 unemployed walking the streets.' As the ship was launched, effigies of Fraser and Nixon hung from the bow. Amid the crowd of workers, sadly, were placards reading: 'Why give our jobs to the Japs?'[42]

Three and a half years later, the vehicle unions faced a crisis in Sydney when GMH decided to close its Pagewood car assembly plant, threatening 1,500 jobs. While the economy as a whole was by this time in an upswing because of the 'resources boom', the car industry was slumping, and GMH set about rationalising its operations. Pagewood was its oldest assembly plant and would cost $100 million to modernise, the company claimed. In June, the *Financial Review* broke the news that GMH had told the federal government that the plant would close, although it had supposedly not bothered to inform the state ALP government.

Stung by the news, Wran accused Fraser of 'treachery' and threatened to stop buying GMH cars, while the State Secretary of the Vehicle Builders' Union (VBU), Joe Thompson, warned of 'massive retaliation' if Pagewood closed.[43] As with the dockyards issue, Wran's righteous anger was just for show; apart from image-building, its main purpose was to persuade car workers that they should look to the government for salvation rather than to industrial action. To enhance the impression that the state government was on the job, Industry Minister Don Day flew off to the USA, where he went through the motions of lobbying General Motors' top management.

Joe Thompson's warnings had slightly more substance. When shop stewards discovered that 500 cars had left the plant in a week, compared to the normal 120, the union imposed bans on the removal of any further vehicles. Next, it banned the unloading of GMH cars arriving on rail trucks for sale in NSW and said that it would consider halting all rail transport of the company's vehicles. Later, the Labor Council threatened to ban dismantling of equipment when the plant was shut down. While this was hardly the 'war' between the unions and GMH which Labor Council Secretary Barrie Unsworth claimed was on the cards, it did suggest the impact that a concerted industrial campaign might have made. Indeed, there were those in the union movement who called for a general strike, although Bob Hawke was quick to explain that the problem was too 'complex' to solve by such simple means.[44]

In the absence of an escalating campaign of industrial action, the union effort was repeatedly pushed into largely empty talk of boycotts: boycotts by the Wran regime, by local councils (a few of which did take such action) and by union members at large. Militants such as the VBU's Paul Ford called for more determined action, saying: 'we have to fight to keep this plant open'.[45] This would have required very different methods of struggle: a serious occupation of the plant; visits to other workplaces to organise solidarity strikes; or calls for the bosses rather than the workers to pay for an economic crisis in the bosses' own capitalist system. Ford and a few others inside and outside the plant argued for a struggle along these lines, but Joe Thompson had the resources of his union office and of Trades Hall, whereas the militants were disorganised and isolated. It had become increasingly clear that the VBU officials' real agenda was simply to extract the best possible redundancy deal.

The Budget can be Stopped

FRASER HAS MADE A BIG MISTAKE.

Riding high after his election win, he thought he could really slug us in this budget and get away with it.

At the same time Fraser looks weak for the first time in months. Withers has got the axe, and Dunstan and Dickie have resigned. The Liberal Party is in crisis.

And now two powerful publications, the Bulletin and the National Times, have accused Fraser himself of lying.

The Government can be fought, and it can be beaten. The strikes and demonstrations this week are the biggest mobilisation of the working class since the Medibank fight of 1976. And we only lost that one because Bob Hawke was more interested in playing tennis than building a fighting movement.

If anything, the situation today is more promising. Not only have we got a more militant leadership in our own Trades Hall, but the Labor Councils in Sydney and Brisbane have taken a far more militant stand this time than in 1976.

Next week, we will have a mass delegates' meeting. Every job should be represented, with delegates mandated to vote for national strike action. A *real* general strike, not the piss-weak affair of 1976, can put an end to Fraser and his anti-worker government.

Today, we can expect a large and militant demonstration. Let's make the most of it. There is no point in just listening to speeches. There is no point in marching to some boring place on the edge of the city, like Parliament House or the Commonwealth centre.

Only two blocks from Bourke St. Mall is the Stock exchange, in Collins St. That is where the real power behind Fraser is located. That is one of the few places in Australia where there were celebrations when the budget was announced.

That is where we should march. It is time the power of the Australian working class was used to confront the employers, and the policies of unemployment, inflation and despair they represent.

International Socialists leaflet August 1978

A horror budget

If the unions were ever going to stage a real fightback around issues of poverty, unemployment and government cutbacks, their best chance was the 1978 'horror budget'.

Having announced big tax cuts in 1977 in order to win that year's election, Fraser reversed himself a year later under the influence of Treasury Secretary John Stone, announcing steep increases. Stone thought that cutting the budget deficit would help to attract foreign investment. In the same budget, Fraser produced yet another new health policy, abolishing Medibank Standard. Despite some talk of 'Medibank III', Medibank had actually been scrapped. While analysts generally saw the new health policy as somewhat more equitable than the system introduced amid the sound and fury of 1976, the changes served to revive much of the working class bitterness surrounding healthcare issues.

These major initiatives were accompanied by numerous smaller annoyances: petrol, beer and cigarette prices were to rise; a range of welfare payments would be cut; and nine-month delays for home ownership assistance were to be matched by a $77 million cut in money for welfare housing. Only those unemployed who had dependents got any increase in their benefits, and pensions were to be indexed annually instead of every six months. The 'vampire's budget', as John Halfpenny dubbed it,[46] summed up everything workers disliked about Fraser. Here was an opportunity to unite all the anti-Fraser forces and give the bastard a bloody nose.

Within 24 hours, waterside workers in Port Adelaide and Melbourne had walked off the job, and hundreds of Melbourne construction workers had taken to the streets. Within two days, the ACTU was reported to be 'canvassing rank and file reaction...to decide whether to call a 24 hour national stoppage.'[47] Raw eggs and a paint bomb narrowly missed the Prime Minister as 600 demonstrators greeted him outside a business luncheon. When Bob Hawke expressed a personal view that workers would prefer more moderate alternatives to a general strike, it sounded rather like wishful thinking, as the momentum of protest continued to build. An Adelaide protest rally drew 7,000 people. Fraser was jeered at a football game in Melbourne.

Sydney saw an initial protest march on 17 August. A mass meeting of railway workers at Chullora the next day called for a national stoppage. Three days later, they stopped work, along with watersiders, metal workers, the Garden Island dockyards, printers and meatworkers, to attend a 10,000-strong rally in Town Hall Square. Speaking alongside Neville Wran, the ALP's new leader

Bill Hayden told the crowd that Malcolm Fraser was displaying 'a total lack of regard for the people'. Several hundred of the people decided that Fraser's big business supporters were equally to blame; they marched down George Street to the Stock Exchange:

> The demonstrators arrived at the Exchange at 2:15 pm, cramming into the narrow corridor on the ground floor that led from O'Connell St. They surged towards the glass door tearing fixtures from the wall. One person sprayed slogans onto the lift doors and on the walls. All the slogans were the same: 'Make the rich pay.'[48]

Of 10 people arrested, two young socialists, Martin Hirst and Phil Lee, had severe charges laid against them. It took a long political campaign to eventually get the most serious charges dropped.

On the same day as the Sydney events, police arrested 129 people attempting to march from Brisbane's King George Square after an anti-budget rally. The struggle over Queensland Premier Joh Bjelke-Petersen's ban on street marches (discussed in the following chapter) was underway.

Fraser claimed that ALP leader Bill Hayden was deliberately stirring up the trouble. By 1978, this sounded pretty inane. The Hayden leadership was not likely to stir up anything. Indeed, Hayden cynically pointed out that some of the Stock Exchange demonstrators had carried placards reading 'Sack Hawke, Hayden and Wran'. It was not, as he suggested, that these were 'closet members of the Liberal Party'.[49] Quite simply, a lot of people who hated Fraser were beginning to wonder whether the rightward moving ALP leaders were much better. Their problem was they lacked an alternative political organisation that *did* want to incite unrest and was big enough to do so effectively.

While the Canberra pollies traded nonsense, Melbourne's THC was organising a rally in the Bourke Street mall. Although the unions didn't call stoppages, 8,000 people turned up. After some speeches, the organisers led the crowd to state parliament. They were appealing for it to disperse when, in a smaller scale re-run of the 1975 breakaway march, teacher activist Julie Ingleby called on the crowd to proceed to the Stock Exchange. One thousand or more heeded the call. As in 1975, the IS popped up at the front of the march. Yet, once again, they were able to accomplish little with their apparent leadership, because they were still too small. Finding itself faced with locked doors and rows of police, the crowd milled about aimlessly before eventually breaking up. As at the time of the Constitutional Crisis, there were angry people looking for a lead, but there was no one both willing and able to provide it. Only the left union leaders could have done so, and they had once again gone home.

The rank and file of Victorian unions kept calling for action. One thousand shop stewards and job delegates came to a mass meeting at Festival Hall, but the left unions had now decided to dampen the unrest, so John Halfpenny offered the shop stewards a motion demanding that the ACTU organise half-day national stoppages each week. An alternative call for a one-week strike, previously endorsed almost unanimously by 700 workers in the Latrobe Valley, was not put to a vote, although several delegates spoke for it. Halfpenny's motion was less militant than it sounded, because a campaign of repeated short stoppages can easily lose momentum. His later suggestion that 'the government could ride out a one-week general strike but they could not ride out half-day stoppages every week,' was not really very sound.[50] Still, weekly stoppages would have sent a powerful message to the government, except for the fact that Trades Hall had no intention of holding them.

The THC endorsed the plan only insofar as it, too, requested action from the ACTU. It was counting on the national union leaders to bury the plan. Sure enough, a special telephone hook-up of the ACTU executive on 1 September made short shrift of the idea, and another opportunity to challenge the Fraser regime had been squandered.

Wollongong's 'out of workers'

The finest industrial fightback against sackings occurred in Wollongong on the NSW South Coast towards the end of 1982. In September, Australian Iron and Steel (AIS) announced that, because of a deepening slump in demand, 250 people would be retrenched, with another 500–700 job losses possible; shortly after that, BHP announced that 206 Kemira miners were to lose their jobs. Wollongong had already been prostrated by recession and unemployment, so these announcements were the last straw for many local trade unionists. Graham Jones, then a rigger at Port Kembla, recalls the feelings of resentment:

> Over the years, BHP had made vast profits and siphoned them off into resource investments. Then when the steel industry went bad they started to cry poor – said they couldn't cross-subsidise.[51]

Six thousand southern district miners struck for 24 hours. Seven bus loads of them travelled to Sydney to occupy some of BHP's offices before proceeding

Right to Work march Wollongong to Sydney 1982

Miners rally South Coast NSW October 1982

to parliament, where they called for nationalisation of the mines. Unimpressed, AIS announced two weeks later that 285 final year apprentices would be without jobs at year's end. Concluding that conventional strike action would have little effect on employers already running production down and holding large stockpiles, the Kemira miners resolved on a different tactic: they occupied their mine. After their first night of occupation, 1,000 workers from other mines turned up to demonstrate in support. A day later, 4,000 miners rallied at the showgrounds, where union president Bob Kelly declared that 'eventually, we are going to have to storm Parliament House.'[52] Sensing the popular mood, the *Illawarra Mercury* also backed the occupation.

On 21 October, 10,000 South Coast unionists packed the showgrounds to vote overwhelmingly for lightning strikes in the steelworks and mines, with a minority demanding stronger action. By this time, the union leaders had met with Neville Wran and BHP and concluded that only federal intervention could resolve the issue in their favour; so, on 26 October, 2,000 unionists boarded trains for Canberra. Three bus loads also travelled from Newcastle.

The plan was for a conventional rally, with Bill Hayden speaking, but the marchers went right past the speakers' platform, hopping over barricades and charging up the stairs to the glass doors of Parliament House. 'It was a real good turnout,' says Graham Jones, 'you could feel the adrenalin pumping.' Finding the doors locked angered the crowd: 'We thought, stuff this, this is supposed to be the people's parliament, we have a right to put our case.'[53] In a 'mad surge,' they began to heave against the doors, which cracked, then opened. The marchers poured inside. After Fraser refused to speak to them, they eventually went back out, but the political impact was considerable. Three days later, the Kemira miners, who had also seen their occupation mainly as a political pressure tactic, came out of the pit after 16 days underground to a heroes' welcome.

The October struggles on the South Coast probably contributed to a Coal Industry Tribunal decision granting better redundancy pay to the Kemira miners. However, their decision to occupy was important, quite apart from that result. After seven years in which organised workers had done relatively little about sackings, this time they had stood and fought, a fact that was not lost on the employers or the government.

Wollongong was also the launching pad for the last round of protest marches of the Fraser era, initiated by the Wollongong Out Of Workers' Union (WOW), one of the more successful of the unemployed groups. It grew out of a collection of graffiti artists called Young and Pissed Off, and its first major action was a 100-kilometre, week-long 'march for jobs.' The marchers were greeted in Sydney by a 20,000 strong rally, after Cockatoo and Garden Island dockyards came out for the day along with several metal shops and groups of building workers.

WOW went on to lead the 1983 Wollongong May Day march and join a nationally organised hunger strike in Canberra on the occasion of the new Labor government's first budget. Treasurer Paul Keating set the tone for a new era of Labor rule by ignoring their pleas completely, announcing that he would increase the youth unemployment benefit by a mere five dollars. The hunger strikers invaded the National Press Club where Keating was speaking the following day. They were thrown out.

This display of arrogance by the new Labor government brings us back to a question which began the chapter: how could the Fraser Government survive such high levels of unemployment – compounded by attacks on social welfare – for seven years? After all, many of the components for an effective resistance were present. The government's manipulation of prejudices against 'dole bludgers' had become less effective over time; a range of activist groups had sprung up; and there was a large mobilisation against the 1978 horror budget. Workers in the dockyards and the car industry fought battles against redundancy which showed some potential. Later, the Kemira coal miners showed how a workplace occupation over sackings could be used to launch a political campaign. At every crucial moment, however, Fraser was helped by the official leaders of the labour movement.

Neville Wran's posturing about the Newcastle dockyards and Pagewood was duplicated, in a sort of shadow-play, among the union bureaucracy; then, after the ACTU had suffocated the 1978 anti-budget protests, Bill Hayden went into the 1980 election offering economic prescriptions only a little to Fraser's left. Bereft of jobs, unemployed workers found themselves bereft of leadership as well. An episode in the Fraser Government's last months brought this home with particular cruelty. The Socialist Left Council in Northcote (Melbourne) ordered the UWU to vacate their offices; when they refused, police threw them out in a dawn raid and bulldozers moved in. BLF officials, having banned demolition, made no real effort to enforce the ban. The UWU, although they claimed grandly to represent all of the unemployed, had far too few forces to resist. Their supporters were left staring at a flattened building, embodying more than a few flattened hopes.

ACTION FOR CIVIL LIBERTIES IN QUEENSLAND

8.
Queensland: battles with Bjelke

Perhaps Malcolm Fraser's aggressive new right-wing politics came as less of a shock in Queensland, where most people were already acclimatised. They had long lived under a Country/National Party government so rock-ribbed that the rest of the country often thought them a bit peculiar: a maverick state, populated by politically backward 'banana benders' who chose a crank, Premier Joh Bjelke-Petersen, to rule them. These rather offensive stereotypes helped to sustain a political myth that the government was somehow unique in its reactionary politics – even 'fascist' – making Bjelke-Petersen impossible to defeat or dislodge. We shall seek to penetrate the myths, to grasp the premier's real strengths and weaknesses and to show how Queensland workers could have considerably shortened his reign. The first step is to ask just how different this state was, and why.

Queensland's economy rests more on agriculture and mining than Australia's as a whole. It is politically and economically decentralised. Brisbane dominates less than other state capitals, because rival port cities have grown up along the coast, equipped with secondary industry for processing primary products. The railway system does not radiate from Brisbane. Instead, spur lines run inland from the coastal towns.

The state's Brisbane-based commercial and banking capital remains too weak to dominate industry, while profits from mining and agriculture flow to Melbourne and Sydney or abroad. Economic ownership is less concentrated than in the southern states. Manufacturing remains underdeveloped, as does the industrial working class. The weakness of the local bourgeoisie, in turn, has meant that foreign capital is more influential than in other parts of Australia. These features, distinctive throughout the 20th century, became more pronounced in the 1960s and early 1970s:

> After a series of clumsy and unsuccessful attempts to encourage manufacturing investment...Queensland eventually experienced its own foreign investment boom – but in mining, not manufacturing. In 1963 the total value of mineral production in Queensland (excluding gold) was $109 million...in 1976 it totalled $1,136 million. Foreign controlled firms dominate the mining sector in Queensland, and account for 85 percent of value added [which] compares with the Australian average of 58.9 percent.[1]

This peculiar economic structure helped to ensure that the National Party was stronger than its Liberal Coalition partner, as well as having a decisive impact on the labour movement. The fragmentation of capital made parliamentary Labor the natural governing party up to the mid-1950s, yet Labor rule was no threat to capital. Outside Brisbane, the dominant force in the industrial movement was the arch-conservative AWU, which largely set the tone inside the ALP.

'Given the rural bias of the Queensland economy,' writes Ross Fitzgerald, 'Labor grew from a combination of early bush workers, shearers, cane cutters, miners and itinerant railway navvies,'[2] becoming essentially a rurally-based, politically conservative organisation. The weakness of manufacturing meant that fewer overseas migrants were drawn to the state in the postwar decades, making for a somewhat insular culture.

Sections of the working class were capable of very militant struggles, for example, in the 1948 rail strike, but this aspect of the labour movement had little resonance in the upper levels of the ALP. It had been a Labor government whose police had attacked the railway workers. ALP governments were just as right wing in other fields. In 1941, Labor Premier Forgan Smith had compromised Queensland University's independence by stacking the University Senate, and he had campaigned demagogically for 'states' rights' against Canberra. ALP governments had kept Aboriginal and Torres Strait Islander peoples in a state of semi-slavery for decades. In 1954, then Labor Premier Vince Gair had created the Literature Board of Review, with its extreme censorship powers. Thus, the typical characteristics of the Bjelke-Petersen regime were largely inherited from parliamentary Labor.

It was also the ALP who had introduced a gerrymander favouring rural electorates. When the great Labor split of the 1950s brought the conservatives to power, the incomers were able to turn this to their own advantage – assisted by a historic decline in Labor's traditional mass base in provincial areas following mechanisation of rural industry. The gerrymander's main victim had always been the Liberal Party, representing the Brisbane bourgeoisie and middle classes, whose political clout was modest.

In the 1970s, Labor remained as conservative as ever. Attempts to launch a Socialist Left faction ran into bureaucratic repression from the party's leadership. The Socialist Left then looked to federal intervention to help it put the ALP on a more progressive course; but, while the federal leadership did intervene in 1979 to revamp the Queensland branch, it was the centre faction that benefited rather than the left. (For Hayden, modernising Queensland Labor was primarily a matter of style and organisation, rather than politics; politically, one could argue that Hayden, in pushing the federal party steadily rightward in the late 1970s and early 1980s, was bringing it into alignment with its Queensland branch.) The state ALP was an obstacle to every important struggle, although sections of the Labor left played a very valuable role at times.

The Bjelke-Petersen regime was the high point of National Party rule. Probably the main thing distinguishing the Nationals from preceding Labor governments was their close links to multinational capital; but because these were mostly mining companies, this was consistent with the earlier pattern of domination by rural industries. The government did achieve significant economic development, again largely within the framework outlined above: bauxite mining at Weipa and an aluminium smelter at Gladstone, with runaway property development on the state's south-eastern coast representing the closest thing to real urban development. Because Joh based himself on these rural, mining and real estate interests, he had a certain independence from the urban bourgeoisie and the more progressive political life of the capital city.

At the same time, however, this base was narrow enough to make it somewhat fragile. As long as politics remained largely electoral, the gerrymander gave him power based on a rural electoral rump; when faced with social or industrial struggles, Bjelke-Petersen could become politically isolated. And he faced a series of such struggles, partly because economic development did have some flow-on effect in Brisbane, resulting in a growth of the working class and the liberal middle class. These groups carried much of the resistance to Bjelke-Petersen in the 1970s and 1980s.

In some ways, the industrial and social protest campaigns of the era were broadly similar to those in the southern states: workers fighting union-bashing, Indigenous people demanding land rights, women defending the right to abortion. Even the most distinctive issues – civil liberties and the right to march – were tied to national politics, because one of the premier's aims in banning protest marches was to combat the anti-uranium movement that had grown so strong in the south. What made Queensland struggles distinctive was partly the premier's autocratic and repressive style of government and partly an underlying vulnerability because of his minority electoral base: when a big campaign took off, it seemed that it could finish him. For both these reasons, people who began to fight tended to become radicalised. Queensland was the only place where the revolutionary left grew during the Fraser era. In those years, it was both the most reactionary and the most radical state, a case of 'combined and uneven development'.[3]

One consequence was that both left and right in Queensland showed some potential to exercise leadership nationally. In his various political and industrial adventures, Bjelke-Petersen had objectives extending beyond the state, including a hunger to establish himself as the leader of the national political right – a goal that became explicit much later in the 'Joh for PM' fiasco of 1987. Queensland was something of a social laboratory for extreme right-wing policies. Had Bjelke-Petersen enjoyed more unambiguous success in the period 1975–82, it might have strengthened Fraser's hand; conversely, to fight Bjelke-Petersen was to strike a blow against the right nationally. Had the left been able to decisively defeat the government, something that looked possible more than once, this might have set an example for, or even revitalised, a labour movement that was in decline Australia-wide. In this complex sense, too, Queensland must be understood as part of, rather than 'different to', the rest of the country.

This is not to deny Bjelke-Petersen a certain distinction. Joh was certainly a character. He championed quacks like the 'cancer specialist' Milan Brych; he was incoherent and he was autocratic. We joked that Queensland didn't have daylight saving because 'the sun shines out of Joh's bum, and he's not getting up early for anyone'. But Bjelke-Petersen was no fool. He had a great talent for *political polarisation* and directed his idiosyncrasies to great effect.

He polarised Queenslanders against southerners and the provinces against the capital, counting on the fact that any electoral backlash would occur in Brisbane, where it would merely weaken his hapless Liberal Coalition partners. Over his years in power, he gradually reduced the Liberals to an impotent fragment, finally ruling without them. Liberal backbencher Rosemary Kyburz complained:

> The Premier uses us to give him the numbers to prop up his own rural rump. But we are nothing more than dogs running after bad meat.[4]

In the Whitlam era, Bjelke-Petersen liked to agitate against the 'socialists' in Canberra, an endeavour at which he excelled. Whitlam's fall in 1975 presented a dilemma. The arrival in the Lodge of a tough-talking fellow conservative deprived him of a target to polarise against, so he turned his attention to the streets of Brisbane.

The ban on street marches

Civil liberties and the right to march were not new issues in Queensland. Although the Coalition had come to power in 1957 promising to rectify Labor's poor record in protecting civil rights, they had defaulted on these promises when the 1960s antiwar protests brought clashes between police and antiwar demonstrators. In March 1966, police arrested 26 people for violating the *Traffic Act*, which required protesters to seek a permit to march, hold meetings or display placards on any road. In response, staff and students from Queensland University held an illegal march, ensuring further confrontations that ran broadly parallel to civil liberties struggles in the south such as the mass hand-outs of illegal leaflets in Melbourne in 1968-69 which won the right to distribute literature in the streets.

During the 1971 Springbok tour, Bjelke-Petersen declared a State of Emergency, and police implemented it with dispatch, provoking Police Commissioner Ray Whitrod to criticise the 'shoot low and lay them out approach' of the government and his own cops.[5] In 1976, Whitrod again fell out with his associates, ordering an investigation into the nationally televised bashing of a demonstrator, only to find himself overruled by the premier. Finally, a gung-ho police raid on the hippie commune at Cedar Bay near Cooktown forced him to quit, warning that Queensland showed signs of becoming a police state.

In September 1977, Bjelke-Petersen was ready to provoke new storms. He announced that demonstrators refused a permit to march would no longer have the right of appeal to a magistrate. They could only appeal to the police commissioner, now the hardliner Terry Lewis. The proposal had come from Liberal frontbencher Charles Porter, but the premier embraced it with relish. Political street marches, said Joh, were 'a thing of the past':

> Nobody including the Communist Party is going to turn the streets of Brisbane into a forum. Protest groups need not bother applying for permits to stage marches – because they won't be granted... You can shout yourselves hoarse in [King George] Square. Don't bother

applying for a march permit. You won't get one. That's government policy now.[6]

Bjelke-Petersen's announcement came in a political climate already laden with conflict. In August, his government had made an unprecedented direct appearance at the national wage case to oppose wage rises for 'militant unions'. Storemen and Packers' organiser Ted Zaphir was on trial for alleged pressure tactics while seeking to enforce a union shop, and the unions were outraged. The premier, attempting to build on his Cedar Bay 'triumph', announced a stepped up anti-drug campaign. Opponents of uranium mining had brought to Brisbane the same protests that were gripping southern capitals. The campuses, to be sure, seemed relatively quiet: ABC general manager Talbot Duckmanton told a Brisbane conference that students were no longer as 'revolutionary' as they had been a decade earlier. Joh Bjelke-Petersen was about to stir them up.

His immediate goal was to polarise the electorate around law-and-order sentiment for the state election planned for later in the year. He also hoped to crush the local section of the anti-uranium movement, in the interests of his mining industry backers. Finally, he aspired to leadership of the conservative political push that had gained momentum nationally since 1974. Bjelke-Petersen did succeed in partially deflecting the anti-nuclear agitation, but at the cost of creating a new protest movement.

It began at Brisbane's two universities. Shortly after the shock announcement, students met to plan their response. On 7 September, hundreds attended campus rallies followed by a brief, token march. There were no arrests or confrontations, but that would soon change. On 15 September, the government rammed its legislation through parliament, with Labor leader Tom Burns complaining that he'd had only one minute to study it after the first reading. (At one point, Burns shouted 'Sieg Heil' at Bjelke-Petersen, who retorted: 'He sticks up for the revolutionaries.') On 22 September, 21 people were arrested as police prevented an attempted march through the centre of Brisbane. On 12 October, the students tried to march again. When stopped, they filtered through to King George Square, where they sat and linked arms. Amazing scenes ensued:

> A student was addressing the police with the megaphone, saying that murderers and rapists were going free while police were standing around uselessly... As police hands grabbed for the megaphone, the students passed it to friends and it was tossed among the massed students like a basketball. A heavyweight

QUEENSLAND: BATTLES WITH BJELKE

210 ARRESTED IN QUEENSLAND MARCH

BJELKE PUTS THE BOOT IN AGAIN

210 people were arrested in Brisbane last Saturday, 3 December, for attempting to march peacefully in protest against the Queensland Government's ban on political street marches.

These latest actions by the police bring the number of arrests since the ban was instituted on 4 September to more than 800. This is the largest number of arrests ever made for a single cause in the entire history of Australia.

The arrests in Brisbane on Saturday were executed with the most ferocious display of violence on the part of the police witnessed so far. Now that Bjelke-Petersen's government has been returned to parliament by virtue of its notorious gerrymander, there are no holds barred on the police. The demonstrators from the 1500 strong rally in Fred Patterson Square (formerly King George Square) were kicked, punched and otherwise assaulted as they attempted to march up Albert Street. Women had their clothes torn off and one person has been hospitalised with injuries.

Following the pattern set by the last two large scale demonstrations, bail has been excessively high. This is part of the Bjelke-Petersen government's ploy to deplete the finances of the civil liberties movement in Queensland and thus render it politically ineffectual. Total bail so far paid out is now more than $30,000.

BJELKE AND THE BOOT

The mass arrests in Queensland show only more forcefully the contempt in which Bjelke-Petersen holds civil liberties and any organised opposition to his government's policies. The Liberal Party and State Labor Party are still effectively dissipated in the parliamentary arena and Bjelke's boldness knows no bounds. Despite mounting opposition from wide sections of the public — the churches, community groups, liberals, unions, the anti-uranium movement, the left and even members of the Liberal-National Party coalition, Bjelke-Petersen refuses point blank to lift the ban.

WHAT'S IN IT FOR JOH?

Obviously, it's not part of an electoral strategy. Bjelke doesn't have to face the people at the polls for another three years. Nor is it simply the act of an irrational and cantankerous provincial despot. Nor is it just that Bjelke doesn't like people marching in the street. Only 'left' political marches have been outlawed.

QUEENSLAND: BATTLES WITH BJELKE

RALLY and MARCH
THE REAL STORY
NOT THE PETERSEN MYTH

PETERSEN'S QLD IS A STATE WHERE YOU CANNOT PARTICIPATE IN A POLITICAL MARCH, ATTEND A MEETING IN A PARK, OR EVEN HAND A LEAFLET TO ANOTHER PERSON WITHOUT FEAR OF POLICE VIOLENCE OR ARREST

WHAT VIOLENCE?

The possibility of violence occurring in street marches is purely speculation, and based on no evidence other than the clash with police since the introduction of the march ban.

Where does the violence come from?

With the implementation of the present legislation there has been an increase in violence, created by continual confrontation between police and demonstrators.

This was most evident on October 22nd. last year when national demonstrations against Uranium were held, and only in Queensland did they result in violence.

44,000 marched in the streets of Sydney and Melbourne without arrests and violence. 5,000 tried to march in Brisbane when violence broke out because of the ban on marches by the Qld. Government.

THE LAW HAS CREATED VIOLENCE NOT THE DEMONSTRATORS.

LET'S SHARE THE STREETS

The disruption to traffic by the next march, if it were allowed, would be minimal. It would take only 15 - 20 minutes, if that, for a march of 3,000 people to pass any one given point.

The march route, and time for the route, have been widely advertised. Thus people should be aware that, if they do not wish to be inconvenienced, can take an alternative

WHO ARE THE RADICALS?

Yes, some groups are communist and marxist, but so what?

Groups and individuals that protest against the restriction on street marches represent a variety of political beliefs.

Would Bjelke-Petersen call the following groups communist:

Church organisations
Branches of the R.S.L.
Educationalists

Environmental groups
High School Student groups

Other supposed communists include:
Young Nationals
Young Liberals
Young Labour

Other supposed communists include:
Archbishop Arnott
Archbishop Rush
Dean George

All these people have questioned the stand taken by Bjelke-Petersen and the Queensland Government.

All groups and individuals whether they be right-wing, left-wing, communists or just concerned about the state of Queensland are uniting in their opposition to the ban. Such unity in the future is necessary to abolish a violent law.

Stuff your ban, Bjelke...

WE'RE MARCHING!

The Battler
PAPER OF THE INTERNATIONAL SOCIALISTS
ISSUE NO 39   1 OCTOBER   PH (03) 33-4142   20 CENTS

BJELKE-PETERSEN mobilised one-fifth of the entire state's police force to "defend" the streets from the "threat" of anti-uranium demonstrations. These thugs-in-blue loved every minute of it.

INSIDE: — How we won the right to speak in the '30's.

THE thin veneer of democracy has never looked more transparent than in Queensland right now.

That fearless crusader for Christianity, anti-communism and unhindered exploitation — Joh Bjelke-Petersen — has just stripped away one of the few democratic liberties we have.

On September 4 he announced...

"Don't bother to apply for a march permit. You won't get one. That's Government policy now...

"The day of the political street march is over. Anybody who holds a street march, spontaneous or otherwise, will know they are acting illegally."

A mere eighteen days later, one thousand demonstrators in Brisbane's King George Square found out just what he meant.

As soon as they lined up to march to Parliament House to protest against Bjelke's announcement, the 700 police — one-fifth of Queensland's police force — moved in and arrested the leading rows.

At the same time, Special Branch agents sprinkled throughout the crowd began picking out people and arresting them.

In all, 31 people were arrested, including an Anglican priest, a mother with her baby — and an undercover Special Branch agent who the cops grabbed by mistake!

The thirty protestors appeared in court next day. Four of the five women arrested were stripped, not once but twice, in full view of passing male cops and made to squat naked on the floor.

The official government line has been to stress the "disruption" that marches cause to traffic. But both Bjelke-Petersen and his supporters have made the real reason clear.

It's to clamp down on left-wingers in general — and especially the rapidly growing uranium movement

ADMITTED

As Bjelke-Petersen himself announced in Parliament, "... the streets of Brisbane will not be turned into a forum by the Communist Party or anyone else."

Bjelke admitted on September 5, "We were warned that anti-uranium demonstrations like the one in Sydney today were being planned for Brisbane. That's why this action has been taken."

Bjelke-Petersen's intentions are perfectly clear. The thirty arrests are just the latest in a long line of repressive actions.

Actions that include the conviction of Ted Zaphir, the Cedar Bay police rampage, the prosecution of the Seamens' Union on behalf of Utah, police bashing of student demonstrators and blacks, and refusal to pass on Federal funds to Queensland women's groups.

Bjelke isn't just some strange Queensland peanut headed for obscurity. He's acting as front man for Malcolm Fraser.

If Bjelke-Petersen gets away with it in Queensland, Fraser will soon be trying it nationally.

Together, they're out to smash all struggle against the bosses and their economic offensive.

They're out to wreck any movements we can build before it gets off the ground.

Well, we've got news for Bjelke. There's too many of us who can't afford to just sit back and trust in his tender mercies. There's too many of us who have no alternative but to fight the degradation of the system he represents.

There'll always be more of us to take up the fight — more than Bjelke's prisons could ever hold.

Ban all you like and arrest all you like, Bjelke-Petersen. WE'RE MARCHING!

policeman trampled over the seated students after it. Students
grabbed his ankles and he went down, collecting punches on the
way. Other police rushed in to rescue him. He was dragged bodily
from a struggling mass of students who still held on to his ankles.
Angry police then moved in on students who had assaulted the
man. Students linked arms and refused to let him go. Police grabbed
a girl student by the hair and flung her aside.

At the height of the melee, Queensland University lecturer Dan O'Neill called to the police: 'You've done something important for Queensland tonight. You've just radicalised a whole new generation of students.' This was more than mere phrasemongering. The civil liberties movement produced a political ferment unprecedented since the Vietnam war, and not only among students. John Minns recalls:

the small Brisbane left suddenly found itself in organising meetings
of hundreds which went on until the middle of the night, and it was
able to mobilise thousands of people – all in the course of a few
weeks.[7]

Bjelke-Petersen's response was to red-bait the movement's leaders, many of whom were well-known campus leftists – such as Dan O'Neill, whose history dated back to civil liberties struggles in the 1960s. The premier also warned against that 'well-known Communist Graeme Grassie' along with his comrade, Carole Ferrier, 'an extremist, revolutionary type of individual and a well-known member of the International Socialists.'[8] Joh's red-baiting did touch on a real feature of the movement: a layer of activists was not only moving rapidly leftwards, but producing some Marxist revolutionaries.

In the early stages, the government was tempted to suppress protest in King George Square itself, which the demonstrators were using as a rallying point. (Charles Porter reportedly wanted to declare it a public thoroughfare.) The police sent plain-clothes officers into the crowds to stir up trouble; TLC president Harry Hauenschild alleged that they had voted for march resolutions, then begun arresting those next to them. After the November 11 rally, the *Courier-Mail* reported this exchange:

A young bearded man smoking a pipe told police in a foreign
accent that he had been a policeman in Germany, but at least

the police in Europe were thinking people. A plain clothes policeman replied: 'You're a Nazi.' The young man said: 'If you call me a Nazi I'll call you a pig.' Police then said: 'That's it' and arrested him.

Most government MPs didn't seem to mind police thuggery. Frontbencher Bill Knox would say in 1978:

> If people show anti-social behaviour, they should be checked out. Police should be given a free hand. If it means shooting people on the spot, it is excusable.[9]

The official union movement showed little concern at first. When they held a general stoppage and 5,000-strong rally for Ted Zaphir, the union officials made no attempt to link union rights with other civil liberties, actively discouraging any suggestions for a street march. Initially, students carried the campaign, with marches from Queensland University preceding the first three rallies. The movement's composition began to change from 22 October, the date of a major anti-uranium rally. This was the first of many occasions where people concerned with other issues found themselves forced to confront the march ban. The uranium issue had aroused considerable interest among organised workers, especially in the maritime unions. When a large crowd attempted to march from King George Square, another drama unfolded:

> In a military-style operation, hundreds of police massed in position... As the marchers pressed forward and chanting grew stronger, police [called] on them to disband... The chant grew stronger: 'What do we want? The right to march. When do we want it? Now!' Dozens of people ran towards Queen Street and senior police acted: 'Get in and arrest them.'

With left-wing Senator George Georges among 418 arrested, these events had a sensational impact in parts of the labour movement. By this time, too, the state election was approaching. The election atmosphere brought to the surface a lot of working class anger towards Bjelke-Petersen and the political right. Civil liberties activists called another rally for 11 November, the day before the election and the second anniversary of the Kerr Coup. It proved to be the biggest rally of this stage of the campaign. Of the 197 arrested, most gave blue collar jobs as their occupations. Eleven days later, one of several people arriving to spend time in jail after refusing to pay fines told reporters: 'We regard ourselves as political prisoners.' They later said that other prisoners had given them 'a tremendous cheer' on their arrival.

These workers were not following any lead from the ALP or the TLC. Terrified of an electoral backlash, both Tom Burns and the TLC had opposed the rally and march, with the TLC devoting itself instead to a tame indoor meeting. Bjelke-Petersen promptly pounced on their timidity, saying:

> the TLC decision to hold its next protest in Festival Hall was a wise one. With the Zaphir case protest in the Roma Street Forum, it made the second time Trades Hall had proved the Government's point that street marches were unnecessary.

But the size of the 11 November mobilisation and the participation by significant numbers of unionists embarrassed the Trades Hall Executive, and the state election disproved ALP fears of a voter backlash, producing a substantial swing against the government. The TLC now felt obliged to deal with the campaign's leaders – organised in the Civil Liberties Coordinating Committee. Trades Hall agreed to co-sponsor a rally on 3 December for both the right to march *and* trade union rights. Union activists at a delegates' meeting in late November demonstrated considerable enthusiasm and defeated their leaders' efforts to rule out a march or open platform by 55 votes to 45.

Unfortunately, most union officials were again spooked by the prospect of confrontation, doing little to build the rally on the job, so the crowd was smaller than on 11 November. Still, an important precedent had been established. Civil liberties and union rights were now linked, and the right to march had become a union issue. Left-wing activists in the campaign, seeing the importance of union involvement and recognising that it would have to be built independently of Trades Hall, had already begun visiting workplaces. In six months, they addressed over 100 job and union meetings.

The TLC and ALP leaders deplored Bjelke-Petersen's repression, but it was another eight months before events obliged them to give even token support to civil disobedience. Still, the 1978 May Day march (a traditional, therefore legal, event) showed that a movement was continuing to grow outside their control. The leftist 'Red Contingent' formed the core of a 5,000-strong unofficial section of the march, constituting perhaps a majority.

Debating strategy

Arguments also raged within the civil liberties campaign itself. The most left-wing position, as described by Carole Ferrier and John Minns, saw the ban as:

> one aspect of the assault on the democratic rights of those groups which most needed the streets to express solidarity and protest: women's liberation, [Black people], anti-uranium activists and the organisations of the working class...we argued that by pursuing a militant course – marching and if necessary getting arrested – the issue could become a focal point for anti-State government sympathies.

They also emphasised the importance of the working class and opposed subordinating either militancy or class politics in order to appeal to 'moderates' such as the Young Liberals or the churches.[10]

Others wanted to concentrate on the single issue of the right to march, while favouring more cautious tactics such as letters to concerned groups and a few rallies, preferably off the streets. Most ALP members in the campaign and union officials such as Hugh Hamilton of the BWIU supported variants of this approach initially, as did the Communist and Socialist Workers' parties. Debates on whether to march illegally preceded every rally until March 1978, polarising one group of activists after another. The resistance to marching steadily lost ground, because it was continually voted down at civil liberties meetings and the rallies themselves. This reflected the rapid process of radicalisation. 'Given that the Labor left and the Communist Party opposed marching for some time into the campaign,' says John Minns, 'it astonished everyone (especially us) that the IS and a few independents consistently won the votes to march.'[11]

There was also a pacifist current, which believed that the campaign's greatest strength lay in winning over the churches. They favoured disobedience but didn't want it to be militant, preferring small 'guerrilla marches' to mass confrontations, which they saw as 'mindless knee-jerk leftism'.[12] The pacifists seldom won these arguments among the activists, who mostly recognised that only a movement prepared to *polarise right back* at Bjelke-Petersen had a chance of defeating him.

The first half of 1978 was comparatively quiet. When police prevented the Concerned Christians from singing gospel songs in April, the government was embarrassed, and when an April Fool's Day rally voted not to march, the massed police looked rather foolish. A Bundaberg dentist marched at 2:45 am down a quiet street with his dog Jaffa (illegally, because he and Jaffa had been denied a permit), giving everyone a good laugh. In June, Griffith University students outflanked the cops with an unannounced march. But such pinpricks couldn't move the government. Only a return to mass struggle could do that.

In July, the ALP squandered a perfect opportunity to get the masses back into the streets. When the party applied for a march permit for 8 July, the government called its bluff and granted one. After two days of panic, Labor cancelled the march, advancing comical excuses: they believed that 'two busloads of gay rights demonstrators would come from Sydney', apparently a mortifying prospect; Tom Burns suggested that the permit application had been 'a ploy', although he could not explain the point of this tactic.[13] More probably, the ALP leaders were haunted by memories of the large unofficial contingent at May Day and the invasion of the official May Day platform by various protesters, including women angered by sexist remarks. They feared that, in the event of a new mobilisation, they would again be challenged by militants to their left. In any case, Bjelke-Petersen profited a second time from the cowardice of organised labour's official leaders. The *Courier-Mail* scoffed:

> The Labor Party has made itself look idiotic... Indeed, its belief that there might have been disruption of the march by militant groups goes part of the way towards supporting what it has declared to be insupportable – the principle of banning street marches which could lead to street disorder.[14]

The ALP's retreat emboldened the government and its police, who promptly took the offensive, arresting 31 people at a women's liberation demonstration on 22 July. There had been no attempt to march, so the police attacked the crowd of 250 on the grounds that the use of 'obscene language' could have upset passers-by. The protest movement struck back one month later with an illegal march attempt following an anti-budget rally. As the anniversary of the march ban rolled around, Queensland was entering a new season of unrest, with a new organisation taking the lead: the Civil Liberties Campaign Group (CLCG), led by Senator Georges and based in the Labor left, was attracting up to 200 people to its meetings.

The high points of the second round were two mass mobilisations on 31 October and 7 December. By this time, because of the growing involvement

Sydney protesters rally in support of Queensland marchers March 1978

of trade unionists and the Labor left, Bjelke-Petersen faced a movement of national importance. ALP politicians and leading union officials of various political hues were turning up to march, even including right-wing NSW TLC secretary John Ducker. Queensland maritime unionists were now strongly committed. The march on 31 October featured a seven metre long banner reading: 'Unionists: Defend Democratic Rights.' When seamen were jailed after refusing to pay fines, their union shut down Queensland's ports, forcing shipping companies to pay the fines anonymously. The maritime unions stopped work for the 30 October rally, then held a 600-strong mass meeting to demand another, union-based mobilisation for December. These events coincided with mass picketing by meatworkers against the export of live cattle, which led to brawls with police, and with a prolonged brewery strike. Then, with the general temperature rising, the TLC voted for a march on Thursday 7 December, to be backed up by a stopwork.

By now, Bjelke-Petersen was feeling the heat. Angus Innes, a Liberal well known for his opposition to the march ban, won the Sherwood by-election, with the National Party coming fourth. The financial cost of enforcing the ban (cops, courts, jails etc.) was also mounting: over two years, it was conservatively estimated at $5 million.[15] There had been attempts by the Liberals, and even some National Party backbenchers, to retreat during the previous year, but the premier had shrugged them off. Now, Bjelke-Petersen himself felt obliged to make a concession. Although the TLC had not applied for a permit, the police offered one for Saturday morning.

The more conservative elements at Trades Hall were attracted to this offer, but Georges, the CLCG and the maritime unions opposed accepting it, arguing that the unions must show solidarity with other, weaker groups that were being systematically denied march permits. Also, a weekday stopwork and rally would have far more impact. Their views prevailed. Despite desperate appeals from Bjelke-Petersen, who booked a series of radio and TV spots, Brisbane saw its largest civil liberties rally: 4,000 participants and 383 arrests, with most of those arrested being blue collar unionists. There were also illegal marches in Rockhampton, Mackay and Collinsville.

The first half of 1979 was again relatively quiet. The burden of court cases following the mass arrests had combined with the steamy Queensland summer weather to bring a lull. Even so, March saw one portentous event: when police arrested three protesters on International Women's Day, constable Michael Egan threw his hat into the air and went to a demonstrator's aid. 'I knew I'd had a gutful and didn't want to be a copper any more,' he said. Egan revealed that 'most of the violence in the early days [of the campaign] was police provoked', and confirmed earlier claims that, in addition to the intimidating presence of the Queensland Special Branch, the police had sent provocateurs into the crowds of protesters to 'stir them up'.[16]

In July, a confidential National Party report recommended ending the march ban, which it acknowledged was: 'seen by a large section of the public as provocative'.[17] When July also saw another round of mass arrests, apparently presaging a new spring of unrest, the writing was on the wall. The government would have to manoeuvre carefully to retreat without admitting an embarrassing defeat. When the Campaign Against Nuclear Power sought a march permit for Hiroshima Day, the police knocked them back; they then granted one for a Nagasaki Day march at 6 pm. It was the first authorised protest march in Brisbane since September 1977. On 13 September, the police allowed 250 students to march against Fraser's failure to raise tertiary allowances. The permit limited the numbers and prohibited placards with sticks or metal rods; marchers with red flags had to put them away.

Queensland remained a repressive state, with civil liberties circumscribed. But Joh Bjelke-Petersen's attempt to drive dissent from Brisbane streets had failed.

Tom Burns' inept handling of the issue sealed his fate as Labor leader. His replacement, Ed Casey, was no improvement. Casey came from the ALP's traditional rural base, and his politics showed it. When he proposed an electoral redistribution, it retained the gerrymander; he voted for the *Justices Act*, which granted virtual immunity to state MPs; he condemned strikes in support of the 35-hour week; and the abortion issue allowed him, for a fleeting moment, the satisfaction of stealing a rightward march on Joh Bjelke-Petersen himself.

The campaign for abortion rights

In the realm of social mores, Queensland's conservative status was well established. The government reaffirmed the point quite conspicuously in 1976–78 when right-wing pressure groups wrecked two education projects. Encouraged by the sacking of four teachers on minor drug charges in 1976 and the subsequent persecution of gay teacher Greg Weir, a coalition of fundamentalist Christians and other rightists led by Mrs Rona Joyner took the offensive against a primary school social studies course called 'Man: A Course of Study'. Joyner, who believed that 'children don't go to school to learn to think,'[18] saw this course as an attempt to socially engineer children into dangerous social views and, ultimately, into socialism. After some honourable resistance in a few schools, the education system abandoned the course.

Joyner next turned her attention to the Social Education Materials Project. Her two organisations, STOP and CARE, objected to discussion of unmarried mothers, divorce, alternative lifestyles and homosexual marriage and to the 'secular, humanist, socialist philosophy' behind them.[19] Bjelke-Petersen, who knew a bandwagon when he saw one, promptly joined the attacks. He added, for the benefit of dissenting teachers: 'They have been warned and already 700 of their colleagues are unemployed in Queensland.'[20]

Queensland's abortion laws matched this repressive climate. In other states, changing attitudes and women's growing social power had forced through reforms after 1969, but Queensland continued to ban abortions. There was a degree of tolerance in practice as the police turned a blind eye; importantly, Children by Choice alleviated the pressure for law reform by organising to make referrals interstate a simple procedure: giving women in Brisbane, who would have been the heart of any campaign to change the laws, the option instead of a quick trip to NSW in case of pregnancy.

The Bjelke-Petersen Government had no pressing desire to upset the status quo, but two developments prodded it into activity. The activities of Greenslopes Fertility Clinic, which had performed abortions since 1977, became widely known in 1979. This was around the time the anti-abortion Lusher motion was before federal parliament, so the Right to Life (RTL) probably decided that it should show the flag in Queensland. In August, its best known member, Ed Casey, produced a petition demanding the clinic's closure and declaimed about the 'massacre of the innocents'.[21] Bjelke-Petersen and his more redneck ministers like Russ Hinze could not bear to be outflanked on the right by Casey, so they sent Health Minister Bill Knox off to draft amendments tightening up the legislation. Alison Anderson records:

> After several months of secrecy and rumours, the draft Bill finally reached the joint parties for preliminary discussion. Liberal MP Rosemary Kyburz caused a sensation by leaking its contents to the press. Proposed clauses included long jail sentences with hard labour for doctors, nurses, social welfare workers or even friends who helped a woman to get an abortion; restriction of all abortions to public hospitals, with compulsory notification of all occurrences to the Department of Health; the only grounds for a legal abortion were to be the imminent death of the woman concerned.[22]

Public outcry forced the government to allow three other grounds for abortion (rape, incest and proven deformity of the foetus), but even these were still hedged about with restrictions.

Pro-choice campaigners began gathering their forces after Casey's August speech. There was plenty of potential support among the public: Labor MP Bob Gibbs tabled a petition with over 3,000 signatures calling for free, safe, legal abortion on demand. But while RTL had a well-oiled machine, the new Women's Campaign for Abortion (WCA) had to start from scratch. It remained fairly small for several months, partly because of doubts that the Bill could really be as bad as was rumoured.

Others were also active. The Labor Women's Organisation, unlike Casey, stood on party policy and opposed the Bill, as did Children by Choice. These organisations also called for repealing the existing law, subject to conditions of medical supervision and conscience rights. Others opposed the Bill as being unenforceable or too restrictive. WCA distinguished itself partly by its stand for medically safe abortions, freely available and free of charge. However, its most distinctive features were its militant tactics, along with its emphasis on the rights of women as workers and its orientation to the trade union movement. Through WCA's efforts, many unions passed motions against the Bill or affirming women's right to choose. Some donated money, joined pickets or arranged jobsite meetings. Some union leaders endorsed the argument that this was an industrial issue, just like the right to work, but took no action. When WCA called a picket outside parliament in December, 13 union officials endorsed it. The TLC carried a resolution opposing the Bill and gave its assent to formal liaison between WCA and the Working Women's Charter Committee.

This was useful preparation; but the struggle first took on greater proportions in March 1980, as the first reading drew near. The National Women's Advisory Council passed a pro-choice resolution by a large majority. The issue dominated Brisbane's International Women's Day march, which 600 people joined. The demonstrators defied police instructions by unfurling large banners, 200 metres in length, before the end of the march. Fifty also marched in Townsville. Unmoved, the conservative parties pushed through a motion calling on the government to 'make sure the lives of unborn Queensland children are protected.'[23]

On 17 April, a crowd of women students rallied outside the parliamentary annexe, then sent a delegation inside to seek discussions with several ministers and with Rosemary Kyburz. Of the ministers, only Llew Edwards agreed to see them. Labor member Kev Hooper also spoke to them; one of the delegation,

Judy McVey, reported that he had called them 'broken down lesbians and man-haters'. The Queensland branch of the Australian Medical Association warned that the Act threatened a 'grave infringement of human rights', although the rights of doctors seemed to weigh at least as heavily in their considerations. They were alarmed by provisions that allowed for doctors to be struck off for advising patients in ways that *might* frustrate the Act, even if they were not actually breaking the law. On 28 April, the Women's Electoral Lobby called for a boycott of Queensland if the Bill proceeded. At the end of the month, there was another demonstration outside the parliamentary annexe, where police grabbed three protesters when the crowd pushed into the forecourt.

By this stage, some leading conservatives were already uneasy about the Bill. National Party State President Sir Robert Sparkes announced that he was against it 'in its reported form', while Russ Hinze remarked: 'I don't think it's got a hope in hell of getting through.' Some of the Liberal backbenchers were becoming increasingly unhappy as they read the mood in their electorates. By the end of April, four had promised to oppose it.

The first weeks of May saw further cracks in the government's facade. The Liberal Party's state organisation demanded that the Bill be scrapped. Party President Yvonne McComb said that more than 40 executive members were 'very unhappy'. Then, as 2,000 people packed the Town Hall on 17 May to show their hostility to the Bill, National Party management called for a secret ballot of MPs. It had become clear that a majority of Joh's own party opposed the Bill. In a public vote, he could hold the line; in a secret ballot, he would be rolled.

On 19 May, 5,000 RTL supporters marched through city streets, but few politicians were fooled by this apparent show of strength – the RTL crowd, bussed directly from church, was passive and not really representative of widespread public sentiment. Even as they marched, there were rumours that 12 Liberal backbenchers and four ministers were now against the legislation. Finally, on 20 May, a pro-choice crowd marched on parliament following a rally in King George Square.

The pro-choice campaign had been consumed by a debate over militancy, with some arguing that 'violence' would alienate ordinary people. Others believed that a militant campaign would build momentum. The 20 May action proved the fears of the 'moderates' to be groundless. Vicki Spiteri, one of the demonstrators, recalls:

> Groups from the office buildings joined the march. Many of these women had never been to a demo before. There they were in

their high heels, straight from work, and they wanted to attack Parliament House.[24]

The *Courier-Mail* reported: 'Demonstrators chanting pro-abortion slogans stood for four hours outside the gates... Arrests began as demonstrators attempted to tear down the gates.'

Inside parliament, Bjelke-Petersen put on a confident face. After two Liberal ministers announced that they would vote against the Bill, Russ Hinze set to work counting heads. He found that the government might fall short. Overnight, the phones ran hot, and Bill Knox had more bad news for Bjelke-Petersen next morning: on instruction from Liberal members, he was no longer moving the legislation as a government Bill. He would only move it as a private member's Bill. This freed ministers from the dictates of Cabinet solidarity. When the vote finally took place, 19 government members voted against, including four Liberal ministers and four National backbenchers. Ed Casey, meanwhile, had decided that 'loopholes' in the legislation were a pretext for opposing it after all!

Militancy in the streets had built the struggle, as it had in the civil liberties conflict. It had not only shown the movement's determination; contrary to the fears of the faint-hearted, it had also helped to attract support from a wider range of working class people.

Land rights and the Commonwealth Games

Earlier disputes had shown what an intransigent foe Aboriginal and Torres Strait Islander people had in the Queensland Government. Bjelke-Petersen was implacably hostile to land rights. To him, they were 'pure Alice in Wonderland'. If implemented, they would lead (nightmarish prospect!) to an independent Indigenous state in the Northern Territory, while the Northern Land Council (NLC) 'could hold mining companies and the entire nation to ransom'.[25] The premier was not always this lucid. In a 1981 confrontation, a member of the Queensland Aboriginal Advisory Council told him: 'That was our land since time began, even before the first Europeans landed here.' Bjelke-Petersen replied:

> But if you didn't have the American soldiers in the last war none of us would be here. You wouldn't be here. I wouldn't be here. You can't always use that argument indefinitely.[26]

The state's race relations were a national issue because, in this as in everything else, Bjelke-Petersen sought to give a lead to the political right throughout Australia. They became an international issue with the approach of the September 1982 Brisbane Commonwealth Games, as calls mounted for a boycott. South Africa's exclusion from the Olympics offered a precedent for politicising the Brisbane event, and Fraser's call for a boycott of the Moscow Olympics following the Soviet invasion of Afghanistan undermined the conservative parties' traditional 'keep politics out of sport' arguments. Plus, it was a classic protest opportunity, with TV crews arriving from around the world.

In 1981, Aboriginal representatives visited New Zealand to talk with anti-apartheid groups. In April 1982, the national Federation of Land Councils sent Les Malezer and Bob Weatherall to Africa to 'convince Commonwealth countries that Queensland has a racist government.'[27] But the delegation soon discovered that African governments were no more principled than our own. The Black states decided to come to Brisbane on the grounds that Australia had been 'a leader in opposing South Africa's apartheid policies,'[28] missing the point that one purpose of Malcolm Fraser's forays into African affairs was to distract attention from the racism in his own country. However, the boycott campaign did stir up political interest. It also prompted a certain amount of right-wing hysteria, with accusations that Libya was backing Aboriginal terrorists with a secret Maori army, trained in Cuba, somehow involved. (One unfortunate Maori, Raymond Renatta, was deported in March 1982 amid this agitation.) The claims were a classic beat-up, but they created the climate for further propaganda labelling Black protests as 'blood in the streets terrorism.'[29]

This laid the political basis for draconian 'security' measures under the *Commonwealth Games Act*. The Act gave the police virtual siege powers in large areas of Brisbane, including both university campuses and a 42-kilometre marathon route, as well as carte blanche authority to protect a wide range of 'notified persons' (VIPs). This included the right to search homes without a warrant and detain people without trial. The ALP charged that references to 'prohibited things' could be used to arrest wearers of political t-shirts and badges.

Although the Indigenous advocates were disappointed that no boycott eventuated, they pressed on with their protests. In August 1981, the Foundation for Aboriginal and Islander Research Action (FAIRA) organised a rally for land rights which marched twice: once illegally and a second time along the permitted march route. FAIRA's tent embassy in King George Square attracted international interest, volunteers from North Queensland communities and 'enormous support from white people too.'[30]

QUEENSLAND: BATTLES WITH BJELKE

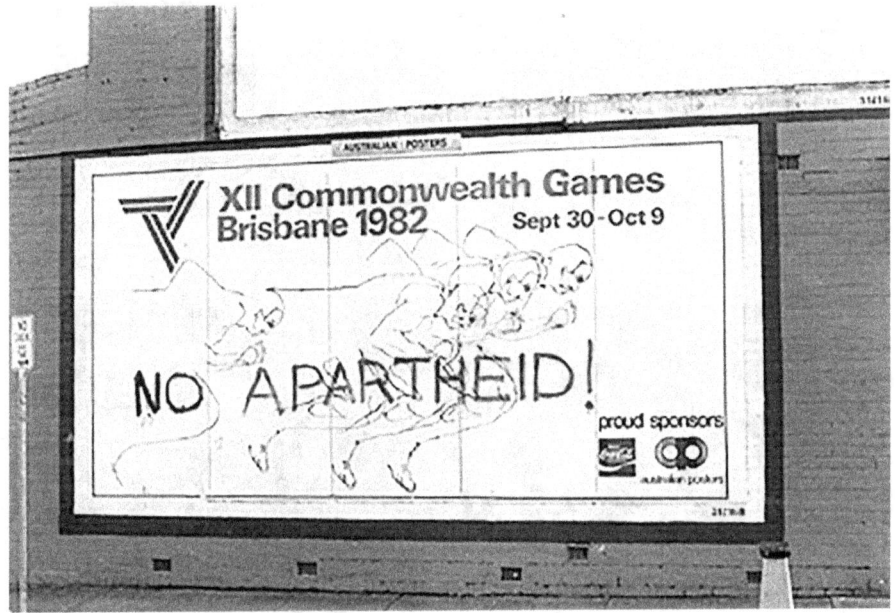

'No apartheid' graffiti painted by the photographer John Ellis on a billboard in Brisbane 1982

In April 1982, 300 people turned out for another rally. Indigenous people in Brisbane formed a Black Protest Committee, and white sympathisers launched a Land Rights Support Group. When Bjelke-Petersen visited New Zealand, he was met by demonstrators. Brisbane Black leaders insisted that they intended a peaceful protest, but many realised that, in activist Mick Miller's words, the police might 'try and provoke us...it is *their* game to bash people.'[31]

Anticipating international scrutiny of Queensland's much criticised Aboriginal and Islander legislation, Bjelke-Petersen hit on a way to confuse the issue: he declared in March 1982 that he would grant what he called a type of land rights under the title of Deeds of Grant in Trust. Aboriginal and Islander reserves would be abolished and their titles transferred to elected community councils, which would also manage them. This plan met none of the key criteria laid down by Canberra for land rights. Boundaries of reserves could be changed by the Lands minister or government; security of tenure wasn't guaranteed; and the Deeds could be revoked at any time. The government hoped that the manoeuvre would give some of the more conservative communities the illusion of land rights, while not really restricting opportunities for developers. In this it failed, because all sections of the Aboriginal movement condemned the plan.

So the case for demonstrating was as strong as ever as the Games approached. Tension was also mounting. British tabloids reported that 'dozens of helicopters' were ready to transport police armed with machine guns to confront demonstrators.[32] This was wild overstatement, but the government probably hoped that its elaborate preparations would discourage militant protests. If so, it hoped in vain. It was true that Indigenous leaders in Brisbane were rather cautious – initially, the Black Protest Committee wanted to confine things to a cultural festival – but more determined activists managed to inject greater fighting spirit into the actions, which encouraged white supporters to be more adventurous as well.

QUEENSLAND: BATTLES WITH BJELKE

BLACKS '76

DEMANDS:

* SMASH THE QUEENSLAND ACTS
* LAND RIGHTS NOW
* END POLICE BRUTALITY
* SMASH RACISM AND SEXISM
* ALL BLACKS ARE POLITICAL PRISONERS

For over 200 years the Australian Blacks have been oppressed by white people. Those days are fast drawing to a close. Blacks are now beginning to stand up for their basic human rights. If you are white, you are an oppressor of Australian Blacks, by reason of your very existence in Australia. Think about it - Do Blacks get the same education as you, the same housing? the same health care (including diet) ? and so it goes on, in almost every issue you care to mention, Blacks have been deprived by whites for 200 years now. If you are not doing something to solve the disgusting racial problem in Australia, you are then part of the problem.

There is a growing awareness in the Black community of who their oppressors are and the various forms of oppression that are inflicted upon them. This awareness hasn't just been gained in recent years but has shown itself ever since the white people colonized Australia. Now it is revealing itself in an increasingly more vocal expression for certain inalieable rights - the ones listed above are but a few of the many required to restore Black self - respect and dignity.

Blacks have said what they want, and how, and why, and when, in short, they have laid it on the line for all to see. They have done all they possibly could peacefully do to achieve these demands. The responsibility to answer their demands with action and understanding belongs to every Australian. It is how the world will judge us. But more importantly, it is how Aborigines will judge us.

SMASH THE QUEENSLAND ACTS

personal experiences of a young Black woman.

Most of us know about the Queensland Aborigines and Torres Strait Islanders Acts that rules over us and our lives. We've been trying to get rid of them for 8 years and haven't had any luck. The white people don't live under this sort of act like all of us do. You ask your mother and father or any old people about the way they had to go up to a white man and ask if they could go to town to buy clothes for themselves and their kids and other things they needed and see what they say about the Act. I could tell you what my mother told me; she told me she couldn't leave the reserve until the reserve until she w as married and so she was sent to other reserves to work, like washing for the white man and his wife and working for them and that was her job to get herself some money to buy herself some clothes and other things that she needed as well.

We are all still trying to get away from the Act, but we still have to keep on fighting those white cunts from ruling our lives. So don't just sit on your ass, get off it and show that you don't want white men telling us what to do.

LAND RIGHTS NOW

The right to unqualified possession of Aboriginal land- sacred areas, Dreamtime places, and traditonal sites- is as basic to Blacks as the right to worship in any church (or not at

Southwest Queensland Aboriginal leader Ray Robinson, finding that the police were stingy with march permits, promptly announced that 'Aboriginal... [people] will march where and when they want'.³³ Two weeks before the Games began, a civil liberties group carried out street theatre, combined with an illegal march. On 25 September, prominent Aboriginal public servant Charles Perkins called for marches without permits, although he met immediate disagreement from Aboriginal Liberal Senator Neville Bonner. (The Liberals later rewarded Bonner for his efforts to restrain the protesters by moving him to an unwinnable position on their 1983 Senate ticket.)

On Sunday 26 September, some 3,000 people, Indigenous and non-Indigenous, marched through Brisbane in a legal procession. They showed a measure of defiance by holding two unscheduled sit-downs in the streets. Two days later, they marched again. The police had granted a permit at the last minute: it was the first weekday daytime march granted a permit since 1977. Again, there were two sit-downs in defiance of permit restrictions. The police almost certainly relented on the daytime permit because militants had won the debate in the Aboriginal camp at Musgrave Park. The Black Protest Committee had resigned, making way for a new leadership called the National Black Unity Group, who were more prepared for confrontation.³⁴

The protesters concluded the week's actions with an illegal march which saw 500 people converging on the Games site at the Queen Elizabeth II stadium. Afterwards, one arrested demonstrator, FAIRA executive officer Bob Weatherall, declared: 'I'm only guilty under white law. I'm not guilty under Aboriginal law. I have the right to walk on my own land.'³⁵

The 1982 general strike

No matter how numerous the challenges to Queensland's right-wing government – over civil liberties, abortion or land rights – only one group in society had the muscle to seriously threaten Joh Bjelke-Petersen, and that was the trade union movement. The power industry unions in particular went toe to toe with him several times. From 1977 at the latest, it seems clear that Bjelke-Petersen had set his sights above all on smashing union power.

In October 1977, as the confrontations over street marches were beginning to mount, Bjelke-Petersen announced that government policy for the November state election would include the 'right to work'. He meant the term in its US usage, as an attack on the closed shop and unionism generally. The same Charles Porter who had sponsored the march ban motion put the proposal to the joint parties' meeting. The conservatives were in no hurry to act on the issue, however; perhaps they feared, as the Labor minister Mr Fred Campbell told the Liberal Party state convention in April 1978, that they would only weaken politically moderate unions while leaving left unions with greater muscle to dominate the union movement.[36]

A successful strike by Gladstone power workers in August 1978 appears to have stirred the premier's anger: he began talking about outlawing strikes in essential services. Within a year, Russ Hinze had prepared an Essential Services Bill.

The Bill gave the government sweeping powers. It could order an immediate return to work; sack anyone defying such an order for more than 48 hours; make collection of strike funds illegal; allow firms to sue for damages; assert direct government control of industry; deregister unions; and impose fines. Unionists could not choose jail rather than paying fines, so the way was open for the state to seize their property. Asked about the possibility of a general strike in response, Hinze was pugnacious: 'Let's see how good the union leaders are.'[37]

To pass such a law was one thing, to enforce it quite another. The unions gave notice almost immediately that they would resist, calling a job delegates' meeting on 18 October. On 23 October, Bjelke-Petersen lashed out at the power workers, declaring: 'we have reached the stage where work must surely be regarded as a contract'.[38] Three days later, the new Act became law. The unions remained defiant. In November, 2,000 trade unionists rallied in Roma Street Forum, while another 1,000 assembled at Ipswich. Then, in December, the power workers again stopped work...and Cabinet was not game to use its new powers.

The government let a further opportunity go by in March 1980. The power workers struck for 48 hours over the government's attempt to buy off key operators by offering them higher pay if they would guarantee power supplies during any emergency. Again, Bjelke-Petersen retreated. The first great confrontation did not come until 1982, during a campaign for the 38-hour week.

The power workers had already won a shorter working week. As late as July 1982, other unions and the government appeared to have reached an agreement on shorter hours, although railway workers were showing some dissatisfaction over the rostering changes they were being asked to accept. Bjelke-Petersen first stalled on the question of timing; then, when the unions protested, he withdrew his offer altogether. Probably, the decline of industrial militancy nationally that had resulted from the onset of recession encouraged him. But the unions began preparing for industrial action, with the railway

Queensland general strike 1983

Queensland general strike 1983

workers announcing a 48-hour stoppage from midnight on Sunday 15 August. The AWU, which had not been previously involved, called a stopwork of its government employees to consider action. By Monday, thousands of workers were on strike, but it appeared to be simply the latest round of an ordinary industrial campaign – and one being conducted against a background of trade union retreat all over Australia, owing to the emergence of a sharp recession.

Although Bjelke-Petersen declared a State of Emergency, he had done so before without acting on it. He also spouted aggressive rhetoric, announcing that union leaders would 'be knocked down in the rush of men wanting to get back to work,' presumably because of promises that 'anybody who turns up for work will have a job forever.'[39] Those who did not would face suspension, said Bjelke-Petersen. But Queensland workers were used to hot air from the premier. Bjelke-Petersen's attempt to make a hero out of Cairns railway employee Ian Stiff, who had announced his intention of scabbing, was nothing new either; earlier in the year, ALP Senator Jim O'Keefe had read into *Hansard* sections of a telephone conversation in which Joh praised apprentice electrician Steve Pearson for planning to sabotage power strikes.

So it was easy to discount his threats to use the Essential Services legislation and suspend workers. The *Courier-Mail* called them 'melodrama' and reported that quite a few members of Cabinet had cold feet.

It is unlikely that building workers' leader Hugh Hamilton took his own words any more seriously when he warned: 'The government has gone crazy... if anyone is sacked the industrial action will widen.' The union officials did not intend to mount a very militant campaign. At mass meetings on the Monday, they argued for a 24-hour stoppage instead of the 48 hours job delegates were demanding. They succeeded in winning over the Brisbane meeting, and most government workers in the capital returned to work after a day. In regional meetings, however, in the absence of the top officials, it was a different story. Townsville, Mackay, Bundaberg and Maryborough all voted to stay out for 48 hours. In Ipswich, a meeting greeted the union leaders with abuse and voted almost unanimously for the longer stoppage. The contrast with Brisbane was impressive; it suggested that the rank and file were fairly keen.

Only at the end of Monday, with the news that Bjelke-Petersen – encouraged by the union officials' retreat – had indeed suspended 3,500 railway workers, did this dispute suddenly became something out of the ordinary. On Tuesday 17 August, the premier moved to deregister 11 unions. These moves immediately brought new life to a fading union campaign. When TLC secretary Fred Whitby said that Cabinet 'must be smoking opium' to provoke the unions like this, many Queenslanders thought that he had a point.

The railways stayed closed; car workers, oil workers and coal miners walked off the job; and the AWU decided to bring its members out, as did glass and metal unions. The maritime industry stopped dead. Most important of all were the massive power cuts which shut down basic industry, seen as symbolising the strength of the working class.

Within a day, Bjelke-Petersen had begun to soften his stand, saying he would consider withdrawing the suspensions if the strike ended. By Thursday, according to the *Courier-Mail*, the Cabinet was contemplating the fact:

> that its Essential Services Legislation was ineffectual, having been told that deregistration moves against unions, fines on unions and the right of private citizens to sue for loss caused by strikes were impossible to enforce.

An unnamed minister lamented: 'It has been put to the test and found very wanting.' Columnist Ken Blanch revealed that the premier was so fearful of union militancy that he had rung a local Gladstone journalist to 'check the union climate in the city' before visiting to open a new aluminium smelter.

On Friday 21 August, the government capitulated. Talks in the Industrial Commission had failed to win any compromises from the unions, so Bjelke-Petersen unilaterally reinstated all the suspended railway employees and revoked all the *Essential Services Act* provisions. The Joh Bjelke-Petersen who appeared on television that night was a far cry from the arrogant bully Queenslanders were used to seeing. 'He had his head down,' socialist and union militant Mark Gillespie later recalled, 'none of the usual ranting and raving. A quick announcement, and he walked off.'[40] It seemed that a historic turning point might be at hand.

The TLC met over the weekend and decided to call a general strike, in support of the claim for shorter hours but also effectively demanding that Bjelke-Petersen step down. Hugh Hamilton is said to have pushed hard for this decision. In itself, an escalation did not seem unreasonable: with the government on the defensive, it made sense to seek further concessions. The trouble was that the union officials had not laid the basis for such a dramatic politicisation of the dispute, nor were they prepared to do so now.

The successful fightback that had rocked Bjelke-Petersen had been partly a spontaneous upheaval independent of the TLC, and there was no guarantee that the TLC could keep it going by fiat. Moreover, it had been largely *defensive*:

workers not immediately concerned with the 38-hour week had seen the suspensions as an outrage and had shown basic solidarity. It did not follow that they endorsed the other demands of the struggle.[41] The step to an *offensive* mass strike for shorter hours and to bring down Bjelke-Petersen would have required new efforts at mobilisation. The union leaders had to argue for the new demands, or at least give the militants on the job the green light to do so, and the process had to begin immediately. Finally, the momentum of industrial action by key unions had to be maintained. The TLC faced up to none of these problems.

For several reasons, therefore, a general strike was unsustainable. Probably, for all their talk of an indefinite stoppage, the officials intended it as merely another 48-hour affair. They were gambling that they could keep the rank and file out for that long without special efforts and that this would be enough to force a government cave-in. One key decision revealed the miscalculation: rather than maintain the existing strike momentum, they sent the electricity and power workers back to work over the weekend. When power was restored in large areas that had been previously blacked out, it had a great psychological impact. While the TLC claimed that the move would help to get the public on side, it was actually a signal that the trade union movement wasn't entirely serious about confronting the government.

By the time mass meetings assembled, there was a certain unevenness in the strike front. Certainly, the meetings were well attended – by about 6–10,000 in Brisbane – and all but unanimously voted for the official motions, but momentum quickly began building for a return to work. The leaderships of key federal public service unions voted not to join in. The Printing union executive endorsed the strike but hastened to reverse its position when it met resistance from members at Queensland Newspapers. Coal miners voted for 24 or 48-hour strikes rather than indefinite action. The AWU pulled out. On Tuesday, after a stormy meeting, the TWU followed suit.

It was still a very large stoppage, with a majority of unions participating, but this was observance rather than a struggle with forward momentum. The fact was reflected in a complete absence of political rallies by workers or anyone else, although a few hundred students at Queensland University went on strike in solidarity.

At this point, the TLC might still have rescued the situation by pulling the power workers back into the dispute. Coal handlers at the power stations wanted to join in. Brisbane Council bus drivers were also prepared to act. However, escalation was far from the union leaders' minds; rather, they hastened to end the strike at midnight on Tuesday. The railways stayed out longer, and various bans stayed on in support of the shorter hours demand, giving Hugh Hamilton a tenuous pretext for denying that the TLC was backing down. Privately, however, union officials conceded a 'technical retreat'.[42]

The collapse of the general strike allowed Bjelke-Petersen to restore his position and even to claim that the Essential Services provisions he had so ignominiously withdrawn had somehow helped him to prevail. The way was open for more aggressive National Party rhetoric, with Robert Sparkes calling for a 'specially trained elite group of military technicians' to combat power strikes.[43] And, while a successful general strike could have created space for a huge response to the protests at the Commonwealth Games a month later, its failure meant that the land rights campaign had to confront a newly confident government on its own.

For those of us on the far left who had often glibly advanced the general strike as a revolutionary tactic, these events were an education in the complexities of the class struggle. A general stoppage can be immensely powerful, shattering the will of the ruling class and its politicians; but, because it creates such an all-or-nothing, winner-take-all situation, it can also bring defeat and demoralisation if it isn't properly fought. Thus, in the Medibank confrontation, Bob Hawke had used a politically passive one-day general strike as a safety valve to deflate a promising industrial movement.

In Queensland, the union officials had turned initial victory into defeat in a curious bout of bureaucratic adventurism. The lesson for revolutionaries was that a general strike can only successfully challenge the power of capital and the state when the momentum of a working class movement is high and still rising – and when the movement's leaders have used the previous struggles to educate at least a sizeable minority of workers in the political implications of the industrial campaign. Union officials of the conventional type, with their bureaucratic mentality and political ties to the existing social order, cannot and will not do this. That, after all, was precisely the reason why the revolutionaries were fighting to build a movement of their own.

The failed general strike opened the way the for a greater tragedy. While the battle had left the government's anti-union legislation and the ruling class mentality associated with it somewhat dented, these still remained essentially intact. Bjelke-Petersen was to make use of both to smash the power workers during the early Hawke years, in the South East Queensland Electricity Board (SEQEB) dispute of 1985, a defeat that enabled the long-term decline of Queensland's labour movement.

9.
The oppressed fight back

Unity among the oppressed is, in a phrase from Brecht, 'that simple thing so hard to achieve'. But there is at least a starting point in the fact that their struggles so often overlap. In the Fraser era, Indigenous Australians spoke from anti-uranium platforms and were keen to take a shot at Joh Bjelke-Petersen. Women were active in strikes, from the Latrobe Valley to the Pilbara, and thousands of them took strike action in government offices and schools. Women led campaigns against environmental destruction. Every mass struggle was enriched by the migrant groups involved, who were sometimes very important indeed: for example, 80 percent of the Pagewood factory workforce were from migrant backgrounds. The lesbian and gay (later LGBTQI+) movements emerged in the wake of women's liberation and would have been virtually inconceivable without it.

At the start of the 1970s, the various movements against oppression tended to see themselves as part of a wider struggle to change society as a whole. This was partly because of the existence of a mass antiwar movement, to which everyone felt they belonged. It was also partly due to the high levels of industrial struggle, which gave people confidence in the labour movement as a force capable of seriously challenging capitalism. Even when the antiwar campaigns had ended, and the class struggle was in decline, the various movements continued to cross-fertilise. Take, for example, the emergence of protests against the Miss Victoria Quest in the early 1980s, where women's demands intersected with those of people with a disability. Demonstrators invaded the stage with placards, pointing out that the quest created an image of a supposedly ideal woman; people with a disability found that impossible to live up to. Provocative actions like these helped to change social attitudes significantly.

Gay Liberation contingent at Land Rights demonstration Sydney 1982

This book reflects the overlap between many struggles. The Aboriginal-led demonstrations at the Brisbane Commonwealth Games appear in the Queensland chapter – as they must, because the struggle against Joh Bjelke-Petersen was not a whites-only affair. Similarly, I consider feminism's impact on the peace movement in an earlier chapter.

There was much common ground, but the 1970s was also the decade that entrenched the idea of *independent movements* of the oppressed. At the start of the decade, radical activists had emphasised the importance of understanding the specific oppression of Indigenous people or women and of mobilising specific movements for the rights of each. These initiatives were valuable in opening up new fronts in the struggle against capitalism and developing critiques of the prevailing social order – so valuable, perhaps, that it was easy to lose sight of their limitations. By the early 1980s, the belief that 'autonomous' movements were needed for every oppressed sector had become an article of faith on the left; similarly, readers will automatically expect a history of the era to include several specific discussions of such movements.

Such discussions may help to ensure that particular oppressions and particular struggles are more fully treated, but the obsession with autonomy also reflects the defeats of the 1970s and 1980s. As the various challenges to Fraser exhausted themselves, and particularly as organised labour looked less and less like a force capable of challenging capitalism, most people involved in fighting oppression withdrew into sectionalism. Autonomy theories made a virtue, not to say a shibboleth, out of what was really a retreat. The growing fragmentation made the 'movements' weaker – if one could still apply that term to what might, by the 1980s, be small action groups, lobbies trying to extract concessions from the welfare state, or (at worst) mere trendy networks designed to advance careers.

As the fragmentation continued, the 'particularism' sometimes became very particular indeed, because there were Black women, lesbians with disabilities, elderly migrants and so on, anticipating the later emergence of identity politics. 'Each attempt to claim representativeness for a particular oppressed group finds that that group must be further broken down,' observed marxist-feminist Ann Curthoys in 1986.[1] She explained how this could undermine our ability to develop a coherent alternative to the existing social order:

> It is argued that nothing of value can be said about the position or policies of a particular group of people other than by members of that group. Thus only women can say anything of value about the

position or the strategy of the women's movement, only Aborigines likewise... And so we are reduced to categories which supposedly define us...we become white heterosexual women, or black homosexual men, or whatever... Analysis is in this way confined to a smaller and smaller canvas. Attempts to understand experience across gender and ethnic lines become rarer, and when they exist are open to condemnation and ridicule... Our problem now is how to regain a belief in the possibility and effectiveness of collective action across gender and racial boundaries, without losing that understanding of specific cultural situations that we have so painfully begun to acquire.[2]

This discussion of Indigenous Australians, migrants and sexual politics takes that challenge as its starting point. In the Fraser era, different oppressed groups found themselves under fire and resisted. Given the prejudices in society, they sometimes needed separate organisation.[3] The history shows, however, that winning victories in the struggle mostly required *unity*, for which the soundest basis was working class solidarity.

Aboriginal and Torres Strait Islander people

Aboriginal and Torres Strait Islander people[4] have been besieged for two centuries. Under Whitlam, some of the pressures abated; under Fraser, they again began to mount. In central Australia, Aboriginal people accounted for 663 out of 889 registered jobless in 1976, while the federal government estimated that out of 30–35,000 Indigenous people in the workforce nationwide, about 14,000 were unemployed. Mike Braham, director of the inner-suburban Chippendale community centre, described the consequences in Sydney, particularly for those in the grip of hire purchase companies:

> Things are so tough here that about 12 people a week come to borrow a dollar or two for milk or a bit of food to see them through... After seeing the way the blacks are hounded, hunted and impoverished I'd put South Africa on a pedestal.[5]

The Aboriginal Medical Service reported that 25 percent of children under five in nearby Redfern were so malnourished that they would suffer brain damage, and 20 percent of children had spent more than two months in hospital before their first birthday.⁶ A continent away, in Perth, the Princess Margaret Hospital had admitted 20 percent of the city's Aboriginal children in 1974, more than half of them undernourished. Things were no better in more remote areas; the infant mortality rate for Northern Territory Aboriginal people was 75 per thousand live births, compared to 16 for whites.

Black communities were often locked in conflict with the police. In August 1977, Brisbane police invaded two hostels and arrested activists, attacked a camp of homeless where they threw several elderly people into the river, then picked a brawl in the Ship Inn in Woolloongabba. When Black people at the Inn gave a rather good account of themselves in the fracas, the cops retaliated with a wave of harassment and arrests, charging three people with attempted murder.⁷ In rural areas, the police complained bitterly about the role of the Aboriginal Legal Service in monitoring their work and documenting abuses. At that time, of course, the extent of Black deaths in custody was not so widely known.

The land has an immense importance for Aboriginal and Torres Strait Islander people. The demand for land rights goes back a long way, but it was the struggles of the 1960s and 1970s that made it front page news. It formed the more important of two battlefields, with calls for better welfare provisions and community control constituting the other. Neither battle was easily won.

Aboriginal people's political and social power was generally fairly limited. They had long been a small minority of the population, although a more recent trend encouraged proud self-identification. They did not form an important voting bloc outside the Northern Territory; nor have a middle class with economic leverage; nor dwell in sufficient numbers in any urban area to use riots or the threat of them to put pressure on the state (as the ghetto Blacks in the USA had done). The 1976 census estimated a population of 14,000 Indigenous people in Sydney, the highest urban total. Apart from a declining presence in the outback pastoral industry, they lacked industrial muscle. In all these ways, they were in a far weaker position than, for example, migrant workers or white women.⁸

Consequently, external support was particularly important. Indigenous people needed positive publicity, both in Australia and overseas, and solidarity from sections of white society, particularly trade unions and social movements such as that against uranium mining. Unfortunately, backing from these sources declined during the Fraser years. Attempts to gain widespread international publicity during the Brisbane Commonwealth Games were a failure – partly, it seemed, because Fraser had managed to buy immunity on the issue of

Australia's Indigenous people by conspicuously condemning racism in southern Africa. The unions were losing confidence in their ability to fight, while the anti-uranium campaign began to sag from 1978.

Whitlam's reforms had encouraged some Indigenous people to look to Canberra for help. But, while the Fraser Government proceeded with legislation to grant large areas of land in the Northern Territory, Fraser scaled down Whitlam's Act, despite a 1,000-strong Alice Springs protest rally. Aboriginal communities were no longer to control all roads running through their land, and Fraser gave the Northern Territory Government the power to pass laws on the day-to-day operation of land rights. (In 1978, the Territory passed laws allowing certain whites to enter Aboriginal lands without permission.) Most crucially, the Fraser version omitted a clause granting land rights based on need. This meant that people living in towns, whose connections with particular areas had been destroyed, and those who worked and lived on cattle stations could not establish land claims.

In every other area, Fraser had only disappointments to offer. The Aboriginal Medical Service which had documented the grim health situation in Redfern applied for a grant to improve the local people's nutrition but received only half of what it wanted – from a Department of Aboriginal Affairs (DAA) that finished 1976 with considerable unspent funds. The 150 Aboriginal housing associations that Whitlam had encouraged were obliged to dismiss employees. The government refused to fund a health service based in Darwin, pleading a lack of cash; it took two sit-ins at the DAA office to win some limited funding. Despite the jobs crisis, the government wound down the activities of the Department of Employment's Aboriginal section, then demoted an Aboriginal public servant who commented publicly on the cutbacks.[9]

Fraser also scrapped the National Aboriginal Consultative Council. In its place, he convened a National Aboriginal Conference. Altered electoral boundaries gave more weight to people in traditional rural areas, apparently in the hope that they would be less demanding than the urban activists.

Cuts to programs in 1976 were so severe that leaked public service documents expressed fears of 'a sharp reaction in the [Black] community',[10] and this was only the start. By 1982, Indigenous Australians were $213 million short of what Fraser had promised them in 1975. Spending on Aboriginal Affairs in the 1981–82 budget was over 35 percent lower in real terms than under Whitlam.[11] The first minister, Ian Viner, gradually exhausted his credibility; so Fraser put Fred Chaney in charge. The *National Times* naïvely boosted him as 'the best Aboriginal Affairs minister since...Arthur Phillip',[12] but Aboriginal people in

Redfern had a more realistic view of the Chaneys of this world. 'They never leave their offices in North Sydney,' said Sylvia Scott of Murrawina ('Black woman') preschool. 'Fred Chaney has been in Redfern once: we expect to get a letter next year just on election time.'[13]

It was hardly surprising that many communities joined the 'outstation' movement, turning their backs on the marginal position white society allowed them and seeking to build new lives away from white-controlled centres. But others chose, or were obliged, to stand and fight, as symbolised by the 1976 decision to set up an 'Aboriginal embassy' in Canberra for the first time since 1972.

It was at Aurukun on the Gulf of Carpentaria that the Fraser Government prepared the most bitter disappointment for Aboriginal people. The strong Aurukun community had learned from the experience of nearby Weipa how destructive mining could be, and they had fended off mining companies in the past. After Whitlam's fall, a consortium of these companies secured a mining lease from the Queensland Government. This violated written promises from that government that no mining would go ahead without the community's consent, making the people particularly determined to resist. Fourteen of them occupied an airfield and mining camp at Tipperary, while some trade unions expressed support.

The community took legal action and won in the Queensland Supreme Court, but Premier Bjelke-Petersen then appealed successfully to the Privy Council in Britain. The state government seized direct legal control of Aurukun and Mornington Island reserves from the churches (who had been too sympathetic to the Indigenous cause for Bjelke-Petersen's liking) and sent in administrators in May 1978. The traditional owners refused to let administrators leave the airfield, occupying community facilities to show that they intended to control their own affairs.

The Aurukun community expected Canberra to help them – after all, hadn't Fraser told a national Aboriginal conference that 'we will not fail these people'?[14] Federal parliament did pass an Act in April allowing community control of Aurukun and Mornington Island reserves, but Bjelke-Petersen simply responded by declassifying them: they were technically no longer reserves. Reluctantly, the Aurukun and Mornington Island Councils agreed to a six-month trial of the new system. Before the six months had expired, however, Bjelke-Petersen dissolved both councils, replacing them with his own agents; meanwhile, his government had constantly meddled in their affairs and withheld funds.

THE OPPRESSED FIGHT BACK

Aurukun banner and Land Rights demo Sydney 1982

On 16 May, the Queensland parliament passed an Act giving Bjelke-Petersen the power to sack the local councils and deny basic legal rights. Despite pleas from Aboriginal Liberal Senator Neville Bonner, Minister Ian Viner blandly announced that the federal government would accept Bjelke-Petersen's actions. In fact, the Fraser regime appeared to be implicated itself; *The Age* reported:

> Mr Viner said he and his opposite number, Queensland's Local Government minister, Mr Hinze, had worked hard on the legislation and it should be given every chance to work.[15]

Fraser had the power to declare the communities self-managing and free of state control. He refused to do so, preferring to posture about ending white rule in Zimbabwe. In 1979, four more Queensland reserves at Yarrabah, Kowanyama, Cherbourg and Mossman Gorge asked Canberra to declare them self-managing, to no avail. On the contrary, Canberra continued negotiating with the state government without reference to the communities. Fred Chaney met with Aboriginal Council members, who told him that the 50-year leases Bjelke-Petersen had provided were no substitute for full land ownership. Chaney replied arrogantly that there was 'too much sloganising' going on.[16] He undoubtedly had the same attitude towards uranium mining.

Ranger and uranium

Uranium mines have cost Aboriginal people dearly, beginning with the postwar mine at Rum Jungle in the Northern Territory. This contaminated about 100 square kilometres of the Finniss River flood plain. In the 1970s, the miners again turned their attention to Aboriginal land, after finding huge deposits in Arnhem Land. This was a beautiful region populated mostly by traditional owners, and the local people feared that mining could ruin it and them. Oenpelli Council chair Silas Maralngurra argued:

> Balanda [white man] push, push, push, – soon pubs everywhere and they will kill the race – look at the Larrakia. Darwin is their country, and they are living on the rubbish tip.[17]

Lucrative royalties (up to $25 million a year) could not begin to compensate, and the Commissioners believed that the traditional owners 'would happily forgo the lot in exchange for an assurance the mining would not proceed.' While recognising that the traditional owners of the Ranger site and the NLC were opposed to the mining of uranium, the Commission concluded that 'their opposition should not be allowed to prevail.'[18] The Commission, after all, belonged to Fraser, who wanted mining to go ahead. Aboriginal people would have the right to negotiate the terms, but not to refuse. If they refused, Fraser would install an arbitrator, and they risked losing the land along with the *Land Rights Act* and the NLC.

The NLC was negotiating under duress. Even so, it had two sources of bargaining power: the determination of Northern Territory Indigenous communities to resist; and their links to Black and white supporters in the southern cities. There, the land rights struggle was allied with the movement against uranium mining – raising in turn the prospect of trade union action. The Black women's paper *Koori-Bina* advised:

> There are two ways in which we must proceed. First we must support the Aboriginal communities in developing the kind of determination and solidarity that began the modern land rights struggle... The other way to proceed is to enlist the support of the white Australian working class culminating in union action to prevent the destruction of our lands. It was from the unions that the Gurindjis obtained their greatest support... The Land Councils

are aware of the critical need for union support and have asked supporters in the southern cities to ask for union bans.[19]

Initially, the union response looked fairly encouraging, so the government moved decisively to cut the links to the south.

NLC chair Galarrwuy Yunupingu, along with two traditional leaders from Oenpelli, had decided on a speaking tour to coincide with anti-uranium demonstrations in Melbourne and Sydney at the end of March 1978. When he heard this, Ian Viner summoned Yunupingu and the NLC's white manager, Alex Bishaw, to a conference. After the meetings, at which pressure from Viner was apparently complemented by advice from Bishaw and Charles Perkins to scrap the tour, Yunupingu cancelled it.

Marcia Langton, general secretary of the Federal Council for the Advancement of Aborigines and Torres Strait Islanders, responded sharply to this retreat, writing:

> the repercussions are many, the most serious being the severing of ties with southern and urban blacks, and the consequent concession to the government-propagated myth of 'southern stirrers'.

The NLC, said Langton, was 'a victim of the power game of the government and the mining companies'.[20] It was not to be the last time.

Negotiations proceeded until September 1978, when Stephen Zorn, a professional negotiator, initialled a draft agreement with the government. It provided for substantial royalties (although some thought that Zorn could have done better), but the environmental safeguards left much to be desired. There was also wide scope for the government to decide whether it was 'impossible or impracticable' for the miners to meet them. Zorn told the NLC that the deal was not as good as it should have been but cited the 'constant threat that the government would use arbitrators and take away what had been gained in the negotiations.'[21]

Yunupingu reported that Fraser had threatened to stop Aboriginal people from going back onto tribal lands: 'They threatened us. It was long, tough and hard.'[22] The NLC accepted the deal 'under protest', as its deputy chair Gerry Blitner put it. Even as it did so, there were signs of mounting dissent.

In Darwin, police had removed Black and white demonstrators from the Ranger office. Telegrams arrived from four Aboriginal communities demanding

Indigenous activist at MAUM march, 3 August 1978

the right to send representatives to the NLC's deliberations. After these concluded, eight communities sought an injunction restraining the Council from signing the agreement, forcing it to review the issue. One thousand Indigenous people arrived in Darwin to protest the deal. Traditional landowners at Oenpelli voted to reject it, and 300 people from Goulburn Island angrily confronted Yunupingu. The NLC then agreed that the communities would be fully consulted about any agreements. Consultations would include those living outside Oenpelli but with a traditional interest in the land.

The government was obliged to further apply pressure, inducing Yunupingu to call a secret meeting at a remote location. On the second day, the Council met with Viner, who again secured its reluctant acceptance of the agreement – but very much on the understanding that the final say depended on the communities. Only two delegates voted against, but one of the dissenters, Leo Finlay, indicated that the decision was actually quite vague:

> There was never an actual motion. We put up our hands but no one knew what exactly we were agreeing to. I relied on the Oenpelli people because I knew they were strong and would not let the NLC rush them.[23]

Viner and some of the Council then flew to Oenpelli, but no real consultation took place. Only four of the 30 or more traditional landowners were present; the rest refused to appear. Silas Maralngurra left the meeting in disgust. After addressing those present, and without actually seeking their consent, Viner flew to Darwin and announced that they had agreed to uranium mining.

Later, in order to force through a mining project at Nabarlek in 1980, the government announced special legislation to forestall a likely legal victory by Aboriginal owners. A year later, it rushed through further legislation to change the boundaries of Kakadu National Park, so that mining companies could again pursue the almighty dollar with impunity. The anti-uranium campaigners in the south protested, but they were themselves a declining force by now.

In a 1977 interview, Bruce McGuiness of the Aboriginal Co-operative in Melbourne had warned about uranium mining:

> They put up the pretence of consultation. They do it all the time.
> They have no intention in the first instance to listen to what Aboriginal people are saying.[24]

It had not taken very long for Ian Viner and Malcolm Fraser to prove McGuiness right.

Noonkanbah: 'If we all stand together'

The Northwest was the last Australian region apart from the central deserts to be invaded by Europeans. As they did elsewhere, white pastoralists who arrived in the 1880s imposed a system of virtual slavery. Finally, after the famous 1946 strike in the Pilbara, wage labour came to the Aboriginal workers of the Northwest. The exploitation did not end but took on new forms. When Aboriginal people became eligible for social security benefits in the 1960s, the pastoralists found ways to channel much of the cash into their own pockets. In 1969, the standard pastoral award was applied to Aboriginal station hands, following the historic Gurindji strike of 1966, but with a 'slow worker' provision allowing employers to pay as little as $20 per week.

By this time, there was considerable unrest on the stations. Most Aboriginal people in the Kimberley either walked off or were evicted, gathering at the nearby township of Fitzroy Crossing. One of these groups was from a station called Noonkanbah.[25] At Fitzroy Crossing, they found only squalor. What hopes the people held for the future lay in the land demands they began making in

One of the first big Land Rights marches, which brought together the issues of Land Rights and uranium, Melbourne 1976

1972 and 1973, encouraged by the growth of the national Black protest movement and the more enlightened policies of the Whitlam Government.

In 1976, the Noonkanbah station was advertised for sale. The Aboriginal Land Fund Commission acquired it and placed it in the hands of the WA Aboriginal Lands Trust. A 200-strong Black community returned to the station in September; finding it very run down, they set about restoring it. Over the next two years, their confidence grew. But these years also saw a renewed interest in the region's mineral wealth. WA Premier Charles Court, who had built his career on resource development, was keen to crown it with major projects in the Kimberley. Court had no patience with opponents:

> Interviewed in 1977...he remarked that before any development project could begin, three things had to happen: first, the site would be deemed sacred or of historical significance to some group; secondly, the trade union movement would place it under a black ban; and thirdly, conservationists would declare it the last remaining location of some rare species... Challenged on his basic beliefs, his reflex action was to portray opposition as left-wing conspiracy or anarchistic dementia.[26]

By May 1978, 497 mineral claims had been pegged on Noonkanbah station without any consultation. One company interested in exploring for oil was Amax, a multinational with strong links to BHP and CSR. In October 1978, Amax selected a drilling site which it apparently believed would not infringe sacred sites. The WA Aboriginal Heritage Act allowed for protection of any 'sacred, ritual or ceremonial site', but the legislators had probably understood this to mean specific features, narrowly defined. At Noonkanbah, by contrast, as anthropologist Kingsley Palmer reported after visiting there:

> although certain places...were recognised as being of particular importance for one reason or another, the whole land was recognised as being endowed with spiritual essence.

Capitalist society with its drilling projects could not be reconciled with the community's culture and tradition. Peter Bindon of the Western Australian Museum reported this after touring the area. Sent back to try again, he reported a second time that 'the whole area within which any drill hole could be located by the company falls under the influence of the sacred sites.' A long, intricate tug of war followed. At times, Amax seemed ready to pull out, but Charles Court dug in his heels.

In May 1979, the Noonkanbah people sent a representative, Dicky Skinner, to Perth with a petition against Amax:

> These people have already made the place no good with their bulldozers... They mess up our land. They expose our sacred objects. This breaks our spirit. We lose ourselves as a people.

The petition made a media splash. Skinner followed it up with an address to the WA TLC, which carried motions of support and sent letters to Amax and CRA. But, around the same time, Cabinet met and reaffirmed its hard line. 'I do not want either the local or the overseas people in Amax to feel I have not personally followed this matter through,' wrote Court. Acting Minister Dick Old formally instructed the state museum to give its consent, whereupon the government authorised the company to drill.

On 15 June, a company representative sought access to Noonkanbah station but was turned back at the gate after verbal exchanges. This event made the Perth papers, and either Court or the company apparently decided on a tactical retreat. The issue disappeared for almost nine months. In 1980, having won an election, Court was ready to try again; in March, contractors entered the property, accompanied by police. However, resistance was also stiffening.

Sympathisers rallied at St George's Cathedral in Perth. The relevant unions recommended bans on all work for the Noonkanbah drilling. The most important were the TWU, whose members would have to transport a rig from Broome, and the AWU, which covered the drilling crew. Bob Hawke called on Amax to pull back, while the AWU suggested that all nine oil rigs operating in WA could be closed down if drilling at Noonkanbah went ahead. The unions' assertiveness reflected the strengthening of their industrial position between 1979 and 1981. Noonkanbah was delighted. The community wrote:

> So we are very pleased that all these people are coming out to help us, the Trade Union mob trying to stop Amax, and all the other people. That never happened in the first place. If we all stand together like this we can be friends and have respect for each other.

Ivan McPhee and Nipper Tabagee came from Noonkanbah to Perth to address supporters, including the TLC. Later, some 30 fringe dwellers from

Swan Valley briefly occupied the city's main cemetery, saying that their sacred sites deserved the same respect as white cemeteries. Another Perth demonstration of 500 people took place on 2 April. Back at Noonkanbah, a session of Aboriginal song and dance lasting until 3 am gave the local people enough of a psychological advantage to intimidate the contractors, who departed the site when the community confronted them the next day. This unexpected victory had an impact on Indigenous people around the country. Said poet Jack Davis:

> For years we had been demonstrating for land rights. I think to most blacks the call for land rights was slightly nebulous... But what happened at Noonkanbah seemed to solidify their feelings.

The links with trade unions continued to improve, but rank and file support outside Perth was limited. In April, Dicky Skinner met in Derby with a two-person TLC delegation who had toured workplaces to assess the level of support:

> The labour force in the Kimberley was largely ununionised and anti-Aboriginal, and it became clear that the muscle would have to be applied at higher levels to be successful.

In some cases, unionists' main motivation was to settle old scores with Charles Court.

Even so, the prospect of union intervention worried Amax. In late April, there was speculation that the company was getting cold feet. Noonkanbah also showed signs of becoming an international issue, after Jim Hagan of the National Aboriginal Council addressed a United Nations sub-committee in Geneva, with US television networks picking up the story. But Court was tenacious. In May, he visited Noonkanbah personally to talk to the Aboriginal owners; the exchange left both sides as far apart as ever. In July, Amax transported a water drilling rig to the site, despite a token blockade by the local people.

July also saw the first of two defections by prominent Aboriginal activists. John Toby, who had previously led a struggle against attempts by CRA to mine diamonds at Argyle, suddenly made a private deal with the company, for which the Kimberley Land Council condemned him. It was an ominous precedent.

At 1 am on 7 August, a convoy of 49 vehicles set out from Perth. Near Karratha, police arrested six picketing union officials. In Roebourne, 40 Aboriginal people protested as the convoy passed. Two more union officials were arrested at Port Hedland. Then, just north of the town, 160 Indigenous protesters blocked a bridge, and police had to push them back. Another 200 protesters greeted the convoy near Broome. The Noonkanbah community also decided to oppose the convoy: 60 men established a blockade at Mickey's Pool, where the road dipped into a sandy creek and no detours were possible. After a night-long standoff, police and Aboriginal police aides cleared the blockade. The cause seemed lost until the news came through that the drilling crew, all trade unionists, had met and voted not to work the rig. Court's hard-line tactics had exploded in his face.

Six months earlier, the AWU had unionised the crew on this rig. They were not particularly pro-Aboriginal, but some of them felt that important union principles were at stake. During several meetings, they stood their ground while CSR, under ACTU pressure, announced that it would not operate the rig without the union crew. Amax, after talks with Bob Hawke, was again willing, if not eager, to pull out, but Court had an ace yet to play: he arranged for Amax to transfer its rights to the state government, which then passed them on to a $2 shelf company. The technicality got CSR off the hook, so drilling could go ahead with a new crew. Court also chose his moment well. For some time, his government had secretly been cultivating Ken Colbung, chair of the Aboriginal Lands Trust. Colbung, who had previously backed the Noonkanbah community, suddenly called on them in August to lift the ban on drilling, arguing that Aboriginal sites were not at risk.

Court chose that day to start the drilling, and Bob Hawke immediately made conciliatory noises, forswearing any 'retribution'. That was to be expected; this man would soon preside over 'national reconciliation' – then sell out the Indigenous people in 1984 by scrapping plans for uniform land rights legislation. The bravery of an isolated Aboriginal community, together with the honourable actions of a small minority of trade unionists, had given Court a tremendous battle; but the wider union mobilisation that could have defeated him did not occur. It was fitting that, after this disgraceful chapter in Australian history, the drilling at Noonkanbah yielded a dry hole.

A fight on many fronts

Indigenous people also fought for their rights on many smaller fronts. In New South Wales, a 1976 Land Rights Conference elected an independent Land Council and demanded the abolition of the Lands Trust, an unrepresentative body to which the Wran Government had granted a small area for lease. Council president Allan Woods was one of a group occupying 56 acres owned by the Lands Trust at Llandilo near Penrith. This linked the land rights struggle directly to the needs of homeless Indigenous people in Sydney, because the

Indigenous demonstration about welfare and land rights 1982-83

Gunya Way Council, organisers of the occupation, were simultaneously applying for funds to build emergency dwellings for the homeless.

In 1980, Indigenous people joined other protesters at Middle Head Beach in a campaign to stop sandmining. Along with the environmental issues, the protesters were concerned about a sacred site at the southern end of the beach. It was quite an event:

> The dredging goes on, but the backdrop is quite extraordinary – mass confrontations, mass arrests, songs of solidarity ringing through the forest, protesters falling out of trees as bulldozers push them down. Whites and Aborigines, united in passionate defence of the beach, have broken down the barriers between them in a way that is unprecedented in the area.[27]

In 1982, the Redfern Aboriginal Legal Service launched a supreme court action demanding the return of nearly 10,000 hectares taken from Black people between 1893 and 1968. Around this time, there was also violent unrest in both Redfern, where residents fought back against police harassment, and the country centre of Moree. The Head of the NSW DAA, Aboriginal activist Pat O'Shane, described as 'justifiable under the circumstances' a riot which broke out after the shotgun death of one man and the wounding of two others.[28]

Following the unrest, Attorney General Frank Walker said that the answer was land rights. The NSW Government did not get around to passing a sort of land rights Bill until 1983. This ensured that NSW Land Councils got 7.5 percent of land tax receipts, but it also had major drawbacks. Lands under private ownership or lease were left untouched. Traditional owners had no right to claim crown land being used for other purposes, no right of access to sacred sites or traditional hunting grounds, and no rights to minerals or royalties. Two thousand people marched in vain against these limitations.

In Victoria in 1979, Aboriginal protesters blockaded Framlingham Regional Park near Warrnambool over claims for 1,000 hectares of forest. A year later, they allied with white environmentalists to warn of the dangers posed by Alcoa's giant aluminium smelter at Portland. The Gunditjmara people feared the destruction of relics and disturbance to sacred sites and were prepared to confront police about it. Their leader, Christina Frankland, won some legal battles along with eight other women. For her trouble, she and about 50 other people were later driven out of Portland by racist harassment.

In 1978, after mass demonstrations, the Pitjanjatjara of South Australia won their claim to 160,000 square kilometres complementing areas they had gained under federal legislation in the Northern Territory. But the Tonkin Liberal government, elected in 1979, allowed the legislation to lapse. It took a further campaign, with the Pitjantjatjara Council bussing demonstrators into Adelaide, before they got their land in 1981 – without the right to veto mining.

In January 1979, the Northern Territory Central Land Council lodged a claim for Uluru (Ayers Rock) and the surrounding areas. Their case was powerful. Tourist industry spokesperson Keith Castle conceded that it was 'common knowledge, and we accept this, that there are areas of deep significance to the [Aboriginal people] around Ayers Rock.' But there were vested interests involved, too: Barry Bucholtz of the Ayers Rock Chalet warned that 'if they say they want a piece of the action, it will be machine guns at 40 paces.'[29] While a victory for the traditional owners could not be denied in this case, Bucholtz summed up perfectly the logic of a social system that never gave an inch where it could avoid doing so.

Against this system, Indigenous people could make only limited gains on their own. In fact, they desperately needed *allies*, in the environmental movement for example, but especially in the white working class. Because union support for the Aurukun people never went beyond statements of principle, Aurukun could be isolated. In the Ranger disputes, Indigenous people had more meaningful support in the anti-uranium movement, with its strong working class component. Fraser recognised the threat that this posed to his plans and sought to weaken the links. Finally, at Noonkanbah, it was union action that came close to foiling the WA Government's attacks on land rights. Still, these struggles were all defeated, because the solidarity actions were not effective enough; it was another indication of the need to rebuild the labour movement on a new basis, with better leaders.

Migrants

Although their trials generally couldn't compare with those facing Indigenous Australians, immigrant workers had a hard time in the 1970s. In mid-1977, for example, *The Age* reported that migrants (especially women) feared reprisals from employers if they reported discrimination on the job; that non-English speakers had immense difficulty participating in unions because the unions made little effort to meet them half way; and that 'more than 30 percent of Melbourne's migrant population is doomed to permanent poverty.'[30]

The philosophy of 'multiculturalism' was coming into fashion. The cultural tolerance it encouraged was an advance on previous attitudes, but the Fraser Government found ways to reconcile it with conservative policies. Although the 1978 Galbally Report did advocate for a range of programs for migrant communities, it also found ways to pay for them at migrants' expense. Money saved by axing tax rebates on remittances to families overseas more than paid for all the new outlays, which were kept low by relying on volunteers in the communities to deliver the new services. Moreover, the services were pretty limited. While Galbally called for the preservation of migrant cultures, which he defined in rather grand terms, the only practical measures he recommended were facilities in libraries, cultural agreements with other countries, and a bit of money for ethnic art from the Australia Council. The report devoted only four out of 122 pages to the mass unemployment which was savaging migrant communities.[31] Fraser's main political objective in developing 'multicultural' policies was to build links to middle-class community leaders, then use them to coopt the various migrant groups.

In other words, it was 'autonomy' in the service of the status quo, and the government was not so tolerant of those migrants who wished to challenge any aspect of the social order. Australia kicked out Italian journalist Ignazio Salemi after he came forward to declare himself an 'overstayed' migrant during a government amnesty – which had been announced with the words: 'You have nothing to fear.'[32] Immigration Minister MacKellar decided, for reasons never disclosed, that Salemi was an exception. Probably, the journalist, who was involved with the migrant welfare group FILEF, had been singled out because of his membership of the Italian Communist Party. Days after the Salemi decision, an exiled Malaysian student leader, Hishamuddin Rais, was forced to leave Australia although he risked jail on returning to his native country.

Fraser was committed to substantial levels of immigration to fuel economic growth, but that hardly precluded racism. 'We do have a non-discriminatory policy,' said MacKellar, 'but it's a selective one.' An analysis of statistics concerning where people came from and where officials were stationed revealed a bias in favour of Europe and the USA, and the high premium on family reunion naturally favoured families of migrants already in Australia, who were mostly white.[33]

In 1979, Fraser's attempts to prosecute 148 people, mainly Greeks, for social security fraud exploded in his face after revelations that the Commonwealth Police had engaged in entrapment and illegally recorded telephone conversations. The government had stopped social security payments to 720 people, prompting protests from the Greek community. The paper *Neos Kosmos* said that a New Year's message from MacKellar 'reminds us of the Mafia, which kills and then sends flowers to the funeral of its victims.'³⁴

Nothing, however, quite compared to the paranoia about Indochinese 'boat people'. Whereas southern European migrants were becoming a familiar and comparatively accepted part of the Australian scene by the mid-1970s, Indochinese refugees had to start from scratch. Even arguments *for* Asian immigration could make concessions to yellow-peril logic. A committee chaired by Fraser's adviser Owen Harries warned of:

> a possible future situation where Australia came under strong pressure to accept more migrants, refugees and guest workers than it wanted from the over-populated parts of Asia.

Harries believed that Australia would be better placed to 'resist' the pressure if it had been 'non-discriminatory and relatively liberal' in its immigration policy.³⁵ This subtle racism in government reinforced more overt prejudices elsewhere.

Minor cultural differences became bogeys, as when four Vietnamese men were prosecuted for killing and eating a dog, and 40 hostile demonstrators (claiming to defend the rights of animals!) turned up outside the court. Ridiculous accusations were levelled against the Indochinese. Some alleged that the boat people were arriving with gold bars; these turned out to be paper thin gold tiles worth about $60 each. Others alleged that they were prostitutes, drug-runners, covert communists or anti-Hanoi fascists. Sections of the left found the latter theory a convenient excuse for capitulating to the paranoia, with Tom Uren, a prominent fan of the 'gentle' Vietnamese regime, accusing the refugees of seeking a soft life.³⁶ A more mainstream ALP figure such as Brian Burke, later WA premier, could claim that they were 'not genuine refugees' and call on the federal government to 'halt this refugee flood'.³⁷

Most of the charges were baseless. While the earliest groups to leave Vietnam had contained some affluent people and adherents of the previous regime, those arriving later were far more likely to be peasants or fisherfolk. The 'genuineness' of political or 'economic' refugees hadn't been queried with other groups of new arrivals; why was it suddenly so important when dealing with Asians? And although unpleasant experiences with the authoritarian Hanoi Government predisposed many of them initially to anti-communism, they generally showed little interest in the right-wing Vietnamese Association on arrival.

In addition to the streak of racism long embedded in Australian culture and historically associated with the White Australia policy, popular fears were exacerbated by economic insecurity. Just as women were accused of taking men's jobs, so migrants were blamed for unemployment. A 1981 poll asked people to nominate their greatest fears about the country's development. The same poll had been held a decade earlier, and two changes stood out: a 10 percent increase in those citing economic problems, and an eight per cent rise in those citing immigration and race.[38] The intersection of the two explained why Cliff Dolan of the ACTU reported Sydney workers as saying, 'send the bloody wogs home and there'd be more jobs for us.'[39] Dolan called such talk 'ridiculous', but unfortunately added: 'if the government does not cut the immigration program and cut it drastically, the tensions will inevitably increase.'[40] Like many other labour movement leaders, Dolan apparently believed you could combat racism by capitulating to it.

This was not only immoral but short-sighted. Paula Kelly of the Indo-Chinese Refugees Association pointed out:

> Of course, when the Vietnamese arrive they are right wing, anti-union. But because most of them get jobs in factories, they soon see that for their own future, trade unions are the thing. They are quite happy to fight for better conditions, for jobs – as long as they understand the issues. Many of them are beginning to understand how trade unions work. Recently, they kicked out an anti-Vietnamese delegate in the Tramways Union. At another company, they organised and took action against a shop steward they accused of making sweetheart deals with the bosses.[41]

Two wildcat strikes

Given their subordinate status in much of the union movement, it was not surprising that migrant workers often had to resort to unofficial strike action. In those areas where they had been largely frozen out of the official structures of the unions, this very fact enabled them to burst into the leadership of particularly militant struggles. The most impressive example during the Fraser era was the 1981 strike by women at Kortex in Melbourne; because that dispute summarises the entire argument of this chapter, I discuss it at the end. However, two other struggles, by male workers, also illustrate the point extremely well.

In January 1977, labourers on Sydney railway construction sites began

THE OPPRESSED FIGHT BACK

Ford Broadmeadows (Melbourne) strike 1981

agitating for pay and conditions comparable to those enjoyed by builders' labourers. They also wanted 32 hours' wet pay per month – payment for time lost due to wet weather – and an end to arbitrary sackings and transfers. (Management was using transfers to break up job organisation.)

This was a disparate group of largely overseas-born workers. In a letter to NSW Premier Neville Wran in July, they estimated that:

> of the approximate number of 300 men on strike only about 20 are White Australians. We have a number of Aboriginal men, one Black South African and the rest of us are from European countries.[42]

At various stages, English speakers from both factions of the BLF appeared on the scene. Talented young Irishman Sean Cody was an early leader of the struggle; unfortunately, Cody turned out to be a careerist who disappeared when offered a full-time position with the pro-Gallagher BLF office. Later, Bob Pringle, former official of the old NSW branch, appeared on the scene and played a valuable leadership role.

From a distance, these two high-profile individuals appeared to dominate events. In reality, while the workforce was delighted with the leadership they provided at times, the core leaders of the strike were themselves mostly

Mediterranean migrants. The most important single figure was Tony Perera, who had a history of radical activity in the Canary Islands. Each language group (Yugoslav, Arabic, Greek and Spanish) had its own leaders and interpreters and the mass meetings were multilingual affairs. This generally suited the militants, who controlled the translations, although the defection of a leading Arab at one point cost them a swag of votes.

The AWU office was largely indifferent until the first big strike hit Eastern Suburbs Railway sites in March. Two men had been sacked for refusing to operate concrete pumps for substandard pay, and 300 workers stopped work in their defence after job delegates organised a march through the underground tunnels to bring out the construction sites. Fitters and plumbers stopped in solidarity, and even some clerks joined them. After a week, the two were reinstated, with the Commission promising an early hearing on their claims.

On returning to work, the labourers began consolidating their job organisation, formally electing an Action Committee. When management offered gangers' positions to key delegates on the Chalmers Street site in an attempt to buy them off, they refused to abandon their members. May saw more disputation, including bans on concrete. Management organised a bogus meeting to throw out Tony Perera as delegate, with AWU Secretary Charlie Oliver hastening to recognise the new rep, but the Action Committee simply held another meeting to reinstate Perera.

In July, after they had brought out additional construction sites at Meadowbank, Chullora and Clyde and marched on the Industrial Court, the workers won some of their claims. The Public Transport Commission (PTC) agreed to give a week's notice before any dismissal; to ensure that there would be no standdowns because of wet weather; and to increase weekly pay by up to $13. It also recognised the Action Committee. The delegates immediately approached the carpenters' unions about forming an inter-union committee, but these unions' full-time officials stymied them.

The PTC hadn't given up yet. Management went to the AWU officials to seek a different agreement, so it took a further mass meeting of the labourers, a march on the minister's office and continuing strike action before the PTC reconfirmed the original deal. This was consistent with the workers' previous experience of the Labor government. In the July letter to Wran, they had written: 'We wonder if you are giving us this treatment because you think that we are just WOGS and anything is good enough for us.'[43] But the 'wogs' had shown Wran a thing or two.

Carworkers in Melbourne could have hurled the same accusations at their management. The vehicle building industry had long employed migrants at poor wages and under oppressive conditions. Partly because of this, it had been an industrial volcano. The Ford plant at Broadmeadows had a history of industrial explosions, with spontaneous strikes in 1963, 1969 and 1973. The 1973 upheaval led to stronger organisation on the job: 'in the next years there were a lot of small actions and after each stewards would resign and be replaced by more militant ones.'[44] In 1981, 41 VBU shop stewards, most of them militants, met regularly. There were Australian-born workers among them, but the migrants tended to take the lead in combativeness.

In 1981, the ACTU claimed a $30 rise for all workers. At Ford, the workforce decided to take the claim seriously. Despite active hostility from their union officials, the stewards were able to lead a six-week strike.

The strikers defied threats from the company to withdraw their annual leave and a previous pay rise; a mass meeting called in response to these threats culminated in a demonstration outside Ford's head office. VBU and ACTU officials, however, were manoeuvring so diligently to secure a return to work that senior shop steward Frank Argondizzo denounced them publicly as 'bureaucrats with big cigars in their mouths.'[45]

Ford's next move was to get the Arbitration Commission to order a secret ballot. Both the ACTU and the VBU had policies against secret ballots during industrial disputes, on the grounds that workers could best make democratic decisions at open mass meetings after hearing debate, whereas secret ballots meant that workers voted as atomised individuals under pressure from the media. While they criticised the move for the record, however, the union officials went along with the secret ballot, which resulted in a narrow majority for returning to work – by 169 votes out of 4,000.

This needn't have been the end of the struggle. At a subsequent mass meeting, the shop stewards pointed out that at least 850 workers hadn't voted, including many who never got ballot papers. The meeting voted overwhelmingly to fight on and, initially, comparatively few of the strikers actually went back to work. But the media created the impression that the strike front had crumbled, and this became a self-fulfilling prophecy over the following days.

The shop stewards' organisation had not been sufficient. To withstand all the forces opposing them, the militants needed a much wider strike committee capable of organising a boycott of the secret ballot or mass pickets in defiance of the results. They also needed solidarity from the wider labour movement. They weren't well enough organised to mobilise this either. Even so, they were proud of their strike. 'What we have done has been a lesson to workers all over Australia,' said shop steward Habib Haddad, 'we have stood up to the boss and said: We won't be treated like animals.'[46]

Habib Haddad was not just addressing fellow migrants. The Eastern Suburbs Railway and Ford struggles were important assertions of strength and pride by non-English-speaking migrant workers, but these workers had never seen the English-speaking workers who joined their strikes as having different interests. They needed and sought the solidarity that only class organisation could provide.

Women and sexual politics

Until Fraser's election, the women's movement had enjoyed the illusion of steady progress. Although the Whitlam Government was in political retreat on this front as on most others, a surge of funding for International Women's Year in 1975, together with laws allowing federal funds to go directly to women's health centres, had enabled a range of women's service projects to go ahead. In NSW alone, health centres opened in Bankstown, Parramatta, Wagga Wagga, the Blue Mountains, Newcastle and Gosford.

In the wider social context, these were relatively minor concessions; to feminists, they assumed considerable importance. Fraser's arrival seemed to place them under threat. Having grown accustomed to pressing for new initiatives, women suddenly found themselves battling to preserve what existed. In May 1976, under the banner of his 'new federalism', Fraser handed control of funding for the refuges and centres to the states, ensuring widespread cuts. His government's only new initiative on women's affairs in the first year was a family allowance scheme, which fitted neatly into the conservative ideological framework of the Coalition parties and whose payments, not being indexed for inflation, rapidly declined in value.

Even so, Anne Summers was unduly pessimistic to think that 'women's affairs ceased to be a political issue at the end of 1975.'[47] This might have been partly true for the Canberra parliamentary scene, but women's liberation – or feminism as it was coming to be called – remained a major force in much of society. Eva Cox was closer to the mark in her insistence that:

> very few people now disagree with our basic claims on child care, employment, maternity leave... And the movement and its issues are no longer regarded as coming from a ratbag fringe.[48]

It would not be so easy for the new government to roll back these gains.

In fact, it was clear by the end of 1976 that the welfare network would survive. Summers herself reported: 'There are now 24 women's refuges, two working women's centres, five rape crisis centres and at least six women's health centres.'[49] Rather than destroy the various centres, the Fraser Government had essentially continued Whitlam's strategy of using them to defuse and incorporate women's struggles. If the centres were given just enough funding to survive, Fraser could get feminists to deliver welfare on the cheap. Contrary to some people's hopes, the centres were not a breeding ground for radical politics. Bon Hull of the Women's Health Collective in Melbourne had said flatly in early 1975:

> We would never open again... We didn't change one single thing. We were just providing a nice friendly service for women. Where we fell down was on politicisation.[50]

There was no shortage of politically charged questions to fight around, however. One of them was abortion. Polls repeatedly showed that most Australians favoured liberal abortion laws, but well-organised anti-choice RTL forces were able to keep the issue in contention. It was literally impossible to prevent abortions: the Royal Commission on Human Relationships estimated that 40–80,000 illegal abortions had taken place between 1965 and 1970.[51] At stake were the rights of poor and working class women, who found it hard to get around restrictive laws without resort to backyard butchers and, beyond that, the issue of who in society was to make 'moral' judgements.

Women – and men – had to rally repeatedly for the right to choose during the Fraser years. Harassment of abortion clinics was not unusual in the mid-1970s, with demonstrators shouting at women entering the Fertility Control Clinic in East Melbourne. Sydney clinics received a series of phoney bookings. Population Services International in Sydney was firebombed. Meanwhile, government policy made life harder for those seeking abortions: in 1978, parliament abolished bulk-billing except for pensioners and allowed health funds to exclude certain items, making abortions more costly for working class people.

But the attempts to turn back the clock were defeated. While the struggle in Queensland, already discussed, was the most spectacular, pro-choice forces won most other battles nationwide.

In early 1979, National Party backbencher Stephen Lusher moved a parliamentary motion demanding a ban on medical benefits for abortion, except where the mother's life was in danger. It was so poorly formulated that Lusher

Demonstrators for abortion rights Sydney 1979

MAY DAY 1980
DEMONSTRATE
AGAINST THE
RIGHT TO LIFE

ABORTION PLATFORM

at the Yarra Bank after the Mayday march. Speakers will include Rae Norris from Brisbane, on the struggle there against Bjelke-Petersen's new repressive anti-abortion laws

DEMONSTRATION

The Right to Life are rallying at the Treasury Gardens, then marching to the Royal Women's Hospital and to Parliament House. We intend to march from the Yarra Bank and meet them there. Join us!

FREE ABORTION ON DEMAND

Counter demonstration against RTL May Day march 1980. The leaflet calling the event was put out by Gay Trade Unionists, Young Gays, VPSA Reform Group and the International Socialists. Note the handwritten headings. The Battler argued the case in a leaflet earlier on IWD and then reported the May Day event afterwards

the battler

PAPER OF THE INTERNATIONAL SOCIALISTS

SPECIAL SPECIAL — THE OPPRESSED FIGHT BACK

NO RETURN TO THE BACKSTREETS — ABORTION ON DEMAND — Women's Voice

LEAFLET LEAFLET

MARCH 8 — INTERNATIONAL WOMEN'S DAY

International Women's Day originates back in 1907 when women in the USA organised a women's day demonstration, demanding rights for women. They laid the basis for future demonstrations by women garment workers in New York demanding the right to vote, the 8 hour day and an end to the conditions of the sweatshop. Since then there have been many fights by women workers for equal pay, suffrage, the right to work and to organise and for abortion rights.

Rally for Free Safe Legal Abortion on Demand

State Health Minister Bill Knox is to introduce an anti-abortion bill into parliament. The bill, due to enter parliament this year, will only allow abortions to be performed in public hospitals. Yet it has been proven that clinics have a better safety record with abortion operations than hospitals. The bill makes no provision for an increase in staff to cope with more abortion operations. The result will be that it will be even harder to get abortions in Queensland. This is an **extremely repressive legislation that hits hardest at working class women and must be fought.** It is working class women who can at least afford to travel interstate for the operation or to be forced out of a job in the process.

WHY THE ATTACKS ON ABORTION RIGHTS?

Faced with an economic recession, the Australian ruling class is playing the old game of divide and rule — scapegoating women workers, the unemployed and minority groups. The onslaught against women this year has taken shape in moves to pass repressive anti-abortion laws which, if enforced, would take women out of the workforce. Just to be able to work women need abortion rights. That's why abortion must be a central issue for this International Women's Day.

ABORTION — AN INTERNATIONAL ISSUE

Conservative governments throughout the world have moved to pass anti-abortion legislation. The Muldoon government in New Zealand succeeded in 1977 in prohibiting abortion. In Britain however, with a strong pro-ab... campaign, Trade Union Council support, and mass demonstrations, the government...

AUSTRALIA'S TORIES FOLLOW SUIT

RIGHT-TO-LIFE RALLY ROUTED

IT'LL BE a long time before the Right-to-Life dares to march in Melbourne on May Day again!

A thousand pro-abortion demonstrators confronted two thousand Right-to-Lifers outside Parliament House on Sunday May 4.

By Rae Norris

THE POLICE moved in at Parliament House as soon as the Right-to-Life had left.

lost votes on technicalities. Still, the debate was intense. Liberal James Bradfield warned of 'an abortion supermarket' if Lusher failed. Stewart West from the Labor left retorted that the anti-abortion push talked about the right to life: 'but it fails to consider the right of a woman to her own life.' There was much more on both sides, but Lusher lost the vote overwhelmingly, 98 votes to 23.

Lusher conceded that his opponents had won an important victory, saying: 'there will probably have to be a reassessment of what influence the Church and moral groups have over the Legislature.'[52] Pro-choice activists built on their success by holding demonstrations on the 'International Day of Action' at the end of March, well aware that future battles were likely.

Later in 1979, the Fraser Government prosecuted 14 doctors, supposedly for defrauding Medibank. However, most had worked in feminist abortion clinics and referral centres, and their supporters alleged that the prosecutions amounted to political harassment. In the same year, the Administrative & Clerical Officers' Association (ACOA), the Commonwealth public service union, adopted a policy supporting women's right to control their fertility. The anti-abortion side was able to force a plebiscite and get the policy scrapped in 1981. It seemed to be an endless struggle, one which was fought out twice on Melbourne streets in the early 1980s.

In 1980, the RTL decided to march on May Day. This proved to be a major tactical error. The left were also in the streets in large numbers, and a crowd of about 1,000 marched up from post-May Day march festivities at the Yarra Bank to confront them. Charging past police horses, the counter-demonstrators proceeded up Bourke Street to Parliament House, where they pushed their way into the RTL throng. While the anti-abortionists were more numerous, the families bussed in after Sunday mass were hardly prepared for a street battle. Little or no violence occurred. The RTL's supporters found themselves eyeball to eyeball with leftists chanting 'Not the church, not the state, women must decide their fate!' and dispersed.

Two years later, a few hundred pro-choice demonstrators again challenged a smaller RTL march. They managed to occupy a position at the front of the anti-abortion crowd, then 'led' the march with banners proclaiming women's right to choose. Once again, a street confrontation ensued near parliament. This time, the police prevailed on the RTL to retreat into Fitzroy Gardens. Both events presented dilemmas for some feminists, because they challenged certain preconceptions: the RTL had mobilised thousands of female marchers, while the counter-demonstrations had been led by socialists rather than feminists and contained large numbers of men. It *was* a women's issue, in being profoundly linked to female oppression; at the same time, it was a *class* issue, because bans on abortion most affected working class people. Finally, it was an issue dividing people on *political* lines, independent of gender. There was no single 'women's side', and feminist autonomy theories were spectacularly irrelevant. If you wanted to defend abortion rights, you needed the widest possible unity between all women and men prepared to fight.

The growth of women's liberation had provoked a reaction from the political right, which provided another eloquent confirmation that there was no monolithic 'women's side' to sexual politics. When people associated with the right-wing National Civic Council established the Women's Action Alliance (WAA), it attracted a significant female membership. WAA claimed to particularly champion the needs of housewives (supposedly ignored by liberationists), and its first public meeting in Melbourne did attract a large crowd. One analysis of WAA's membership found a large proportion were:

> young wives and mothers living the suburban dream on a new housing estate. Some, until recently, had been independent wage-earners... Now that these women have chosen motherhood...they feel ignored by the community and without any status in it. The early 1980s recession with rising interest rates and unemployment made them feel extremely vulnerable.[53]

The group's declared priority was defending the economic interests of single-income families, for example, by lobbying for higher family allowances and spouse rebates. So WAA was clearly in the National Civic Council tradition of offering a conservative, family-oriented but – in some ways – socially aware program.

Babette Francis' Women Who Want to be Women (WWWW), founded over dinner at her Toorak home, was a rather different outfit, strongly anti-abortion in emphasis and with some half-baked intellectual pretensions. The group proclaimed a 'third stage of feminism' – which, on closer examination, seemed to be drawn largely from the pages of the *Women's Weekly* – and presented a cake to the Fraser Government with pink icing inscribed: 'To the men of the House from the women in the home.'[54]

The right and left currents, both female, fought it out in 1979 for control of Fraser's token advisory body, the National Women's Advisory Council (NWAC). Over 4,000 women had registered for a NWAC conference planned for November as part of the United Nations Mid Decade for Women. But the organisers cancelled it, claiming that no suitable venue was available. Right-wing groups had apparently swelled the numbers with block registrations. The right had also managed to get a number of anti-abortion amendments through pre-conference workshops. Alarmed by a Melbourne *Age* article about these developments, 400 women gathered in Melbourne to set up a lobby aimed at countering the conservatives, but the composition of the new Coalition for Women's Rights showed that the dangers did not only come from the far right.

The Coalition's founders included the 'Business and Professional Women' and, when it drew up a ticket for elections to the next conference, company director and Liberal Party activist Eve Mahlab appeared at its head. There were no workers on it at all. Contrary to those who defended the ticket as clever tactics for achieving unity against the common foe, it was really a political capitulation to the Liberals. Organising on the basis of a classless 'sisterhood', the feminists had legitimised the party of Malcolm Fraser. They had also won 11 out of 15 places, but the government simply added extra conservatives to the conference, so all the compromising went for nothing.

Fortunately, it later became clear that the threat from right-wing groups had been exaggerated. A 1981 survey of 300 Melbourne housewives, supposedly these groups' best hunting-ground, showed that 46 percent approved of the aims of women's liberation as they understood them, but the approval ratings for WAA and WWWW were only 3 and 5 percent respectively.[55]

Women in the working class

Despite economic stagnation, the number of women working continued to rise. This was partly because of an increase in part-time employment, and partly because some women were forced to seek work when their husbands were retrenched. As their numbers grew, they also became more combative.

Nurses began to shed the Florence Nightingale image, taking to Sydney streets as early as 1976 (see Chapter 4). At Royal Brisbane Hospital in 1979, they wore street clothes instead of uniforms while banning non-essential clerical work in protest against the demotion of their matron. The protest actions later widened to include work-to-rules and stopwork meetings; after six months, they forced the Queensland Government to dismiss the hospital board. In Sydney in 1982, nurses and other health workers led protests of up to 10,000 people against government plans to close two hospitals. Stopwork action prevented the closure of Gloucester House at the Royal Prince Alfred, saving 200 jobs. The Royal Australian Nursing Federation scrapped its long-standing no-strike commitment, and several hundred nurses marched through Newcastle in 1982 to show their anger over cuts in health services.

In 1976, 500 female public servants stopped work in South Australia in protest against unequal pay scales. There were even sporadic attempts to form unions among prostitutes, although these apparently failed because 'it was too complicated – and too many muscles were flexed', presumably by pimps.[56]

However, the largest struggles by women were mixed struggles involving unions representing both sexes. Between 1970 and 1975, the number of female union members increased by 50 percent, while male membership only increased by 12 percent. By 1980, nearly 32 percent of trade unionists were women. The trends are best documented in the white collar and professional sectors, where 'proletarianisation' and 'feminisation' went together, with both trends linked to growing industrial militancy. For example, the number of female staff in DSS doubled from 1976 to 1983, while the number of males rose by just over 50 percent.[57] These were also the years in which DSS saw its first industrial action. DSS staff had first applied work bans in 1977, then held a service-wide stoppage in 1979 over anti-union legislation. The growing militancy culminated in a prolonged strike in 1981.

While women in ACOA were underrepresented among workplace delegates, they still made up 20–25 percent of these by the 1980s. They were an important part of the rank and file unrest that propelled a new Reform Group leadership to power. The Reform Group, in turn, championed such issues as child care. One of its leading figures, Ann Forward, became the first woman to hold a federal office in ACOA. Her success owed far more to united organising by both sexes than to any separate women's grouping; the establishment of separate women's committees in the union was a result, rather than a cause, of the Reform Group's success.

As women workers' numbers and confidence grew, the official union structures began responding to their demands. Unions began electing more female officials. Jennie George became secretary of the NSW Teachers Federation. Jan Marsh became ACTU industrial advocate, having made her mark in 1978 by winning a crucial test case for maternity leave and protection against dismissal on account of pregnancy. The arrival of these officials was not decisive in itself; Jan Marsh, for her part, let it be known that she was not 'vociferously libbish'.[58] More important were the new avenues opening up for rank and file activists. The white collar unions funded a Working Women's Centre in Melbourne, while a Women's Trade Union Conference in Sydney in August 1976 attracted 500 delegates, mostly from white collar unions but also some from the AMWU.

Health cuts rally Sydney 1979

URN ON THE LIGHTS
ACK FRASER
FRASER'S HEALTH PLA
NEVER
SUCC
AN EVEN
SUPPORT N.S.W.
LABOR GOVT.
AGAINST
FRASER'S HEALTH
CUTS

The AMWU delegates reported that the participants were:

> prepared to fight...as part of the labour and union movements to strengthen the whole movement. They want unions to give leadership in mobilising women workers.

Some were planning to organise around the Working Women's Charter (officially adopted by the ACTU in 1977) and wanted action 'at the grassroots level'.[59]

The Working Women's Charter campaign created local activist groups in most states. In 1977, 300 delegates attended a national Charter Campaign Conference. The ACTU called a special unions' conference in 1978 to discuss the Charter's demands on equal pay, child care, union training and other issues. With only 62 out of 132 unions bothering to attend the latter event, however, it became clear that progress would not come from relying on the top union structures. It *would* take action at the grassroots – and, fortunately, there was quite a bit of that. In Sydney, for example, a rank and file newsletter called *The Paper Factory* spoke for 'clerical workers who want to see a society where sexism has no place'.[60] In Melbourne, the paper *Women At Work* interviewed Gail Cotton of the FPU, who had organised factory meetings to set up Charter committees:

> I asked for volunteers for the committees and was inundated. In some places there were more women wanting to be on the committee than there were places. I had the ACTU Charter translated and I used an interpreter, so we could discuss the Charter point by point. It was a fantastic boost of confidence... They all endorsed the Charter, but they were really more interested in what they could do. In one factory they decided to draw up their own Charter. One demand was that every job in the factory had to be open to both males and females.

Cotton continued:

> The next thing will be to hold meetings of all the workers to explain what the committees have been doing and to get men and women to work together.[61]

While the Charter drew its initial inspiration from a specific focus on women's oppression, Cotton recognised that winning demands based on it required unity between both sexes on the job.

Women still faced discrimination, but they were winning victories. In the mid-1970s, they overturned the rules that said only men could drive Melbourne's trams, after a stiff fight inside the union. When the Rockhampton Council in North Queensland sacked Janine Marshall because she was married, the Municipal Officers' Association got the award varied so that it couldn't happen again. Although Janet Oakden never got to be a train driver in NSW, Deborah Wardley, backed by demonstrations, forced Ansett to employ her as a pilot. An increasing number of young women took apprenticeships as auto-mechanics or fitters. And Wollongong saw an important struggle against job discrimination at BHP.

Women had long been 'underemployed' on the NSW South Coast. Nevertheless, when mass unemployment arrived in the 1970s, they were often accused of taking men's jobs. Despite this hostile environment, a Jobs For Women campaign took on BHP in 1978 and again in 1980. Having applied for work in the steel mills and been knocked back, they lodged a complaint with the NSW Anti-Discrimination Board, circulated petitions in the steelworks, marched in the streets and set up a 'tent embassy' in front of BHP's employment office. The campaign involved quite a few migrants, for whom the rigours of the steel mills were less daunting after their experience of clothing sweatshops. While some men were hostile, others backed them: one of the campaigners, Slavadenka, later recalled with satisfaction:

> the cold windy night...when we have given leaflets to the men... We asked them, 'How you feel the womans to work with you?' They says, 'Great, why not?'[62]

Finally, the company gave in. Within a year, 700 women were working in the steelworks. This, of course, was by no means the end of the tale: the leaders were given heart-breaking labouring jobs in an attempt to drive them out. These tactics failed, but BHP needed only to bide its time till the next industry downturn; when that arrived at the end of 1982, the company simply applied the 'last on, first off' rule and retrenched them.

Forty-four of them went to the Anti-Discrimination Board. They might have demanded reinstatement, but they decided against it because this could lead to other people being sacked, thereby undermining traditional trade union principles embodied in the 'last on, first off' rule. It might also have strengthened the 'women-take-men's-jobs' argument. Instead, they successfully demanded compensation on the grounds that the company's previous refusal to hire them had cost them seniority. This way, they could avoid undermining solidarity with their male fellow workers.

That solidarity could be important. In 1978, 15 female canteen staff at Williamstown Dockyard struck for a week because of delays in their pay, whereupon the dockyard's 1,500 male unionists came out in their support. 'We didn't ask the men to go out,' said Monica Cullinan. 'But we've always gone out for them and they stuck behind us on this issue.'[63] The canteen staff went to the Arbitration Commission when their case was heard, carrying placards and wearing badges saying: 'Unions are for women, too!' Their strike won not only compensation for the delays, but also the right to be paid weekly instead of fortnightly.

A 1981 ACTU women's conference gave some measure of progress made. The ACTU's president Cliff Dolan was on hand to open proceedings. The 140 delegates agreed that equality of opportunity was yet to be achieved, both in industry and the trade union movement, but it was clear that women's concerns had gained much greater recognition. In the same year, the ACTU Congress carried a motion for 'free safe legal abortion' by 528 to 392 after intense debate. For the first time, it mentioned migrant women under the Migrant Workers' Policy. A conference on 'Sexism – an Industrial Issue' held by Victoria's three teacher unions in 1981 had 250 attendees.

Of course, as organisations functioning on capitalist terrain, the unions were infected with sexism. Because they were also an expression of the class struggle, however, they remained the most important single vehicle for working class women to make gains. These gains were mostly won by fighting alongside men, with women frequently in the leadership.

Lesbians and gay men

Having won victories in the early 1970s, lesbians and gay men feared a backlash in the second half of the decade. For a time, it seemed to be happening. In 1976, *The Age* reported that police had used entrapment to make mass arrests at a beat at Black Rock beach. In 1977, the Queensland Government banned Greg Weir from teaching for being an outspoken member of the Kelvin Grove Homosexual and Lesbian Student Teachers Group. There were demonstrations supporting Weir in Melbourne and Sydney, but the ban stayed. In early 1978, it emerged that, following the murder of a gay man in Newcastle, the local police had investigated other homosexuals not connected to the crime. In

Brisbane, the police launched a wave of harassment against lesbians and gay men in their ranks.[64]

The attacks reached their peak in Sydney in mid-1978. After a successful gay solidarity march and public meeting in June, crowds turned out in Taylor Square for a Mardi Gras parade. Police attempts to curtail the event succeeded only in turning it into a second demonstration, to which they responded by arresting 53 people. The *Sydney Morning Herald* helpfully published the names and occupations of those arrested. Around this time, Victoria banned the book *Young, Gay and Proud* from its schools.

But 1978 also saw unprecedented levels of resistance. Protest meetings over the arrests drew 400 people in Sydney; several hundred demonstrated in Melbourne; 50 rallied in Brisbane. Then 1,000 people marched through Sydney on 15 July, and police again set upon them. Undaunted, the movement returned to Sydney streets in August after its national conference. The conference participants had decided to march on the footpath on a quiet Sunday afternoon, but the police still surrounded the crowd. After ordering it to disperse, they moved in almost immediately, beginning to make arrests before anyone could leave the scene – in fact, leaving the scene without walking into the arms of hostile police was almost impossible. Supposedly, they had acted to prevent the demonstrators disrupting an anti-abortion rally underway in Hyde Park. Ironically, this happened anyway, because the RTL organisers cancelled their march on police advice.

The attempts at intimidation were not working. November saw a strong march in solidarity with Californians opposing the homophobic Briggs initiative. In July 1979, Gay Solidarity Week climaxed with the largest mobilisation seen to that time: 5,000 people chanted and danced their way through Sydney streets during a festival which, as the Mardi Gras, was to become an annual event. In early 1980, a large street march concluded the Summer Offensive for Gay Rights. For the community, and for a lot of other people, to succeed in holding these processions was an important victory for freedom of political and cultural expression.

With the police faltering, the guardians of morality cast about for other forces. They placed their hopes in British morals campaigner Mary Whitehouse, who toured Australia in September 1980. A Coalition Against Repression (CAR) set out to oppose her, beginning in Adelaide. CAR organised forums, radio programs, two rock festivals, pickets and a fundraising dance during her Adelaide visit, while Melbourne saw a public meeting and demonstration. But Sydney was, inevitably, the main battleground.

Rally protesting Mardi Gras arrests Sydney 15 July 1978

Her visit to Sydney University was a disaster for the organisers, with Whitehouse supporters outnumbered by protesters. The same happened at a 'shoppers' rally.' Her main march on 24 September was not quite so tiny, and 600 people did join a 'March for the Child'; but, compared to the thousands who had joined previous Festival of Light processions, both events were dismal flops. The CAR protesters provided most of the highlights, including a spectacular pie-throwing.

Tensions between lesbians and gay men persisted throughout this era, primarily because sexism persisted among gay men. Clearly, however, beating off the right-wing attacks had improved conditions for fighting that sexism. That fight had required a united mobilisation of lesbians, gay men and quite a few straights – in opposition to reactionaries of both sexes.

Around the same time that lesbians and gay men were fighting right-wing attacks in the late 1970s, they were also beginning to win support in the unions. As early as 1973, the NSW BLF had banned work at Macquarie University when a homosexual student was excluded from the Robert Menzies College. Of course, the BLF was a rather unusual organisation. The first breakthroughs in other areas came in the second half of the decade in clerical and teacher unions, with the ACOA Reform Group (public servants) backing anti-discrimination policies in 1978 and the Australian Teachers Federation doing the same in 1979. In 1980, the Plumbers and Gasfitters followed suit, and the NSW Labor Council decided to support law reform.

In October 1980, cafeteria staff at Melbourne University stopped work to demand reinstatement of a gay student, Terry Stokes, who had been expelled from Graduate House. Not only formal union policies, but rank and file workers' attitudes, were changing: they could be won to the fight for gay rights. That was partly a consequence of the courageous struggles waged by lesbians and gay men, but these were hardly 'autonomous'. They had generally relied on mobilising other people in their support, something that they could do more readily because of the favourable climate created by the wider struggles of workers and social movements since 1968.

Migrant women workers: building unity

Migrant women are among the most oppressed workers. What better test, for the argument about autonomy versus unity, than three strikes among female migrants during the Fraser era?

In June 1977, 39 cleaners at BHP, members of the MWU, struck on receiving dismissal notices from the Newcastle Cleaning Company. The company had lost its contract to Keir Cleaning, after BHP approached Keir about cutting costs. The new employers wanted to employ 16 full-time employees, instead of the 39 part-timers who had been working there, and to cut back the total number of hours worked by the workforce as a whole. Newcastle Cleaning had itself previously carried out cuts in hours and staff, putting the cleaners under immense stress. Some of those not sacked had still been forced to leave the job temporarily, forfeiting long-service entitlements. This time, they took collective action.

They arranged pickets, collected money and spoke at lunchtime meetings at other workplaces. One of the barriers to their organising had been the division between migrant workers and Australians; before the strike, each group had been blaming the other for their problems on the job. In the course of the dispute, these divisions were forgotten for a while.

Half of the cleaners were from Yugoslavia. One with enough English language skills became a union delegate and translated for the others. Unity was emerging in the struggle.

Theoretically, the dispute was with Keir's. In reality, BHP's pressure for lower costs was the root of the problem, but BHP steadfastly refused to meet the union, so the strikers decided to take matters into their own hands:

> They entered the building through a side door [and] walked quickly through the corridors until they came to the purchasing officer's comfortable office, and demanded to see him. They were told he was unavailable [and] they then occupied his office... As an outcome of the occupation, the purchasing officer agreed to meet with the union.[65]

In August, the Arbitration Commission decided that 18 full-time workers would be employed – a small victory for the cleaners. Just as importantly, the strikers returned to work much better organised, with four union delegates. The company was obliged to move two of the delegates to day shift and promote the two others to leading hands in order to undermine this assertion of union power.

Laundry workers at the Hospital Laundry and Linen Service in Murdoch (Perth), all migrants, struck early in 1982 over demands for a 35 hour week, $30 and some additional benefits. This strike was defeated by the use of scab labour and the failure of the wider union movement to organise solidarity, a failure which partly reflected the general ebbing of militancy following the 1981 metal trades agreement (see Chapter 11). In addition, gender loomed large as an issue. According to Janet Greenwood, 'the women I have talked to have unhesitatingly said, "It's because we are women"'[66] that they faced obstruction not only from employers, but also from the Trades and Labour Council.

It is evident from Greenwood's account, however, that the problem was not men per se. The local union organiser was ignorant on some issues but clearly sympathetic. Most importantly, while the TLC's Disputes Committee said that the strike would be unlikely to attract support from other unions, this was mainly a problem with the full-time officials:

> The strikers know they received support from other unionists but see it as coming from the rank and file. Ordinary union members in Western Australia contributed between $6,000 and $8,000 per week to the strike fund.

Clearly, these women didn't need autonomy. On the contrary, their main complaint was that they 'were told again and again we were on our own.' What they needed was some way to build solidarity with other rank and file workers, male and female.

The 1981 textile workers' strike at Kortex in Melbourne was part of the 'wage push' militancy at the start of the 1980s. It was also influenced by leftist currents within the Turkish immigrant community. One of the Kortex workers had a husband working at Rowntree's, where the unions had won a pay rise through industrial action, while others had husbands involved in the tumultuous unofficial strike at Ford. Some were members of the left-wing Victorian Turkish Labourers' Association. The printing shop next door was on strike. These were strong influences on a workforce which itself had little trade union tradition.

The strike began when officials of the Textile Workers' Union failed to show up for discussions on a $25 pay claim. Angered, women at the Albert Street factory walked out anyway and made plans for a mass picket. The following Monday, they not only picketed in Albert Street, but marched to another nearby Kortex factory to bring it out on strike. Emboldened by success, they began to discuss issues beyond the original $25 claim. Sandra Bloodworth recounts:

> They wanted an end to the compulsory 'bonus' system [which] meant that if you didn't get the extra amount of work done for the bonus, you were sacked... They wanted a canteen so they had somewhere decent to have lunch and tea breaks so they didn't have to smoke in the toilets... They wanted the right to visit the toilet

Striking migrant women at Kortex (Melbourne) in 1981. They danced on the picket line and sang songs about the need for solidarity and cutting out union officials' tongues

the battler
$25 NOW
NO MONEY
NO WORK

when they chose and for as long as they chose. The existing system was two visits a day, and these for only three minutes. And perhaps the most galling of all was the compulsory donations they had to make for the bosses' birthdays. They wanted that stopped.[67]

The fight for pay was now a fight for dignity as well. They got no help from the union, but here was a case where women's lack of union tradition had its advantages. Not being used to looking to the union to solve their problems, they were capable of bypassing it when they needed to. When the union officials refused to bring out non-strikers working inside, the women's response was to strengthen their picket lines. They were unconcerned about looking respectable, and they welcomed participation by 'outside' leftists. Management hired enforcers to escort strikebreakers in to work; but they found that the women were able to win many non-strikers over by steady argument.

Finally, no longer able to ignore the dispute, the union officials called a mass meeting. The employers sent busloads of workers from other factories to stack it. They circulated multilingual leaflets arguing for acceptance of the $13.50 the Arbitration Commission had awarded the whole industry. Their thugs were inside the hall. The strikers refused to be intimidated. They occupied the stage, brandishing placards and chanting slogans. They made such a row that the thugs were withdrawn. The women then demanded a vote by division and won it. The union officials had to make the dispute official, closing down all three Kortex factories.

At a second mass meeting two days later, the bosses supplied the officials with a list of employees so that they could vet people. Once more there were non-strikers present, and some of the enforcers were again inside. A donnybrook ensued. The officials announced a secret ballot, leading to a second uproar. The strikers were against secret ballots on principle – believing that everyone should show where they stood in front of their fellow workers – and also didn't trust the union leaders. When it became clear that the ballot would proceed, they participated, but neither side was so naïve as to treat it as an exercise in democracy:

> When the vote came out it was 365 for staying out; 362 to go back – out of a meeting of no more than 500! The officials had set it up, so they had to accept the vote...this victory had depended on the fighting spirit of the young women... Some of them had fought their way in and voted up to ten times.

Management and the union officials now cooked up a third meeting, to be held with selected workers inside the factory. This meeting proved impossible to stop, and it yielded a return to work, but the workforce were offered an extra $11.50 to be paid in three months. Just as importantly, perhaps, the climate inside the factory was transformed, with the workers electing shop stewards and gaining some improved working conditions. On the last day before the Christmas break, the women stopped for a party, for the first time ever.

Whereas migrant women had traditionally been seen as meek and passive, Kortex showed how that could change in struggle. The women's family relationships changed too: men visiting the picket fell in behind the women's leadership, bought coffee and minded children. At home, the men took over child care and domestic chores to free their wives for strike agitation.

It was a dispute that drew together many strands – migrant issues, women's oppression and class – in a struggle to which arguments about 'autonomy' could add nothing. But then, there were no feminists present to raise them. Whereas women's liberation had embraced the 1975 Everhot strike as a cause célèbre, the feminists were conspicuous by their absence at Kortex. This was disappointing but not surprising, because the women's movement was shifting conspicuously to the right. It was not alone in that: much of the left was doing likewise. The next chapter considers why.

10.
Issues on the left

The Australian left generally welcomed the crisis of the 1970s, in the firm expectation that its influence would grow.

Despite a certain ebbing of political radicalism after 1970, the left forces still maintained a considerable presence. The Victorian Socialist Left faction was a major force inside the ALP, the CPA had temporarily arrested its historic decline, and the various groups further left were still gaining organisational strength. These currents should have been able to make strong advances after 1975, when so many people were questioning the society around them.

Although conventional industrial disputes had declined with the onset of recession, they were still higher than in, for example, the Hawke era. Strikes over Whitlam's dismissal and Medibank showed that workers were still capable of exceptional militancy. What's more, socialist ideas had a considerable currency among active trade unionists. When Jeff Hyde, a Chrysler shop steward from Adelaide, visited the Latrobe Valley strikers, he told the local paper quite unselfconsciously: 'The working people...could run this country far better than it is being run now.'[1] On the face of it, conditions were favourable for the emergence of powerful new left-wing currents in the working class.

The left had plausibly attributed the strength of capitalist ideas among most of the population to decades of postwar prosperity; the economic crisis, then, should have presaged a boom in socialist politics. Whitlam's dismissal and Fraser's rise posed the question of political power quite starkly, so that the far left did not seem far fetched when it argued that 'we live in the era of socialist revolution.'[2]

The economic slump did combine with the political events of 1975 to generate both a ferment of ideas and an enthusiasm among large numbers of

Poster conflating Fraser's right wing politics with fascism

workers for a decisive confrontation with the employers and the political right. Yet, after seven years of battles with Fraser, the main political beneficiaries were not the left, but rather the political centre, the politicians who sought a new era of reconciliation between capital and labour.

The socialist movement, far from having grown, was in steep decline by 1982. The ALP Socialist Left had become just another factional machine, while the CPA had lost key union leaders such as John Halfpenny and Laurie Carmichael and was soon to discuss dissolution. Intellectuals, too, were in retreat. Academic Marxism, which had flowered briefly in the 1970s, was giving way to 'post-structuralism', with its hostility to systematic politics. Revolutionary Marxists had established only a small presence in the labour movement and could not hope to stem the rightward tide. So weakened was the socialist movement that, when a sizeable minority of Labor supporters became disillusioned with the Hawke Government in the mid-1980s, they turned not in the direction of socialism, but to political currents lacking any substantial connection with the left or the working class –the Australian Democrats or various forms of liberal or single issue politics.

Earlier chapters have identified some reasons for this decline. Above all, it flowed from the defeats organised labour and the social movements suffered after 1975. Workers who had once been able to rely on localised industrial pressure to extract pay rises found themselves floundering in the face of generalised recession and battered by defeats. Rather than moving leftward under the impact of the crisis, their ideas drifted rightward as they lost confidence in their own strength. They were increasingly tempted to rely on bureaucratic manoeuvres and on voting Labor rather than fighting the system. Movements which had once hoped to confront social and environmental problems through class struggle met a similar fate.

These setbacks, in turn, discouraged those intellectuals with an orientation to the working class or the social movements, while making it easier for academic Marxists to defect in the direction of the next intellectual fad. As for the small army of left and movement activists who had emerged from the Vietnam war era, they were showing signs of fatigue by the end of the 1970s. Many had been intensely active for a decade or so, only to find that they were achieving less and less as time went on, in terms both of winning victories and of recruiting to the causes they championed.

Important as they were, however, such factors will not quite suffice as explanations for the drastic decline of the left over just seven years. On the one hand, the upheavals of 1975–78 represented a series of opportunities to *reverse* the pattern of defeat and decline; but these were largely wasted. Prominent leaders of the industrial and political left bore considerable responsibility for that, as we have seen. On the other hand, politics is not a simple reflex of social trends. Politically sophisticated people on the left were generally part of formal or informal organisations and networks and carried on debates in specialised publications. These structures insulated them somewhat from the pressures of the society around them. They should have managed more than a token resistance to the rightward tide. Some did, but the majority collapsed with remarkable speed into support for Labor Party policies designed to subordinate the needs of workers and oppressed people to the interests of capitalism.

This debacle was only possible because most of the left was itself infected from the start with reformism: the view that the system could be reformed from within. Its apparently radical ideas concealed considerable common ground with the dominant capitalist ideology, so it could slide without any great theoretical ruptures from a 'left reformism' associated with considerable militancy to a 'right reformism' which endorsed the pro-capitalist policies of the Hawke Government. There were some forces seriously committed to revolutionary socialism, and the critique in this chapter draws on their arguments; but they mostly remained marginal in practice throughout the Fraser era.

From women's liberation to feminism

Politically, the early Women's Liberation Movement (WLM) owed much to the left. Its founders included members and ex-members of the CPA (for example, Joyce Stevens and Zelda D'Aprano) as well as independents influenced by Marxist politics, such as Anna Yeatman. The Maoists of the Worker-Student Alliance and the Trotskyists of the Socialist Workers' Party were influential in building the early WLM groups and in their public actions. Initially, the movement as a whole saw itself as allied with the wider left in a struggle to fundamentally change society, as indicated by its very name, which carried echoes of Vietnam and of Paris 1968.

Accordingly, the movement generally saw left-wing men as allies. They were active within Adelaide Women's Liberation as late as 1971, reflecting the local movement's view that 'women's liberation is human liberation', that men and women were both oppressed by the capitalist state, and that 'women's liberation was not a feminist movement narrowly confined to the struggle for equality with men in present society.'[3] Similarly, early issues of movement papers like *Mejane* and *Vashti* carried the odd article by male contributors.

The early movement showed a strong interest in class politics. It held one of its first national conferences in August 1971 to coincide with an ACTU conference; its members were often concerned to establish links with working class women; and, as late as March 1976, an International Women's Day speaker could say:

> We live in a male-dominated society which is also a capitalist society... Governments are there to uphold capitalists' position and to ensure that they make continuing profits. They don't make exceptions for women...they divide them off in classes as they do men. If women were in power and maintained capitalism they would still be divided from each other by classes.[4]

From the early 1970s, however, two factors had begun to push the movement away from these socialist and revolutionary influences. One was the growth of the movement itself. Young women poured into it, drawn largely from the universities and from professional and other skilled occupations. Most of these saw gender as a more important issue than class, making them a suitable audience for a growing radical feminist current. While socialism remained important for some time, the radical feminists increasingly set the agenda for movement debates with their argument that all women, as a sex, were involved in a power struggle with men and should put aside issues of race and class:

> As the Female Liberation Movement must cut across all (male imposed) class, race and national lines, any false identification of women with privileges that are really male (such as whiteness or class etc.) will be fatal to our movement.[5]

At the same time, Whitlam's government was widening the scope for welfare activity and for bureaucratic careers. This was the second factor. Funding for health centres and similar projects expanded, particularly during 1975, International Women's Year. Elizabeth Reid became Whitlam's Women's Adviser. While many activists remained critical of the welfare focus and also of Reid, the seeds of ambiguity had been sown. Moreover, the new welfare network provided a certain material base for the activists and so conferred an illusion of power; one could imagine that, contrary to the warnings of socialists, the oppressed might achieve their ends through the existing state machine.

Women's liberation demonstration Sydney 1975 links women's liberation to socialism

The Constitutional Crisis and Fraser's rise to power shook such illusions severely. Capital and labour mobilised their forces for struggle, so the politics of class suddenly overshadowed everything else. The WLM feared that its key accomplishments were under threat but found itself relatively powerless to influence the outcome. While Fraser did not dismantle the welfare network, his attacks, along with the economic recession, did bring home to many of the activists that their health centres and other institutions represented dependency more than power. Rather than moving away from reformism, however, a discouraged and disoriented women's movement responded by shifting decisively to the right, in an ideological *démarche* that took on two main forms.

Radical feminism continued to gain ground with its view that all women could and should be united against men and their supposed system of 'patriarchy'[6] on the basis of a 'female culture'. Sometimes, there was rhetoric about a feminist revolution, but this perspective was always left rather vague;[7] beneath even the most radical pretensions lay a logic of accommodation to existing society. As the IS' Janey Stone argued in 1974, the search for a female culture seemed so vital because it 'amounts to the only thing that does cut across all class, race and national lines for women'. But she pointed out that, to the extent that such a culture existed, it was precisely the embodiment of traditional, sexist models of femininity:

> As radical feminism has grown and developed it has retreated
> more and more into the female role... Articles are written attacking
> thought and theory as 'male'. Women 'suddenly' develop an interest
> in crafts, particularly those not exactly traditionally regarded as
> unsuitable for females, e.g., weaving or crocheting.[8]

Related to this was radical feminism's obsession with the personal sphere. By insisting that 'the personal is political', the early WLM had made important points about the political implications of everyday life. But, by the mid-1970s, the terms of the argument had changed. Joyce Stevens and others pointed out:

> sections within the movement developed a tendency to ignore
> what they as individual women did not experience...condemning
> everything outside individual women's personal concerns as 'male
> power games' or, at best, secondary to and derivative from this
> individualised 'personal'.[9]

Such subjectivism had an appeal to people losing confidence in the labour movement, but it could not lead to any strategy for social change. By default, the activists kept drifting into piecemeal reform projects. Meanwhile, despite Fraser's cuts, there were still various explicitly reformist avenues within, or associated with, the state machine. Sara Dowse had succeeded Elizabeth Reid and stayed on under Fraser, making the Women's Affairs Branch inside the PM's Department the nucleus of a network of women's policy units throughout the public service. Inevitably, such work in the bureaucracy brought new conservatising pressures.

When the government moved to establish the NWAC in 1978, feminists in the working party decided that the Council should not be elected. Fearing both 'damaging conflict' among women and the organisational strength of the right, they decided that:

> it was better for the government to make the appointments, and to rely on these relatively conservative women being radicalised by prolonged exposure to the issues during consultation processes.[10]

This was a long way from the combative spirit of the early days.

These 'femocrats' were joined by numerous other careerists. Lesley Lynch reported that the 1979 Women and Law Conference had revealed a 'new breed of feminist legal women' whose talents and energy were admirable but who displayed 'an unhealthy respect for the overall legal system'.[11] Another contingent was moving into business. In the decade ending in 1978, the number of females in administrative, executive and managerial positions had risen by 18 percent. In 1978, garment entrepreneur Vera Randall became the first Australian Veuve Clicquot 'business woman of the year'. Such trends helped to explain why one founder of Sydney Women's Liberation told Anne Summers: 'We've become more conservative. It is as if we had to be very extreme to discover the possibilities. Now we've become more realistic.'[12]

It was the same in electoral politics, which appeared more important as the social movements declined, particularly after a swing to Labor in the 1980 elections. Female leaders of all the major parties ranging from Labor's Joan Child to National Party president Shirley McKerrow came together at a 1981 seminar, at which 'ideological differences disappeared'.[13] The story was little different out on the hustings. Take the 1980 ALP candidate for Dundas: a feminist, whose research found the electorate to be rather conservative. She thus felt obliged to present a respectable image that 'would not in itself be a challenge to the lifestyle of the majority of voters in the electorate':

> Our major pamphlet featured a picture of a smiling mum in a neat skirt and jumper surrounded by three smiling children... I acquired various items of dress to fit this image [and] became very conscious that I had created a monster and was even buying her clothes.[14]

What good was a feminism that feared to challenge conservative lifestyles? To be sure, there were still plenty of activists wearing jeans and raising hell. But the difference in principle between militancy and moderation, let alone reform and revolution, was eroding steadily. Susan Eade noted that, as early as 1976, one Canberra discussion group had decided: 'the old distinction between reform and revolution is obsolete and irrelevant' and dismissed the 'socialist revolution propagated by the male left as pie in the sky'. In the wake of the Constitutional Crisis, the Canberra feminists had arrived at an 'anarchist-reformist concept of the revolution.'[15]

This was a fair description for the politics of much of the movement nationally – with the added proviso that the anarchism lay mostly in the style, while reformism increasingly dominated the practical politics. Over the next couple of years, most people stopped referring to liberation, and the WLM ceased holding general meetings in the capital cities around 1978.

Meanwhile, socialist ideas steadily lost ground. The majority of women identifying as socialist, including many in and around the CPA, had made a fatal concession quite early by trying to reconcile conflicting ideologies with an arbitrary amalgam – calling themselves socialist-feminists or, in the case of the more theoretically inclined, marxist-feminists. The implication was that socialism was fundamentally flawed but could be fixed with a feminist admixture. In reality, socialism and feminism were pointing in different directions.

The resulting ambiguities plagued the socialist-feminist journal *Scarlet Woman*. This publication contained valuable partial critiques of radical and reformist feminism, and the editorial collective saw race and class as important issues. But *Scarlet Woman*'s backers were as incapable as the radical feminists of arriving at a strategy for social change. Even attempts to establish an ongoing organisation foundered in the face of basic disagreements – not surprising, given that their theory was essentially a cut-and-paste affair. After years of chewing over, the concept 'capitalist-patriarchy, socialist-feminism's almost mystical beast' remained largely undefined.[16] At the 1980 Women and Labour

Conference, Pat Gowland's attempt to provide an answer got no further than the lame conclusion: 'A tentative application of a Marxist-feminist theoretical framework is possible.'[17] So how could you work out a strategy for fighting the beast? No wonder the *Scarlet Woman* editors had to concede that: 'we have obviously felt more confident about our feminism than our socialism.'[18]

In fact, 'hyphenated' feminism was in deep decline by the early 1980s. Ann Curthoys lamented:

> As time goes on, one after another of former marxist-feminists has announced her conviction that the two theories cannot be integrated or made compatible, and that if a choice has therefore to be made it has to be for feminism.[19]

That choice was being made despite glaring weaknesses in feminist theory and practice. Talk of sisterhood, for example, looked rather facile alongside the frequent and often bitter conflicts among feminists. (*Scarlet Woman* reported 'vitriolic attacks' and sectarian battles over 'the one true line.')[20] There were even sharper conflicts once you looked outside the movement's own ranks. Not only were there right-wing women's groups, but the right-wing forces could invade feminist territory and hijack feminist formulations. In 1980, a group of conservative women physically occupied the Alice Springs Women's Centre, complaining that the Centre ignored 'the very separate needs of white women'; the occupiers also mouthed 'platitudes about Aboriginal autonomy.'[21] It was not much longer before some anti-abortionists began to use the term feminism.

The hope of uniting all women was not merely utopian; it could lead to reactionary conclusions. When the Australian Social Welfare Union tried to get award coverage of NSW women's services in 1982, some in the movement attacked them for compromising feminist 'autonomy'. Union structures were hierarchical, said the critics, and 'therefore patriarchal.'[22] But perhaps the most outrageous and revealing episode occurred in the aftermath of a 1981 'Womyn, Patriarchy and the Future Forum', where Black participants warned the audience that racism lurked just beneath the surface in the movement. This raised a few hackles, and one Pam Stein replied as follows:

> Certainly as a radical feminist *I am* trying to destroy black cultures – if they keep trying to uphold the cultures of patriarchy... I am racist to the extent that I believe there are two races – women and men,

and I hate the men who are destroying our race...[women] should be analysing this and eliminating our murderers.[23]

The statement was as ignorant as it was insensitive. Misled by a patriarchy theory which saw all men as oppressors, Stein thought that Aboriginal women should see *their* men in this role, but that was nonsense. There was evidence that Aboriginal society had been free of sexism before white colonisation,[24] and there was little doubt that sexism in *modern* Indigenous communities resulted from the pressures of the white society around them.

Aboriginal men who had to cope with racist violence, illness and malnutrition hardly qualified as oppressors by any standard, and Aboriginal women understandably resented attempts by comparatively affluent white feminists to paint them as such. The existing women's movement had little allure for the many women prominent in the Black movement, who repeatedly declared, as Pat O'Shane did in 1976, that 'racism is the greatest problem facing them in this society.'[25]

To their credit, numerous feminists rushed to dissociate themselves from Stein's diatribe. Jocelyn Clarke responded by stating: 'I have no common ground with some of the other women who call themselves radical feminists.'[26] Well said, but where did *that* leave the female culture and a united women's struggle?

Although the dangers and contradictions of reformist and radical feminism were becoming obvious, that did not reduce their influence. Occasional wistful pleas for a return to some concept of liberation fell on deaf ears. By the early 1980s, feminism was no longer necessarily left wing. Its academic representatives often displayed what Anna Yeatman called 'the usual sort of academic snobbery towards those...whose ideals and values are embedded in practice.'[27] In addition to the political factors discussed above, this had a social basis, which Ann Curthoys explained in an insightful passage:

> As I grew older, and gained greater job security and a higher level of pay, I saw my feminist friends around me experiencing the same process. We...had become established. We became public servants, journalists, teachers, academics, librarians, social workers and so on. We published magazines, saw the correct films, attended the correct meetings, and had consciousness-raised ourselves to think correct thoughts... The women I'm speaking of were, then, in terms of the society they lived in, highly privileged people... Yet how did this group, these friends

of mine, see themselves? They saw themselves as oppressed, as victims, as underdogs.[28]

To be sure, as Curthoys herself noted, teachers or librarians were still part of the working class. Oppression was a tangible reality for many of them. But the fact remained that numerous feminist leaders and trendsetters had gained a foothold in the capitalist system. As they did so, their theories shifted ground in subtle fashion, slipping into categories which that system could accommodate.

Nationalism: a road to the right

Nationalism is a traditional feature of Australian labour politics, usually in close alignment with reformism. The connection is logical: both nationalism and reformism look to the existing nation state and seek to strengthen it. However, in the late 1960s and early 1970s, the Maoists of the Communist Party of Australia (Marxist-Leninist) (CPA-ML) sought to construct something resembling a *revolutionary* nationalism.

During a genuinely revolutionary phase in the 1920s, Australian communists had opposed patriotism, dismissing references to the 'spirit of Eureka' as a 'meaningless bleat'.[29] Later, Stalin's 'people's front' policies of the mid-thirties were designed to lure Western social democrats and sections of the Western bourgeoisie into alliances with the USSR and had committed the Communist Parties to various forms of nationalism. At the same time, Stalin steered them towards parliamentary strategies. Still, they could resist fully embracing the patriotic-reformist logic because they had a reference point outside their own society: their first loyalty was to a foreign ruling class in the USSR (or, later, China). In the postwar decades, demands for 'national independence' were vehicles for challenging US influence and gained a new (although ultimately spurious) revolutionary colouration because of the examples of Vietnam and China.

Trading on the ultra-revolutionary image of the Chinese cultural revolution, the Maoists were able to serve up a potent cocktail combining national chauvinism (blaming everything on 'the Yanks' or on Japan) with revolutionary slogans. They traded on a certain disquiet in both the bourgeoisie and the labour movement about the surge of foreign investment since the late 1960s. On this basis, they were able to recruit a layer of radical students whom they organised into the Worker-Student Alliance (WSA). WSA saw the main enemy as US imperialism but, as its name implied, still retained an orientation to class struggle.

Commonwealth Government Clothing Factory protest at proposed closure 1981 uses nationalist and pro-company arguments

HY SELL A
ACTORY THAT
AKES PROFIT
AND WE GET
THE
COBURG TRUCK PARTS

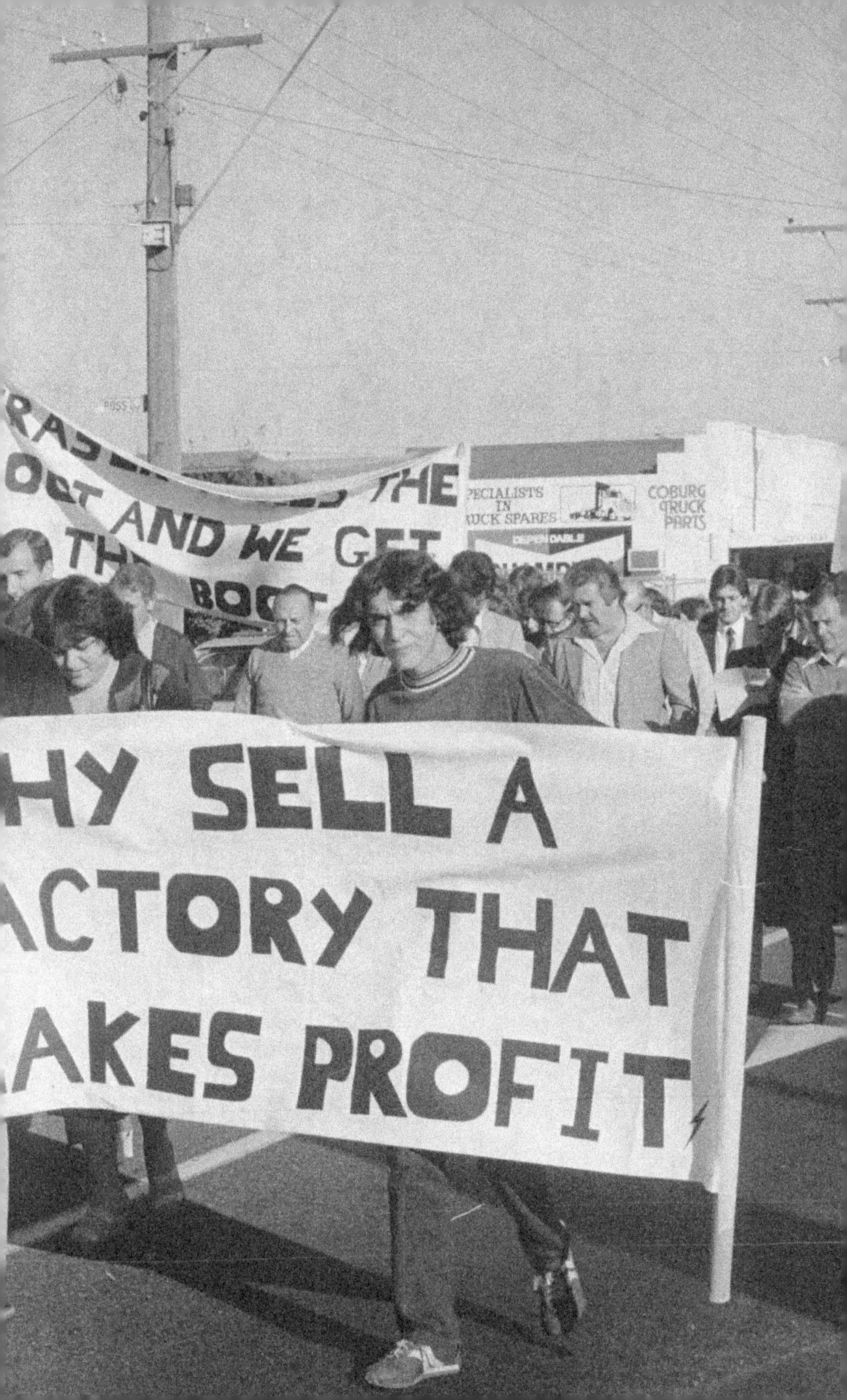

USE LYNCH'S RAZOR TO CUT HIS OWN THROAT

FACTORY
Contour Razors
ADVANCE AUSTRALIA WHERE
R.G.G.F.
FRAZER MEANS UNEMPLOYMENT
WE NEED SUPPORT.

PROTECT AN
AUSTRALIA'S

SU

DING

EXPAND A.N.L.
SHIPPING LINE.
STAY PUT ITS OUR JOBS

By 1975, however, the nationalist politics were beginning to predominate. At the height of the Constitutional Crisis, the Maoists tried to take the big Melbourne demonstration to the US Consulate, claiming that US machinations lay behind John Kerr's actions. Over the next few years, they threw themselves into building an Australian Independence Movement (AIM), campaigning for Blinky Bill to replace Mickey Mouse as King of Melbourne's Moomba festival and arranging for Matilda the boxing kangaroo to knock out Uncle Sam on May Day platforms. Their *Independent Australian* magazine promoted Australian businesses in an attempt to woo a supposedly 'patriotic' section of the bourgeoisie, alongside cultural discussions attempting to revive a narrow version of the 'Australian legend'. For a time, the Maoists won considerable sympathy for this venture, partly because opportunist elements in the wider labour movement were also promoting nationalism in order to derail the class struggle.

But it was an awkward enterprise. The AIM had to promote Banjo Paterson, despite his racism, and somehow blur the fact that traditional Australian nationalism had been closely linked to genocide against Aboriginal and Torres Strait Islander people and to the 'yellow peril' anti-Asian syndrome. In an otherwise useful book about early resistance to colonisation, Fergus Robinson and Barry York even hypothesised that convicts and Indigenous people (the 'first Australian patriots') could have made common cause against British colonialism – although they had no evidence worth mentioning.[30] The AIM also had to draw obscure distinctions between supposedly progressive Aussie rock music and the 'imperialist' variety coming out of the USA – never mind that they were largely indistinguishable, or that the latter stemmed from the culture of the USA's Black people. The whole argument was also very narrow, because the bush ballads or celebrations of Australia's invention of the stump-jump plough meant little to the growing section of the working class born overseas, while increasing numbers of women rejected the sexist strand in traditional Australian culture.

The hoped-for alliance with 'patriotic capital' that was supposed to compensate for this proved elusive. It was hard to identify any significant bourgeois figures interested in forming a block with the Maoists, although they had brief hopes for financial high-flyer Gordon Barton. More typically, the *Independent Australian* devoted its attention to sections of small business, such as small wineries or the Independent Publishers' Association. Even these were not easy to woo, and the AIM began to drop any mention of socialism or left politics in a desperate attempt to maintain credibility with them.

So the Maoists and their umbrella organisation were already on a reformist course when the whole attempt to construct a revolutionary nationalism collapsed abruptly, because the reference point outside Australia changed. In the course of the 1970s, Beijing tilted decisively towards the West. Mao and his successors began seeking allies among the Western bourgeoisie, and Maoist parties like the CPA–ML came under pressure to accommodate to their own national ruling class. China's new nemesis was the Russians, so the new Australian leader Malcolm Fraser, stridently anti-Soviet, became a potential ally. As the implications of this turn worked their way through CPA–ML theory, the Maoists had to make some bizarre adjustments. Even their assessment of the Constitutional Crisis had to change.

The main culprit remained US imperialism, but the reasons ascribed to Washington for dumping Whitlam shifted subtly. Originally, the Maoists had cited Whitlam's inability to control the unions and his economic nationalism. His softer line on the USSR was mentioned in passing. By 1978, in an effort to rationalise what had become an absolutely obsessive anti-Soviet line, the CPA–ML was insisting that 'superpower contention' had been the main factor. Whitlam had been dumped because he was too pro-Soviet.

Because the anti-Soviet Fraser had replaced Whitlam, this line of argument opened the door for the Maoists to align themselves with the new government. They did so indirectly. In November 1977, they slammed the ALP for its 'even-handed' attitude to the two superpowers, because: 'in circumstances where Soviet social-imperialism is advancing…that unavoidably means assisting Soviet social-imperialism. Hence this Labor Party attitude menaces the independence of Australia.' To be sure, the conservatives were also lackeys of imperialism. 'But where is the greater danger?' This question needn't be answered explicitly, because they had insisted two months earlier that the Soviets were 'the greatest menace to Australia.'[31] By the late 1970s, the Maoists and their AIM were panic-mongering about the machinations of the Moscow Narodny Bank.

In addition to isolating them from pro-Soviet sections of the left, these formulations outraged others who knew that Fraser's anti-Soviet rhetoric underpinned Australia's *own* imperialism abroad and anti-communist attacks on the labour movement at home. Foolish attempts to link women's liberation to 'Australian independence' didn't help. The crudity of the arguments, the downplaying of socialism and the accommodation to Fraser (plus ructions over internal Chinese politics) provoked the more left-wing elements of the AIM to break away, and the CPA–ML lost most of its 1960s recruits.[32] The growing isolation of the Maoists left the field free for more overtly reformist forms of labour movement nationalism.

One curious case was their sometime academic fellow traveller Humphrey McQueen. McQueen's first book had ripped into Australian nationalism, but he had drifted steadily rightward over the years. By the early 1980s, he was firmly on a nationalist and reformist course. His book *Gone Tomorrow* was a milestone in this evolution. *Gone Tomorrow*[33] explored many issues with some flair, nonetheless returning repeatedly to the evils of foreign capital. McQueen looked to the more enterprising domestic capitalists to pose an alternative, at one point launching into a celebration of Rod Carnegie's efforts to Australianise CRA, the local subsidiary of Rio Tinto Zinc, then moving along to this astonishing passage about one of our most bilious local reactionaries:

> Despite Lang Hancock's reactionary attitudes, Australia's working people would have been much better served if he, and not foreign investors, had owned the Pilbara since his profits could be recycled through Australia thereby creating jobs; and even if he invested all of his mining profits in Asian factories which then took jobs away from Australians, our balance of payments could benefit from these repatriated profits...

Having embraced Australian capital, why be shy? Australian *imperialism* was more charming still!

McQueen was too sophisticated to imagine that 'economic independence' alone could solve the country's problems:

> After getting the benefits for Australia there remains the question of how to distribute them to Australians... Welfare spending and employment are two of the obvious ways of achieving this goal.

With these provisos, he was content that 'economic nationalism is a practical program for rescuing the welfare of Australia's working people.' Socialism might be desirable as an added extra, but McQueen had clearly lost faith in it. 'Bitter disappointment arose when racism, sexism and other inequalities survived the establishment of socialism in Russia or China,' so, consequently, 'reform is more likely to be attempted than is revolution.' Unlike the CPA-ML, McQueen could see faults in Mao's China, but the fact only hastened his reformist evolution.

In the mainstream of the labour movement, nationalism had seldom taken on quite so left a face as that initially presented by the Maoists. Its historic role was to divert attention from the class struggle against the Australian bourgeoisie and to facilitate class collaboration in the supposed national interest. As an ideology, it perfectly suited the needs of the trade union bureaucracy, the ALP machine and Labor MPs, who liked to employ the rhetoric of struggle (against foreigners) while containing industrial militancy and social protest at home. In the Fraser era, union and ALP leaders used nationalist rhetoric to divert working class anger after the Constitutional Crisis, then to lock their rank and file supporters gradually into reformist projects whose culmination was the ALP–ACTU Accord.

Soon after Whitlam's fall, the unions began searching for alternative economic perspectives to counterpoise Fraser's monetarism. Their first resort was traditional Keynesian policies. Tom Uren lectured groups of workers about the 'multiplier effect', and the first major union document – the AMWU's 'People's Budget' of 1976 – relied on calls for public spending and public works. But this wasn't credible among the ruins of the big-spending Whitlam Government. A system in crisis lacked the resources to make such concessions, so the traditional reformist projects could not deliver the goods. Something else was needed to restore enthusiasm. The AMWU leaders found it in a particularly paranoid version of economic nationalism.

The union's 1977 publication *Australia Uprooted* was a mass-distribution pamphlet. The main appeal of its crude and uncertain economic arguments lay in dire warnings that foreign-owned multinationals were out to destroy Australian industry by turning the country into a 'vast quarry', while Fraser was doing these foreigners' bidding by cutting wages.[34] Although further pamphlets were needed to flesh out the arguments and add a veneer of sophistication, the immediate political problem had been solved: the AMWU had an excuse not to fight the Australian bourgeoisie. Instead, it argued, metal workers must *unite* with that bourgeoisie to defend domestic manufacturing from the multinationals' infernal plans.

The conspiracy theories had little basis in reality. Although Fraser did look primarily to resource development to drive the economy, he did not intend to destroy the rest of industry. According to Industries Assistance Commission measurements, average rates of protection for manufacturing, which had been 27 percent in 1975, were still 23 percent in 1980 and rose again to 25 percent in 1983. At the very time the AMWU was launching *Australia Uprooted*, the government was introducing new protectionist policies for manufacturing

YEARS OF RAGE

The arguments in *Australia Uprooted* influenced other unions: here the NSW Teachers Federation

industry. But these simplistic theories held considerable appeal for workers losing confidence in their ability to fight the class struggle.

A range of left intellectuals stormed onto the new bandwagon. Ted Wheelwright and Greg Crough elaborated critiques of foreign ownership of capital; the short-lived 'resources boom' gave the arguments about de-industrialisation and becoming a giant quarry a superficial plausibility; and a complex argument about currency values (the 'Gregory Thesis') gave them some theoretical sustenance. AMWU researcher Ted Wiltshire argued for a 'total package which includes a commitment to Australia having a viable manufacturing industry', including nationalisation and controls on private finance plus restructuring of manufacturing industry through state intervention.[35] By the late 1970s, a large slab of the left intelligentsia was at work on 'alternative economic strategies'.

Many of these writers were, like some of the feminist opinion-makers discussed above, worn-out or disillusioned radicals now entering comparatively privileged careers. This helps to explain an intellectual accommodation to capitalism. But, to be fair, their enthusiasm for alternative strategies also derived from an understandable desire to put forward something *positive*. With its endless array of negative slogans (stop this! ban that!), the left did sometimes remind you of Groucho Marx singing: 'Whatever It Is, I'm Against It'. The challenge was to find alternatives that really challenged the status quo. This, the left intelligentsia largely failed to do – nor *could* they, on a nationalist basis.

Australian nationalism has always had a reactionary dynamic. In the colonial era, it was closely linked to racism, and its supposed hostility to British imperialism usually amounted to complaints that Britain was betraying the white race in Asia. In the 20th century, it has become an ideological support for Australia's own imperialism. The goal of making this country economically competitive fitted naturally together with the attempts by both conservative and Labor governments to intensify the exploitation of labour.[36] All of the alternative strategies, therefore, tended to collapse into the logic of capitalism, despite their authors' best intentions.

They also had another fundamental weakness: to some degree, they all sought to shut out the pressures of the world economy through investment guidelines, tariffs or other forms of state control. But isolating Australia from the international economic division of labour would have immense costs, as Marxists like Rick Kuhn pointed out:

> Multinationals' investments have extended the scope of Australian industry and employment in the past. If the country is to survive without infusions of overseas capital while industry and employment are maintained, then the social rate of savings would have to be increased. That is, the amount available for workers to consume will have to be cut. This would especially be the case as capital equipment produced by protected local industries would be more expensive.[37]

Moreover, calls for greater economic isolation would have to be sold to a fair section of Australian business, and overseas interests would have to sit idly by and allow themselves to be frozen out. None of that was at all likely – but then, these proposals were never likely to be acted on anyway. The fading of the 'resources boom' allowed the argument to shift to new ground. Having built a consensus about the need to strengthen manufacturing, the ALP and union lefts could turn their attention to the details of that project. It was, after all, in the 'national interest'. Later, under Hawke, the emphasis was on national competitiveness, but the underlying logic was the same. Here, too, the politics of nationalism meshed neatly with the economics of reformism.

Militancy uprooted

The alternative strategists, whatever their intentions, simply contributed to diverting or dampening the class struggle. Some key union leaders seized on their ideas with enthusiasm, precisely because they offered a particularly subtle attack on the industrial militancy of the Australian working class – which would not be easy to subvert, partly because unionists who had been hammered by Fraser would be reluctant to forgive and forget. An additional factor was the union leaders' own earlier statements. While even the best of them had always operated within an essentially reformist framework, the days of giddy militancy around 1968–75 had seen some pretty radical posturing. John Halfpenny, for example, had declared as late as 1976 that 'the interests of workers and management correspond only by accident' because class conflict was 'inherent in the capitalist system'.[38]

So the first attempts to reconcile workers to the capitalist system had to assume the most left-wing possible guise. Laurie Carmichael made a fair fist of this in 1977 when *Australia Uprooted* appeared: he argued that its economic proposals were actually vehicles for a transition to socialism. After all, they called for some nationalisation of industry associated with 'an extension of worker control'! Carmichael spoke vaguely about mass struggles to back up the policy proposals. While he and other left officials did little to mobilise workers, the rhetoric of struggle helped to provide left camouflage for a shift to the right.[39]

Further camouflage was soon required. Lest workers take seriously the talk about socialism and mass struggle, the ideologues of the official labour movement moved quickly to replace both concepts with pale imitations. This became easier as the 1970s wore on, because workers were losing confidence in their own ability to win gains. The reform projects of the early Whitlam years had had a certain substance to them; if the capitalist system had kept growing, reforms within it might well have continued to improve the lives of the working class. By contrast, the new proposals were intellectual fairy floss. The economy was not going to return to the growth levels of the postwar decades. If a growing number of militants nevertheless put their faith in the new arguments, it was because they saw few alternatives.

First came a sustained attack on basic industrial militancy. Railways union research officer Roger Jowett told a conference organised by the Trans-National Co-operative in 1978 that strikes over wages lacked the ability to 'mobilise, unite and educate workers.' After all, wages had not even been mentioned at the last ACTU Congress. Rather, workers must take the offensive with alternative economic plans and engage in the 'progressive conquest of power.'[40]

That might appear to take the struggle away from the dismal lowlands of 'economism' towards revolutionary heights; in reality, the conquest of power was increasingly used to mean a social contract with the next Labor government. And this was the second part of the exercise. Ex-communist Winton Higgins extolled the Swedish model: a powerful trade union federation, together with social democratic governments, was supposedly achieving a transition to post-capitalist society.[41] For most of the following decade, Sweden was a lodestar for sections of the labour movement, until an emerging Swedish crisis in the late 1980s put paid to the illusions.

There was talk of 'revolutionary reforms' – but, of course, these dare not be too revolutionary. No-nonsense union officials like Bruce Hartnett understood that 'a socialist strategy for Australia must include...firstly, an alternative economic program which is realistic, credible and achievable.' This was to be implemented under capitalism with the aim of achieving full employment and rising living standards.[42]

Hartnett later moved along to a management job at ICI Australia, and we are still waiting for the full employment. It was actually the alternative economic strategies which lacked realism; in particular, they ignored the need to dismantle the power structures of the system and replace them with new and very different ones. In retrospect, it is clear that the whole alternative-strategy literature was a vast fantasyland. Although some of the reforms were worth fighting for, others were essentially technocratic. In any case, the measures proposed could no more abolish capitalism by themselves than Sweden's social-democrats could genuinely commit to introducing socialism. Far from leading to a 'conquest of power', the various plans for industry merely provided insights for politicians and bureaucrats, while demoralising or coopting militant workers.

In the early 1980s, writers closer to the ALP centre seized on some of the insights to help rehabilitate Laborism intellectually. One vehicle was a series of *Labor Essays* edited by Gareth Evans, two volumes of which focused on policy. Written amid a temporary revival of industrial militancy during the 'resources boom' (see next chapter), the 1981 edition still presented a fairly left-wing face, paying lip service to socialism and seeking to forge links with the rightward moving alternative strategists.

Economist Barry Hughes offered sophisticated arguments against wages militancy. Increasingly, he argued, inflation was wiping out wage gains. Moreover, the wage–price spiral of the 1970s had allowed affluent professionals to get ahead at workers' expense. On the other hand, if a government incomes policy achieved falling inflation while fully indexing wages, workers could gradually make gains because 'current money wage increases, reflecting past higher inflation, will be more than enough to keep up with present price rises.'[43] The argument was incredibly neat, as long as you trusted Labor to maintain full wage indexation.

Bruce Hartnett advanced a complementary argument, acknowledging in passing that wages were important but warning that, without a wider focus, wage claims could merely reinforce the existing social order:

> The wage claim maintains the momentum in the system, keeping it running and distracting both unions and their members from the underlying issues relating to the concentration of power and decision-making in a few hands.[44]

Better, he said, for unions to undertake challenges to that concentration of power, as the BLF had done with its Green Bans. This was a fair point and sounded rather daring. Alas, he then launched into a proposal to use union super funds to prop up manufacturing industry, making it obvious that his real aim was 'interventions' in bureaucratic forums designed to cement new alliances between capital and labour.

In the same volume, moreover, Chris Hurford essayed a frontal attack on socialism:

> The likelihood that Australia's institutions could be developed to replace the present mechanisms of the private sector within any foreseeable period is remote indeed. No political strategy for such radical change, which bears any concrete relationship to Australian reality, presently exists. Accordingly, we must turn to a strategy which can germinate within the confines of the existing and prospective attitudes of Australian people.[45]

The socialist references had only been intended to lure the gullible. Labor wanted ideas for administering the system, not for challenging it; while some insights could be extracted from the alternative strategies, they must be set firmly in a capitalist framework. In any case, the party had lost interest by 1983 in cultivating those to its left. Industrial militancy had collapsed with the return of recession in 1982, and most of the intellectual and trade union left had thoroughly compromised itself. The 1983 edition of *Labor Essays* was full of shadow ministers and conventional social democratic proposals. Ralph Willis wanted more expansionary macro-economic settings, Barry Jones wanted better industry planning – and socialism did not rate a mention.

The intellectual eclipse of the left ran parallel to its political decline inside the ALP. The left factional apparatus was quite strong, but its underlying strength had been sapped by years of failure, both in politics and in industry. Hampered by the vacillations of key union officials, the left had failed to stop the Newport power station, failed to stop uranium mining, failed to save Medibank and lost the Latrobe Valley strike. The unions did win a series of battles between 1978 and 1981, as we'll see in Chapter 11, but these were not fought on a very political basis. The final settlements, with their no-strike deals, renewed the trend towards class collaboration –in turn helping to weaken working class organisation at the grassroots.

When a CPA industrial publication complained in 1982 that 'shop floor organisation has not expanded', this was a euphemism for disastrous decline: actually, there were 'few if any effective self-acting shop committees'.[46] But without organised strength at the base, the left could not hope to shape politics at the top. This was already becoming apparent by 1980, when the *National Times* announced that 'the lions of the left are gone':

> The days when Jim Cairns was its prophet, Lionel Murphy its brains and Tom Uren its organiser are history. For the first time in decades the left in recent years cannot deliver to one of its own any of the four leadership posts inside the parliamentary party.[47]

The left could no more determine policy than it could control key positions, a fact which the 1982 ALP national conference mercilessly exposed. The conference dumped the party's previous blanket opposition to uranium mining, refused to take a serious pro-choice stand on abortion and ran away from endorsing a capital gains tax. The left at least made some effort to hold the line on uranium, but it was hugely embarrassed when one of its key leaders, Bob Hogg, made the running for the pro-uranium forces. By this stage, it was only an isolated minority within the ALP left – with some small groups outside the party – who still thought seriously in terms of challenging the capitalist system.

With the left in decay, the politicians at the top could flaunt their right-wing views as they moved towards power. Hayden traded on his reputation as the budget-slashing Treasurer of 1975, while Hawke boasted that he would take a hard line against the unions. In case the bourgeoisie was still a bit uneasy, Labor had a new star every boss could love: Paul Keating. 'Labor's OK, look at Keating,' said one business leader. Another, Hugh Morgan of Western Mining, announced that he 'would be pleased to have someone like Keating as our minister'. His fellow mining magnate, Sid Londish, called Keating: 'the type of person we really need in power.'[48]

Once Labor had politically neutralised the forces on its left and built bridges to the right, all that remained was to articulate a new strategy for Australian capitalism. The ALP leadership had been debating this since February 1979, when Bob Hawke told the party's economics committee that 'a comprehensive, equitable incomes policy' should become Labor policy.[49]

At the party's Adelaide conference in July of that year, Hayden negotiated with the left to steer through a more leftish sounding call for an incomes policy to 'achieve a more equitable distribution of our national wealth and income, with the commitment to supporting the maintenance of real wages.'[50] This was a factional rebuff to Hawke, but the incomes policy concept was becoming entrenched. Besides, Hayden was not serious about maintaining, let alone improving, living standards. His refusal to commit a Labor government to full wage indexation brought ructions with the ACTU from time to time.

As the prospect of a Labor government drew near, the leaders of the industrial and political wings flirted repeatedly with each other. Hayden raised the social contract issue at the 1981 ACTU Congress, around the same time as the AMWU began talking about their 'social wage' campaign. In February 1982, Hayden explicitly hailed the latter as a significant step towards his own plans for a prices-and-incomes deal; in July, Labor's federal conference endorsed the concept in principle; and later in the year, prominent ALP politicians appeared at union meetings pushing the 'social wage' concept. In September, the ACTU and party leaders released a discussion paper containing the gist of what eventually became the Prices and Incomes Accord.

These results were not surprising, given the close links between the ALP politicians, the trade union officialdom and other closely related groupings remote from the working class rank and file. The July 1982 conference brought together approximately 150 delegates and proxies, of whom 65 were MPs, 34 were union officials, 13 were party officials and 10 were practising lawyers (many, no doubt, MPs-in-waiting). Individuals in this milieu might take a consistent left-wing stand; as a social whole, it was grafted into the existing social order, making it a vehicle for capitalist ideas. Hawke's 1983 election win was this bureaucratic layer's hour of triumph.

At first, of course, the Hawke ascendancy also seemed to be a victory for the working class itself – a fact owing much to the upheavals which gripped industry at the start of the 1980s.

YEARS OF RAGE

PRIVILEGE
LIB MODEL
HANDOUTS
NO JOBS
KICK THE POOR
AID THE RICH
BASH THE UNIONS
RUSH INTO URANIUM
WOMEN + KIDS LAST
IGNORE ABORIGINES
EXPAND A.S.I.O.
BLAME UNEMPLOYED
HIDE BEHIND THE BIG LIE

IS THIS THE COAT FOR YOU?

348

Authorised by Ailsa O'Connor, 22 The Broadway, Elwood. Printed by Walker Press, 23 Smith St, Fitzroy

11.
A union revival

No matter how bleak things seemed around 1978, there were grounds for hope if you knew where to look. The sharp union defeats of the early Fraser years, especially Medibank and the Latrobe Valley strike, had sent industrial militancy into a sharp decline which had seemed far reaching, even irreversible. Yet, in reality, organised labour's basic strength remained intact. Amid high unemployment, workers might not be confident about claiming wage rises, but the unions had deep roots and were hard to dislodge from key positions. This was demonstrated in 1977 and 1978 when five individual right wingers tried to break open several closed union shops, typically claiming some issue of conscience. In reality, their objective was to weaken the unions. While some saw their efforts as a Liberal conspiracy, Alec Kahn's assessment was more plausible:

> It is hardly likely that the Liberals would have picked stooges as easily discredited as Krutulis (a member of the nutty, extreme right-wing Workers Party), Latham (hated by his workmates), or Kane (twice saved by his union when sacked for drunkenness). A far more likely explanation is that the atmosphere the Liberals had created... simply encouraged these glory-seekers to come out one by one.[1]

The first battle was brief. When swimming instructor Kerry Ferguson refused to join the Municipal Employees Union (MEU) at Holroyd Council in Sydney, 160 MEU members refused to work with her; after a 10-day strike, the council stood her down until she successfully applied for conscientious objector status. The union then accepted her employment, but Ferguson resigned, claiming harassment.

The next conflict, at Broken Hill, was much more protracted. After Noel Latham reported a subordinate for refusing to clean a bulldozer's radiator (the man claimed it wasn't his job) the unions' Barrier Industrial Council fined him $50 for 'dobbing'. Latham declined to pay, so the AMWU refused to renew his membership, and council employees refused to work with him. Litigation produced a compromise settlement; but, when Latham returned to work in September 1977, 90 council workers walked off the job. In the face of such resistance, no court could reinstate him. When Latham had earlier asked the NSW Industrial Commission whether any 'lawful document' legitimised such union power, Justice Cahill replied: 'That is a rhetorical question. What I have been pointing out is what happens in Broken Hill.' Claude Forell found that Latham had little support from local people, who detested him 'as a scab and a stirrer.'[2]

Latham's frustrations were shared by several would-be heroes in Victoria. In 1977, Paul Krutulis gained an exemption from union membership from the Arbitration Commission as a conscientious objector, only to find that tramway workers at Kew planned to stop work as soon as he appeared. Commissioner Cohen then recommended his dismissal, saying that she 'had to deal with the reality of the situation.'[3] Krutulis later became president of a group called People Against Communism, before being murdered in September. Krutulis departed the scene to be followed in early 1978 by motor mechanic Jack Kane, who had crossed a picket line at a Melbourne City Council depot. The AMWU forced the Council to sack him before it would end the strike.

In September of the same year, Barbara Biggs succeeded in provoking a confrontation in the tramways where Krutulis had failed, by refusing to join the union and causing 100 unionists at Brunswick depot to go on strike. The union executive had arranged token action confined to this depot, but the members wanted more. The strike spread to Preston; then 2,000 trammies at a mass meeting voted for an indefinite strike amid 'rowdy outbursts'. When Biggs complained at being excluded from the meeting, a female conductor told her: 'We should have let you in, love. You would have been torn to pieces.'[4]

A range of anti-union forces now raised their heads. *The Age* ran a letter headed 'Boorish Hullabaloo of Yelping Pack of Union Yahoos'. The Industrial Relations Bureau threatened to intervene, and Industrial Relations Minister Tony Street made ritual accusations of union 'blackmail'.[5] As late as 6 September, *The Age* argued that the union faced 'an almost unwinnable contest'; but on the same day, the *Access Age* short letters column showed that the tide was turning: seven out of eight letters were hostile to Biggs. As the industrial defiance spread, union arguments were gaining ground. It emerged that Biggs had been a member of the Liquor Trades Union, which exploded her claims to be a conscientious objector, and some past legal offences came to light, shattering her pose of high moral principle. Five restaurants refused to serve her, while passers-by abused her in the street. Biggs finally settled for a clerical job in the Transport ministry, and the trammies had again saved their closed shop.

The Industrial Relations Bureau eventually prosecuted the AMWU over the Frank Kane affair but was faced with a firm ACTU stand that proved it ineffectual. Although Noel Latham later won some damages in court, this had little industrial impact. Perhaps the greatest losers were the People Against Communism, whose short involvement with Paul Krutulis was followed by a flirtation with Barbara Biggs. The group had looked silly enough before these catastrophic liaisons.

The tide turns: from Sydney to Paraburdoo

Getting rid of scabs was essentially a defensive exercise, but the unions came closer to taking the offensive in telecommunications in 1978, when Telecom had announced a $2,000 million plan to computerise its exchange system. The technicians' union, ATEA, said that the new system eliminated the need for a maintenance crew at each exchange, because regional Exchange Maintenance Centres (EMCs) would service up to 14 of them. The resulting redeployments would impair promotion opportunities, so the ATEA banned repairs and maintenance in early August 1978. Its main target was Telecom's revenue recording devices, which had recently been centralised and were particularly vulnerable.

The ATEA's peculiar strengths help to explain why it could take the lead for the unions as early as 1978. As a public sector union, it was not directly affected by unemployment. Members had elected new federal and state leaderships in the mid-1970s, and the new leaders in Victoria had fought a victorious struggle over work organisation, boosting their members' confidence. The union's ability to target sensitive telecommunications facilities meant that it could directly threaten business profits and even the functioning of the Stock Exchange. In addition, the ATEA was fighting over the consequences of technological change, at a time when much of the public was worried about them. So the Telecom workers had a considerable reservoir of public sympathy.

In mid-August, management started standing down technicians, but to little effect. The union bans, by contrast, proved very effective. By 21 August, telecommunications in NSW and Western Australia were near collapse, and Telecom was losing $1 million a day in revenue; a few days later, the breakdowns had spread to Victoria and South Australia, placing Malcolm Fraser under increasing pressure to act. But what was he to do? Union-bashing rhetoric found little resonance among a public enjoying free long distance calls. When Communications Minister Tony Staley warned that the dispute could endanger planned cuts in charges, the threat was hollow, because the cuts were necessary to get the public phoning off-peak. When Fraser had the army set up special equipment at his Nareen property so that he wouldn't be cut off from Canberra, he looked all the weaker. Union solidarity was growing, with telegraphists at the Sydney main post office stopping work and Adelaide telephonists threatening to walk out if asked to do technicians' jobs.

Finally, the Arbitration Commission sealed a partial union victory. Bob Hawke got an agreement that Telecom could negotiate independently of Canberra, and management promptly softened its stand. It accepted a union plan to create Exchange Support Centres alongside the EMCs and made concessions regarding job satisfaction, career opportunities and classifications. A final sticking point was back pay for 4,000 stood down ATEA members. The union doggedly demanded this concession, which was political dynamite because it would destroy standdowns as an effective management tactic. Finally, Justice Gaudron found a loophole: 70 percent of those laid off had not refused to do their own jobs, only to scab on their mates. These got back pay.

The union also won a measure of control over new technology. ATEA officials were premature in boasting that: 'the technology will be settled on our basis, not theirs,'[6] because the trialling would yield further disputes, but they had a right to feel pleased.

A year later, the ATEA won a second round, this time over pay. The union wanted a $20 per week rise. The government resisted, responding to union bans by proclaiming the *Commonwealth Employees (Employment Provisions) Act* (CEEP). This gave Telecom the power to suspend or sack employees engaged in industrial action, as well as providing Bob Hawke with an opportunity to enter the dispute and broker a settlement through a work value inquiry. A sizeable minority of the membership voted against the settlement, with Queensland branch secretary Alan Muir arguing that the claim could have been won through direct action; members were militant and confident 'right up to the end of the dispute.'[7] Even so, the union did relatively well out of its work value case, while Fraser's impotence was again exposed. Proclaiming CEEP had achieved nothing. The government had chosen not to use the previous year's standdown tactics, and now it avoided using the more drastic provisions of CEEP. A mere seven hours after the Act's proclamation, a Full Bench had agreed to the work value inquiry, effectively warning Fraser to back off. The unions took this as a clear signal that the tide was turning in their favour.

Union power was increasing because the economy had started to revive. In fact, from about 1979 onwards, Malcolm Fraser was suggesting that prosperity was just around the corner: that an international oil crisis was forcing up energy prices and signalling a 'resources boom'. Phillip Lynch's Department of Industry and Commerce reported that planned investment in mining and manufacturing into the 1980s exceeded $22.6 billion.[8] While the resources boom turned out to be overrated and short lived (only $6.5 billion of that total was 'firm') and, even at its height, left unemployment at 5.6 percent, it did tighten the market for skilled labour, enhancing union bargaining strength. Employers were tempted to concede union claims on the basis that they would make up the cost through increased profits later on.

Logically, this equation first made itself felt in the mining industry. At Utah Development Company's four open cut coal mines in central Queensland, 1,750 members of the Combined Mining Unions (CMU) imposed overtime bans in February 1979, followed by guerrilla stoppages in March. Next came a six-week strike – and the company began offering money, first $17, then $30. But the unions flatly refused the attached conditions, particularly company demands that everyone work 'continuous rosters', a series of seven-day shifts. They would not make this sacrifice for any amount of money. They ran their strike well, meeting weekly to pass stern, unanimous motions against continuous rosters, while the CMU liaison committee toured NSW mining towns to raise funds and secure moral support. This was an impressive effort, given that few of the open cut miners had previous union experience.

Malcolm Fraser kept a low profile, although Joh Bjelke-Petersen made dark references to communist involvement. Bob Hawke eventually sought to play his famous mediator's role, but cautiously, because the miners weren't likely to swallow an unsatisfactory settlement. Finally, in July, the company conceded $35 plus productivity and Christmas bonuses, along with various fringe benefits, abandoning its call for continuous rosters. Many informed observers recognised the productivity trade-offs, which appeared superficially to be a gain for the company, to be bogus, a mere device to get around the indexation guidelines.[9]

The Utah dispute intersected with a curious battle over taxes. Threats to apply fringe benefits tax to miners' rent subsidies led to a six-day strike by all coal miners in Queensland during 1979. On a visit to Blackwater, Fraser assured the mining communities that they could 'sleep tight at night' without worrying

about the issue,[10] but he later backtracked, so the strike resumed in 1980. During a visit, Doug Anthony and John Howard were bombarded with eggs, and one demonstrator got Howard in a headlock.

The miners invited their wives to attend meetings and vote on some issues, so the women strongly backed the strikers. Not one, wrote a journalist, was 'sour, sad, disappointed, doubtful or weak in attitude or action.'[11] Polls showed almost 60 percent of Australians supported the strike; money poured in; and the Japanese miners' union TANRO sent the strikers a sympathetic telegram. They stayed out for 10 weeks before achieving a compromise settlement.

The Pilbara was another new mining area with highly profitable companies and a raw and rebellious workforce, a region where:

> yesterday's disputes are re-fought today with new union convenors and new supervisors. Or companies find themselves stuck with a tough union convenor who cuts a dashing figure among a membership turning over at up to 100 percent a year.[12]

An era of rapid expansion in iron ore mining between 1966 and 1973 had been followed by a phase of consolidation and slower growth. The two phases had also seen the establishment and consolidation of strong combined union committees among the shop stewards at all the iron ore sites, which were largely independent of the state union leaders 2,000 kilometres away in Perth.

By 1979, Hamersley Iron management had decided that it was time to break the shop stewards' power. They were concerned about a looming recession in the Japanese steel industry, which would eventually reduce the demand for iron ore. The workers, on the other hand, seeing a still highly profitable industry while hearing talk of a resources boom, had decided that it was time to squeeze the company.[13]

The workforce was dissatisfied with its industrial agreement and impressed with the victory at Utah. They were also angered by two leaked company documents citing plans to cut housing subsidies and contract out cleaning services – and containing insulting proposals to 'encourage local convenors towards activities which will constructively occupy them and channel their efforts away from strike agitation, whilst satisfying their ego.'[14] The company was clearly making plans to smash local union organisation, but events were to show that these plans were premature. Union mass meetings voted by 98 percent for strike action. They also resolved:

> We reject the concept of negotiations and the company's counter claims, and withdraw our labour indefinitely or until such time as the negotiating committee receives a realistic offer from Hamersley Iron.[15]

Apart from a 40 percent wage increase, the union log also contained four 'non-negotiable' demands for better conditions. This was a big blue, but it might have remained little known without political intervention by the state government. Two weeks into the strike, several union officials travelled to Karratha to attend a mass meeting. The police had warned that the meeting was illegal under the WA *Police Act*, because they had no permission from the police commissioner – a blatant provocation, because the police had refused a union request to telex for this very permission. Police arrested Laurie Carmichael and another official, Jack Marks, on their return to Perth and eight others later in Karratha.

Unionists throughout the north-west promptly walked off the job; the AMWU made plans for a national stoppage; and, finally, the ACTU called for a 'day of national protest' on 21 June. It was the occasion for some aggressive comments from Jack Marks, who said that, if the arrested officials were penalised: 'there will be little moving except the palpitations in the parliamentarians' hearts.'[16] But, rather like the final Medibank strike three years earlier, the national stoppage was a token event. Because the national response was bureaucratically run from the start, and the mood in the working class was more apolitical, it had even less impact. Those arrested were later given trivial fines, quickly paid by an anonymous donor. Still, for Hamersley Iron workers – suddenly national heroes – these events meant a morale boost, a flow of donations and renewed determination.

Immediately afterwards, the company offered concessions on the date of commencement and meal breaks, but the workers did not budge. It was all still 'non-negotiable'. The strikers' wives were organising, and they had published a 'Message to Women Everywhere' arguing the union case, having learned a lesson from an earlier strike at Mt Newman:

> At that time a few staff members' wives had started an anti-strike women's committee to drive a wedge between males and females in the working class... There is no doubt that the activity was detrimental to the struggle at Mt Newman, and the women at the Hamersley sites were not going to let it happen again.[17]

The company had been prepared for a long dispute but had clearly underestimated its adversaries. With the two sides deadlocked, outside forces came into play. Conservative politicians in Perth and Canberra threatened to shut down the entire iron ore industry; Senior Commissioner Kelly hinted at deregistration; Bob Hawke contacted CRA's managing director Rod Carnegie; and WA TLC secretary Peter Cook began to play a greater role in the negotiations, which became partly a search for a face-saving formula to get around the unions' 'non-negotiable' stance. On 1 August, they struck a deal. It provided substantial pay hikes ($30 to $40), and the unions got their way on most other issues, prompting the AMWU journal to proclaim a 'great victory'.[18]

The rank and file were not so sure. While the agreement in principle was ratified at all sites, Paraburdoo and Tom Price greeted the full package with a large 'no' vote. It took some frantic activity by the negotiating committee to turn the situation at Tom Price around. (At Paraburdoo, a second vote was avoided.) The mining sites were unhappy that the pay rise didn't cover their strike losses and that the agreement allowed house rents to be indexed to CPI; many thought that Hawke and Cook had sold them out. So the miners' strikes were not 100 percent victories, contrary to some union claims; but, like the two Telecom disputes, they seemed to show that the union movement had turned the corner.

The big wage push

The year 1979 found unionists talking about a 'wage push' to make up for the fall in real wages suffered in the early Fraser years. For some time, employers and politicians had been telling workers that 'excessive' wages had caused recession and unemployment, but the case was far from watertight. A survey by Commonwealth Industrial Gases following a 17.5 percent currency devaluation in 1976 showed that Australian wages were below those paid in Canada even before the dollar fell; after devaluation, they were well below those paid in Japan.[19]

More immediate and telling comparisons appeared in the press later in the decade. In 1978, when average weekly earnings were just over $11,000 per year, Malcolm Fraser was earning $80,000 and Joh Bjelke-Petersen more than $60,000.[20] In 1980, the *National Time*s announced that 'executive pay is skyrocketing', while *The Bulletin* declared bluntly:

> the bosses have been doing better than the workers in the last five years, with corporate profits growing at a much greater rate than both wages and inflation.

Top executives were reaping the rewards:

> The list of perquisites that go with the job of chief executive is growing longer: company-paid superannuation, a prestige car, low-interest loans, company credit cards and a generous entertainment allowance are considered to be the bare essentials.[21]

As economic recovery boosted their bargaining power, trade unionists were less inclined to tolerate these double standards. It was time wages rose. At the same time, ironically, the Fraser Government was pushing the other way, by arm-twisting the Arbitration Commission to reduce wage indexation hearings from quarterly to six-monthly intervals. Something had to give, and it did. The indexation barrier sprang a leak.

Workers in factories around the country began securing over-awards directly from their employers. When the AMWU's Jim Baird said in late 1978: 'we are winning increases of between $5 and $7 in over-award campaigns in thousands of shops,'[22] he might have exaggerated, but the trend was undeniable. In industry-wide bargaining, such informal deals were not yet an option, but a legal loophole appeared in their place: section 7(a) of the indexation principles, which allowed higher pay for a change in work value.

In the Latrobe Valley dispute, Commissioner Mansini had interpreted this section very narrowly, but Justice Robinson loosened it again in a 1978 waterfront case by giving every wharfie in Australia an $8.60 pay rise. The decision was based on the 'value of the whole industry'.[23] By October 1978, 2,000 employees of the NSW Electricity commission had won a $7 rise based on work value. By early 1979, the rush was on. Two-thirds of transport workers in the airline industry won increases of $8 to $11, which then flowed on to other drivers, who in turn set a benchmark for storemen and some fitters.

In 1975–78, about 95 percent of all wage movements had come through wage indexation decisions. Now, the indexation system was suddenly in doubt. No matter how willing Malcolm Fraser might be to fight to the last drop of their blood, the bosses were more inclined to make commercial decisions. Ruling class backing for Fraser had always been fragile; it had largely held together as long as he could win. Now he looked like a loser. An employer representative lamented:

> We only have two choices – give it all round now and carry the extra cost, or fight it all the way and carry the cost of continual industrial disputation. My personal opinion is that we'd be better off giving it now.[24]

Nor could Fraser count on public support. Philip Lynch might claim that the community was 'sick and tired' of industrial unrest,[25] but it also seemed to be sick and tired of government posturing – and, anyway, large sections of the community were themselves striking for higher pay. In 1979, Jim Baird told the Arbitration Commission that the metal unions planned a 48-hour strike, after

67 mass meetings attended by 35,000 metal workers: 'the biggest gathering of workers that I ever recall.' The flow-on logic was irresistible, said another union official: 'Our members are not crazy. They saw what happened in relation to the transport workers where they got the $8.'[26] The 'magic $8' was rapidly becoming a community standard.

The ACTU Congress opened in September 1979 with much of the union movement charging ahead. Naturally, Bob Hawke wished to appear to be leading the charge, so he warned the government that, if it believed in the free market for business, it must expect unions to exploit the market where they could. The Congress announced an 8 percent productivity claim and signalled its rejection of those indexation guidelines which restricted collective bargaining. There was increasing talk of bargaining outside arbitration. The writing was on the wall for wage indexation. Having eroded its benefits while workers were on the defensive, Fraser had little hope of convincing them to stick by it now. A remarkable wool handlers' dispute showed this beyond any doubt.

In December 1979, that colourful figure Justice Staples awarded rises of between $12.50 and $15.90 to Storemen and Packers in the wool industry. This was well above the $8 figure, which had by now become a virtual 'phantom guideline'. As recently as the previous month, metal workers had received $7.30 to $9.30. But the labour market was still tightening, and Staples did not intend to be an '$8 automaton'. The 1907 Harvester judgement had sought to 'ensure the workman food, clothing, frugal comfort, provision for evil days, etc', and Staples' award placed a wool storeman with a wife and three children just $24.90 above the poverty line. 'Are these rates fair, reasonable or extravagant? I leave that to others to judge.'

Staples was on the way to outraging the entire arbitration hierarchy. What irked them was not so much his sympathy for workers, which was not consistent by any means, but his exposure of the system's logic – or lack of it. With wages being set in response to industrial pressure, the old arbitration formulas were losing credibility:

> What shall be the measure? It may not be discovered in the profitability of the enterprise and not in the increased productivity... It may not be an adjustment to the burden of taxation on the wage earner nor reflect any movement in the cost of living...nor may it derive from a comparison with rates paid in other industries... I shall simply select a figure as Tom Collins selected a day from his diary and we shall see what turns up.

The Fraser Government was horrified, as was the National Farmers' Federation. Together, they encouraged the wool brokers to appeal, and the Full Bench threw out Staples' decision, causing a lengthy strike. Ultimately, the brokers agreed to pay $10.75 to $12.75. Given that most workers were paid at the lower end of the range, this was not dramatically below the original decision. Moreover, the deal was only for one year, whereas Staples' award would have applied for two – which, amid the wage spiral of the time, was a big plus for the unions. 'We should have given in to the bastards in the first place,' lamented the wool brokers.[27] It was a conclusion numerous employers began to draw as the wage push rolled on.

In some ways, this conclusion was premature. There was still substantial unemployment, so any downturn in the economy could rapidly puncture working class confidence. The level of rank and file job organisation had not revived significantly, so it would not be hard for the union officials to turn off the tap of industrial struggle when they decided that the time was right. Finally, the disputes of 1979–81 were overwhelmingly about bread-and-butter issues. There was little political radicalism, either from the rank and file or from the left union officials. This burst of militancy at the start of the 1980s was both limited and fragile, but it was not until the resources boom came to an end that the weaknesses became clear.

Campaigning for shorter hours

As workers gained confidence on the wages front, they began thinking about a shorter working week. This was an area of hard-won conquests. In launching a booklet on the 35-hour week, AMWU president Dick Scott reminded his audience of the battle for 40 hours, quoting the 1947 Arbitration judgement:

> It has been the historic role of employers to oppose the workers' claim for increased leisure… The arguments have not changed much in 100 years. Employers have feared such changes a threat to production; a limitation upon industrial expansion; and a threat to internal and international trade relations. And history has invariably proved the forebodings of employers to be unfounded.[28]

Initially, the issue was linked to problems of unemployment and technological change. When the Bank Employees announced a campaign for the 30-hour week in 1978, NSW secretary Allan McArdle said:

> The Telecom dispute brought our situation to a head... Our first priority in this campaign is to protect those working in the industry. Our second is to create new employment.[29]

The 35-hour week campaign at the Altona Petrochemical Complex in Melbourne showed in practice how shorter hours could create jobs.

The Altona dispute dated from 1974, when two oil refineries had granted a 35-hour week to bring conditions into line with their US parent companies. Despite an 'understanding' that the deal would not flow on to other plants, Australian Carbon Black nearby had a 35-hour week by September 1975. The other plants wanted it too but won nothing in the difficult years from 1976 to 1978, despite months of bans, partly because management undercut strikes by using staff labour.

Finally, in August 1979, with the industrial climate improving for the unions, workers at Union Carbide more or less spontaneously decided to keep staff labour out by occupying their plant. Management were beside themselves. Said electrician Vic Williams: 'There was people rushing around sacking us left right and centre. Some people were sacked about ten times.'[30] Australian unions had little tradition of occupying workplaces, yet here 55 men staged a 51-day sit-in. The occupation became a cultural event, when a Sunday barbecue outside the gate was turned into a rally and festival, attracting performers like Frank Traynor's Jazz Band and Redgum, along with a large crowd to buoy union morale.

With the company threatening to use punitive sections of the Arbitration Act, the occupation ended on 16 October after a close vote. Although Vic Williams had argued to continue the struggle because 'we were shifting the management and our strength was developing,'[31] union organisers convinced the majority to await an onsite investigation by Justice Coldham.

Coldham's July 1980 report resolved little, and the dispute seemed set to bog down in arbitration once again. But two days later, BFGoodrich management decided to use staff labour during a 48-hour stoppage; the unionists in the plant went on an indefinite strike; and a second blue was on at Altona, where every unionist in the complex agreed to a $25 per week levy for the Goodrich workers. The strikers set up tents at the plant entrance, and Goodrich became the next battleground.

The strike lasted 18 weeks before the issue again came before the Arbitration Commission. This time, the Commission was ready to settle the dispute, but it wanted some semblance of productivity offsets for shorter hours, forcing the

Union Carbide: 35 hour week struggle

by Bruce Hanna

In 1974 oil industry workers achieved a 35-hour week based on increased productivity. But the same has not happened in the closely associated petro-chemical industry, dominated by big multinationals like Union Carbide.

Since 1961, the petro-chemical industry has enjoyed a productivity increase of about 400 per cent! And Union Carbide's Australian profits rose by 25 per cent last year to $6,598,000.

As one woman said outside the plant, the 35-hour week "is crucial in the light of the current unemployment situation. We have to think about jobs for the future generation, that is, for our children. If the men do not win a 35-hour week now, they never will."

Workers share this concern. "If you look at the state of the economy and the half million unemployed, the 35-hour week should have been brought into the industry a long time ago," said one. "In Sunshine alone there are over 2,500 without a job."

About fifty Union Carbide workers at Altona, Victoria, are in their fourth week of occupying the plant, as they continue their campaign for a 35-hour week without loss of pay.

Fitter Don Calderwood says: "Continued scabbing by supervisors has forced us to take over the plant. We just got sick of it."

Union Carbide has a top-heavy workforce, designed especially to provide scab labor during strikes. There are two supervisors for every seven workers.

"The staff are shitting themselves," one worker told me through the locked gate. "Now that we've occupied the place they are useless to the company, and their jobs are threatened too."

The company has sacked the occupying workers, and threatened them with liability for lost profits. Repressive anti-union laws are also being invoked at their heads. "You don't realise just what legislation there is until you become involved in it," says Don (see *Tribune*, Sept 26).

But workers are confident that such a move would unleash a massive counter-attack from the trade union movement. There is a healthy strike fund, and people are bringing food and money to the front gate. "Support is building up more and more with each stage," says Don.

Across the Tasman

Interstate travellers have stopped by to lend support, and workers have received encouraging phone calls from as far as Brisbane. When the New Zealand relatives of one instrument fitter read about the occupation they rang across the Tasman to find out how it was going.

Union Carbide is losing $60,000 a day and threatens to close the plant. "These Yank multinationals are all the same — as soon as they can't have everything their own way they threaten to close down."

But fighting this multinational company is a real "multinational force" of workers from India, Greece, Malta, Italy, Finland, Holland, Scotland, Ireland, Wales, England, New Zealand and Australia.

Bags of rags

And spirits are high after a rough first night when "we had to sleep anywhere we could find. Some slept sitting in chairs or on cartons, with bags of rags for pillows."

Then bedding and other amenities were passed over the fence and the Altona workers settled down for a long-term occupation of the $80 million factory.

After the first morning, one young fitter said: "This is great. It's the first time I've had breakfast in eleven years."

But, as Don puts it, "we aren't

The fifty maintenance workers, trades assistants and operators don't know how long they will be forced to stay in. One is due to be married in seven weeks, and a fellow worker suggested the marriage might have to be performed through the fence.

But when the occupation started, anyone with family problems had to go out, even though that meant staying out while the others stayed in.

The occupiers have TV, draughts, chess, cards, badminton, and table tennis to break the monotony. Hundreds of books have been donated, and a charity lined up to

• Every day workers' families arrive to keep them company

take them when the dispute is over. Every day workers' families arrive to keep them company. While I was there one small child squeezed between the locked gates and hugged his father before retreating outside.

Tasty guards!

Union Carbide has hired six full time guards to patrol the fence, but no one is sure whether they are there to keep the workers in or others out.

A tent has been put up outside for visitors, and barbecues and concerts are regular events. The workers are in good humor. Big Luke, an electrician, came to the gate after their own barbecue, licking his lips and asking: "Have you got any more guards there?"

In 1936

The workers' wives and supporters have seen a film about a struggle in the US against General Motors in 1936, showing just how ruthless big corporations can be. Women played a massive role in that dispute too — men and women workers who occupied the GM plant there were subjected to intense pressure and capitalist propaganda, accused them of having a big orgy. Women were tear gassed as they fought police in the street, and the National Guard came out with machine guns and cannons...

Solidarity

The Altona situation is not as desperate as that, but the dedication and solidarity of the workers and their families is the same.

The 35 hour week is going to make more jobs and give people more leisure time. It's long overdue and only the capitalists have anything to lose.

INSIDE:
China: 30 years on p 12, 13
Newcastle's Star War p 16
Zimbabwe women p 11

Report on Union Carbide workers Tribune 3 October 1979

parties to conjure up a series of trade-offs everyone could live with. Opinions differed on how real the trade-offs were, with many unionists insisting privately that 'we didn't give anything away, not really.'[32] Certainly, it was a major victory on the employment front, creating 100 new jobs. Unfortunately, the wider union movement did little to build on this accomplishment.

In fact, the wider 35-hour week campaign was plodding along rather slowly. The ACTU, now headed by Cliff Dolan following the launch of Bob Hawke's parliamentary career, was reluctant to argue an industry-wide case in arbitration, preferring to translate productivity increases into earlier retirement or increased long-service leave. And, notwithstanding the new eagerness among the rank and file, the top union body was in no hurry. 'The ACTU approach,' wrote Bob Carr, 'seems to envisage progress made over 10 years.'[33] In mid-1980, fearing that the Arbitration Commission would delay the national wage case, the ACTU executive instructed the metal unions to postpone their campaign, only to find the membership so restive that mass meetings refused to comply.

The Fraser Government tried to stiffen the employers' backbone with threats to refer sweetheart deals to the Prices Justification Tribunal or to have the Industries' Assistance Commission review firms' tariff arrangements. Given the balance of industrial forces, however, this had little impact. In fact, almost immediately after the threats, two tobacco companies announced a shorter working week. The Metal Trades Industry Association (MTIA) was more effective than Canberra. MTIA propaganda attacked union claims that shorter hours would create jobs, countering that they would *cost* jobs by bankrupting small shops. This counteroffensive made a considerable splash and enabled many employers to hold the line for a while.[34] At the end of 1980, the number of employees working a 40-hour week had fallen only slightly.[35] 'At present, we are two immovable objects waiting for a breakthrough,' said Society of Engineers' Secretary, Terry Addison. But, with the economy still strengthening, Laurie Carmichael correctly predicted a 'crescendo' for 1981.[36]

The government's last serious attempt at resistance was in late March 1981, following ratification of the Altona deal. The *Financial Review* reported that ICI planned to negotiate with the Chemical Workers. In Cabinet, Fraser canvassed various punitive options, including a special tax rate and a reference to the Industries Assistance Commission; for its part, ICI stoutly denied that it was negotiating with the union and suspended $900 million worth of investments because of government threats. ICI Chair Milton Bridgland was summoned to Canberra. Patrick Weller relates:

Fraser, Lynch, Peacock and Kemp held a long and bitter discussion with him. Fraser brought to bear the full weight of his position, his harrowing aggressive style and his argumentative vigour.[37]

Government pressure finally forced the company to agree to a joint press release opposing the 35-hour week.

However, the union campaign was becoming unstoppable. On the very day the press release appeared, Fraser met with the ACTU. Employer spokesman George Polites warned Fraser that: 'while business was still resisting, survival might eventually require it to give in.'[38] In the same month, the Full Bench voiced fears that 'industrial reality' would ensure a wide flow-on of shorter hours, regardless of whether real productivity offsets were achieved,[39] and it was proved right when metal workers at Fox Manufacturing in Sydney gained the 35-hour week for trivial productivity offsets. By June, the deal had flowed through to Fox Brisbane. Wives of Brisbane metal workers were circulating a letter backing the campaign.

In May 1981, the MTIA said that it was under fire from its members for not negotiating an orderly retreat; by October, it had capitulated. Alcoa conceded a 36-hour week, blaming the government for not providing tax relief to help it resist union pressure. By this time, the shorter hours struggle had effectively merged with the wage push: increasingly, the target was 38 hours, which was won together with a wage rise. In most cases, actual hours didn't decline; instead, more hours were simply paid at overtime rates. Fraser finally threw in the towel in 1982. In April, Cabinet had secretly decided to soften its opposition; in June, it began negotiating a 38-hour week for those of its own employees still working 40.

On paper, all of these deals included productivity offsets. The truth was that many were bogus. An employer survey found that only one-third of companies which cut hours had actually secured cost offsets, and even those had recouped only 20 percent of the cost. Although employers did benefit through reduced absenteeism and better morale, the campaign had clearly ended in a union victory.[40]

In another sense, however, it was disappointing. Originally, the unions had promoted the 35-hour week as a solution to unemployment. 'Let's have shorter hours and more jobs!' wrote Laurie Carmichael,[41] and the Altona petrochemical workers had gone out and done it. By 1981, however, this aspect had been largely obscured. This was partly because of the merging of the wages and hours issues (if shorter hours meant more overtime, no new jobs would result) and partly reflected the benefits to employers (if productivity rose, there was less incentive to hire labour). Workers who understood these facts took the job creation aspect less seriously, while a tightening labour market made it seem less urgent.

There was also a political weakness. The issue had been held up as a panacea: shorter hours would create more jobs without seriously challenging the prevailing social order. In reality, the government was deliberately using unemployment as part of its anti-inflation strategy, and a strong case could be made that unemployment was an essential part of the capitalist system, providing a 'reserve army of labour'. Left union leaders knew this but generally didn't dwell on the logical implication – that a political struggle was needed to make the government and employers create jobs even where it wasn't profitable.[42]

The shorter hours/more jobs argument was largely ideological window dressing for a campaign whose real objectives were narrower. The new phase of working class confidence should have been an opportunity to reverse the rightward trend that had dominated Australian industry and politics since 1974; but, by the early 1980s, most union leaders were beginning to seek a new accommodation with the bosses, as the 1981 metal trades settlement was to show.

A backlash fails

In these years, it seemed that all of industry was in ferment. The scope of the industrial unrest could be gauged from a small item in the *Sydney Morning Herald* of 10 July 1981, citing strikes affecting milk, eggs, cinemas, hospitals, driving tests, taxation, Telecom and transport.

Sections of the middle classes were so perturbed by this wave of industrial agitation that, for a short time, a big anti-union backlash seemed to be on the cards. After a large anti-union demonstration in New Zealand, led by 22-year old sales representative Tania Harris, right-wing forces called similar actions in Australia. Many unionists believed that the conservative parties or employer groups had a hand in these developments, although there was no hard evidence. Sales manager Leanne Hayward emerged as Sydney's answer to Tania Harris; in Brisbane, it was Housewives' Association leader Gabby Horan.

Initially, the media showed some enthusiasm, especially Rupert Murdoch's *Daily Telegraph*, which generated much of the blanket publicity required to get some 30,000 people marching through Sydney. Despite a small counter-demonstration, the event was largely peaceful. In Brisbane, however, counter-demonstrators fought police, and numerous arrests ensued. The media tone

Insurance workers join the industrial ferment in 1980

then shifted perceptibly. Letters to the papers were mixed, with quite a few pro-union correspondents and others worried about deepening social divisions, a point *The Australian*'s Buzz Kennedy urgently sought to reinforce. While he thought that the marchers' message 'needed to be said... I don't think it should be said again. This way lies danger.'[43] Some other commentators were worried that, among the self-styled 'We care' marchers in Sydney, 'no one seemed to care that a party of Nazi supporters also took part.'[44]

Melbourne's procession was set for a day later. Already, the opposition had grown, with wharfies stopping work for 24 hours while leftists announced a counter-mobilisation. Now the organisers began to back-pedal. Spokesperson Nola Baker told a bemused public:

> this is not an anti-strike march. We believe in unions and we believe in the right to strike. What we are hoping is to instil national pride.[45]

These confused signals apparently discouraged a lot of their supporters, especially those from small business who *were* anti-union. The prospect of street clashes probably kept others away. A relatively small march was harassed by counter-demonstrators, who managed to get a 'Hands Off The Unions' banner in front of the procession.

A small minority of militants had beaten back the anti-union push with relative ease. This was only possible because the government and employers were well aware of the strong position the mainstream of the union movement was in because of the resources boom; still, the backlash had failed – and, contrary to the usual fears of labour movement bureaucrats, the aggressive response of pro-unionists hadn't alienated public opinion. The next day's letters to *The Age* were generally critical of the right wing, with one correspondent declaring bluntly: 'I am tired of people griping about the unions.'[46]

In federal parliament, the government failed to extract much mileage from the issue, which was dissipating quickly. A final anti-strike mobilisation in Perth attracted fewer than 1,000 people. As they marched, the ACTU executive was formulating its own pointed comment with reference to right wingers' professed sympathy for Polish Solidarity: 'It is hypocrisy to laud Polish workers and support their right to strike, and then criticise Australian workers who strike for legitimate reasons.'[47]

The ease with which the anti-strike mobilisation was beaten back indicated that the power of the ideological right was in decline – a situation in which the unions could have taken the offensive politically. But the union officials

A UNION REVIVAL

Halfpenny (to the left of the placard) and Carmichael (behind the placard) at the IRB 1979

showed no interest in doing so. From these and other experiences, some rank and file militants concluded that it was time to challenge the union leaders.

Rank and file insurgencies

Rank and file discontent was fairly widespread. At the height of wage indexation, pay rises had fallen behind inflation, and what rises workers did get seemed to come directly from the Arbitration Commission, with little union input. In 1979, *The Bulletin* noted that:

> many workers, especially those who wrested heavy increases from employers during the wages boom of the early 1970s, now have the impression their unions are doing nothing for them.[48]

As workers' industrial strength grew amid the resources boom, some rank and filers gained the confidence to translate that accumulated discontent into action. This explains why grassroots unrest could increase alongside the good pay settlements which *were* achieved after 1979.

Leaders of the AMWU were shocked when maverick Dusty Miller turfed out veteran organiser Jim Baird in a 1979 election. Miller had a left-wing background but ran a rather right-wing campaign, attacking the CPA by name. However, his win suggested not so much a *political* trend as a general mood of discontent. His attacks on the CPA were only partly red-baiting. He also appealed to membership feeling that the 'communists' Halfpenny and Carmichael were fake lefts. Two years later, John Halfpenny only narrowly gained re-election against another outsider.

These poll results reflected a largely unfocused dissent that could not take the union movement forward. A more politically coherent opposition movement was needed to challenge the unions' rightward drift, and it needed to base itself squarely on the mobilisation of the rank and file in struggle. A number of rank and file insurgencies in these years displayed some of the necessary features; unfortunately, none of them could put it all together.

One area that showed promise was the Sydney building industry. Militants widely despised the leadership of Steve Black, installed by federal intervention in 1974. In 1978, the remnants of the old NSW BLF made a determined push to regain control from the pro-Gallagher forces. Because the officials were accused of ballot-rigging, the 'Builders Labourers For Democratic Control' demanded a court-controlled ballot. This group had strong support on a number of building jobs, including the Qantas site in central Sydney and the big Bondi Plaza project – sites where they had led and won numerous struggles. Given this favourable starting point and the officials' poor image, they expected to win the vote. Unfortunately, while the big sites were a good base for launching industrial action, election campaigning required a far-flung canvassing apparatus. Here, the officials had a big advantage. About 30 organisers went door to door securing votes from the more apathetic members, ensuring that the existing leadership was returned by 687 votes to 481.

The electoral defeat need not have been a disaster. The sizeable opposition vote was a demonstration of strong support from the militants, which they could have presented as a moral victory, then used to launch new struggles on the job. The trouble was that the dissidents had relied heavily on an electoral win, which they presented as the solution to their problems. The loss demoralised them. In the aftermath, the jobsite opposition to Black and Gallagher declined, while high-profile individuals from the old NSW branch, such as Jack Mundey and Joe Owens, began to look to government deregistration moves to destroy Gallagher for them.

Electoralism had its dangers; however, even truly massive rank and file mobilisations couldn't guarantee success. In 1980, officials of the MEU in Melbourne were astonished when a crowd of angry members stormed into their union's offices after a rally and occupied it for several days. A rank and file group had emerged amid general discontent after MEU officials took a trip to Europe, supposedly to study garbage collection methods. Rebel organiser Rhonda Pryor alleged:

> they were accompanied by a contractor and paid by a contractor [who] wants to introduce a system of garbage collection in Melbourne that is going to put our members out of work.[49]

Petitions forced the leadership to call a mass meeting, which saw further stormy scenes, but the rank and file group was never able to dislodge the MEU leadership. Contract labour became an increasing problem. When garbos at Waverley City Council tried to resist, MEU members held a city-wide strike in their support, but a compromise arrangement by the union executive once again left them isolated. The dissidents were unable to channel the upsurge of rank and file militancy effectively because they lacked a clear political direction.[50]

This was not surprising. Whereas the high point of class struggle in the late 1960s and early 1970s had seen quite political – and left-wing – mass campaigns over Vietnam, Clarrie O'Shea, Green Bans and the like, no such political radicalisation occurred during the 1979–81 union offensive. Workers were not even involved in political campaigning at the level of the anti-uranium struggles of 1977–78. Despite the unfavourable circumstances, there were some on the left, most importantly the IS, who did try to build a more political rank and file opposition movement in teacher and public service unions. Their small numbers and relative isolation meant that their achievements were strictly limited, but their experiences offer some hints as to what a larger revolutionary party might have accomplished.

The conservative leadership of the Victorian Secondary Teachers' Association provoked increasing ferment in 1981, under union president Peter Vaughan. The union had allowed teachers to be forcibly transferred from Seaford-Carrum High School and had overturned a number of decisions made by mass meetings. Some militants, including Tess Lee Ack from the IS and Gerry Beaton from a different socialist background, launched an oppositional rank and file grouping, dubbed Teacher Solidarity in allusion to the Polish events of the time.

Teacher Solidarity argued for the union to present a log of claims, in place of its traditional ad hoc campaigns, and to fight around it in more determined fashion. At mass meetings, the group was able to get 30 to 40 percent of the vote, and the log of claims idea was eventually accepted. However, the log simply became a new vehicle for the same old style of conservative union campaigns. And, while Teacher Solidarity rightly argued that mobilising rank and file members in struggle was more important than 'changing the faces on the Central Committee,'[51] the reality was that the group could not win ongoing leadership of rank and file teachers either. Ultimately, the main beneficiaries of this period of rank and file unrest were a trendy group of aspiring bureaucrats who toppled Vaughan at an ensuing election.

Socialist organisations such as the IS and its allies could not accomplish much more among public servants, although the unions in this sphere were going through a crisis that offered some opportunities.

Growing staff numbers and the increasingly 'proletarian' nature of their work had brought public service clerks a greater union consciousness in the 1970s. Traditional leaderships in the 'staff associations', who had trouble coping with the transition to trade unionism, were caught between the aggressive cost-cutting measures of the Fraser regime and their members' rising militancy after 1975.

Fraser applied strict staff ceilings, used the Productivity Control System in DSS to increase the pace of work, had cut maternity leave and had eliminated paternity leave. New legislation made it easier to sack public servants. State governments also tightened up. The union response was limp at best, and quite a few members wanted to do something about that.

In 1976, Victorian members of the ACOA set up a Reform Group. This group was primarily devoted to winning control of the state branch by electoral means, which it accomplished over the following decade, but it contained a left-wing minority oriented to building militant workplace organisation. Its success encouraged dissident factions elsewhere, the most important being two 'Action Groups' in NSW and the ACT. Their joint paper, *Grey Collar*, circulated widely. Socialists were prominent in the Grey Collar current.

Another spin-off appeared in the Victorian Public Service Association (VPSA), where young socialist Jeff Soar and three others called a meeting to discuss uranium mining. After 20 Victorian public servants marched on Hiroshima Day 1978, the group used this initial base to set up a small ginger group in the VPSA. Unfortunately, although the group was able to tap a certain mood of dissatisfaction among the wider membership – Jeff Soar won an astonishing 47 percent of the vote for General President – this mood remained largely passive. Soar's big vote contrasted sharply with a turnout of fewer than 60 when the Reform Group called a demonstration against staff ceilings. Like Teacher Solidarity, this VPSA Reform Group was too peripheral to mobilise workers in struggle.

The Grey Collar group in ACOA did have greater success during a 1981 dispute in DSS. ACOA members had imposed work bans in DSS and were demanding extra staff. The government, which had defeated similar bans elsewhere by standing down unionists, decided to use the same methods in DSS. NSW members then walked off the job. Grey Collar agitated successfully for a union-wide stopwork meeting, and over 1,000 members turned out in pouring rain. Having failed to break the union campaign, the government escalated, announcing that it would use the CEEP legislation. ACOA called a 24-hour stoppage, together with the clerical assistants' union APSA.

Grey Collar convinced DSS delegates to call for extending the stoppage. On Wednesday 9 December, union members at a packed meeting in Sydney Town Hall endorsed the proposal, despite strong opposition from their officials. Following the meeting, several thousand of them marched through city streets behind the Grey Collar banner. Workplace delegates set about organising pickets, and over 100 unionists, led by the rank and file group, assembled outside

DSS headquarters on Friday, chanting slogans and singing 'Solidarity Forever'. The ACOA officials eventually regained control of the dispute, because the militants had no organisation outside NSW and the ACT, and NSW members finally voted to return to work at a second mass meeting on 19 December. A militant tradition did remain in Sydney DSS offices, providing the basis for another rank and file rebellion in 1988.[52]

During the dispute, the Grey Collar group had attracted 60 public servants to a rank and file conference which presented the revolutionaries with an opportunity to explain what they were trying to do. Rick Kuhn summed up their perspective:

> The central purpose of a rank and file organisation is to change what are accepted as 'reasonable' policies and actions...by offering a pole of attraction on the left: a pole in terms of the ideas put forward and also an organisational focus... By building the groups, through recruiting militants, the opportunities for greater contact with other workers grow – it becomes easier to discuss politics with more of them and to involve them in action... It is through such action that consciousness changes, opening the way, not only to militant trade union consciousness but also revolutionary class consciousness.[53]

This was a reasonable summary of how rank and file organising can contribute to the building of a revolutionary movement; unfortunately, it didn't take adequate account of the revolutionaries' own small numbers. But even a sizeable revolutionary party would have found it hard going at the end of the 1970s. Although workers were militant, they were no longer very interested in radical politics. The second half of 1981 was to show that even the militancy concealed a certain fatigue among the rank and file.

From indexation to collective bargaining

The year 1981 was full of turning points. Halfway through it, the indexation system collapsed. In December, the first elements of an alternative system appeared.

In April, the Arbitration Commission had reviewed the wage guidelines and accepted a government submission to close the 'work value' loophole. This defied industrial reality, because union bargaining power was high. Telecom technicians and tradespeople demonstrated this when they won pay rises of up to $23 outside the system. A flow-on scramble ensued. 'To hell with indexation,' said the TWU's Harry Quinn. 'That's gone out the window.'[54] By late July, 50,000 truck drivers were on strike. Postal workers and Telecom clerks were also pursuing industrial campaigns. As a consequence of his much-vaunted resources boom, Fraser had lost control of wage fixing. He was forced to stitch up a special deal to resolve the first Telecom dispute (after an agonised 13-hour Cabinet meeting) and he was about to openly ditch the guidelines. A last try at sabre-rattling drew the story out a bit.

Industrial Relations Minister Wal Fife told the ACTU on 22 June that the government intended to use the CEEP Act against the Telecom clerks and to deregister the TWU. Cliff Dolan was aghast. Using CEEP in DSS was one thing, but the unions in Telecom had greater muscle; deregistration moves would only enrage the TWU. 'It will be like a red rag to a bull,' Dolan warned.[55] At the time, a major dock strike also loomed because of threatened standdowns. Frantic to restore industrial peace, Dolan rang both Fraser and Justice Moore and arranged a crisis meeting, then dodged union transport bans by travelling to Canberra in a RAAF plane.

According to the *Sydney Morning Herald*, Moore said that he would see whether the dock strike could be deferred (and this is what happened). With one problem addressed, Dolan next advised the government to back down on CEEP and on deregistration of the TWU. Fraser, by now aware of his weak position – and also keen to resolve the crisis so that he could attend Charles and Di's royal wedding – agreed on the spot, after which some haggling occurred over a new anomalies loophole for the wage guidelines. The Prime Minister and the ACTU President emerged from the meeting as the best of mates, with Fraser suggesting that a new era of peaceful collaboration was at hand.

This interlude was extremely short lived. The Arbitration Commission, which had begun questioning the viability of wage indexation as early as 1979, now decided that because 'the commitment of the participants to the system is not strong enough...the time has come for us to abandon the indexation system.'[56] The Fraser Government now ditched its interventionist wages policy. For the next year or so, Canberra looked to the market to set wages, hoping vainly that the big gains made by the strongest unions would not flow through to the weaker ones once the centralised framework was scrapped. This retreat was camouflaged as conforming to the Liberals' professed free-market philosophy, but it fooled very few.

With indexation gone, the wage push proceeded through collective bargaining and culminated in the December 1981 metal trades agreement. The metal unions and employers had negotiated a $41 rise in two instalments and a 38-hour week. The federal government went through the motions of opposing this, then tried to limit the flow-ons, with minimal success. Within days, the building industry had announced a deal involving $31.30 and 38 hours. After ratifying the metals deal, the Commission set a 'going rate' of $20 to $30 in four decisions. Average weekly earnings, which had risen by 13.5 percent in 1980–81, leapt by another 16 percent in 1981–82.

At the time, many saw these settlements as signalling an even stormier wage offensive for 1982. However, the metal trades agreement had another side, as the *Sydney Morning Herald* pointed out:

> The agreement is regarded as the most significant advance for employers in industrial relations for 30 years. It is tied to a pledge – which the unions have said they will do their best to honour – that there will be no additional wages or conditions claims for 12 months.

Any problems would be dealt with through a disputes procedure, with the Arbitration Commission as a last resort. Automatic quarterly cost-of-living adjustments, which the unions had originally seen as essential compensation for the no-claims provision, were quietly dropped. Reportedly, the no-claims arrangement had been 'drawn up and offered by the unions themselves in response to suggestions by the employers'.[57] There was no serious resistance from the ranks to this sacrifice of the unions' freedom of action. Building unions announced within days that they had something similar in train for their industry.

These agreements turned union officials into industrial police. By April 1982, Bert Evans, spokesman for the metal employers, was gloating:

> There have been occasions where employees on the job have sought to raise the question of wages but very properly, without exception, the metal unions have been quick to point out to the members that they voted on the agreement and are bound to honour it.[58]

Thus had management and the union officialdom negotiated their own formula for industrial peace; if Fraser had lost his grip on industrial relations, the vacuum did not last long.

On the contrary, both sides of the industrial divide had tired of strife. If the bosses were forced to recognise that the unions could not be crushed, trade unionists drew remarkably few optimistic conclusions from their victories in

1979-81. Even the militants were feeling bruised from years of confrontation. While the decline in militancy during 1975-78 had concealed the underlying strength of unions, the runaway union offensive of 1979-81 had also concealed serious weaknesses. The metal unions' enthusiasm for compromise partly reflected the decline of manufacturing under Fraser, but there was a conciliatory mood among virtually all the union officials by the end of 1981.

Despite the temporary opportunities afforded by the resources boom, officials had thoroughly grasped the fact that Australian capitalism could not grant continuing wage rises and restore profitability at the same time, and they were not in the business of uprooting the system. As we have seen, insurgent groupings among the rank and file were seldom strong enough to challenge them, and organisation on the job had continued to deteriorate during the 'wage push'. Consequently, it did not take much of a turnaround in the economy to pull the rug out from under the militancy of the time. In late 1981 and early 1982, unemployment had stopped falling and begun to creep upwards, a development which had a rapid sobering effect on workers.

The AMWU's next initiative reinforced the trend. In February 1982, the union issued a call for union action to win lower taxes, interest rates and health charges, along with higher pensions and better social welfare. John Halfpenny even threatened industrial action. But the new 'social wage' campaign was not what it seemed. As the Melbourne *Age* reported, it was really designed to lay the basis for a 'social contract' arrangement when Labor won government:

> The AMWU would be the first union to agree...that in return for positive government action in areas such as taxation and health payments...the unions would moderate wage claims. The unions and the ALP refuse to call such an agreement a social contract – but that is what it amounts to.[59]

The exhaustion of both sides in the class struggle was opening the way for a new era of class collaboration. And the pace quickened in the course of 1982, as a new recession took its toll on both the remaining pockets of industrial militancy and the electoral prospects of the Fraser government.

12.
The more things change...

The resources boom, such as it was, turned to bust in 1982. The economy contracted sharply, pushing unemployment above 10 percent, while inflation remained in double digits. This new recession might have been enough in itself to ensure Fraser's 1983 election defeat.

Actually, his government had been in decline for some time. A certain exhaustion of the government was inevitable after seven years. In capitalist politics, the spoils of office open the way for corruption, leading to damaging scandals. The policies that seem coherent at first begin to unravel under the pressure of events, causing ministers to fall out. Meanwhile, the Opposition refashions its policies and image, while voters begin to forget its past sins. So it was with Fraser.

The scandals began early. Before the 1977 election, Fraser forced Treasurer Phillip Lynch to resign because his business associates appeared tainted by shady land deals in Victoria. In 1978, former deputy whip Don Cameron effectively accused frontbencher Eric Robinson of manipulating an electoral redistribution. Robinson survived, but the ensuing investigation brought down Senator Reg Withers, and *The Bulletin* published charges that Fraser himself had heavied Robinson to change his evidence.[1] Ian Sinclair came next: in 1979, this National Party heavy resigned from Cabinet after special investigator Michael Finnane accused him of forgery and suggested delicately that Sinclair was prone 'to give evidence which is untenable'.[2] Finally, in 1982, the Costigan Royal Commission tipped a huge bucket on the government's handling of tax evasion.

Fraser had supposedly spent years preparing an attack on tax cheats. In August 1975, the Commissioner of Taxation had authorised the Deputy Crown

Solicitor in Perth to act against 'bottom-of-the-harbour' schemes, but little happened thereafter. The instructions to prosecute, wrote Costigan, were found in 1982 'relegated to a bottom drawer where I was told they had rested undisturbed for the past five years.'[3] This had allowed a $6 billion explosion of cheating, at the very time that the government was campaigning against 'dole bludgers' and pontificating about financial rectitude. After Costigan's report, Fraser rushed to prepare legislation, but he was caught between two fires. Workers despised his hypocrisy; business hated him for making the legislation retrospective.

These pressures spurred on a fragmentation process that had slowly gathered pace since 1978, when complaints surfaced that Fraser was too authoritarian. 'You mistake command for leadership,' one frontbencher told him.[4] He was said to go over ministers' heads to consult public servants, and he certainly didn't hesitate to dump colleagues and antagonise people – to the point where he had assembled a fair collection of enemies within government ranks by about 1981. There were also ructions between the Coalition partners, due mostly to rivalries at state level but fuelled by resentment among Liberal backbenchers at their grazier PM's chummy relations with the Nationals.

The result was a whiff of that same instability that had so damaged Whitlam, prompting a Liberal minister to say: 'It's not the policy or the general direction of the government which is in trouble, it's the management of the government.'[5] He was mistaken, however. While the crisis of management was real, it could have been handled had Fraser's economic strategy not collapsed. His government's credibility depended heavily on economic success, because of its peculiar starting point.

Malcolm Fraser had won power in brutal fashion. While only a minority loathed him for it, most of the electorate was uneasy; even in the business world, some had voted Liberal with a bad taste in their mouths. Liberal Senator Chris Puplick later observed:

> A large proportion of the country always believed, even after the 1977 and 1980 elections, that the Fraser Government was there because in the first instance it had done something improper.[6]

The electorate would continue to support the government only if it produced results, but the very circumstances of Fraser's 1975 victory made this harder to do. Russell Schneider, a close observer of the government, wrote that a 'worry over the legitimacy of his bid for power...dominated Malcolm Fraser's attitude

THE MORE THINGS CHANGE...

Anti-Fraser banners at a demonstration 17 October 1980

Protesters continue to dog Fraser after five years in office. Present to open a nursing home, he entered the front under heavy escort and a barrage of abuse and later was hurried out through a back door

to his years in office.'[7] The consequence, according to John Howard, was that 'we did not always succeed in practising what we preached.'[8] Liberal 'dries' as well as the ALP have developed this line of argument to suggest that Fraser was a failure from Day One, both in fiscal policy and in industrial relations. It is not necessary to be so simplistic.

Certainly, there were early deviations from the Prime Minister's announced path of fiscal austerity, such as the tax cuts offered in the 1977 election (and soon withdrawn). A look at successive budget deficits, however, shows that his assault on government spending did achieve some initial success. The deficit had peaked at $3,500 million under Whitlam. Under Fraser, it fell to $2,719 million in 1976–77. It rose again but fell to $2,033 million in 1978–79 and $1,110 million in 1980–81, finally hitting a low of $549 million in 1981–82 amid the short-lived prosperity of the resources boom. Moreover, Fraser undoubtedly won important victories over the unions in his first years in power. The government's problem was that conservative fiscal policy and union-bashing did not address the core of the deep problems facing Australian capitalism.

A sharp downturn in 1974 brought on the agony of the Whitlam Government. Deficit spending aided a temporary revival by 1976, but recession returned once the Fraser regime had administered savage cuts to government programs. A better performance between 1978 and 1981 was followed by yet another sharp downturn, the worst since the Great Depression. It was hardly what those voting Liberal had hoped for.

The government's strategy had been based on fashionable theories that linked wages, inflation and unemployment closely together; Fraser thought that he could solve economic problems by reining in union power and 'fighting inflation first'. The facts did not confirm the theories. A dramatic surge in inflation had taken place in 1974, about the same time as a major wage offensive by the unions. While something like a 'wage–price spiral' undoubtedly occurred, much of the inflation was in such areas as food prices, where union demands were not decisive. Unemployment rose in the mid-to-late 1970s, weakening workers' bargaining power and forcing wages down, which took some pressure off prices. After falling for a time in Fraser's early years, inflation began to rise again from 1979 – rather too early to be blamed on the 'wage push'.

Inflation and unemployment were sometimes combined in a 'misery index', an eloquent statistic. The two most miserable years were 1975, when Fraser swept to power promising to restore prosperity, and 1983, when Fraser fell to a new Labor leader making similar promises. Given that union militancy figured so greatly in political life, it is equally interesting to consider the levels of disputation. These also marked the beginning and end of the Fraser era. A huge wave of industrial militancy contributed to Whitlam's crisis, and strike levels were still high in 1975. After a boost to the 1976 figures because of the Medibank strikes, disputation did fall away considerably as the recession hit home, remaining low until 1978. At the first sign of economic revival, however, strikes burst out all over, showing that the unions remained quite strong.

Thus Fraser was unable either to solve the economic crisis or to smash the unions. From the bosses' point of view, he could be forgiven the first. The more sophisticated among the bourgeoisie realised that the crisis was worldwide. Most voters, however, were no more prepared to accept this excuse from Fraser than from Whitlam. Their dissatisfaction was complemented by a growing ruling class disillusionment with Fraser's handling of industrial relations. The employers disliked brawls with the unions unless they yielded results, and the 'wage push' of 1979-81 convinced many that his methods were flawed. As early as 1980, when Bill Hayden ran a capable election campaign against Fraser, the electoral pendulum was clearly swinging back to Labor. By 1982, the government was deeply worried. They particularly feared Bob Hawke, who was now in parliament.

Fraser also paid the price for creating false expectations during the resources boom. In 1981, he had expressed a 'determination to see that the prosperity flowing from these great ventures will lift the living standards of every Australian family'[9]; alas, the fleeting resources boom had generated little enduring wealth. At the same time, his last assault on the public sector – the 'Razor Gang' exercise – had achieved only small savings at a high political cost.

So, by 1982, a personally unpopular Prime Minister, with few permanent achievements to show for years of hardship and confrontation, found himself driven back to old-fashioned deficit spending in an effort to lift the economy out of recession and buy votes. The monetarism he had embraced in 1975-76 was sloughed off, to reveal the Keynesian within. In a curious combination of 'too much, too late', he tried a giveaway election budget, full of tax cuts and concessions, with many welfare benefits boosted by up to 50 percent. He also funded an ambitious new airport at Brisbane. The pork-barrelling continued through the year and into 1983, until the *Sydney Morning Herald* was moved to sarcastic jibes about this 'born-again Keynesian':

> The name of his game is now job creating capital works. First were the employment projects funded from the proceeds of the wage freeze on Federal public sector wages. Then the speeding

Razor Gang protest Bendigo, probably May 1981

BENDIGO
THE RAZOR
FRASER
THE
WILL BENDIGO SUPPORT THE ORDNANCE

YEARS OF RAGE

RAZOR REPORT

Campaign Against Public Sector Cuts

Vol. No. 1, Friday 28 August, 1981

Working for a viable public sector.

The Campaign Against Public Sector Cuts (CAPSC) was formed at a Public Meeting at the Collingwood Town Hall in early May. The meeting was called by the Victorian Council of Social Services (VCOSS), and was a direct response to the 'Razor Gang' report. The Steering Committee of CAPSC is an open committee. Regular attenders of the meetings include workers affected by the cuts, members of welfare organisations, members of the ALP and other political parties, members of various trade unions and community organisations such as the Childcare Federal Funding Campaign, and many concerned individuals.

CAPSC was formed to fight the philosophy of the present government which is to give as much money as possible to the private sector at the expense of the public sector. This is an attack on both workers and the users of the services provided by the public sector. Included in the platform of CAPSC are the following principles:
o Support for the establishment of a viable public sector responsive to the needs of its users and the workers within it.
o Support for the principle that people should have the right to the provision and control of vital services which affect the quality of their lives.
o Support for the principle that the Federal Government must retain responsibility for the provision of community services, and must not devolve that responsibility to State or Local Governments without the provision of adequate funds.
o Calls for and support to trade union action against cuts in socially necessary public spending.

CAPSC believes that the public sector plays an integral role in both the economy and society and that the community and its workers should exert control over their environment, including consultation over the servicing of our rights to health care, education, housing etc.

We see our role as changing the terms of the debate away from reactive positions on the 'Razor Gang' or federal or state budgets, to developing clear policies on services that meet the needs of the community.

Campaign Against Public Sector Cuts broadsheet 28 August 1981

up of the Alice Springs to Darwin railway building. Then the offer of $500 million for an alternative to the Franklin Dam. Then the $640 million water resources program. Finally a $166 million program to celebrate the Bicentennial – although doubtless there is more to come.[10]

The government was locked into even more spending, because it had underestimated both the emerging drought and the unemployment payouts which the recession would necessitate. The budget deficit, already swollen by falling revenues, blew out so spectacularly that Liberal right wingers moaned privately about Fraser the 'closet centralist socialist'.[11] For another government, this would have been embarrassing enough. For Malcolm Fraser, it was a fiasco.

A freeze on wages

In the industrial sphere, 1982 did seem to bring the government some success. While the unions had shown their strength in the economic upturn, recession had tipped the balance of forces against them once more. In November, the government seized on rising jobless figures to argue for a clamp on wages, and Fraser called a special Premiers' Conference for 7 December to consider a national 'wage pause'. Although National Party leader Doug Anthony spoke vaguely about restraining 'other incomes',[12] it was soon clear that professional incomes, interest and dividends would be inviolate. Wage earners would bear the burden of sacrifice.

The core of Fraser's plan was a freeze in the public sector. Government wages would be pegged and the savings used to create jobs, with some of the money going to the states as bait to lock in the premiers, including those from Labor states. The public sector would then set the pace for private industry. The economics was shaky – by reducing consumer demand, the pay freeze might destroy more jobs than it created – but the proposal was primarily political. It legitimised the argument that wage rises caused unemployment. To the extent that Bill Hayden, the ALP premiers or the ACTU went along with Fraser's plan, Fraser would gain the labour movement's imprimatur for this contention.

The freeze took some selling. Employer groups knew that this sort of measure had failed before, because the pent up wage pressures had exploded in 'catch-up' claims once the clamps came off. It was likely to provoke calls for price control, the last thing business wanted to hear. The Labor premiers seized the opportunity to demand expansionary fiscal and monetary policies as trade-offs. Even federal Cabinet was divided on the specifics: Treasurer John Howard wanted to legislate an immediate private sector pay freeze, while Ian Macphee, now in the Industrial Relations portfolio, preferred 'to basically complete the community round [of pay rises] and then say there will not be any more increases for 12 months.'[13] The Arbitration Commission seemed to agree with Macphee when it gave cost-of-living increases to 15,000 waterfront workers on 20 November. About 2 million other workers were in the 'wage queue' behind them.

On 23 November, the ACTU hinted that it would comply. Its president Cliff Dolan went through the motions of 'rejecting completely' the concept of a wage freeze and reaffirming union policy of maintaining real wages, but the ACTU secretary Peter Nolan was telling reporters: 'we would be stupid to say we were unbending.'[14] Two days later, the Arbitration Commission signalled its own acquiescence by granting only the first instalment of an oil industry pay rise. Towards the end of the month, the ACTU went further, suggesting that it would accept a six-month freeze if the savings went to a 'national employment fund' or were in exchange for other job creation measures along with price control. None of these proposals had a hope of being implemented. Their sole impact was to legitimise the freeze concept and the wages-cost-jobs ideology behind it.

After some theatrics, the Premiers' Conference produced a messy compromise: a six-month freeze for most workers, 12 months for some, with limited job creation. The Arbitration Commission decided to allow some workers a limited 'catch-up'. On the other hand, federal government employees copped a 12-month freeze imposed by legislation. Employees of the non-Labor States faced a similar fate. The Wran Government showed its egalitarian principles by exempting state MPs from the restrictions; they got 7 percent from January. But, despite Cliff Dolan's attempt to dismiss the freeze as an 'absolute farce...political gimmickry at its worst,'[15] it was very effective politics and put the unions on the defensive. Sensing this, a number of employer bodies announced plans for further attacks on wages and conditions.

The unions held a flurry of consultations. In January 1983, they launched a limited, job-by-job campaign for higher wages in the metal, transport and building industries. They claimed to be winning some rises in the field, but there was no attempt at a generalised campaign to raise wages for the mass of Australian workers. In the oil industry, unionists met only frustration.

The oil workers had an excellent case. Their employers had signed an agreement in September providing for an initial pay rise, to be followed by a second instalment on 1 January. The second instalment had then fallen foul of the wage freeze. Not a little annoyed at this, electricians at Victoria's largest fuel supplier, the Shell refinery at Geelong, began an indefinite strike. Maintenance workers at the Clyde Shell refinery in Sydney placed overtime bans. On 28 January, the ACTU's oil industry tactics committee endorsed these actions, proposing also a series of bans for the whole industry and calling a delegates' meeting for 2 February to plan action against Bass Strait oil production.

Although the ACTU tried to portray the oil dispute as a one-off event with no flow-on implications – Simon Crean of the Storemen and Packers gave the government an explicit assurance to that effect – it was actually a test of the government's resolve. Macphee sharply rebuffed Crean. The oil workers were quite determined, and an interesting confrontation was developing. By early February, employer representative John Welch was complaining that TWU bans had disrupted fuel supplies to the Australian National Railways in Tasmania. Amoco, Caltex and Shell had been put 'out of the market' in Melbourne and Adelaide.[16]

Then Fraser called a general election for March, and a relieved Simon Crean immediately defused things:

> It has always been our intention to hit the government hard in this campaign, and now it makes more sense to assist in knocking the Liberals right out of government.[17]

He was pleased to announce the following day that Bob Hawke had 'prevailed on us for restraint,'[18] and Crean did his best to suggest that electing a Labor government would ensure a wage rise. Despite the recession, the unions appeared to have the muscle to challenge the wage freeze, but the officials had no great desire to do so, for reasons we'll consider below. The industrial action dissolved as all eyes turned to the election campaign.

To the polls

The conservatives' electoral fortunes had peaked by 1977 at the latest (Labor had won NSW as early as 1976), and the first hints of decline began to appear with the Victorian land scandals. At the start of the 1980s, Labor began to roll the conservatives steadily back. Under Bill Hayden's leadership, the ALP won seats in the 1980 federal poll, then John Cain led it to victory in Victoria in 1982. Cain's win was to be expected, given the air of decay and ineptitude surrounding the Victorian Liberals (Sam Lipski wrote that 'the State and its capital are gripped by a psychology of defeat'[19]). Even so, losing the 'jewel in the Liberal crown' was a shock to the Coalition, which was further shaken when Labor went on to win power in South Australia under John Bannon and Western Australia under Brian Burke.

The new leaders were all 'moderate' and pro-business, taking their lead from Neville Wran's successful formula: act like a Liberal, wear a blue suit, and you too can govern. Thus the 1980s era of right-wing Labor government arrived well before Bob Hawke seized the main prize. It would be easy with hindsight to conclude that the ALP's 1983 federal election victory was inevitable – that a 'drover's dog' could have won it. That it was *not* inevitable was demonstrated by the Flinders by-election in late 1982, which was expected to be a triumph for Labor but only brought a modest swing.

Hayden's problem was that, in pulling Labor towards the political centre, he had removed any distinctive policies or even a distinctive 'feel'. By 1983, the electorate wanted a change, but Hayden didn't seem to offer it. Rather, he looked like an erratic opportunist, saying anything to please, as with his uncertain response to the wage freeze. When launching the Flinders campaign, he had denounced the freeze as economic lunacy. Then, on discovering that the Labor premiers were effectively accepting it, as was the ACTU, he began softening his stance: it was now a 'gimmick', but one which the unions should try to make work.[20] Finally, in late January, with the ACTU making noises about backing the oil workers, he sought to harden his position again.

Hayden had trouble responding because he shared Fraser's basic assumption, that wages must fall. Even in the speech declaring the wage freeze a gimmick, he demanded a redistribution of income from wages to profits. Labor actually hoped that, if it won power, it would be able to use the framework set by the freeze to implement the incomes policy it was cooking up with the ACTU. Here, too, Hayden stumbled. Although the substance of the Accord had been agreed for months, the ALP leader couldn't seem to finalise it. The ACTU wanted it to pay lip service to full wage indexation; Hayden feared that this would alarm the business community.

These dilemmas underlay the increasing push inside the party to replace him with Hawke, encouraged by a considerable feeling among ordinary workers that Hawke was more impressive and likely to win. Sections of the media backed it, wanting a more credible alternative to Fraser. Hayden succumbed on 4 February, allowing Hawke to take the leadership just as Fraser was obtaining a double dissolution of parliament.

In policy terms, there was little to distinguish Hawke, but he was better placed to sell the *illusion* of radical change simply by being new. Hayden had spent years establishing a cautious image; Hawke could step into the limelight and act brash. He could make lavish promises without appearing to contradict earlier statements. He could trade on his radical image as a union leader, yet rely on big business to remember that Bob Hawke had always been their mate. Consequently, his campaign slogan of 'national reconciliation' sounded like an innovation instead of a social democratic cliché. Probably the ALP's boldest reform was Medicare (the emotion-charged name 'Medibank' had been left behind), and even this Bill Kelty sold as 'a government scheme which would relieve [employers] of corporate expenditure'.[21]

Hawke wrapped up the Accord then rammed it through a national union conference, opposed by only one delegate, NSW Nurses' Federation secretary Jenny Haines. The vexed issue of wage indexation suddenly resolved itself: real wages would be maintained 'over time', with the union officials joining various consultative and planning bodies in exchange for industrial peace. Hawke floated a $2,750 million economic expansion plan, which sounded like a lot, then largely forgot about the promises in favour of his gossamer campaign theme, 'reconciliation'. Fraser never knew what hit him.

The Liberals had planned to campaign on the slogan, 'We're not waiting for the world', designed to look bold compared with the cautious Hayden. When they found Hawke could outbid them in audacity, the Fraser camp abruptly changed gears. The Accord, once derided as 'paper thin', suddenly became a 'blue-print for union government' giving 'union militants the right to veto across a broad range of government policy'.[22] The Liberals splashed around a picture of Laurie Carmichael shaking Hawke's hand. None of these tactics worked, however, for Fraser was now up against Hayden's dilemma: he couldn't differentiate himself from policies whose substance he had been steadily embracing. The *Sydney Morning Herald* remarked:

> The commendable practice of consulting the social partners in developing economic policies – a practice which Mr Fraser's government engaged in extensively before the last budget – is now portrayed as surrendering responsibility for economic management. Mr Fraser made great virtue of the consultations his government held with the ACTU last year... There was no suggestion then that Mr Fraser was allowing the unions to run the country.[23]

One of Fraser's final rallies, Sydney February 1983

Hawke and the ACTU, meanwhile, left no room for doubt that their Accord would suit business down to the ground. When asked how he proposed to 'control the unions', Hawke said that he could rely on 'peer pressure' among the officials, who had, after all, signed an agreement to 'restrain their claims' in pursuit of 'economic expansion, which is what all unions and business want'.[24] When Cliff Dolan made some unguarded remarks about taxing profits, his new ACTU secretary Bill Kelty quickly declared that the ALP and ACTU were 'never likely to embark on a situation where profits are artificially reduced'.[25]

Dolan himself eagerly endorsed Hawke's assurance that a Labor government would not be a 'handmaiden' to the unions, and when ALP frontbencher John Brown illustrated the point all too well with an attack on 'outrageous' penalty rates,[26] Hawke was unruffled. Labor could afford to relax about these issues in any case. Polling showed that, while the public was still concerned about strikes, years of confrontation had reduced the appeal of union-bashing.

The conservative parties' embarrassment reached an ironic peak when Joh Bjelke-Petersen entered the fray. His hopes of seizing on a rail strike to agitate about the union menace had been dashed when the strike failed to occur. Unionists were 'so mad for power,' complained his Deputy Llew Edwards, that 'they're even acting responsibly.' Nonetheless, Petersen persisted with a 20-minute attack on the Accord, whereupon Labor's Keith Wright rose to:

> quote chapter and verse of previous statements by Messrs Fraser, Bjelke-Petersen and Edwards indicating that they were in favour of precisely the things advocated by Mr Hawke...: co-operation between governments, employers and unions.[27]

Malcolm Fraser wound up a failed campaign at the Princess Theatre in Launceston, the very spot at which he had opened his campaign for the 1975 Bass by-election – his springboard to power. In 1983, it was his last stop before the biggest federal ALP win since Curtin's day.

All that common ground

Convention offers us two conflicting images of the Fraser Government's end. One has Hawke and Labor bringing fundamental changes: reconciliation in place of union-bashing, growth-oriented policies in place of 'fight inflation first'. The other sees Fraser as a closet Tory paternalist, who pretended to be a hard liner but reverted to Keynesianism and dialogue with unions in every crisis. ALP myth-makers naturally prefer the former assessment, while John Howard has implied the latter:

> People often say Malcolm Fraser was elected in 1975 with a mandate to smash the unions, but it was nothing of the kind. The industrial relations policies of the Coalition were as benign and complaisant as ever.[28]

I have suggested a third view. Fraser's initial stance was actually fairly determined. It is true that the sharp monetarist edge in government policy generally came from others such as Stone and Lynch; still, during his first years in power, Fraser destroyed Medibank, cut welfare funding, restricted land rights and forced the unemployed to carry much of the blame for their plight. With Fraser setting the tone and aided by recession, employers were able to defeat major strikes by well-organised groups of workers.

The government was serious, and so were the bosses. But, like most of society, they underestimated the dimensions of the crisis, and they also misjudged the strength of the organised working class. Neither Fraser nor the employers had prepared for the industrial bloodbath necessary for them to attain their objectives. They had wounded their opponents rather than destroying them; when circumstances changed, their opponents had struck back fairly effectively.

As this became clear, advocates of alternative strategies began to get a hearing. Some of these had been vocal all along. In South Australia, the Dunstan Government was exploring workers' participation. John Uhrig, chief executive of white goods manufacturer Simpson Pope, was thinking along similar lines, as was the management of CSR; and the idea was slowly catching on elsewhere. A 1976 survey of top managers found that 39 percent saw 'industrial democracy' as a way of getting higher productivity.[29]

Fraser was never capable of embracing this concept (although a government committee did so in 1980), but it remains important as a sign, amid the class conflict of the mid-1970s, that some executives and policymakers did see advanced forms of class collaboration as an option. Many more became open to some kind of 'social contract' at the start of the 1980s.

Fraser did use some forms of class collaboration from the start: helped by clear signals coming from Bob Hawke even before the 1975 election, he recognised that the ACTU leadership could be allies. The PM's close personal relationship with Hawke, which had once seen them 'sit around at the Lodge working their way through bottles of port,'[30] declined as the ACTU leader emerged as a political rival but was replaced in 1981 by a warm relationship with Cliff Dolan. However, collaboration at the top had limited value if he merely used Hawke or Dolan as troubleshooters, because this could erode their credibility eventually while doing little to weaken the *roots* of worker assertiveness.

When he lost control of the 1979–81 'wage push', Fraser allowed his more moderate ministers to explore ways of regaining the initiative through a more systematic incorporation of the unions. By the end of 1981, these efforts began to bear fruit, partly because the left–militant unions felt that the balance of forces was tilting against them, but also partly because the great majority of union officials from left to right themselves wanted some kind of accommodation. The right wing had wanted it all along, while most of the left had been drawn towards it from 1981 onwards.

Although Carmichael later insisted, rightly, that it was 'nonsense to suggest that my actions in conjunction with a few metal workers in Australia created a massive international recession,'[31] such notions certainly did infect the metal unions in 1982, as they watched rapid job losses follow closely on their successful wage offensive of the previous year. It was precisely at this point that the wages-cost-jobs theory became hegemonic in the Australian trade union movement. Carmichael himself was almost pathetically eager to embrace the new approach, which was not hard for him to do, given that the wage settlements at the end of 1981 themselves contained the main elements of institutionalised class collaboration.

The metal industry award, which traded wage rises for industrial peace, became a model. 'The metal industry award has to be seen to work,' said Ian Macphee in mid-1982. 'This is a compact of a kind that we haven't seen in Australia before.'[32] He sought a wider relationship between the government, the employers and the union officials based on similar principles, pressing the unions at tripartite talks in July for a commitment to hold down wages if the government loosened the purse strings in the August budget. The unions were non-committal but showed enough interest to convince Fraser that he could pull off the wage freeze.

By November, Macphee was suggesting that the wage freeze could become the basis for an incomes policy, including perhaps even a price monitoring mechanism. If his plans were less specific than those Hawke later unveiled, still, the gist was there. And while Macphee never quite won over Cabinet to this perspective, there is no doubt that Fraser was moving towards it, as shown by his November appeal for the wage freeze, which presaged Labor's arguments:

We must shake off the attitudes, the prejudices that have led to too much division in the past. We must unite this nation in one cause based on the dignity and rights of all Australians.[33]

The *Financial Review* did not miss this underlying continuity. During the election campaign, it pointed out that a wage freeze and an incomes policy had a common starting point: 'that in a recession there are limits on the claims that can be made on the national income.' In plain English, wages must fall. And they must be *kept* down when the economy showed signs of reviving:

So a wages pause, if it is to have the longevity ideally required for it to become the basis [for a strong recovery] must be developed into an incomes policy.[34]

Ian Macphee could hardly be blamed, therefore, if he incautiously told a journalist during the campaign that much of Labor's Accord was 'consistent with my approach', that Labor's aim of extending the wage freeze 'does seem to be the same', and that 'I am committed to the ACTU being as strong as possible.'[35] Although it didn't quite fit the Coalition's election rhetoric, it sure fitted the facts.

If Fraser in 1983 had elements of class collaboration in common with Labor, his attacks on certain unions also presaged the Hawke era. His Royal Commissioner Frank Costigan was investigating the Federated Ship Painters and Dockers Union (FSPDU), while his government was laying the basis for deregistration of the BLF.

Of course, there was graft on Australian waterfronts, but Costigan's attempts to portray the painters and dockers as engaged in organised crime were primarily a political attack on a left-wing and militant organisation. For nearly two years, the Commission heard evidence from the union's enemies, most notably one Bill Longley, then serving a prison sentence for arranging the 1973 murder of the FSPDUs' Victorian secretary, Pat Shannon. During that time, the union had no opportunity to reply. After Shannon's successor Jack Nicholls was found shot dead, the union ceased cooperating with the Commission. Costigan couldn't prove anything very damning about the union, but he recycled various tales about dockland brawls and shoot-outs, allowing the media to create the impression of a gangster union. Similarly, a harmless remark by federal secretary Terry Gordon: 'We catch and kill our own' – a fishing analogy illustrating self-reliance – was invested with sinister implications.[36]

Costigan's inquiry into the FSPDU was a curtain-raiser for the main event, a two-pronged attack on the BLF. In Victoria, the Liberals set up a Royal Commission to look into charges of corruption centring on Norm Gallagher while the Fraser Government concentrated on its deregistration plans.

The BLF leadership certainly had its ugly side. Gallagher's destruction of the old NSW branch had made him widely hated in the Sydney labour movement, and his treatment of dissidents elsewhere had not been gentle. The union's political inconsistency had also helped to isolate it; for example, it had changed its mind more than once over the bans on Newport and had moved from banning the US war base at Omega to fighting the FIA for the right to build it. Many union militants were consequently reluctant to defend the BLF. But a close examination of the government attacks made it abundantly clear that, as with the painters and dockers, the government was using its persecution of the BLF to attack the industrial left and militant unionism generally. Whatever you thought of its federal secretary, it was correct to defend the BLF for these reasons.

It was charged that Gallagher had accepted help from various employers in building two Gippsland beach houses. Even if all the charges were true, the alleged total value of $181,000 worth of materials, services and labour was hardly earth-shattering given the long history of rake-offs in the industry. Would anyone have bothered with it had Gallagher belonged to the right wing of the union movement?

There was also another question. 'For these gifts [the employers] expected some quid pro quo,' wrote the *National Times*,[37] yet no substantial evidence was ever forthcoming that the BLF had exempted the supposed contributors from industrial action.[38] On the contrary, the campaign against the BLF was designed to establish in the popular mind the image of a group of mad militants who spared no one. The political nature of the exercise subsequently became even clearer when Gallagher got a jail sentence after the builders and developers had only received good behaviour bonds.

Deregistration moves faltered when the ACTU refused to go along, but this was a temporary hiccup. Once Hawke was in power, Labor governments at state and federal level took them up again, building on the foundations laid under the Liberals. The ACTU, now deep in the Accord embrace with Hawke, collaborated fully, and the BLF faced a withering attack in 1986.

That selective union-bashing occurred alongside the emerging Lib-Lab consensus about deepening class collaboration should not be a surprise. Because some unions might recognise the dangers that Accord-type policies posed to workers' interests and be tempted to stand against them, it was imperative for Hawke to make an example of one or two recalcitrant organisations.

The central aim of the new policies was, after all, much the same as that of the old – holding down wages. In that sense, things had remained the same. By 1982, most of the union movement was capitulating to the argument that economic problems stemmed from 'excessive' wage claims. The 1982 recession did appear to follow on directly from the wage push of the previous years, so it seemed that perhaps the right-wing critics had been correct to blame the crisis of the 1970s on union militancy. In reality, the crisis stemmed from quite different causes, located deeply in capitalist production relations. But to argue this alternative economic theory, which I have briefly summarised in an appendix, was beyond all except the extreme left fringe of the labour movement by 1983.

Hawke at the summit

Having run a largely issue-free campaign, Hawke entered the Lodge with few real commitments. What's more, the Liberals had prepared a gift for him. He had announced that, if the Fraser estimates for the budget deficit proved to be understated, he might reassess policy. After the election, he found a large blow-out, nearly $10 billion foreshadowed for 1983–84 – sufficient pretext to dump what few promises he had made. Hawke then announced plans for his famous economic summit, knowing that the employers as well as the unions would rush to attend.

Although only *The Age* and the *Illawarra Mercury* had endorsed Labor, most of the press had covered Hawke favourably throughout the campaign. They, and the class they represented, were weary of Fraser-style confrontation and liked the idea that Labor could persuade unions to make, as *The Age* put it, 'concessions which would have been unthinkable in the past'.[39]

Some employers were absolutely thrilled about the summit. 'It is obviously a great privilege to be invited,' said Lloyd Zampatti of Tooheys. AMP's Alan Coates said that his mates looked forward to it 'with the greatest goodwill', while the MTIA was taking a 'positive approach'.[40] And well might they feel at home in this gathering, because it was an elite affair. Roughly 40 delegates came from big business, seven knights among them. Women, Indigenous people and youth had a few token representatives, with the unemployed presumably covered by social workers. The organised working class was 'represented' by a selection of top union bureaucrats – that layer that had served them so badly for seven years under Fraser before rushing to embrace the wage-cutting logic of the Accord.

Hawke at the ACTU congress September 1983

The summit was a triumph for Hawke, who dominated proceedings, establishing the 'Bonapartist' flavour of early Labor rule as the ALP–ACTU tag team set the policy agenda, to the mild chagrin of a fragmented and politically disoriented bourgeoisie. There was nothing remarkable in this. Forces apart from big business not only can, but often do set the pace in capitalist society. However, they can only do so over time if they either challenge the power of capital or pursue policies that fit its long-term interests. Laurie Carmichael might still talk of doing the former; the summit showed just how thoroughly the Accord partners proposed to do the latter.

The press reported: 'The ACTU seized the initiative on the central issue of wage-fixing by offering important concessions during the opening session of the summit on Monday.'[41] Bill Kelty announced that the unions would moderate wage demands, then discount them further in exchange for Medicare, and would put off catch-up claims for the wage freeze to an indefinite and hypothetical future. Under centralised wage fixing, said Kelty, extra claims by stronger unions would be suppressed. 'The union movement can't have it both ways.' Just about everyone present loved Kelty's presentation. 'Great speech, great speech,' said Bob Hawke, while the next speaker, CRA's Rod Carnegie, thought it 'incredible'.[42]

The employers had been wrong-footed only in the sense that the unions were rushing to concede their key demands. In an overnight caucus, they hit upon a way to preserve the illusion of hard bargaining: while agreeing on a return to centralised wage fixing, they came out firmly against CPI-based wage indexation. This was pure ideological posturing. The summit could easily dodge the CPI issue, leaving it to the Arbitration Commission.

In any case, a return to full CPI increases did not constitute an immediate threat. It would only occur after the Fraser wage freeze was extended for another six months. Many employers remembered how real wages had declined under Whitlam's indexation system, even *with* full CPI adjustments; they also recalled how readily that system had lent itself to Fraser's 'plateau indexation', with its blatant real wage cuts. On top of all these considerations, the economists had begun predicting an economic recovery. Indexation would be a handy device to block the real wage increases unions had traditionally won during the recovery phase.

What nobody possibly fully realised in 1983 was the extent to which Labor and the ACTU would use the Accord framework to slash workers' wages when the recovery led to balance-of-payments problems from 1985 onwards. By this, as by most standards, Labor in the 1980s achieved Malcolm Fraser's goals more

fully than the conservative parties could do. Nevertheless, we must give credit (so to speak) where it is due. Just as Whitlam's retreats and his wage indexation policy had softened workers up for Fraser's attacks, so the conservative onslaught of 1975–78 inflicted wounds severe enough to make them easier prey for the deadly embrace of Hawke's Accord. Then, towards the end of his years in power, Fraser helped to lay the basis for the Accord itself.

Threads of continuity ran from Whitlam through Fraser to Hawke. What made each era very different politically was not the intent of the politicians but the ebb and flow of class struggle. Whitlam came to power at a time when the bourgeoisie and its politicians had lost control of the working class and social movements; he set about coopting them, then faltered when he lost control of the economy. Fraser thought that he could master the working class and restore prosperity, but the ensuing confrontations served only to exhaust the contending forces.

That cleared the way for new and more successful attacks on the working class under Hawke, which proceeded primarily through the cooptative mechanisms of the Accord but did not preclude certain selective union-bashing. Bjelke-Petersen's Queensland Government was allowed to finally smash the state's power workers in 1985, with only token protests from the ACTU. The BLF was effectively destroyed in NSW, Victoria and the ACT after 1986, with the ACTU leaders' active connivance. Seizing on the more favourable climate, the iron ore mining companies of the Pilbara began undermining workers' job organisation, setting the scene for Robe River's annihilation of its unions. 'National reconciliation' indeed!

For the labour movement and the left, the Fraser era had offered both dangers and opportunities. Struggles which showed the basic economic strength of organised labour in Australian society fended off the most serious dangers. At the same time, however, the main opportunities went begging. A fairly large minority of workers went into the mid-1970s with an ill-defined but genuine belief that the crisis of capitalism was the appointed time for labour to impose its will on a society whose old order was proving bankrupt. A sizeable minority of political activists held similar views. But, in the absence of a mass political movement determined to pull these currents together and lead a struggle for power, this fragmented vanguard could not even seriously challenge the government, let alone prevail.

Exhausted in partial struggles, led down blind alleys by the Hawkes and Halfpennies, the increasingly discouraged militants were tempted by the hope that collaboration between governments, capital and labour could solve their problems. Over the following decade of ALP government, we learned how false that hope was; and, by the early 1990s, Australian society was again in crisis. It was time to revive the rage.

Of course, the official leaders of the labour movement continued to counsel moderation, social harmony and reliance on traditional institutions. Only a brash minority, still small in numbers, advocated militancy, class struggle and revolutionary politics. The history of the Fraser years suggested that this minority was right. Whether the new years of rage might end more favourably than the old depended on socialists' ability to gain a wider hearing.

Appendix:
The roots of economic crisis

If there was one key belief uniting the three governments – Whitlam from 1974 onwards, Fraser and Hawke – it was the conviction that excessive wage levels were responsible for the economic crisis, because they undermined profits and pushed up unemployment. Trade unionists' inability to refute these claims was important in undermining working class militancy and opening the way for the Accord. The argument can only be refuted by challenging the economic logic of capitalism itself.

It is undeniable that, all other things being equal, high labour costs will generally cause employers to shed labour.[1] It is foolish for the left to deny the fact, both because the empirical evidence is against us[2] and because it is reformist to imagine that the system can accommodate limitless rises in real wages, particularly in times of slump.

The union wage offensives of 1974 and 1981 pushed up labour's share of the national product, which in turn reduced profitability. Falling rates of profit, by discouraging investment, were a factor in the recessions which followed. Seizing on these facts, the *Financial Review*'s Michael Stutchbury noted that 'the 1982–83 recession can be labelled a trade union or wage blow-out recession.'[3] But this assessment ignores other important factors. By the time Stutchbury wrote his column, the recession of the early 1990s was well underway, proving that economic crisis could happen even after years of 'wage restraint'. Even in 1982, there were obvious objections to blaming the unions for the economic problems of the Whitlam and Fraser years.

Australia's recessions followed trends in the world economy, which was hit by three major blows in the early 1970s: the end of currency stability; severe pressures on productive capacity and on food and commodity prices; and the

1973 'oil shock'. None had much to do with unions or wage rises. The recession of the early 1980s was precipitated by a second 'oil shock' and tight monetary policies – hardly a consequence of union claims. The resulting international slumps flowed through to Australia.[4]

To be sure, there were also specifically Australian factors, but workers weren't the villains here either. Conventional wisdom has it that the unions went over the top on the wages front during Whitlam's years in power, but this is something of a myth. Under Whitlam, the unions had initially held back, and 1973 saw wages fall slightly behind CPI. Unions only launched their dramatic wage push of 1974 in *response* to the emergence of runaway inflation, caused by such factors as US war spending in Vietnam and a big hike in food prices following bad weather and international shortages.[5]

It is no more sensible to blame the unions for the 1982 recession. The union 'wage push' during 1979–82 was partly a *response* to exaggerated expectations aroused by Fraser about the wonders of the resources boom. The government had portrayed wage restraint as a temporary expedient until prosperity returned, so, if it was now boom time, why not claim pay rises? In any case, the proximate domestic cause of the recession was high interest rates. Partly, this reflected international pressures; to the degree that it was locally driven, we must recall that Fraser had also played an important role in establishing the ideological basis for a tight monetary policy. If this was an opportunist exercise in which he did not entirely believe, that hardly lessens his culpability.

Taking a longer term view, there is another sense in which the government must assume responsibility for the economic malaise afflicting Australia since the 1970s. The Australian economy has lost ground in world trade for most of the postwar era, as its primary products have receded in importance. At the same time, high tariffs ensured that manufacturing remained backward, fragmented and inward looking. A paper circulated by the Jackson committee in 1976 warned that many Australian workers 'work their guts out to keep producing from clapped-out machinery driven from lines of belts similar to those pictured in schoolbooks on the Industrial Revolution.'[6]

Fraser's fascination with resource development at the end of the 1970s stopped him from addressing these problems. He stuck to high interest rates and tight credit, partly because he didn't mind if manufacturing declined somewhat. The idea was that booming exports of minerals would pay for manufactured imports. Instead, the 'resources boom' petered out, and recession ensued.

But surely, lower wages would still have made the economy more competitive? Workers saw little point in boosting international competitiveness if this occurred at their expense, but we now know that the whole argument was false in any case. The wage cuts which Fraser ultimately failed to deliver were achieved under Labor. This improved competitiveness in the short run, but only demonstrated that, in the long run, productivity was far more important. Low wages gave employers no incentive to invest in machinery, so productivity growth lagged.

So much for conventional economics. Marxists could and did raise more penetrating questions. Why should workers make sacrifices? Having brutally attacked the labour movement, Fraser had a hide asking for restraint – the crisis was his problem, not ours. More fundamentally, Marxists wanted to abolish capitalism rather than make it work better. Consequently, they argued for workers to pursue their own interests without regard to the health of an exploitative system. If the system could not accommodate better wages for workers, that was just one more reason for getting rid of it.

The Marxist political arguments were grounded in an economic analysis that centred on capitalist profits. Ian Macphee complained in early 1983: 'the relative share of GDP for wages and profits is now at the same unhealthy proportion which prevailed in the notorious years of 1974-75.'[7] Actually, the profit share was even lower, a devastating result for the government. This was part of a longer term trend that had seen the profit share fall by nearly 21 percent between 1967 and 1983, partly reflecting the relative strength of the working class over two and a half decades.

Taken on their own, these figures might suggest that excessive wages were the cause of the economic crisis, but there is more to the story. While conventional economics emphasises the profit share, Marxist theory focuses on the rate of profit: the rate of return capitalists receive on their investments in labour and means of production. If this is too low, investment stagnates. The rate of profit in Australia fell by *30* percent during the same period.[8] Although the profit share could be portrayed as directly linked to the wages share, the rate of profit could not. Other factors must have been at work in the onset of economic crisis in the 1970s.

The tendency for profit rates to fall is the core of Marx's theory of capitalist crisis. This theory argues that, as capitalism grows, it piles up means of production more rapidly than the labour force expands. But, according to the labour theory of value, only the latter is the source of new values – and thus of profits. Therefore, capitalist growth tends to undermine profitability, in turn discouraging investment and breeding economic crisis. The argument is complex, but the implications are simple: there is little point in workers concerning themselves with the health of the capitalist system. Even if this health is restored, the next growth phase simply paves the way for new crises. As double-digit unemployment returned in 1991 after years of wage-cutting under Labor, Marxists could claim that their theory had been strikingly vindicated.[9]

It is nonsense to blame wage rises for the Whitlam or Fraser recessions or for those of more recent times. The labour movement was, and is, right to defend wages and conditions. Its failure lies in not challenging a *system* that makes crisis inevitable.

Afterword

Rick Kuhn

When *Years of Rage* first appeared in 1993, it was already clear that the class collaborationist politics of the ALP government's Prices and Incomes Accord benefited capital rather than labour. The book's concluding chapter argued that the confrontations between capital and labour under Malcolm Fraser's conservative government ended up exhausting both sides. 'That in turn cleared the way for new and more successful attacks on the working class under Hawke, which proceeded primarily through the cooptative mechanisms of the Accord.'[1] This Afterword traces the extent to which these cooptative mechanisms, many of which Tom identified, as well as new circumstances, shaped the struggles after 1983.

The Accord

The damage to workers' bargaining power when unemployment reached 10 percent, during the 1983 recession, was a factor in union leaders' revised strategy away from industrial action toward even greater a reliance on Labor governments. As an incomes policy, the Accord was redistributive; some money went down, from the employed working class to those in receipt of social security benefits, but most went up, to the capitalist class. Wage-setting arrangements under the Accord cut real pay and soon required that money wage increases for specific industries could only happen at the expense of job conditions which made working life bearable.

Three serious union defeats in 1985 reinforced the logic of the Accord.[2] In February, the conservative state government of Joh Bjelke-Petersen provoked a conflict with the ETU by sacking 1,000 line workers employed by SEQEB. Coal miners and workers in Mt Isa initially took serious strike action in solidarity. But the Queensland TLC called off the solidarity strikes in favour of a doomed legal strategy. The second defeat occurred at the Mudginberri Abattoir in the Northern Territory. While the abattoir's workforce accepted a shift to individual contracts, rather than the industry award, the Australasian Meat Industry Employees' Union did not. From May, the union tried to picket the employer back into compliance with the award. There was very limited solidarity action, even from other unionists in the industry, and the picket was called off in September in the face of court-imposed penalties on the union. In July, workers at Dollar Sweets in Melbourne began a picket over a claim for a 36-hour week, which was outside the Accord rules. The picket lasted 143 days but, in the absence of any solidarity action, the picketers and their small but militant union, the Federated Confectioners Association, were also defeated.

The process continued in 1986. The Hawke Labor government, state governments, employers, courts and other unions combined to smash the BLF for its failure to comply with the Accord. A similar coalition, supplemented by the use of the Australian Airforce to scab, defeated the efforts of the Australian Federation of Airline Pilots to defend pay and conditions in 1989.

The centralisation of wage fixing under the Accord accompanied these setbacks for unions and likewise undermined unions' strength in workplaces. From the late 1980s, union restructures and amalgamations increased the weight of full-time union officials in the movement still further, constricting rank and file control over workers' own organisations.

Although workers' objective capacity to take effective industrial action improved with the economic recovery, strike action declined after the 1983 recession. For the first time in Australian history, workers did not achieve substantial real pay gains during a period of sustained growth. Real average weekly earnings and, even more so, real award wages, were lower in 1989-90 than in 1982-83.

The class collaborationism of the overwhelming majority of union officials that Tom documented not only continued to be a feature of class relations in Australia but increased. It is now generations since most union leaders had personal experience of sustained strike action. The tendency for them to owe their jobs more to patronage networks (especially through the ALP), rather than to experience as workplace activists, has intensified.

What Treasurer Keating called 'the recession we had to have' in 1990-91 deepened the decline in working class combativeness institutionalised by the

AFTERWORD

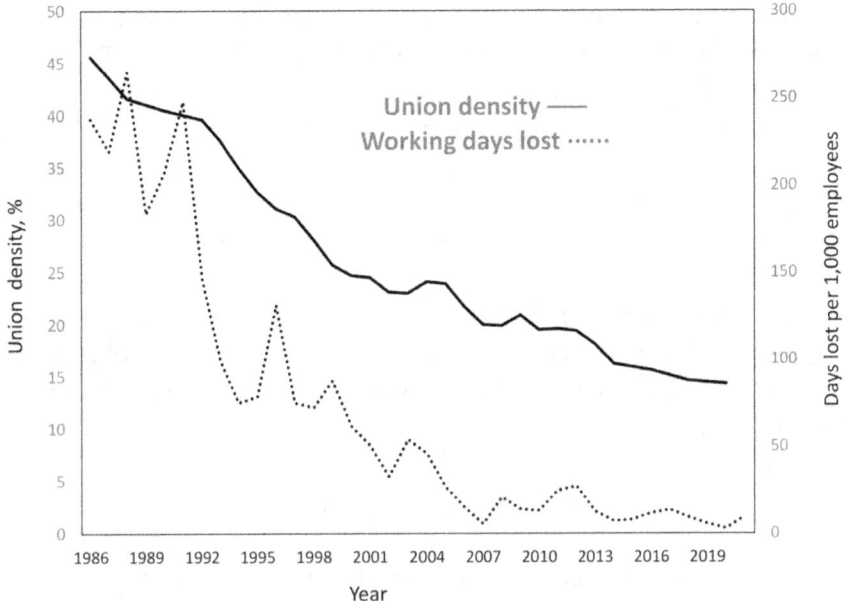

Sources: Australian Bureau of Statistics 6325.0 Trade Union Members, 1996; 6310.0 Employee Earnings, Benefits and Trade Union Membership, 1999, 2000, 2003; Trade Union Membership, August 2020 (NB data discontinuity in 2004)

Accord. In terms of unemployment, although not contraction of gross domestic product, this was the most serious economic downturn in Australia since the Depression of the 1930s. The levels of industrial action and union density (the proportion of workers in unions) between 1986 and the early 2022s are shown in the figure.

The extent of strike action fell unevenly until the global the financial crisis of 2007-09, despite the prolonged period of sustained economic growth since Keating's recession. It has then bumped along a low levels. The fall in union density has been more even, reaching just 12.5 per cent in 2022.

In 1992, the Liberal Victorian Government of Jeff Kennett provoked an important exception to the fall-off in workers' fights. The movement resisted Kennett's privatisations of state assets, school closures, and sacking of public servants as well as legislation that excluded many working conditions from industrial agreements and curtailed workers' rights to strike or picket. There was widespread industrial action and rallies of up to 150,000 protesters. But, apart from two one-day, state-wide stoppages, the campaign was not coordinated across different sectors and the sectional action fizzled out within a few months.[3]

Labor's approach to land rights paralleled its handling of working class interests: protestations of support combined with attacks in practice. The Keating Government's 1993 Native Title Act was a blow against Indigenous people because it limited the effect of the High Court's 1992 Mabo decision. This nationally operative legislation contrasted with the far more generous Northern Territory Land Rights Act, drafted by the Whitlam government in response to the activism of Indigenous people and their supporters, but passed, in watered down form, under Fraser.[4]

Three episodes of broader union mobilisation and several protest campaigns, including the largest protest movement in Australian history, punctuated the years when John Howard was Prime Minister and showed the potential for a shift in class relations.

Harassing Howard

Union officials only began to take the mobilisation of their members seriously after the defeat of the Keating Labor government in March 1996, as Howard's conservative government prepared anti-union legislation. But the campaign was cut short when outraged workers and Indigenous activists had the temerity to attempt entry into Parliament House during the ACTU's 'Cavalcade to Canberra' on 19 August 1996.[5] Instead of building on the rage, union leaders denounced the display of militancy and backed off; the *Workplace Relations Act* was passed.

Emboldened, the Howard government continued its attacks on workers. It conspired with Patrick Stevedores to exclude Maritime Union of Australia (MUA) members from the corporation's operations. Patrick dismissed all its dock workers and replaced them with scabs in April 1998, provoking a national response. Workers from other industries joined wharfies on picket lines and contributed funds to sustain the sacked employees. The high point of the confrontation came at East Swanston Dock in Melbourne: the police were hemmed in by 4,000 picketers on one side and 2,000 construction workers, who had marched in from the city, on the other side. The dispute inspired the song *Roll On*, by punk band The Living End, as police failed to break the picket. In the context of widespread solidarity action, the courts subsequently reinstated the unionists.

Here was an opportunity to restore working class self-confidence in their capacity to defend or extend their wages and conditions through industrial action. But, despite this position of strength, the leaders of the ACTU and MUA signed a deal with Patrick that eventually halved the labour force, reduced conditions and increased the pace of work. Union officials had secured their place in the industrial relations system, for the time being. But their class collaborationist approach, so-called 'strategic unionism', meant that this was at the expense of workers' jobs and conditions.[6]

The treatment of refugees became a major political issue during the 1990s. In 1992, the Keating government introduced legislation which required detention of all non-citizens who were in Australia without a visa, including applicants for refugee status. Despite protests against the new policy, Labor intensified the attack on refugees in 1994 by making it possible to detain them until they died. In 1999, as the number of imprisoned asylum seekers rapidly rose, protests and breakouts by the detainees themselves triggered and sustained a campaign against the policy, particularly by 'Refugee Action' groups in several cities. Other protest and refugee welfare organisations emerged later.[7] The size of the demonstrations and marches initiated by the campaign organisations have fluctuated between handfuls and many thousands in the years since.

The Howard government made its refugee policies an issue during the lead-up to the 2001 election.[8] The ploy had a significant racist component, as the vast majority of those affected were not white. His government subsequently denied anyone who arrived in Australia by boat without a visa the right to apply for refugee status; started shipping all such people offshore, to be imprisoned in Australian-funded concentration camps in Papua New Guinea and Nauru; and began to force boats or their passengers back to their countries of origin. In 2005, however, scandals over the deportation of an Australian citizen, Vivian Alvarez Solon, and the imprisonment of a permanent resident, Cornelia Rau, together with continued demonstrations, shifted public opinion about refugee policy.

Elected in December 2007, Kevin Rudd's Labor government ended boat turnbacks and off-shore detention, while maintaining mandatory jailing, only for his successor as Labor prime minister, Julia Gillard, to reinstitute the imprisonment of refugees on Pacific islands in 2012. Her successor, Rudd again, declared: 'As of today, asylum seekers who come here by boat without a visa will never be settled in Australia'.[9] When the Liberal–National Coalition returned to office in 2013, it reinstituted the boat turnbacks. But the efforts of human rights and support organisations, along with protests by refugees and the Refugee Action groups, maintained pressure on Australian governments to cease their inhumane and racist treatment of people seeking asylum. Among the first acts of Anthony Albanese's Labor government in 2022 was to return people headed to Australia on a boat to Sri Lanka, without assessing their refugee status. Echoing Rudd, Albanese insisted that 'people who arrive by boat will not be settled here.' His government, however, later decided that refugees who had earlier been granted Temporary Protection Visas could stay permanently.[10]

The international anti/alter-globalisation movement gained momentum with the Battle of Seattle protests against a World Trade Ministerial Conference from 30 November ('N30') 1999. In Australia, the national mobilisation from 11 September ('S11') 2000, to protest the World Economic Forum's gathering of corporate bosses, politicians and top public servants, was a significant upward blip in social struggle. For three days, thousands took to the streets of central Melbourne. After 20,000 protesters laid effective siege to the event's venue on the first day, police attacked those barring entry on the second day. Victorian Labor Premier Steve Bracks participated in the Forum and defended the police violence. The union movement was divided: ACTU President Sharan Burrow addressed the dignitaries, but the Victorian THC had endorsed the campaign and, on the second day, thousands of unionists marched in support.[11]

The alter-globalisation movement, with its anti-capitalist politics, stalled after Al Qaeda crashed planes into the World Trade Center in New York and the Pentagon in Washington. The US Government used those attacks as a pretext for invading Afghanistan in 2001 and then Iraq in 2002–03, igniting the largest antiwar movement the world had ever seen. The Howard government sent Australian armed forces to participate in both military campaigns.

The Australian Greens were active in building the antiwar movement. Many unions verbally supported the campaign and encouraged members to attend rallies. There were union contingents and speakers. But union involvement in the organisation of demonstrations was much less than during the Moratorium movement against the Vietnam war. The ALP, on the other hand, supported the invasion of Afghanistan, while arguing that the invasion of Iraq was illegitimate only because the United Nations had not endorsed it. Some Labor parliamentarians dissented and, eventually the party leader Simon Crean spoke at a rally.[12] This was a minor and passing deviation from the bipartisanship of Labor and conservative parties in foreign policy since the 1970s.

Australian workers turned up to the protests in huge numbers, mostly as individuals rather than in organised union blocks. On the weekend of 15 February 2003, there were demonstrations in many countries. Up to half a million marched in Sydney: the largest demonstration in Australian history. Around 200,000 took to Melbourne's streets. The invasion of Iraq began a few days later, despite the massive protests, and the movement subsided. Against majority opinion in the country, Australia became one of the very few members of the USA's 'coalition of the willing' invaders.[13]

A new Howard government policy in 2004 prompted an initially less dramatic but more sustained and, eventually, massive and successful response. It inserted a definition of marriage as only being between a woman and a man into the *Marriage Act*. Community Action Against Homophobia mounted street and other protests in Sydney, while Equal Love groups were set up to organise the militant campaign in other cities. Australian Marriage Equality concentrated on the respectable lobbying of politicians and paid advertising, criticising the other groups' confrontationist rhetoric and tactics – designed to draw more people into activity.

Labor governments between 2007 and 2014 did nothing to modify the law. The 2011 ALP Conference in Sydney did favour marriage equality but allowed its parliamentarians a 'conscience vote' on the issue, capitulating to the minority of homophobes among its members and union affiliates. Ten thousand demonstrators, mainly mobilised around the marriage question but including refugee supporters, chanted 'Shame Labor shame' outside the conference venue.[14]

Marriage equality was only achieved in 2017 under the conservative Coalition government of Malcolm Turnbull, after the movement was boosted by repeated protests in Australia and equal marriage legislation in other countries (including Spain, Canada, the USA, Sweden, Argentina and Ireland). The scale of the campaign dramatically increased as the Liberal Party, under pressure, shifted its position, and the Labor Party and even corporate CEOs joined in. But the ALP still did not require the bigots in its own ranks, especially those associated with the leadership of the right-wing shop assistants' union, to vote in favour of the amendment.[15]

The third upsurge in union action under the Howard government contributed to the defeat of the conservatives at the November 2007 election. The initial slogan of the Your Rights at Work campaign organised by the ACTU was 'Your Rights at Work, Worth Fighting for'. The focus was opposition to the government's WorkChoices legislation, which further undermined minimum conditions of employment and union rights. There were rallies across the country and 250,000 people attended one in Melbourne in November 2005. But, a year later, the slogan was modified to 'Your Rights at Work, Worth Voting for'.

Restricting rage, making myth under Labor

After the election, the Rudd Labor government filed off some of the rougher edges of the WorkChoices legislation, but left fundamental features intact, including secret ballots for industrial action and restrictions on union officials' rights to enter workplaces. Although the policy was renamed 'Forward with Fairness', it was in fact 'WorkChoices Lite'.[16]

Continuity with its conservative predecessor was also a feature of the Rudd government's treatment of Indigenous Australians. This even applied to the policies associated with Howard's failed attempt to replay his 2001 election victory with a racist stunt, now directed against Aboriginal people. Loudly asserting bogus claims about paedophile rings, the government sent the army to occupy Indigenous communities in the Northern Territory. The package of policies that formed the Northern Territory Intervention overrode self-government; restricted land rights; imposed external bureaucratic controls over their inhabitants' lives, including their incomes and access to alcohol; and suspended the *Racial Discrimination Act*, along with other laws that secured Indigenous people's rights. With union support, many hundreds of people around the country demonstrated against the Intervention shortly after its launch. The incoming Rudd government maintained Intervention policies. These remained an issue for participants in large, annual Invasion Day marches and other protests against the oppression of Indigenous Australians for two decades. In 2022, the Albanese government wound back only some aspects of the Intervention, which had been costly both in terms of money and damage to the quality of Aboriginal people's lives. Some forms of income management continued, including leases handing over control over their land, which the Howard and Rudd governments blackmailed Aboriginal communities into signing in return for spending on housing.[17]

The ALP mythologises the legacies of Labor governments. In *Years of Rage*, Tom O'Lincoln demonstrates the capitalist logic of the policies pursued by the Whitlam and Hawke governments. This logic has continued. The more recent legends portraying the Rudd and Gillard governments as paragons of progressive virtue are also hollow. The *rhetoric* of Rudd's 2008 apology to the Stolen Generations of Indigenous people, taken from their families as children, contrasted with his government's *practice*, such as the continuation of the Northern Territory Intervention. Attribution of Australia's success in passing relatively unscathed through the Global Financial Crisis of 2007–09 to governments policies contrasts with the way resource exports to China decisively buoyed up the Australian economy. Labor apologists applaud Gillard's 'misogyny speech' of 9 October 2012, which targeted the hypocrisy of Liberal leader Tony Abbott, ignoring the circumstance that the speech was actually made in defence of a sexist former Liberal, who was the Speaker of the House of Representatives.

And, on the same day, Gillard's government eliminated a welfare payment to single parents (overwhelmingly women) once their children turned eight, rather than sixteen.[18]

Another brief surge of struggle occurred in 2011. 'Occupy Wall Street', inspired by occupations of public spaces during the Arab Spring of 2010–11 and the anti-austerity movement in Spain from May 2011, was a protest against corporate domination of politics and society. Movements around the world emulated tactics employed in New York, notably occupations and flash mobs (demonstrations designed to attract attention and disrupt normal activity in a particular location, not publicly announced in advance). In Australia, the movement was strongest in Melbourne. Several thousand people converged on the small City Square and set up an encampment. Police expelled the activists after a week but smaller contingents were able to occupy several other locations in the city for short periods.[19]

International inspirations

There were major mobilisations against the conservative governments of Tony Abbott (2013–2015), Malcolm Turnbull (2015–18) and Scott Morrison (2018–2022). Many of the largest intersected with international movements.

That was less the case for the response to Abbott's austerity measures and other policies: a series of substantial protests across Australia in 2014, starting with the 'March in March'. Outraged, tens of thousands joined protests initiated and organised by people without formal affiliations to the left. The movement was not sustained, as no element with social weight, like the Labor Party, unions or even the Greens, was prepared to seriously build on their anti-Liberal sentiment and momentum, still less to lead the movement in the direction of more militant – let alone industrial – action. After budget protests in May, the movement declined and then petered out altogether.[20]

The powerful intersection between the movement against Black deaths in custody in Australia and the Black Lives Matter movement emanating from the United States reached a high point in 2020, despite COVID lockdowns. The establishment of the Royal Commission into Aboriginal Deaths in Custody in 1987 followed from demonstrations over the police killing of 16 year-old John Pat in 1983 and many other Black deaths. The Commission concluded in 1991 but many of its recommendations are yet to be implemented. The Bridge Walks of 2000, involving more than a quarter of a million people in Sydney alone, reflected very widespread solidarity with Indigenous people. Organised by the

Council for Aboriginal Reconciliation, a government agency, the events made no specific demands but were nonetheless seen as counterpoised to the Howard government's racism. As with Rudd's apology to the Stolen Generations, no substantial changes in the government's policies accompanied or followed the symbolism. Unlike the apology, however, the walks were not just passive spectacles for the many who participated. Annual Invasion Day rallies and marches, mobilising from thousands to tens of thousands around Australia, have been more focused on concrete demands.[21]

The Black Lives Matter movement in the USA, starting in 2014, already had an impact in Australia in July 2016 when thousands protested against Indigenous deaths in custody under the same slogan. The movement escalated in early 2020. After the police murder of George Floyd in Minneapolis, many tens of thousands of Australians joined Black Lives Matter marches against Indigenous deaths in custody in capital cities and many smaller centres, despite concerns about the spread of COVID-19.[22]

In 2022, Albanese's Labor government recapitulated the tactic embodied in the Rudd's Apology. To temporarily disarm those opposed to anti-Indigenous racism and divert their attention and energy, Albanese promised a referendum to enshrine a tokenistic, purely advisory 'Voice' to parliament in the constitution. Serious measures to overcome this Indigenous oppression – Aboriginal and Torres Strait Islander self-determination, comprehensive land rights and massive funding – have never been policies of the parties currently in Australian parliaments.[23]

The US #MeToo movement against sexual harassment and rape also had a strong resonance in Australia. Inspired by the Women's Marches against the inauguration of the profoundly sexist Donald Trump as president in January 2017, many marched in Australian capital cities and again, on a smaller scale, a year later. But the largest protests came in 2021, after former Liberal Party staffer Britany Higgins publicly stated that she had been raped in Australia's Parliament House. On 15 March, tens of thousands joined March 4 Justice rallies across the country.[24]

Meanwhile, the planet has been frying. School strikes for climate, initiated by students in Sweden, spread to Australia in 2018. The response of the Rudd and Gillard governments to global warming had been pathetic. Their conservative successors even tolerated climate change denialism in their parliamentary ranks and spent millions on the fairy story of 'carbon sequestration' (pumping carbon dioxide underground). As the scientific evidence and experience of climate change, in the form of storms, floods, fires and droughts increased, public concern about governments' inaction in the face of global heating intensified. The largest response came from young people.

The first School Strike in Australia, on 30 November, was relatively modest: around 15,000 participated. Because the movement was mainly a protest against federal government inaction, without formal demands that might hurt profits, state and territory Labor frontbenchers climbed on board and endorsed the next one, on 15 March 2019. Up to 150,000 students and adults participated. Environmental NGOs, primarily focused on maintaining respectability and on helping Labor into office rather than building mass activism, contributed resources and thus influenced the school student organisers. Their orientation slowed the pace of the movement. The third strike only happened on 19 September but was huge. Many bosses and the Victorian Labor government gave workers time off to attend and over 300,000 showed up. The pandemic restrictions limited attendance at the events called in September 2020. A year later, the Strike 4 Climate 2021 was pitched as a protest against the federal budget in May. Tens of thousands marched in 47 locations. In comparison with previous Australian protests, the event on 26 March 2022 was small.[25]

Parallel to the Student Strikes, Extinction Rebellion (XR) spread from the United Kingdom. To promote awareness of the climate crisis, XR engaged in street theatre and civil disobedience, a promising step beyond the strictly legal demonstrations and marches characteristic of the climate movement so far. The group grew rapidly in Australia in 2019 and organised stunts and some larger scale actions that mobilised thousands of people. Participation subsided dramatically because of the pandemic and tighter control by the political sect at the core of XR.[26]

It has not been difficult to discern the effects of climate change. From September 2019 through to February 2020, bushfires burned through millions of hectares of Australian farmland, national parks and urban areas, consuming some suburban houses and small towns. A climate rally in Sydney on 11 December drew thousands. As the disaster intensified, Prime Minister Morrison went off on a jolly Hawaiian holiday in December. With health-damaging smoke enveloping many Australian cities, a Socialist Alternative campus front, Uni Students for Climate Justice, called demonstrations for 10 January 2020 to express widespread rage at the Morrison government's indifference and inaction on climate change. Estimates of protest attendance in Sydney alone ranged from 10,000 to 50,000. One week later, thousands protested again.[27]

Since the period covered by Tom's book, there have been many other smaller environmental campaigns, particularly against specific environmentally damaging projects. From 2016, for example, protesters targetted the Adani corporate conglomerate's Carmichael coal mine in Queensland. The Labor government in Queensland facilitated the project, and the mine workers' union supported it. Scaled down from the original proposal, the mine is now exporting coal.[28]

Another consequence of capitalist development, the COVID-19 pandemic, led to the largest avoidable loss of lives since World War II. For a period, the Victorian and Western Australian state Labor governments maintained sensible policies – including border closures, lock-downs and mandatory indoor mask-wearing – that were more effective in saving lives than the responses from the federal and other state governments. But they too eventually prioritised profit-making over human lives. Instead of seriously fighting for health and incomes during the pandemic, many union officials were determined to sacrifice their members for the sake of unity with bosses. In Victoria, for example, the construction workers' union campaigned against shutting down the building industry. The NTEU leadership, together with some vice chancellors, floated a plan to cut tertiary education workers' pay in return for union officials' involvement in university budgeting and empty promises about saving jobs. Widespread rank and file rage at their officials' actions became a revolt, largely thanks to efforts of the NTEU Fightback organising centre, and the proposal was scuttled.[29]

Laboring under illusions, again

As of this writing, the Albanese Labor government maintains its predecessors' commitment to ruling in the interests of the capitalist class. Most fundamentally it has presided over 'the biggest destruction of real wages in Australia since records began,' as inflation reached forty year highs.[30] Although it has formally established a target of reducing carbon emissions by (only) 43 percent by 2030, the government still promotes increased extraction of oil, gas and coal. Offshore detention and boat turnbacks continue. Despite some cooling of rhetoric critical of China, the US Alliance remains the keystone of Australia's foreign policy. There has been no tampering with the Morrison government's decision to buy obscenely expensive nuclear submarines and the associated AUKUS Pact, announced in September 2021.

In 2022, union leaders again enthusiastically mobilised electoral support and financial resources to hoist the ALP into office. But, consonant with the pattern Tom documented and explained, most have shown no comparable or even much enthusiasm at all for industrial action in defence of real wages. Instead of leading concerted fights to sustain real pay, they welcomed the crumbs cast in the direction of the working class in the October 2022 budget and measures of industrial relations reform. The legislation, however, created even more legal obstacles to workers taking strike action and weakened the Better Off Overall Test, under which enterprise agreements can't reduce individual workers' pay and conditions below the standard of industrial awards.[31]

At the time of writing, the government is still enjoying a honeymoon period. But, sooner or later, there will be further episodes of rage and protest against the deepening crises of the capitalist system and the damage it wreaks, such as those Tom documented and explained. The approach he used can assist us in promoting and sustaining future episodes of rage and struggle and to turn them into a revolutionary movement for socialism.

December 2022

Acronyms and abbreviations

ABC	Australian Broadcasting Commission
ACF	Australian Conservation Foundation
ACOA	Administrative & Clerical Officers' Association
ACSPA	Australian Council of Salaried and Professional Associations
ACTU	Australian Council of Trade Unions
AGIC	Australian Government Insurance Corporation
AIM	Australian Independence Movement
AIS	Australian Iron and Steel
ALP	Australian Labor Party
AMWU	Amalgamated Metal Workers Union
APTU	Australian Postal and Telecommunications Union
ARU	Australian Railways Union
ATEA	Australian Telecommunications Employees' Association
AUS	Australian Union of Students
AWU	Australian Workers Union
BHP	Broken Hill Proprietary
BLF	Builders Labourers Federation
BWIU	Building Workers' Industrial Union
CAMP	Campaign Against Moral Persecution
CAR	Coalition Against Repression
CEEP	*Commonwealth Employees (Employment Provisions) Act*
CES	Commonwealth Employment Service
CICD	Congress/Campaign for International Cooperation and Disarmament
CGTLC	Central Gippsland Trades and Labour Council
CLCG	Civil Liberties Campaign Group

CMU	Combined Mining Unions
CPA	Communist Party of Australian
CRA	Conzinc Riotinto of Australia
CUC	Combined Unions Committee
CYSS	Community Youth Support Scheme
DAA	Department of Aboriginal Affairs
DEYA	Department of Employment and Youth Affairs
DSS	Department of Social Security
EMC	Exchange Maintenance Centres
EPA	Environmental Protection Authority
ETU	Electrical Trades Union
FAIRA	Foundation for Aboriginal and Islander Research Action
FEDFA	Federated Engine Drivers and Firemen's Association –
FIA	Federated Ironworkers' Association
FILEF	Federation of Italian Workers and their Families (*Federazione Italiana Lavoratori Emigrati e famiglie*)
FOE	Friends of the Earth
FPU	Food Preservers' Union
FSPDU	Federated Ship Painters and Dockers Union
GMH	General Motors Holden
HEC	Hydro-Electric Commission
IRB	Industrial Relations Bureau
IS	International Socialists
MAUM	Movement Against Uranium Mining
MEU	Municipal Employees Union
MKU	Mary Kathleen Uranium
MOA	Municipal Officers Association
MTIA	Metal Trades Industry Association
MWU	Miscellaneous Workers' Union
MUA	Maritime Workers of Australia
NLC	Northern Land Council
NTEU	National Tertiary Education Union
NWAC	National Women's Advisory Council
PKIU	Printing and Kindred Industries Union
PND	People for Nuclear Disarmament
PJT	Prices Justification Tribunal
PTC	Public Transport Commission
RSL	Returned Services League
RTL	Right to Life

SACK	Society for Asserting the Constitution over Kerr
SEC	State Electricity Commission
SEQEB	South East Queensland Electricity Board
THC	Trades Hall Council
TLC	Trades and Labor Council
TWS	Tasmanian Wilderness Society
TWU	Transport Workers Union
USSR	Union of Soviet Socialist Republics (Soviet Union)
UWU	Unemployed Workers' Union
VBU	Vehicle Builders' Union
VPSA	Victorian Public Service Association
WAA	Women's Action Alliance
WCA	Women's Campaign for Abortion
WLM	Women's Liberation Movement
WOW	Wollongong Out Of Workers
WSA	Worker-Student Alliance
WWF	Waterside Workers' Federation
WWWW	Women Who Want to be Women
XR	Extinction Rebellion

Endnotes

Preface

[1] T O'Lincoln, *Years of Rage*, Melbourne, Interventions, 2nd edition, 2012

Author's Introduction

[1] R. Connell, *Ruling Class Ruling Culture*, Melbourne, Cambridge University Press, 1997, p. vii.

1 Contending classes

[1] P. Raskall, 'Who's Got What in Australia', *Journal of Australian Political Economy*, no. 2, June 1978, p. 7.

[2] G. Crough, 'Small is Beautiful but Disappearing', *Journal of Australian Political Economy*, no. 8, June 1980, p. 4.

[3] One 1986 study influenced by Marxism estimates the main owners of means of production at 0.4 percent of the population, and top managers at 13.6 percent. Even allowing for overlap, the 14 percent total is far larger than the actual bourgeoisie but offers a useful 'ballpark' figure for the ruling class together with those layers closest to it. J. Baxter et al., 'The Australian Class Structure', *Australian and New Zealand Journal of Sociology*, vol. 25, no. 1, May 1989, p. 111.

[4] Crough, p. 5.

[5] Summarised in T. O'Shaughnessy, 'Economic Notes', *Australian Left Review*, no. 58, April 1977, pp. 27ff.

[6] R. Connell and T. Irving, 'Yes Virginia, There is a Ruling Class' in H. Mayer (ed.), *Australian Politics, a Fourth Reader*, Melbourne, Cheshire, 1977, p. 81.

[7] J. Higley and D. Smart, *Elites in Australia*, London, Routledge & Kegan Paul, 1979, pp. 248, 253.

[8] Quoted in K. Tsokhas, *A Class Apart?*, Melbourne, Oxford University Press, 1984, p. 108.

[9] S. Encel, *Equality and Authority*, Melbourne, Cheshire, 1970, p. 350.

[10] Quoted in M. Simms, *A Liberal Nation*, Sydney, Hale & Iremonger, 1982, p. 81.

[11] Tsokhas, pp. 2, 66.

[12] See H. Draper, *Karl Marx's Theory of Revolution*, especially vol. 1, *State and Bureaucracy*, New York, Monthly Review Press, 1977.

[13] Simms, p. 54.

[14] D. Plowman, 'Union Statistics: Scope and Limitations' in B. Ford and D. Plowman (eds.), *Australian Unions*, Melbourne, MacMillan, 1983, p. 538.

[15] D. Horne, *Time of Hope*, Melbourne, Angus & Robertson, 1980, p. 93.

[16] R. Kriegler, *Working for the Company*, Melbourne, 1980, pp. 200 and 254–5.

[17] R. Trahair, 'The Men on the Mine' in A. Bordow (ed.), *The Worker in Australia*, St Lucia, 1977, p. 52.

[18] Quoted in R. Lansbury, 'White Collar and Professional Employees' in Bordow, p. 212.

[19] The statistical profile of the workforce is drawn from census data.

[20] Commission of Inquiry into Poverty, First Main Report, *Poverty in Australia*, vol. 1, Canberra, 1975, p. 20.

[21] Cited in J. Collins, 'Fragmentation of the Working Class' in T. Wheelwright and K. Buckley (eds.), *Essays in the Political Economy of Australian Capitalism*, vol. 3, Australia and New Zealand Book Co., Sydney, 1978, p. 6.

[22] S. Frenkel and A. Coolican, 'Organisation and Decision making in Two Unions' in Ford and Plowman, p. 168.

[23] For a discussion of the role of trade union officials, see T. Bramble, *The Contingent Conservatism of Full-Time Trade Union Officials*, Discussion Paper 11/91, Department of Economics, La Trobe University.

[24] Quoted in D. Jaensch, *Power Politics*, Sydney, Allen & Unwin, 1983, p. 42. David Kemp argued that this class identification was eroding because of a 'strong trend away from the Labor Party among voters from blue collar households, and a somewhat weaker trend towards Labor among voters from white collar households'; D. Kemp, *Society and Electoral Behaviour in Australia*, St Lucia, University of Queensland Press, 1978, p. 352. But, given the 'proletarianisation' of white collar workers discussed later in this chapter, Kemp's case was overstated at the very least.

[25] On the postwar Communist Party, see T. O'Lincoln, *Into the Mainstream*, Sydney, Stained Wattle Press, 1985.

[26] For a discussion and able debunking of these theories in the Australian context, see V. Burgmann, *Power and Protest*, Sydney, Allen & Unwin, 1993, pp. 1–7. For a discussion of what does and does not constitute the 'new middle class', see A. Callinicos and C. Harman, *The Changing Working Class*, London, Bookmarks, 1987, Chapter 1.

[27] Quoted in R. Gordon and W. Osmond, 'An Overview of the Australian New Left' in R. Gordon (ed.), *The Australian New Left*, Melbourne, Heinemann, 1970, p. 19.

2 A new era of conflict

[1] Quoted in Horne, *Time of Hope*, p. 92.

[2] On the international context, see C. Harman, *The Fire Next Time*, London, Bookmarks, 1988.

[3] *The Bulletin*, 22 March 1969.

[4] Quoted in J Hurst, *Hawke PM*, Melbourne, Angus & Robertson, 1983, p. 73.

[5] Quoted in Hurst, p. 86.

[6] Hurst, p. 90.

[7] The far left deserves considerable credit for building the movement in its earlier stages. See A. Picot, 'Vietnam: How We Won Last Time', *Socialist Review*, no. 4, Winter 1991.

[8] B. Scales, *Draftmen Go Free: A History of the Anti-Conscription Movement in Australia*, Melbourne, self-published, 1989, p. 24.

[9] Z. D'Aprano, *Zelda: The Becoming of a Woman*, Melbourne, self-published, 1977, p. 126.

[10] *Australian Financial Review*, 9 September 1970.

[11] I have discussed the Whitlam Government at greater length in T. O'Lincoln, 'The Rise and Fall of Gough Whitlam', *Socialist Review*, no. 5, Autumn 1992.

[12] *The Australian*, 23 August 1969.

[13] Quoted in E. G. Whitlam, *The Whitlam Government 1972-1975*, Melbourne, Viking/Penguin, 1985, p. 215.

[14] *The Age*, 9 October 1974.

[15] Quoted in P. Tulloch, *Poor Policies*, London, Croom Helm, 1979, pp. 43, 45.

[16] See S. Castles et al., *Mistaken Identity*, Sydney, Pluto Press, 1988, Chapter 4.

[17] *The Australian*, 14 November 1972.

[18] *Australian Government Digest*, vol. 2, no. 4, 1974, p. 1197.

[19] *Australian Government Digest*, vol. 2, no. 3, 1974, p. 723.

[20] G. Elliott and A. Graycar, 'Social Welfare' in A. Patience and B. Head (eds.), *From Whitlam to Fraser*, Melbourne, Oxford University Press, 1979, p. 96.

[21] A. Summers, 'Women', in Patience and Head, p. 198.

[22] See Cameron's comments, *Australian Government Digest*, vol. 2, no. 1, 1974, p. 89.

[23] Quoted in B. Hughes, *Exit Full Employment*, Melbourne, Angus & Robertson, 1980, p. 91.

[24] Quoted in Hughes, pp. 41-41.

[25] D. Plowman, 'Unions and Income Policies' in Ford and Plowman, p. 414.

[26] Fraser put it that way when introducing the 1982 wage freeze; quoted in D. White and D. Kemp (eds.), *Malcolm Fraser On Australia*, Melbourne, Hill of Content,1986, p. 193.

[27] In his Deakin lecture; quoted in White and Kemp, p. 111.

[28] M. Fraser, 'National Objectives', *Australian Quarterly*, vol. 47, no. 1, March 1975, pp. 27-32.

[29] Quoted in Hughes, p. 49.

3 Coup in Canberra

[1] G. Freudenberg, *A Certain Grandeur*, Melbourne, Macmillan, 1977, p. 250.

[2] Quoted in Connell, p. 118.

[3] Quoted in P. Ormonde, *A Foolish Passionate Man*, Melbourne, Penguin, 1981, p. 165.

[4] *The Australian*, 5 August 1975.

[5] Quoted in Freudenberg, p. 266.

[6] *Wentworth Courier*, 20 November 1975; reproduced in *Daily Tribune*, 2 December 1975. Punctuation adjusted.

[7] *The Age*, 29 November 1975.

[8] D. Horne, *Death of the Lucky Country*, Melbourne, Penguin, 1976, pp. 18-19.

[9] Quoted in F. Crowley, *Tough Times*, Heinemann, Melbourne, 1986, p. 143.

[10] Quoted in P. Edgar and A. Smith, 'The 1975 Election Campaign', in P. Edgar (ed.), *The Politics of the Press*, Melbourne, Sun Books, 1979, p. 166.

[11] *Sun-Herald*, 31 August 1975.

[12] *The Australian*, 18 September 1975.

[13] *Sun-Herald*, 5 October 1975.

[14] Edgar and Smith, p. 151.

[15] Edgar and Smith, p. 153.

[16] Quoted in C. Lloyd, 'The Media and the Elections', in Howard R. Penniman (ed.), *Australia at the Polls*, Washington DC, 1977, p. 179.

[17] See Edgar and Smith, p. 116.

[18] Quoted in Lloyd, p. 208.

[19] *Illawarra Mercury*, 1 October 1975.

[20] Quoted in Lloyd, p. 183.

[21] *National Times*, 15–20 September 1975.

[22] *National Times*, 15–20 September 1975.

[23] *AMWU Monthly Journal*, November 1975.

[24] *Sun-Herald*, 31 August 1975.

[25] *The Australian*, 15 September 1975.

[26] *Sydney Morning Herald*, 2 October 1975.

[27] P. Kelly, *The Dismissal*, Melbourne, Angus & Robertson, 1983, p. 267.

[28] *Sydney Morning Herald*, 15 October 1975.

[29] A. Theophanous, *Australian Democracy in Crisis*, Melbourne, Oxford University Press, 1980, pp. 329–30.

[30] *Daily Tribune*, 25 November 1975. But others took a similar approach, including me.

[31] *Sydney Morning Herald*, 13 and 15 October 1975.

[32] *National Times*, 3–8 November 1975.

[33] *Nation Review*, 24–30 October 1975.

[34] *The Age*, 21 October 1975.

[35] *The Age*, 17 October 1975.

[36] *The Age*, 17 October 1975.

[37] *The Age*, 21 October 1975.

[38] *Sydney Morning Herald*, 18 October 1975.

[39] *The Age*, 24 October 1975.

[40] *The Bulletin*, 15 November 1975.

[41] *Sydney Morning Herald*, 1 November 1975.

[42] *Daily Tribune*, 24 November 1975.

[43] *Sydney Morning Herald*, 12 November 1975.

[44] Kelly, pp. 285–293.

[45] K. Rowley, 'Marxism and Conspiracy Theories', *Intervention*, no. 8, March 1977, p. 7.

[46] *The Australian*, 12 November 1975.

[47] *The Australian*, 12 November 1975.

[48] *The Australian*, 12 November 1975.

[49] *Courier-Mail*, 13 November 1975.

[50] *National Times*, 24–29 November 1975.

[51] *Advertiser*, 12, 13 and 15 November 1975.

[52] *Courier-Mail* and *The Age*, 12 November 1975.

[53] *The Age*, 14 November 1975 for Cleghorne and Halfpenny quotes.

[54] *The Age*, 18 November 1975.

[55] *Daily Tribune*, 28 November 1975.

[56] *Sydney Morning Herald*, 3 December 1975.

[57] *The Age*, 9 December 1975.

[58] *Sydney Morning Herald*, 7 October 1975.

[59] *The Age*, 3 December 1975.

[60] *The Age*, 1 December 1975.

[61] *The Age*, 25 November 1975.

[62] *Sydney Morning Herald*, 11 December 1975.

[63] *Daily Tribune*, 25 November 1975.

[64] *Direct Action*, 4 December 1975.

[65] *The Age*, 3 and 15 December 1975.

[66] *The Age*, 15 December 1975.

4 Fraser on the offensive

[1] D. Horne, *Death of the Lucky Country*, p. 100.

[2] *Nation Review*, 5–11 December 1975.

[3] Quoted in Hughes, p. 53.

[4] *Sydney Morning Herald*, 31 January 1976.

[5] *Sydney Morning Herald*, 26 March 1976.

[6] *Sydney Morning Herald*, 16 January 1976.

[7] *Sydney Morning Herald*, 26 March 1976.

[8] *Scope*, 29 January 1976.

[9] *The Bulletin*, 31 January 1976.

[10] *Sun-Herald*, 14 December 1975; *Sydney Morning Herald*, 15 December 1975.
[11] *The Age*, 19 June 1976.
[12] *Scope*, 29 January 1976.
[13] *The Bulletin*, 28 February 1976.
[14] *National Times*, 5–10 April 1976.
[15] *Australian Financial Review*, 24 June 1976.
[16] *The Age*, 3 December 1975.
[17] This and the previous two quotes from *Sydney Morning Herald*, 8 April 1976.
[18] *Sydney Morning Herald*, 21 April 1976.
[19] *Australian Financial Review*, 12 January 1976.
[20] *Quadrant*, November 1975, p. 16.
[21] *The Age*, 1 June 1976.
[22] All quotes from the South Coast: *Illawarra Mercury*, 3, 9 and 17 June 1976.
[23] *Australian Financial Review*, 3 June 1976.
[24] *The Age*, 9 June 1976.
[25] *The Age*, 10 June 1976.
[26] Max Costello, interview, June 1976.
[27] *The Age*, 17 June 1976.
[28] *The Age*, 8 June 1976.
[29] *The Age*, 9 June 1976.
[30] *The Bulletin*, 10 July 1976.
[31] This paragraph is a précis from K. Windschuttle, 'Sir, It's Not Often That I Write, But ...' in K. and E. Windschuttle (eds.), *Fixing the News*, Sydney, Cassell, 1981, pp. 109–112.
[32] *Nation Review*, 16–22 July 1976.
[33] *The Age*, 7 July 1976.
[34] *The Health Worker* (Sydney), August 1976.
[35] R. Schneider, *War Without Blood*, Sydney, 1980, Angus & Robertson, pp. 168-9.
[36] *Scope*, 29 July 1976.
[37] *Sydney Morning Herald*, 9 August 1976.
[38] *Direct Action*, 7 October 1976.
[39] *Sydney Morning Herald*, 20 March 1976.
[40] *Sydney Morning Herald*, 27 March 1976.
[41] The last four quotes about anti-Kerr demonstrations are taken from *Nation Review*, 20 May, 17 June, 29 July and 5 August 1976.

5 In the trenches

[1] I. Turner and L Sandercock, *In Union is Strength*, Melbourne, Nelson, 1983, p. 143.

[2] An earlier version of the account of the Fairfax strike appeared in T. O'Lincoln, 'The Struggle at Fairfax', *Front Line*, no. 6, June, 1977. I observed much of the dispute. Unsourced quotes are from my own observation or interviews at the time.

[3] *Nation Review*, 11 November 1976. Emphasis added.

[4] *The Bulletin*, 13 November 1976.

[5] For example, 'A report published in the latest issue of the Communist weekly *Tribune* quotes Mr Don Paget...', *Sydney Morning Herald*, 26 November 1976.

[6] Remaining quotes about the Fairfax strike are from the *Sydney Morning Herald*, 28 October, 5 November, 11 November, 13 November,16 November, 9 December and 17 December 1976.

[7] *National Times*, 20-25 December 1976.

[8] For more background, see J. Benson and D. Goff, 'The 1976 Latrobe Valley SECV Maintenance Workers' Strike', *Journal of Industrial Relations*, vol. 21, no. 2, June 1979, pp. 217-220.

[9] *The Age*, 17 June 1977.

[10] *The Age*, 27 August 1977.

[11] *The Age*, 30 September and 1 October 1977.

[12] *The Age*, 1 October 1977.

[13] *The Age*, 4 October 1977.

[14] *The Age*, 4 October 1977.

[15] *The Age*, 5 October 1977.

[16] Benson and Goff, pp. 225-6.

[17] *The Bulletin*, 29 October 1977.

[18] *The Age*, 19 October 1977.

[19] *The Bulletin*, 26 October 1977.

[20] *The Age*, 19 October 1977.

[21] *The Age*, 20 October 1977.

[22] *The Age*, 8 October 1977.

[23] *Sunday Observer*, 16 October 1977.

[24] *The Bulletin*, 29 October 1977.

[25] Melbourne *Herald*, 19 October 1977.

[26] *Latrobe Valley Express*, 21 September 1977.

[27] *The Age*, 20 October 1977.

[28] *Latrobe Valley Express*, 30 September 1977.

[29] *The Age*, 1 October 1977.

[30] *The Age*, 8 October 1977.

[31] Melbourne *Herald*, 6 October 1977.

[32] *Latrobe Valley Express*, 28 September 1977.

[33] *The Age*, 1 October 1977.

[34] *Latrobe Valley Express*, 26 October 1977.

[35] 'Elizabeth' (pseudonym for Latrobe Valley activist), interview, October 1979.

[36] Melbourne *Herald*, 6 October 1977.

[37] *The Age*, 6 October 1977 and Melbourne *Herald*, 24 October 1977.

[38] *Sunday Observer*, 23 October 1977.

[39] *The Age*, 22 October 1977.

[40] *The Australian*, 15–16 October 1977.

[41] *The Age*, 1 October 1977.

[42] *The Age*, 26 October 1977.

[43] Quoted in AMWU, *The 1977 Latrobe Valley Power Strike*, Melbourne, 1978 (unpaginated).

[44] *The Age*, 26 October 1977.

[45] *Tribune*, 2 November 1977.

[46] M. Ogden, interview, 'The Latrobe Valley Power Dispute', *Australian Left Review*, no. 64, May 1978, p. 15.

[47] *The Age*, 19 October 1977.

[48] 'Shoemaker's Newsmakers', *Latrobe Valley Express*, 26 October 1977.

[49] The result cannot, however, be read as an *endorsement* of the strike, since the Democrats got most of the swing.

6 Workers, peace and the environment

[1] *The Age*, 22 January 1975.

[2] *The Age*, 22 January 1975.

[3] Melbourne *Herald*, 9 March 1976.

[4] *Tribune*, 14 April 1976.

[5] See *The Bulletin*, 29 May 1976.

[6] *Sydney Morning Herald*, 2 December 1976.

[7] *The Age*, 1 April 1977.

[8] *Scope*, 28 April 1977.

[9] *The Age*, 10 May 1977.

[10] *The Age*, 20 May 1977.

[11] *The Age*, 10 June 1977.

[12] *The Battler*, 20 May 1977.

[13] *The Age*, 3 August 1977.

14 *The Age*, 26 August 1978.

15 *The Age*, 29 March 1979.

16 *The Age*, 28 March and 2 April 1979.

17 *The Age*, 24 October 1980.

18 Max Costello, interview, July 1991.

19 *Sydney Morning Herald*, 20 May 1976.

20 *Sydney Morning Herald*, 24 May 1976.

21 *The Australian*, 29 June 1976.

22 *The Age*, 29 July 1976.

23 *Sydney Morning Herald*, 2 August 1976.

24 *Sydney Morning Herald*, 3 August 1976.

25 *National Times*, 6–11 September 1976.

26 *National Times*, 24–29 October 1977.

27 *National Times*, 16–21 August 1976.

28 Ranger Uranium Inquiry, *First Report*, Canberra, 1976, p. 185.

29 *Sydney Morning Herald*, 26 May 1977.

30 *Sydney Morning Herald*, 30 October 1976.

31 *Direct Action*, 14 April 1982.

32 *The Age*, 5 July 1977.

33 *Direct Action*, 7 July 1977.

34 *The Age*, 5 July 1977.

35 *The Age*, 12 and 13 July 1977.

36 *The Age*, 14 July, 3 August and 24 August 1977.

37 R. Martin, 'The ACTU Congress of 1977', *Journal of Industrial Relations*, vol. 19, no. 4, December 1977. The account of the Congress and all quotes are drawn from pp. 425–428.

38 *The Age*, 8 March 1979.

39 *The Age*, 30 and 31 March 1979.

40 *The Age*, 7 April 1979.

41 *The Bulletin*, 16 October 1979.

42 *Sydney Morning Herald* and *The Age*, 14 September 1979.

43 *The Battler*, 29 March 1980.

44 *National Times*, 26 July–1 August 1981.

45 *CANE News* (Perth), December–January 1982–83.

46 B. Probert, 'Social Movements and Socialism' in D. McKnight (ed.), *Moving Left*, Sydney, Pluto Press, 1986, p. 57.

[47] The Campaign/Congress for International Cooperation and Disarmament was founded in 1959 and was heavily CPA influenced if not controlled.

[48] *People for Peace News Bulletin* (Adelaide), vol. 1, no. 2, August 1982.

[49] See comment on use of the terms USSR, Soviet and Russia in the Preface.

[50] *Direct Action*, 14 April 1982.

[51] L. Smith, 'Women and Nuclear Power', *Movement Against Uranium Mining Newsletter*, Melbourne, March 1981.

[52] *The Age*, 7 January 1983.

[53] *The Age*, 7 June 1982.

[54] Hobart *Mercury*, 17 December 1982.

[55] *The Age*, 23 December 1982.

[56] *The Age*, 8 January 1983.

[57] Hobart *Mercury*, 5 February 1983.

[58] Hobart *Mercury*, 28 February and 1 March 1983.

[59] *The Age*, 7 June 1982.

[60] V. Burgmann, *Power and Protest*, p. 200.

[61] *Direct Action*, 24 March 1982.

[62] *National Times*, 30 January–5 February 1983.

[63] Hobart *Mercury*, 8 March 1983.

[64] Hobart *Mercury*, 21 January 1983.

7 'Work or riot': the unemployment crisis

[1] *The Age*, 6 July 1977.

[2] *Daily Mirror*, 16 January 1976, quoted in K. Windschuttle, *Unemployment*, Melbourne, Penguin, 1980, p. 163.

[3] Quoted in Windschuttle, p. 163.

[4] Windschuttle, pp. 211–3, shows in detail how marginal the problem of 'dole cheats' really was.

[5] Windschuttle, p. 169.

[6] *Sydney Morning Herald*, 16 January 1976.

[7] *National Times*, 29 March–3 April 1976.

[8] *The Bulletin*, 27 March 1979.

[9] *The Age*, 6 September 1977.

[10] *National Times*, 30 August–4 September 1976.

[11] *National Times*, 22 July 1978.

[12] Cited in Windschuttle, p. 50.

[13] *National Times*, 5 January 1980.

[14] *National Times*, 30 September 1978.
[15] *National Times*, 6-12 March 1983.
[16] *National Times*, 27 July-2 August 1980.
[17] *The Age*, 6 April 1979.
[18] *National Times*, 22 July 1978.
[19] Windschuttle, p. 146.
[20] J. Schultz, *Steel City Blues*, Melbourne, Penguin, 1985, p. 164.
[21] *The Bulletin*, 13 April 1979.
[22] *The Age*, 9 June 1977.
[23] *The Bulletin*, 17 April 1979.
[24] *Access Age*, 9 March 1979.
[25] *National Times*, 28 August-4 October 1980.
[26] *National Times*, 13-19 July 1980.
[27] *National Times*, 13-19 July 1980.
[28] *National Times*, 23-29 August 1981.
[29] *Direct Action*, 17 February 1977.
[30] *Direct Action*, 9 November 1978.
[31] *National Times*, 6-12 April 1980.
[32] *The Age*, 10 November 1982.
[33] Melbourne *Sun*, 13 November 1982.
[34] *The Age*, 13 November 1982.
[35] *National Times*, 14-20 November 1982.
[36] *Direct Action*, 21 July 1977.
[37] *Sydney Morning Herald*, 14, 16 and 17 August 1976.
[38] Melbourne *Herald*, 1 April 1977.
[39] *Advertiser*, 25 August 1976.
[40] *Sydney Morning Herald*, 1 September 1976.
[41] *Sydney Morning Herald*, 31 August 1976.
[42] Melbourne *Herald*, 1 April 1977.
[43] *Sydney Morning Herald*, 20 June 1980.
[44] *Sydney Morning Herald*, 2 and 3 July 1980.
[45] *The Battler*, 26 July 1980.
[46] *The Age*, 17 August 1978.
[47] *The Age*, 18 August 1978.
[48] *Sydney Morning Herald*, 22 August 1978.

[49] *Sydney Morning Herald*, 23 August 1978.

[50] *The Age*, 31 August 1978.

[51] Graham Jones, interview, July 1991.

[52] Schultz, pp. 50–51. This section largely follows Schultz's account.

[53] Graham Jones (interview) July 1991.

8 Queensland: battle with Bjelke

[1] T. O'Shaughnessy, 'Joh and Don', *Intervention*, no. 12, April 1979, pp. 20–1.

[2] R. Fitzgerald, *From 1915 to the Early 1980s, A History of Queensland*, St Lucia, University of Queensland Press, 1984, p. 3.

[3] Terms developed by Leon Trotsky as part of his theory of permanent revolution.

[4] Quoted in H. Lunn, *Johannes Bjelke-Petersen*, St Lucia, University of Queensland Press, 1984, p. 313.

[5] Quoted in Fitzgerald, p. 568.

[6] Composite quote: *Courier-Mail*, 4 and 5 September 1977. Where not otherwise noted, quotes in the remainder of this section are also from the *Courier-Mail*: 23 August; 15 September; 13 and 23 October; 1, 13, 23 and 24 November; and 5 December 1977.

[7] John Minns, letter, December 1992.

[8] *Courier-Mail*, 7 September 1977; Queensland *Hansard*, 20 September 1977.

[9] *National Times*, 21–7 June 1981.

[10] C. Ferrier and J. Minns, 'Flying Backwards to Queensland', *International Socialist*, no. 8, Autumn 1979, p. 22.

[11] John Minns, letter, December 1992.

[12] M. Plunket and R. Summy, 'Civil Liberties in Queensland', *Social Alternatives*, vol. 1, nos. 6–7, June 1980, p. 79.

[13] *Courier-Mail*, 1 July 1978.

[14] *Courier-Mail*, 4 July 1978.

[15] Plunket and Summy, p. 86.

[16] *Courier-Mail*, 24 April 1979.

[17] Quoted in Plunket and Summy, p. 85.

[18] *Gold Coast Bulletin*, 9 March 1978.

[19] J. Freeland, 'Class Struggle in Schooling', *Intervention*, no. 12, April 1979, p. 39.

[20] Quoted in Freeland, pp. 44–5.

[21] Quoted in A. Anderson, 'The Abortion Struggle in Queensland', *Hecate*, vol. 6. no. 2, 1980, p. 8.

[22] Quoted in Anderson, 'The Abortion Struggle in Queensland', p. 8.

[23] Unsourced quotes here and in the remainder of this section are from the *Courier-Mail*: 14 March; 18 and 20 April; and 4 and 21 May 1980.

[24] Vicki Spiteri, interview, June 1992.

25 *Courier-Mail*, 20 February 1978.

26 *National Times*, 23-9 August 1981.

27 *Direct Action*, 24 March 1982.

28 *Courier-Mail*, 19 September 1982.

29 *National Times*, 21-7 June 1981.

30 Bob Weatherall, interview, June 1992.

31 *Direct Action*, 24 March 1982.

32 Quoted in *Courier-Mail*, 10 September 1982.

33 *Courier-Mail*, 15 September 1982.

34 For background, see *National Times*, 3-9 October 1982.

35 *Direct Action*, 5 October 1982.

36 *Courier-Mail*, 5 June 1978.

37 *Courier-Mail*, 5 September 1982.

38 *Courier-Mail*, 24 October 1979.

39 Unsourced quotes here and in the remainder of this section are from the *Courier-Mail*, between 11 and 25 August 1982.

40 Mark Gillespie, interview, June 1992.

41 One phone poll reportedly showed 86 percent supporting the government on the 38-hour week but only 16 percent supporting suspension of workers (Brisbane *Telegraph*, 19 August 1982).

42 *Courier-Mail*, 25 August 1982.

43 *Courier-Mail*, 3 September 1982.

9 The oppressed fight back

1 A. Curthoys, *For and Against Feminism*, Sydney, Allen & Unwin, 1988, p. 147.

2 Curthoys, pp. 148-9.

3 I am thinking mainly of Aboriginal and Torres Strait Islander people, for whom 'assimilation' has meant genocide and autonomy in the form of land rights is so important. The establishment of community controlled legal and medical services has brought considerable benefits. Even so, autonomy can only succeed up to a point. Community controlled services still depend on funding from the existing state, and that state is capable of revoking land rights if the interests of capitalism require it. I don't believe Indigenous people can ever become truly independent of the state without smashing it. That, however, requires a united revolutionary movement. Regarding other oppressed groups, while I defend their *right* to organise separately and separate services are valuable, I think the fetish of 'autonomous' organisation had become an obstacle to the struggle by 1975. Full discussion of these issues would exceed the ambit of this history - but see the first section of Chapter 10.

4 At the time of writing, terms such as Koori were used for some regional Indigenous Australians, but they do not apply nationally, so they are not used here.

5 *Sydney Morning Herald*, 12 May 1976.

[6] *The Age*, 12 August 1977.

[7] *Direct Action*, 18 August 1977.

[8] Dave Nadel first drew my attention to these points.

[9] *National Times*, 12-17 April 1976.

[10] *National Times*, 28 June-3 July 1976.

[11] *National Times*, 23-29 August 1981.

[12] *National Times*, 20 October 1979.

[13] National Times, 8 December 1979.

[14] *The Age*, 17 August 1978.

[15] *The Age*, 22 August 1978.

[16] *The Age*, 17 April 1979.

[17] Quoted in J. Roberts, *From Massacres to Mining*, Melbourne, Blackburn, 1981, p. 127.

[18] Quoted in Roberts, p. 128.

[19] *Koori-Bina*, vol. 1, no. 5, 1976.

[20] *Direct Action*, 30 March 1978.

[21] *National Times*, 9 and 16 September 1978.

[22] Transcript quoted in *Direct Action*, 28 September 1978.

[23] Statement reprinted in *Direct Action*, 23 November 1978.

[24] *Chain Reaction*, vol. 3, no. 1, 1977.

[25] On the Noonkanbah struggle, I have relied on S. Hawke and M. Gallagher, *Noonkanbah: Whose Land, Whose Laws*, Freemantle Arts Centre Press, 1989.

[26] Bob Reece, unpublished essay quoted in Hawke and Gallagher, p. 97. The facts of Noonkanbah are drawn largely from this book; the other quotes are from pp. 119, 126, 143, 195, 223, 228 and 313. However, the interpretation is entirely my own.

[27] *National Times*, 5-11 October 1980.

[28] *Sydney Morning Herald*, 6 November 1982.

[29] *National Times*, 24 March 1979.

[30] *The Age*, 15 and 17 June and 2 August 1977.

[31] See Castles et al., Chapter 4.

[32] *The Age*, 24 August 1977.

[33] *National Times*, 9-14 January 1978.

[34] *National Times*, 24 November 1979.

[35] *National Times*, 13-19 September 1981.

[36] *The Bulletin*, 19 September 1978.

[37] *The Bulletin*, 4 July 1978.

[38] *National Times*, 28 November-4 December 1981.

39 *National Times*, 24 November 1982.

40 *The Age*, 17 December 1982.

41 *The Battler*, 14 November 1981.

42 *Direct Action*, 28 July 1977.

43 *Direct Action*, 28 July 1977.

44 Carworker quoted in C. Lever-Tracy, 'The Supervisor and the Militant Shop Steward', *Journal of Industrial Relations*, vol. 29, no. 3, September 1987, p. 345.

45 Melbourne *Herald*, 30 October 1981.

46 *The Battler*, 14 November 1981.

47 A. Summers, 'Women' in Patience and Head, p. 200.

48 *The Bulletin*, 11 September 1976.

49 *National Times*, 10-15 January 1977.

50 *National Times*, 10-15 January 1975.

51 *The Bulletin*, 3 April 1979.

52 *National Times*, 31 March 1979.

53 J. Clarke and K. White, *Women in Australian Politics*, Sydney, Fontana/Collins, 1983, p. 173.

54 Clarke and White, p. 179.

55 Clarke and White, p. 195.

56 *The Bulletin*, 28 March 1978.

57 M. Simms, *Militant Public Servants*, Melbourne, Macmillan, 1987, p. 102.

58 *National Times*, 5-11 April 1981.

59 J. Stone et al., *Report on Women's Trade Union Conference*, mimeo, Sydney, 1976.

60 *Women at Work*, August 1977.

61 *Women at Work*, July-August 1978.

62 Quoted in A. Deveson, *Faces of Change*, Sydney, ABC/Fontana, 1984, p. 161. Reproduced verbatim.

63 *Women at Work*, undated.

64 See *National Times*, 27 February-3 March 1978.

65 H. Grace, 'Cleaners' Strike', *Scarlet Woman*, no. 7, August 1978, p. 4 for both quotes.

66 J. Greenwood, 'Besides our Size it's Because we are Women' in *All Her Labours, vol. 1: Working It Out*, Sydney, Hale & Iremonger, 1984. Quotes about the laundry strike: pp. 59, 65 and 68.

67 S. Bloodworth, 'Women Workers Organise', *Hecate*, vol. 9, nos. 1-2; the account of the Kortex strike is taken from this article, which was also produced in pamphlet form as *Sweatshop Rebels*, Melbourne, 1983.

10 Issues on the left

1 *Latrobe Valley Express*, 21 October 1977.

[2] *Direct Action*, 23 October 1975.

[3] S. Kinder, *History of Adelaide Women's Liberation 1969-74*, Adelaide, Salisbury Education Centre, 1980, pp. 37, 41.

[4] *Mabel*, no. 3, April-May 1976.

[5] Quoted in J. Stone, *Perspectives for Women's Liberation*, International Socialists, Melbourne, 1981, p. 12.

[6] For a Marxist critique of this concept, see S. Bloodworth, 'The Poverty of Patriarchy Theory', *Socialist Review*, no. 2, Winter 1990.

[7] Often, it was very confused indeed. See, for example, K. Higgs and B. Bloch, 'Beyond the Clichés', *Scarlet Woman*, no. 3, February 1976.

[8] Stone, pp. 12-13.

[9] J. Stevens et al., 'Being Red - Feeling Blue', *Scarlet Woman*, no. 9, September 1979, p. 10.

[10] M. Sawer, *Sisters in Suits*, Sydney, Allen & Unwin, 1990, p. 42.

[11] L. Lynch, 'Women and Law Conference', *Refractory Girl*, no. 17, March 1979, p. 35.

[12] *National Times*, 10-15 January 1977.

[13] *National Times*, 23-29 August 1981.

[14] M. Hourihan, 'The Compleat Candidate', *Refractory Girl*, no. 23, March 1982, p. 3.

[15] S. Eade, 'And Now We are Six', *Refractory Girl*, nos. 13-14, March 1977, p. 8.

[16] A. Gibbs, 'Symposium', *Scarlet Woman*, no. 15, Spring 1982, p. 22.

[17] P. Gowland, 'Patriarchy, Power and the Mode of Production', *Papers of the Second Women and Labour Conference*, vol. 2, 1980, p. 710.

[18] Quoted in M. Hostal et al., 'Ten Scarlet Years', *Scarlet Woman*, no. 19, Spring 1984, p. 6.

[19] A. Curthoys, p. 103.

[20] *Scarlet Woman*, no. 15, p. 22 and no. 14, p. 7.

[21] *Vashti*, no. 27, Autumn 1980.

[22] Quoted in J. Stevens, 'Class and Gender', *Scarlet Woman*, no. 20, Spring 1985.

[23] *Girls' Own*, no. 3, July-August 1981.

[24] See, for example, F. Gale, 'Roles Revisited' in P. Brock (ed.), *Women, Rites and Sites*, Sydney, Allen & Unwin, 1989.

[25] P. O'Shane, 'Is the any Relevance in the Women's Movement for Aboriginal Women?', *Refractory Girl*, no. 12, September 1976, p. 32.

[26] *Girls' Own*, no. 5, November-December 1981.

[27] Quoted in V. Burgmann, *Power and Protest*, p. 112.

[28] Curthoys, p. 97.

[29] *Workers' Weekly*, 12 December 1929.

[30] F. Robinson and B. York, *The Black Resistance*, Maryborough, Widescope International Publishers, 1977, frontispiece and pp. 120ff.

[31] *The Australian Communist*, May-June 1978, p. 52; November 1977, pp. 45-6; and September 1977, p. 59.

[32] Disputes over the Gang of Four in China were also important, and the CPA-ML's homophobia didn't help.

[33] H. McQueen, *Gone Tomorrow*, Melbourne, Angus & Robertson, 1982; the quotes are from pp. 87, 127, 222, 226 and 229.

[34] Amalgamated Metal Workers' Union (AMWU), *Australia Uprooted*, Sydney, 1977, pp. 11, 16.

[35] T. Wiltshire, 'The Australian Manufacturing Industry', in *TNC Reportback No 3: Labour and the Economy*, Sydney, unpaginated.

[36] I have discussed Australian nationalism at greater length in T. O'Lincoln, 'The New Australian Militarism', *Socialist Review*, no. 4, Winter 1991.

[37] R. Kuhn, *Militancy Uprooted*, Melbourne, Socialist Action, 1986, p. 11. The critique of nationalism in this chapter owes much to Kuhn's discussion, which summarises arguments he made consistently from the late 1970s onward.

[38] *AMWU Monthly Journal*, May 1976, p. 15.

[39] L. Carmichael, interview, 'A People's Programme', *Intervention*, no. 9, October 1977, p. 49.

[40] R. Jowett, 'Labour and the Economy' in *TNC Reportback*.

[41] W. Higgins, 'The Left Social Democratic Challenge', *Intervention*, nos. 10-11, August 1978.

[42] B. Hartnett, 'Towards a Counter-Strategy for Labour' in G. Crough et al., *Australia and World Capitalism*, Melbourne, Penguin, 1980, p. 252.

[43] B. Hughes, 'Trade Unions, Collective Action and Incomes Policy' in G. Evans et al. (eds.), *Labor Essays 1981*, Melbourne, Drummond, p. 121.

[44] B. Hartnett, 'Australian Unions and Socialist Strategies' in Evans et al., p. 48.

[45] C. Hurford, 'Structural Economic Change' in Evans et al., p. 138.

[46] Communist Party of Australia, *A Strategy for the 1980s in the Metal Industry*, Sydney, 1982, p. 5.

[47] *National Times*, 5-11 October 1980.

[48] *National Times*, 20-26 February 1983.

[49] *The Bulletin*, 24 April 1979.

[50] *The Bulletin*, 18 December 1979.

11 A union revival

[1] A. Kahn, 'The Fraser Years', *International Socialist*, no. 11, Autumn 1981, pp. 8-9.

[2] *The Age*, 23 June 1977 for both quotes.

[3] *The Age*, 3 June 1977.

[4] *The Age*, 5 September 1978.

[5] *The Age*, 5 September 1978.

[6] *The Bulletin*, 12 September 1978.

[7] A. Muir, interview, *The Battler*, 4 August 1979.

[8] *The Bulletin*, 9 May 1978.

[9] See *National Times*, 12 August 1978.

[10] Quoted in T. McCarthy, 'The 1980 Central Queensland Coal Industry Housing Tax Dispute', *Journal of Industrial Relations*, vol. 23, no. 2, June 1981, p. 253.

[11] *National Times*, 17-23 August 1980.

[12] *National Times*, 14-20 September 1980.

[13] For background to the dispute, see H. Thompson, 'The Pilbara Iron Ore Industry', *Journal of Australian Political Economy*, no. 21, May 1987.

[14] Quoted in N. Duffy, 'The 1979 Hamersley Strike', *Australian Bulletin of Labour*, vol. 8, no. 4, September 1989, p. 214.

[15] Quoted in Duffy, p. 216.

[16] *The Age*, 13 September 1979.

[17] H. Thompson and D. Bartlem, 'Confrontation in the Pilbara', *Arena*, no. 55, 1980, p. 24.

[18] *AMWU Monthly Journal*, September 1979.

[19] *The Bulletin*, 22 January 1977.

[20] *National Times*, 9 September 1978.

[21] *National Times*, 6-13 December 1980; *The Bulletin*, 15 July 1980.

[22] *The Bulletin*, 31 October 1978.

[23] *The Bulletin*, 31 October 1978.

[24] *National Times*, 14 April 1979.

[25] *The Age*, 7 April 1979.

[26] *The Bulletin*, 26 June 1979 for both quotes.

[27] *National Times*, 23-29 March 1980 for all quotes of the wool dispute.

[28] Quoted in B. Hill, *Sitting In*, Melbourne, Heinemann, 1991, p. 89.

[29] A. McArdle, interview, *Direct Action*, 12 October 1978.

[30] Quoted in Hill, p. 60.

[31] Quoted in Hill, p. 220.

[32] Quoted in Hill, p. 310.

[33] *The Bulletin*, 29 April 1980.

[34] I once caught myself humming the employers' 'Thumbs Down to 35' jingle.

[35] R. Kyloh, *Productivity Bargaining within a Centralised Wage System*, Australian Government Department of Employment and Industrial Relations, Canberra, 1984, pp. 21-2.

[36] *The Bulletin*, 9 December 1980.

[37] P. Weller, *Malcolm Fraser PM*, Melbourne, Penguin, 1989, p. 373.

[38] Weller, p. 375.

[39] Quoted in Kyloh, p. 23.

[40] See Kyloh, pp. 24-6.

[41] *AMWU Monthly Journal*, February 1980.

[42] However, Herb Thompson informs me that, in the Pilbara, 'a more sophisticated debate took place using Marxist criteria, i.e., shorter hours generated incentives for capital to advance the productive forces. Same standard of living with shorter hours was seen by some as a genuine attempt to "abolish the wages system".' Letter, September 1992.

[43] *The Australian*, 10 March 1981.

[44] *The Age*, 10 March 1981.

[45] *The Age*, 11 March 1981.

[46] *Access Age*, 12 March 1981.

[47] *Sydney Morning Herald*, 14 March 1981.

[48] *The Bulletin*, 18 September 1979.

[49] *The Battler*, 26 July 1980.

[50] Ken Howard, interview, February 1993.

[51] T. Lee Ack, 'Rank and File Groups in the VSTA', discussion paper for Teacher Solidarity conference, Melbourne, September 1981.

[52] The story of the 1981 dispute is told in Grey Collar, *The Fight for Jobs*, Sydney, 1981. On the 1988 dispute, see E. Harrison and D. Main, *Fighting Labor's Cuts*, Sydney, 1989, available at https://labourhistorycanberra.org/topic/author/harrison-eris/.

[53] This passage is actually taken from an article written around the same time: R. Kuhn, 'Thin Cats and Socialism', *International Socialist*, no. 10, August 1980, pp. 18-19.

[54] *The Bulletin*, 7 July 1981.

[55] *Sydney Morning Herald*, 1 August 1981.

[56] *Sydney Morning Herald*, 1 August 1981.

[57] *Sydney Morning Herald*, 18 December 1981.

[58] *Sydney Morning Herald*, 4 April 1982.

[59] *The Age*, 9 February 1982.

12 The more things change...

[1] *The Bulletin*, 22 August 1978.

[2] *National Times*, 6 October 1979.

[3] *National Times*, 29 August-4 September 1982.

[4] *The Bulletin*, 13 June 1978.

[5] *National Times*, 10-16 May 1981.

[6] *Sydney Morning Herald*, 9 March 1983.

[7] *The Australian*, 7 March 1983.

[8] *Sydney Morning Herald*, 9 March 1983.

[9] *National Times*, 21 February 1981.

10 *Sydney Morning Herald*, 28 January 1983.

11 *The Australian*, 7 March 1983.

12 *Sydney Morning Herald*, 16 November 1982.

13 *Sydney Morning Herald*, 19 November 1982.

14 *Sydney Morning Herald*, 23 November 1982.

15 *Sydney Morning Herald*, 9 December 1982.

16 *Australian Financial Review*, 4 February 1983.

17 *Australian Financial Review*, 4 February 1983.

18 *Sydney Morning Herald*, 5 February 1983.

19 *The Bulletin*, 4 August 1981.

20 *Sydney Morning Herald*, 19 and 27 January 1983.

21 *Sydney Morning Herald*, 23 February 1983.

22 *Sydney Morning Herald*, 22 February 1983.

23 *Sydney Morning Herald*, 22 February 1983.

24 *Sun-Herald*, 27 February 1983.

25 *Sydney Morning Herald*, 23 February 1983.

26 *Sydney Morning Herald*, 22 February 1983.

27 *Sydney Morning Herald*, 23 February 1983.

28 *The Australian*, 2 December 1991.

29 *National Times*, 29 March–3 April 1976.

30 *Australian Financial Review*, 15 February 1983.

31 *The Australian*, 14–15 September 1991.

32 *National Times*, 30 May–5 June 1982.

33 *Sydney Morning Herald*, 17 November 1982.

34 *Australian Financial Review*, 15 February 1983.

35 *Sydney Morning Herald*, 1 March 1983.

36 For example, 'Dockside Justice: We Kill Our Own', *National Times*, 29 August–4 September 1982.

37 *National Times*, 2–8 May 1982.

38 Former BLF official Brian Boyd claims that there was one minor exemption in 1985. See B. Boyd, *Inside the BLF*, Melbourne, Ocean Press, 1991, p. 178.

39 *The Age*, 4 March 1983.

40 *Sydney Morning Herald*, 12 March 1983.

41 *Sydney Morning Herald*, 13 April 1983.

42 *Sydney Morning Herald*, 12 April 1983.

Appendix

[1] Some firms (or unusually successful national economies) may avoid this by increasing market share.

[2] See, for example, R. Gregory, *Aspects of Australian Labour Force Living Standards*, Copland Oration, 21st Conference of Economists, Melbourne, 1992.

[3] *Australian Financial Review*, 25 March 1992.

[4] V. Argy, *The World Economy in the 1970s: lessons from experience, prospects and current policy proposals*, Sydney, Australian Professional Publications, 1988, pp. 5-16. Argy, who states that he is influenced by conservative theories, nevertheless does not mention wage levels once as a cause of crisis.

[5] B. Hughes, *Exit Full Employment*, pp. 57ff.

[6] *The Australian*, 3 June 1976.

[7] *The Age*, 2 February 1983.

[8] Profit share calculated from National Accounts data: divide Gross Operating Surplus by GDP. For calculation of rate of profit, see the methodology used in R. Kuhn and T. O'Lincoln, 'Profitability and Economic Crisis', *Journal of Australian Political Economy*, no. 25, October 1989.

[9] See K. Marx, *Capital*, vol. 3, Moscow, 1874, Chapters 13-15. On the theory's compatibility to Australia, see Kuhn and O'Lincoln.

Afterword

[1] p. 415.

[2] For the developments described in the following paragraphs, see Tom Bramble, *Trade unionism in Australia: A history from flood to ebb tide*, Cambridge University Press, 2008, p. 139. On the Accord in general, see: Liz Ross, *Stuff the Accord! Pay Up! Workers' Resistance to the ALP-ACTU Accord*, Interventions, Carlton, 2020; Elizabeth Humphrys, *How Labour Built Neoliberalism: Australia's Accord, the Labour Movement and the Neoliberal Project*, Leiden, Brill, 2018.

[3] Catherine Foster, 'Australian Unions Strike Over State Reform Bid', *Christian Science Monitor*, 12 November 1992, online; David Glanz, 'Kennett vs the unions - a fight we should have won', *Solidarity*, 9 November 2012, online.

[4] See Diane Fieldes, 'Mabo - end of terra nullius?', *Hummer*, 1 June 1995, pp. 33-7.

[5] Luke Deer, 'The Parliament House riot of 1996', 1998, https://sa.org.au/interventions/riot.htm, accessed 12 October 2022.

[6] Tom Bramble, *War on the Waterfront*, Brisbane Defend our Unions Committee, 1998, https://www.sa.org.au/node/1575, accessed 12 October 2022; The Living End, 'Roll on', *Roll On* CD 2001, https://www.youtube.com/watch?v=c_-q-KodhAI&ab_channel=WarnerRecordsVault, accessed 12 October 2022.

[7] Jerome Small, 'A history of resistance on both sides of the razor wire', *Socialist Alternative*, 23 September 2010, online. For an account of the refugee solidarity movement, see John Minns' forthcoming book, tentatively titled *An Anatomy of Activism: Building the Refugee Campaign*.

[8] David Marr and Marian Wilkinson, *Dark Victory: How a Government Lied its Way to Political Triumph*, Crows Nest, Allen & Unwin, 2004.

[9] Bianca Hall and Jonathan Swan, 'Kevin Rudd to send asylum seekers who arrive by boat to Papua New Guinea', *Sydney Morning Herald*, 19 July 2013, online.

[10] Anthony Galloway, 'Albanese Government Turns around Its First Asylum Seeker Boat', *Sydney Morning Herald*, 24 May 2022, online; Anthony Albanese, 'Press conference Melbourne, transcript 20 Jun 2022', https://www.pm.gov.au/media/press-conference-melbourne, accessed 22 October 2022; Paul Karp 'Labor to Allow 19,000 Refugees to Stay Permanently in Australia from Early 2023' *Sydney Morning Herald*, online.

[11] James Plested, '20 years on from S11: Looking Back at the Battle of Melbourne', *Red Flag*, 11 September 2020, online.

[12] Simon Crean, 'Brisbane Anti-War Rally Address', transcript, 16 February 2003, https://library.fes.de/aussies/2003/0203/20003649.html, accessed 2 November 2022.

[13] Lisa Macdonald, 'Half a million rally against war in Sydney', *Green Left Weekly*, 19 February 2003, online; Arun Pradhan, 'Almost 1 million Australians march against war', *Green Left Weekly*, 19 February 2003, online.

[14] Louise O'Shea, 'The campaign for equal marriage rights', *Marxist Left Review*, issue 2, Autumn 2011, online; Philip Coorey, 'Labor swings both ways but struggles to pick up votes', *Sydney Morning Herald*, 5 December 2011, accessed via *Factiva*, 26 October 2022; Peter Boyle, 'Labor conference shifts party further right-wards', *Green Left Weekly*, 5 December 2011, online; Louise O'Shea, 'How we won marriage equality', *Red Flag*, 7 December 2017, online.

[15] Michael Koziol, '"We're entitled to be heard": The Labor senators voting "no" to same-sex marriage', *Sydney Morning Herald*, 29 November 2017, online.

[16] Kathie Muir, *Worth Fighting For: Inside the 'Your Rights at Work' Campaign*, UNSW Press, University of NSW, 2008; Tom Bramble, 'We need a new class-struggle unionism', *Socialist Alternative*, November 2011, online; Liz Ross, 'Labor's work laws a kick in the guts', *Socialist Alternative*, October 2008, online.

[17] 'What is the Northern Territory Intervention?', Castan Centre for Human Rights Law, https://www.monash.edu/law/research/centres/castancentre/our-areas-of-work/indigenous/the-northern-territory-intervention/the-northern-territory-intervention-an-evaluation/what-is-the-northern-territory-intervention, accessed 24 October 2022; Meldi Arkinstall, 'Rally condemns NT intervention', *Sun-Herald*, 15 July 2007, accessed via *Factiva*, 24 October 2022; Diane Fieldes, 'The Northern Territory Intervention and the liberal defence of racism', *Marxist Left Review*, issue 1, Spring 2010, online; Human Rights Law Centre, '"Never again": Key laws behind the Northern Territory Intervention to finally end', 15 July 2022; Human Rights Law Centre, 'Failed Cashless Debit Card to end, but financial control of Aboriginal and Torres Strait Islander people continues', 28 September 2022, https://www.hrlc.org.au/news/2022/9/28/failed-cashless-debit-card-to-end-but-financial-control-of-aboriginal-and-torres-strait-islander-people-continues, accessed 24 October 2022.

[18] Jacqueline Maley, '"This is not OK from our first female PM": Gillard's legacy under the spotlight', *Sydney Morning Herald*, 2 October 2022, online.

[19] Timothy Lawson, 'Occupy Australia: thousands turn out across the country', *Green Left Weekly*, 14 October 2011, online; Ray Cassin, 'Why do the Occupiers so preoccupy our masters?', *Age*, 24 October 2011, accessed via *Factiva*, 26 October 2022.

[20] Steve Lillebuen, 'Tens of thousands gather for March in March protest', *Sydney Morning Herald*, 16 March 2014, online; Helen Davidson, 'March in May: tens of thousands across Australia march in budget protest', *Guardian*, 18 May 2014, online; Paul Farrell, 'March in August: thousands rally

ENDNOTES

against Tony Abbott by taking to streets', *Guardian*, 31 August 2014, online.

[21] Elliott Johnston, *Royal Commission into Aboriginal Deaths in Custody: Report of the Inquiry into the Death of John Peter Pat*, 30 March 1991, http://www.austlii.edu.au/au/other/IndigLRes/rciadic/individual/brm_jpp/BRM_JPP.RTF, accessed 27 October 2022; Louise Dodson, 'Marchers bridge reconciliation gap', *Australian Financial Review*, 29 May 2000, p. 3, accessed via *Factiva*, 28 October 2022. On the 2023 Invasion Day marches see Ben Doherty, 'Thousands attend Invasion Day rallies on Australia's national holiday as colonisation debate rages', 26 January 2023. https://www.theguardian.com/australia-news/2023/jan/26/thousands-attend-invasion-day-rallies-on-australias-national-holiday-as-colonisation-debates-rages.

[22] '#BlackLivesMatter hits Australia', Triple J, 17 Jul 2016; Luke Henriques-Gomes and Elias Visontay, 'Australian Black Lives Matter protests: tens of thousands demand end to Indigenous deaths in custody', *Guardian*, 7 June 2020, online.

[23] Gary Foley 'Can the Voice to Parliament deliver radical change?', 7am, 5 January 2023, https://7ampodcast.com.au/episodes/can-the-voice-to-parliament-deliver-radical-change-with-gary-foley, accessed on 15 January 2023.

[24] Jenny Noyes and Arielle De Bono, 'Up to 10,000 join Sydney Women's March as global movement protests Trump inauguration', *Sydney Morning Herald*, 21 January 2017, online; Calla Wahlquist, 'Brittany Higgins addresses March 4 Justice rally as women demand action across Australia', *Guardian*, 15 March 2021, online.

[25] Matt Bungard and Pallavi Singhal, '"Fantastic turnout": School climate strike draws big crowd in Sydney', *Sydney Morning Herald*, 15 March 2019, online; Sherryn Groch, '"More effective than UN": Student climate strike draws thousands', *Sydney Morning Herald*, 15 March 2019, online; Sherryn Groch, '"Learning in itself": Education Minister backs school climate strike', *Sydney Morning Herald*, 15 March 2019, online; Luke Henriques-Gomes, 'Hundreds of thousands attend school climate strike rallies across Australia', *Guardian*, 20 September 2019, online; Jenny Noyes, 'More than 2000 companies give staff time off to attend climate strike', *Sydney Morning Herald*, 19 September 2019, online; Benjamin Preiss and Noel Towell, 'Andrews government gives public servants green light to skip work for protest', *Sydney Morning Herald*, 17 September 2019, online; Mostafa Rachwani, 'School strike for climate: thousands take to streets around Australia', *Guardian*, 15 May 2021, online; Emily Laurence, Heath Parkes-Hupton and Nibir Khan, 'School Strike For Climate rally draws students to Kirribilli House calling for greater action on climate change', *Guardian*, 26 March 2022, online.

[26] James Plested, 'Roger and me – a socialist view on Extinction Rebellion', *Red Flag*, 4 November 2019, online.

[27] Amy Remeikis, 'Scott Morrison's Hawaii horror show: how a PR disaster unfolded', *Guardian*, 21 December 2019, online; Naaman Zhou, 'Sydney climate protest: thousands rally against inaction amid bushfire and air quality crisis', *Guardian*, 11 December 2019, online; 'Bushfires crisis: world rallies to demand climate action as Australia burns – in pictures', *Guardian*, 11 January 2020, online; '"Scomo's got to go": Tens of thousands march for climate action', 10 January 2020, online.

[28] 'Adani: thousands protest across Australia against Carmichael mine', *Guardian*, 8 December 2018, online; Stop Adani, 'Timeline of #StopAdani actions', https://www.tiki-toki.com/timeline/entry/1006867/Timeline-of-StopAdani-actions, accessed 29 October 2022; Peter Hannam, '"Barbaric": Adani's giant coal mine granted unlimited water licence for 60 years', *Sydney Morning Herald*, April 5 2017, online; Tony Maher, 'Labor shouldn't toughen its stance on Adani coalmine, CFMEU head warns', *Guardian*, 15 February 2018, online.

[29] Ben Schneiders and Clay Lucas, 'Construction workers lash out at union over handling of pandemic', *Age*, 12 April 2020, online; Diane Fieldes, 'NTEU Fightback: Rank and file rebellion in a most unlikely union', *Marxist Left Review*, issue 20, Winter 2020, online.

[30] Australia Institute, 'WPI: worst real wage decline this century', media release, 18 May 2022, https://australiainstitute.org.au/post/wpi-worst-real-wage-decline-this-century/, accessed 28 October 2022. This assessment was made *before* inflation peaked.

[31] Department of Workplace Relations, 'Bargaining and improving workplace relationships: Better Off Overall Test', https://www.dewr.gov.au/download/14724/better-overall-test/30841/better-overall-test/pdf, accessed 31 October 2022; Retail and Fast Food Workers Union, 'New IR Laws Deliberately Attack The Lowest Paid', 1 November 2022, https://raffwu.org.au/new-ir-laws-deliberately-attack-the-lowest-paid/, accessed 6 November 2022.

Image Credits

Abbreviations:

JEC	John Ellis Collection
SLNSW	State Library of New South Wales
SWAG	Socialist Workers Action Group
UMA	University of Melbourne Archives

p. iv	Photographer: Janey Stone
opp. p. 1	SLNSW and the SEARCH Foundation FL4512608
p. 3	Cartoon: Mark Matcott. Reproduced with his kind permission.
pp. 4-5	SLNSW and the SEARCH Foundation FL4504251
pp. 8-9	SLNSW and the SEARCH Foundation FL4427703
p. 11	Cartoon: Mark Matcott. Reproduced with his kind permission.
p. 13	SLNSW and the SEARCH Foundation FL4513918
p. 19	John Halfpenny and Bernie Taft at the World Peace Council reception 1974, JEC, UMA, 1999.0081.00105
p. 20	Photo: Michael Elton. From the collections of the SLNSW [d7_16926/Australian Photographic Agency 16926] (Mitchell Library)
p. 24	City of Melbourne City Collection (registration number 1597336)
p. 26	The Commons Social Change Library
pp. 28-29	Courtesy West Australian Newspapers (Image No. WAN-0031385)

pp. 30-31	Student Action for Aborigines bus outside the Hotel Boggabilla, February 1965. SLNSW and the SEARCH Foundation
p. 32	SLNSW and the SEARCH Foundation FL4527239
p. 34	SLNSW and the SEARCH Foundation FL4541061
pp. 40-41	SLNSW and the SEARCH Foundation reference 965301
p. 52	Front cover *The Battler* 19 November 1975. Published with kind permission of Socialist Alternative.
p. 54	Police break picket lines at the *Herald and Weekly Times* strike, August 1975, JEC, UMA, 1999.0081.00533
pp. 64-65	SLNSW and the SEARCH Foundation FL4494638
pp. 66-67	Leaflet SWAG November 1974. Published with kind permission of Socialist Alternative.
p. 70	Photo: SWAG 1975. Published with kind permission of Socialist Alternative.
p. 71	*Scope* 1 December 1975
p. 72	Photos: SWAG 1975. Published with kind permission of Socialist Alternative.
p. 79	*The Battler* election poster November 1975. Reproduced with kind permission of Socialist Alternative.
p. 84	Front cover *The Battler* 17 December 1975. Reproduced with kind permission of Socialist Alternative.
p. 88-89	SLNSW and the SEARCH Foundation FL4504559
p. 94	ACTU Institute https://atui.org.au/2021/07/09/the-1976-strike-to-defend-universal-healthcare/
pp. 96-97	Poster *The Battler* 12 July 1976. Reproduced with kind permission of Socialist Alternative. ACTU Medibank poster. Ephemera collection Ken Mansell. Medibank demonstration poster 1976. Ephemera collection Ken Mansell.
p. 104	Sir John Kerr demonstration, 30 June 1976, JEC, UMA, 1999.0081.00232. Sir John Kerr demonstration, 9 June 1976, JEC, UMA, 1999.0081.00337; JEC, UMA, 1999.0081.00292.
p. 106-107	Protest at Malcom Fraser's visit to Monash University, August 1976, JEC, UMA, 1999.0081.00792.
p. 116-117	SLNSW and the SEARCH Foundation FL4505696, FL4505699, FL4505698
p. 128	Latrobe Valley strike support leaflet. Ephemera collection Ken Mansell
p. 130-131	Reason in Revolt website: https://www.reasoninrevolt.net.au/objects/images/image_viewer.html?d0888,1,1,S,

IMAGE CREDITS

p. 133	Latrobe Valley strike support leaflet. Ephemera collection Ken Mansell
p. 136	Latrobe Valley strike support leaflet. Ephemera collection Ken Mansell
p. 140	Latrobe Valley strike leaflet. Ephemera collection Ken Mansell
p. 144	Cartoon: Mark Matcott. Reproduced with his kind permission.
p. 147	Omega protest site, 8 July 1978, JEC, UMA, 1999.0081.00565
p. 148	Direct Action leaflet. Ephemera collection Ken Mansell
p. 152	Public Servants Against Uranium Mining banner, 3 August 1981, JEC, UMA, 1999.0081.00132
p. 154-155	Banners at Movement Against Uranium Mining march, 3 August 1978, JEC, UMA, 1999.0081.00164
p. 157	Rivna Green (Indigenous activist) at MAUM march, 3 August 1978, JEC, UMA, 1999.0081.00721
p. 164	Photographer: Janey Stone. Reproduced with her kind permission.
p. 166-167	Honeymoon uranium mine rally, May 1982, JEC, UMA, 1999.0081.00918
pp. 170-171	SLNSW and the SEARCH Foundation FL4511781
p. 174	Tasmanian Dam protesters. Tasmanian Wilderness Society at the Dam Site, 17 December 1982, National Archives of Australia, NAA: A6135, K16/2/83/4
pp. 176-177	SLNSW and the SEARCH Foundation FL4431658
pp. 178-179	SLNSW and the SEARCH Foundation FL4428592
p. 184	Poster 'Support Unemployed, Put Fraser on the Dole'. Ephemera collection Ken Mansell
p. 188	Leaflet 'How can trade unions fight unemployment'. Ephemera collection Ken Mansell
p. 195	Anti-Malcom Fraser protest, March 1980, JEC, UMA, 1999.0081.00589
pp. 196-197	Photographer: Tess Lee Ack. Reproduced with her kind permission.
pp. 198-199	SLNSW and the SEARCH Foundation FL4421972
p. 200	Unemployed Workers' Union soup kitchen outside the Arts Centre, 12 December 1978, JEC, UMA, 1999.0081.00410
p. 202	Leaflet for mass meeting and march April 1977. Ephemera collection Ken Mansell
p. 208	IS leaflet on the budget August 1978. Ephemera collection Ken Mansell

pp. 212-213	SLNSW and the SEARCH Foundation FL4434276
pp. 214-215	SLNSW and the SEARCH Foundation FL4429332
p. 218	Action For Civil Liberties leaflet. Ephemera collection Ken Mansell
p. 225	Cartoon: Mark Matcott. Reproduced with his kind permission.
pp. 226-227	Leaflets Queensland late 1970s. Ephemera collection Ken Mansell
p. 228	Front page *The Battler* 1 October 1977. Published with kind permission of Socialist Alternative.
p. 234-235	SLNSW and the SEARCH Foundation FL4365407
p. 243	'No apartheid graffiti' Brisbane billboard, JEC, UMA, 1999.0081.00678
p. 244	Flyer Queensland late 1970s. Ephemera collection Ken Mansell
p. 245	Flyer Queensland late 1970s. Ephemera collection Ken Mansell
p. 248-249	SLNSW and the SEARCH Foundation FL4430232
p. 250-251	SLNSW and the SEARCH Foundation FL4430221
p. 256	Poster Queensland 1978. Ephemera collection Ken Mansell
p. 258-259	SLNSW and the SEARCH Foundation FL4430166
p. 265	Aurukun banner at Land Rights demonstration Sydney 1982, JEC, UMA, 1999.0081.00731
p. 268	Indigenous activist at MAUM march, 3 August 1978, JEC, UMA, 1999.0081.00195
p. 270-271	Melbourne Land Rights demonstration, 1976, JEC, UMA 1999.0081.00878
p. 276-277	SLNSW and the SEARCH Foundation FL4431409
p. 283	Photo: International Socialists, 1981. Published with kind permission of Socialist Alternative.
p. 288-289	SLNSW and the SEARCH Foundation FL4369005
p. 290	Leaflet May Day 1980. Ephemera collection Janey Stone.
p. 291	Leaflet *The Battler* 1980. *The Battler* 17 May 1980. Both published with kind permission of Socialist Alternative.
p. 296-297	SLNSW and the SEARCH Foundation FL4370904
p. 298-299	SLNSW and the SEARCH Foundation FL4504223
p. 304-305	*Alternative News Service*, 10 July 1978. Ephemera collection Ken Mansell. Rally protesting Mardis Gras arrests. Photographer: David Urqhhart. SLNSW FL19878475. Reproduced with his kind permission.
p. 306-307	SLNSW and the SEARCH Foundation FL4369589

IMAGE CREDITS

p. 308	Leaflet for demonstration on 4 November 1978. Ephemera collection Janey Stone
p. 312-313	Photographer unknown. The Battler 23 January 1982, p. 10.
p. 314	Photographer unknown. The Battler 23 January 1982, p. 10.
p. 318	Poster, unknown date. Ephemera collection Ken Mansell
pp. 322-323	SLNSW and the SEARCH Foundation FL4487931
pp. 330-331	SLNSW and the SEARCH Foundation FL4424134
pp. 332-333	SLNSW and the SEARCH Foundation FL4424122
pp. 334-335	SLNSW and the SEARCH Foundation FL4431153
p. 340	Front page *Education*. Ephemera collection Ken Mansell
p. 348	Poster, unknown date. Ephemera collection Ken Mansell
p. 354	Cartoon: Mark Matcott. Reproduced with his kind permission.
p. 362	*Tribune Magazine* Wednesday 3 October 1979, p. 9. Courtesy Trove and SEARCH Foundation
p. 366-367	SLNSW and the SEARCH Foundation FL4412894
p. 369	Cartoon: Mark Matcott. Reproduced with his kind permission.
pp. 370-371	SLNSW and the SEARCH Foundation FL4369991
pp. 372-373	SLNSW and the SEARCH Foundation FL4369992
p. 382	Front page *The Battler* 4 June 1983. Published with kind permission of Socialist Alternative.
p. 385	Demonstration at nursing home 30 March 1980, JEC, UMA, 1999.0081.00617; 1999.0081.00294
p. 386-387	Demonstration at nursing home 30 March 1980, JEC, UMA, 1999.0081.00358
p. 390-391	SLNSW and the SEARCH Foundation FL4423737
p. 392	Campaign Against Public Sector Cuts broadsheet 28 August 1986
p. 398-399	SLNSW and the SEARCH Foundation FL4431632
p. 406-407	SLNSW and the SEARCH Foundation FL4433726
p. 409	Cartoon: Mark Matcott. Reproduced with his kind permission.

Biographies

Tom O'Lincoln

Tom O'Lincoln joined the radical student movement in Germany in 1967 and was subsequently a socialist organiser, unionist and journalist. As a writer, Tom's work spanned political economy, Australian history and Marxist theory. His works include *Into the Mainstream: The Decline of Australian Communism*, *Australia's Pacific War: Challenging a National Myth* and *The neighbour from hell: two centuries of Australian imperialism*. His political memoirs, *The highway is for gamblers*, were published in 2017. Currently living in residential care, Tom continues his commitment to revolutionary Marxism.

Rick Kuhn

Rick Kuhn is a Marxist activist and economist. He won the Deutscher Prize in 2007 for his *Henryk Grossman and the Recovery of Marxism* and was a Reader in Political Science at the Australian National University. A life member of the National Tertiary Education Union, Rick has been involved in social movement and union campaigning, as well as Socialist Alternative and its predecessor organisations, since the 1970s.

About Interventions

Interventions is an independent, not-for-profit, incorporated publisher. We publish left-wing, radical and socialist books by Australian authors. We welcome books which for political or financial reasons are unlikely to be accepted by commercial publishers. Our books cover a wide range of topics including labour history, left-wing politics, radical cultural themes, socialism and Marxism, memoirs, and works about resistance to racism, sexism and all other forms of oppression.

At Interventions we believe radical ideas matter. We want our books to be part of the development of a critical and engaged Australian left.

By highlighting alternative voices, especially those that have been pushed to the margins, we hope to contribute to a greater insight and awareness of the injustices that exist in society, and the many efforts at the grassroots to right these wrongs.

We welcome publishing proposals. If you are interested in submitting a proposal please check out the information for authors on our website https://interventions.org.au/forauthors. If you think your proposal fits our guidelines please follow the submission process outlined there. Please note we are not currently publishing poetry or fiction.

Interventions has no independent source of income and is committed to keeping prices accessible. As bookshops and warehouses close around the world, our future hangs in the balance. By supporting us you will help us keep radical ideas alive and accessible to all. If you would like to support radical publishing in Australia please consider supporting our Patreon. Visit patreon.com/interventions to donate a small amount each month and get some great rewards.

Website: https://interventions.org.au/

Contact us: info@interventions.org.au or use the contact form on the website.

About this book

The Interventions editor and production project manager for this book was Janey Stone with support from Alex Ettling and Phillip Whitefield. Tess Lee Ack assisted with proof reading.

This book was copy edited by Eris Harrison of Effective Editing.

This book was designed and laid out by Viktoria Ivanova of Vik Designs. Viktoria is a communication designer in Melbourne. She is a book publishing fiend, runs Spark Publishing Inc (for art-centric left books) and also designs for Victorian Socialists.

Tom O'Lincoln legacy project

Tom O'Lincoln was born in California in 1947. He grew up in Walnut Creek, east of San Francisco, and attended the University of California, Berkeley. His experiences as an exchange student at the University of Göttingen in 1967-68 had a major impact on the direction of his life. Tom was radicalised and became an activist and a Marxist. In late 1969, he joined the Berkeley branch of the International Socialists (IS). In 1971, together with Janey Stone, he came to Australia. In 1972, he became involved in revolutionary politics in this country, a commitment that has lasted to the present day.

Starting with the small grouping, the Marxist Workers Group, which became Socialist Workers' Action Group at the end of 1972, Tom was a leader and member of various formations which carried through the IS tradition, finally joining Socialist Alternative in 2003. Tom was an activist in many political movements and an active trade unionist as a teacher and in the public service.

Always a keen traveller, Tom witnessed major struggles in Germany, Portugal and Indonesia; he engaged with socialists and activists in countries as far apart as Nicaragua, Peru, Lebanon, Poland, South Korea and the Philippines. He corresponded with, and met, leading socialists in the UK, the USA, Germany and elsewhere. His language skills enhanced this experience – Tom could conduct political discussions in German, Russian, Spanish (with some excursions into Portuguese, French and Croatian) and, later in life, Indonesian.

Tom was a prolific writer. He wrote extensively for left-wing newspapers, magazines and websites, including his own website, which he managed for many years. Tom also translated political material into Indonesian and helped to run an Indonesian language website for 10 years.

Tom's political interests were always very wide. Having settled here, he made Australia his focus. He published books on Australian history, Australian imperialism, the Communist Party of Australia, the left and social struggles. He contributed works on many international topics, with Indonesia being a special interest during the 1990s. He also wrote on Marxist theory and economics, Stalinism and other theoretical subjects. A list of all Tom's longer works is included in *The Expropriators are Expropriated*.

Unfortunately, following a diagnosis of Parkinson's disease, Tom found it increasingly difficult to continue the creative process. He published the last two of his books with help from others. For several years now, Tom has lived in an aged care facility, where he has continued his interest in current events and the development of politics in the world.

Some of Tom's books were published with the help of Vulgar Press. Generally, although various imprints were named, they were effectively self-published, mostly with funds from the Jeff Goldhar Project. When Interventions was set up in 2015 as an independent, not-for-profit radical publisher, we took over Tom's backlist.

All the books prior to 2015 were published conventionally, with print runs determined by finances at the time. This led to variable stock levels, not helped by the failure of the main distributor and the disappearance of some stock. Because several titles are now out of print, Interventions has initiated a project of publishing new editions of all Tom's major works, with new design and new contextual essays. Importantly, these titles will be added to print-on-demand services, ensuring that these political ideas will always be accessible. The content of Tom's books has stood the test of time. His is a literary legacy worth preserving and extending to new audiences.

The books that constitute this project, listed by their first year of publication, are:

- 1985 *Into the Mainstream: The Decline of Australian Communism*
- 1993 *Years of Rage: Social Conflicts in the Fraser Era*
- 1998 *Rebel Women in Australian Working Class History (co-edited with Sandra Bloodworth)*
- 2005 *United We Stand: Class Struggle in Colonial Australia*
- 2011 *Australia's Pacific War: Challenging a National Myth*
- 2014 *The Neighbour from Hell: Two Centuries of Australian Imperialism*
- 2016 *'The Expropriators are Expropriated' and other writings on Marxism*
- 2017 *The Highway is for Gamblers: a Political Memoir*

The last two titles are already available through Interventions print-on-demand. New, enhanced editions of *The Neighbour From Hell* and *Rebel Women* have been published by Interventions in 2021 and 2022 respectively and are now also available through print-on-demand. A new edition of *United We Stand* is planned for late 2023 or early 2024. The remaining two titles are also planned to be reissued as resources allow.

Tom has been an activist, a revolutionary socialist and a Marxist his whole adult life. In his political memoir, *The Highway is for Gamblers* (Interventions 2017), he writes:

> I have been a Marxist for half a century. In that time I have participated in and been witness to great struggles and momentous historical events. I've had the privilege of standing shoulder to shoulder with selfless fighters around the world. Those events and the people involved only confirmed in my mind that human liberation can be won through the mass struggles of the working class.

Tom then asks the question, 'Why be a revolutionary socialist today?' His answer? 'It's a life worth living.' We at Interventions want to keep this legacy alive.

MORE FROM INTERVENTIONS

Without Bosses: Radical Australian Trade Unionism in the 1970s
By Sam Oldham

In the 1970s, rank and file trade unionists pushed the boundaries of their organisations, in some cases setting global precedents. This book revisits many of the better known events of the period, including the almost complete neutralisation of anti-strike laws through mass strike action in 1969, and the famous green bans of the Builders Labourers' Federation. It also details fascinating experiments with self-management and workers' control. At factories, coal mines and building sites across the country, workers 'sacked' their managers and supervisors, taking their workplaces into self-management and running them without bosses. This book overflows with incredible and inspiring stories from a critically important period in Australian history.

Stuff the Accord! Pay up! Workers' Resistance to the ALP-ACTU Accord
By Liz Ross

This book deals with the 1983-1996 ALP-ACTU Accord. This was a landmark program of restructuring Australian capitalism, a social contract between the union peak body, the Australian Council of Trade Unions (ACTU) and the social democratic Australian Labor Party (ALP). It pitched worker against worker, destroyed two unions, oversaw one of the greatest transfers of wealth from workers to employers, gutted union membership and the gains of previous decades. This story of resistance, from the left and workers' perspective, has not been told in full before. It discusses how workers fought back against the attacks on their wages and conditions, their jobs, their unions, and their rights.

MORE FROM TOM O'LINCOLN

Australia's Pacific War: Challenging a National Myth

War is such a nightmare it's hard to believe any war can retain a positive aura for decades. Yet the vast conflict in the Pacific is a shibboleth for Australian politics to this day. Politicians use its appeal to legitimise modern wars. This book questions every aspect of this syndrome.

Into the Mainstream: The Decline of Australian Communism

How are the mighty fallen. At the end of World War II, the Communist Party was a major force in Australian working class life. This book traces the party's decline from an influential movement, plagued by its bureaucratic Stalinist politics, finally drifting into the political mainstream. It offers lessons for socialists today.

The Neighbour from Hell: Two Centuries of Australian Imperialism

This book offers an original study of Australia's 'boutique imperialism'. Far from being servile and passive agents of the United States and Great Britain, Australia's rulers callously seek to extract maximum benefits from calculated interventions in the global capitalist system.

The Highway is for Gamblers: A political memoir

A moving political memoir that is a testament to a life worth living, in the ranks of those fighting for human liberation. It captures the rich political history of the past six decades, written with a pen that burns with indignation against oppression. This is not a nostalgic memoir of reminiscence, but an insight for the activists of tomorrow who hope to change the world.

www.ingramcontent.com/pod-product-compliance
Lightning Source LLC
Chambersburg PA
CBHW071951290426
44109CB00018B/1990